Chen Village

De-Maoification, 1981. A small picture of a deceased village elder discreetly takes pride of place over Chairman Mao.

Chen Village

REVOLUTION TO GLOBALIZATION

□

THIRD EDITION

Anita Chan,
Richard Madsen,
and Jonathan Unger

University of California Press
Berkeley · Los Angeles · London

University of California Press, one of the most
distinguished university presses in the United States,
enriches lives around the world by advancing scholarship in the humanities, social sciences, and natural
sciences. Its activities are supported by the UC Press
Foundation and by philanthropic contributions from
individuals and institutions. For more information,
visit www.ucpress.edu.

University of California Press
Berkeley and Los Angeles, California

University of California Press, Ltd.
London, England

Library of Congress Cataloging-in-Publication Data

Chan, Anita.
    Chen village : revolution to globalization / Anita
Chan, Richard Madsen, and Jonathan Unger.—3rd ed.
        p.   cm.
    Rev. ed. of: Chen Village under Mao and Deng. 2nd ed.
    Includes bibliographical references and index.
    ISBN 978-0-520-25931-7 (pbk. : alk. paper)
    1. China—Rural conditions—Case studies.
    2. Globalization—Social aspects—China.
    3. Globalization—Economic aspects—China.
    4. China—Economic conditions—2000–   I. Madsen,
    Richard, 1941–   II. Unger, Jonathan.   III. Chan,
    Anita.   Chen Village under Mao and Deng.   IV. Title.
    HN733.5.C423   2009
    307.720951—dc22   2008037218

Manufactured in the United States of America

18   17   16   15   14   13   12   11   10
10   9   8   7   6   5   4   3   2

This book is printed on Cascades Enviro 100, a 100% post-
consumer waste, recycled, de-inked fiber. FSC recycled
certified and processed chlorine free. It is acid free, Ecologo
certified, and manufactured by BioGas energy.

Contents

Acknowledgments

This book is the third expanded and updated edition of our study of Chen Village, a community in the People's Republic of China. In it, we bring our discussion of Chen Village up to the latter part of 2007. Our research and writing was made possible over the years by the generous assistance of a great many individuals and institutions spanning four continents. Regretfully, it is impossible here to acknowledge them all. We can only single out these few for special thanks.

We owe our greatest debts of gratitude to two outstanding teachers: Ronald P. Dore, the former PhD supervisor of Anita Chan and Jonathan Unger, and Ezra F. Vogel, the former principal supervisor of Richard Madsen. Their scholarly advice and personal support aided our initial research agenda considerably, and they continue to this day to be our friends and inspiration.

Our research in Hong Kong in the 1970s was carried out at the Universities Service Centre. We wish to express our thanks to John Dolfin, the former director of the Centre, for providing us with a work environment that greatly facilitated our initial research.

We are grateful also to two excellent photographers. During the summer of 1981 Lau Pok-chi of the University of Kansas made a trip on our behalf to the countryside near Chen Village, and his photographs appear as the frontispiece and on pages 15, 44–46, 68, 94, 187, 216, 218, 220, 275, 277, and 283. Thomas Cliff of the Australian National University took photographs in Chen Village during the summer of 2007, and his photos appear on pages 338, 350, 368, 378, 379, 381, 382, 384, and 390. In January 2006 Carla Chan Unger took the photographs that appear on pages 334, 335, 343, and 371. The photo on page 359 was taken by one of our interviewees, Ao, in October of 2007. The three authors took the other photographs that appear in the book.

For Anita Chan and Jonathan Unger, financial support for the project came from the Institute of Development Studies at the University of Sussex, in England; from the Social Science Research Council of the United Kingdom; from the Nuffield Foundation; from the Center for East Asian Studies, University of Kansas; and from the Contemporary China Centre at the Australian National University. For Richard Madsen, financial support came from a National Institute of Mental Health Comparative International Studies Training Grant and a National Defense Foreign Language fellowship. The book was drafted at the University of Kansas, Harvard University, the University of California at San Diego, the Center for Chinese Studies at the University of California, Berkeley, and the ANU's Contemporary China Centre.

Marc Blecher, John Burns, Deborah Davis, and Edwin Lee graciously shared with us notes from their own interviews with Chen Villagers in the 1970s. Mari Fitzpatrick, B. Michael Frolic, Nancy Kaul, Andrew Kipnis, Uldis Kruze, James Nickum, Stanley Rosen, Theda Skocpol, Connie Squire, Judith Strauch, and James Watson read and critiqued various parts of the book. Lam Tao-Chiu, Kaxton Siu, Michael Agelasto, Yang Lieming, and Diana Beaumont visited Chen Village to help us arrange for our fieldwork for this third edition. Much of the final draft of the chapters on the Maoist period was typed by Nancy Kaul and Patrick James. Dianne Stacey, Yu Hong, and Darren Boyd assisted in preparing the post-Mao chapters.

We are especially thankful to our interviewees from Chen Village, who gave us so much of their time and entrusted to us the memories and knowledge upon which the book is based. To them this book is gratefully dedicated.

Prologue

This book tells of the extraordinary changes that have occurred in a southern Chinese community over a period of four and a half decades, from the early 1960s up to 2007. During this time period, China was first swept up in revolutionary Maoist programs and then, after Deng Xiaoping came to power, launched into rapid economic development. Chen Village has experienced, in microcosm, the twists and turns of recent Chinese history, and our book describes a series of often unexpected shifts in the political, economic, and social circumstances of Chen Village residents.[1]

The first edition of the book was published in 1984 and carried the tale of Chen Village up to the end of 1981. Through renewed research in 1989 and 1990 for a second edition, we were able to examine how the village fared during the period of Deng Xiaoping's rule. Continuing our research during 2006 and 2007 for this new third edition, we found that the community is no longer a rural village. The experience of Chen Village under Mao and its transformation in the post-Mao decades comprises a dramatic story—and, as readers will see, one tinged with multiple ironies.

---

[1] To protect the privacy of the villagers and our interviewees, we have altered the village's name and the names of all the people who appear in this book. We have also disguised somewhat the location of the village.

The experiences of Chen Village were, until about 1980, similar to those of a great many other Chinese villages. They were all shaken by a series of tumultuous government-sponsored political campaigns between the mid-1960s and the late 1970s. Our initial study—the first nine and a half chapters of this book—illustrates the impact of these nationwide political movements on one such community. Thus our narrative focuses, chapter by chapter, first upon the Four Cleanups campaign of the mid-1960s, then on the Cultural Revolution turmoil of 1966−68, then the "class struggles" of the Cleansing of the Class Ranks campaign in the late 1960s, and then the events leading up to and past the death of Mao in 1976. In Chen Village, these various campaigns and national upheavals were the dynamos of social, political, and economic change. Even though political campaigns ceased after Mao's death, national policies continued to profoundly affect Chen Village in the subsequent "reform era." Throughout these four and a half decades, the changes in Chen Village were sometimes in the directions promoted by the government. But at other times, as shall be seen, the village reacted in ways that were substantially different from what China's leadership could have ever expected or desired.

Readers should bear in mind, though, that the episodes we relate cannot in any simple or straightforward fashion be considered entirely "typical" of Chinese rural society under Mao and Deng, or typical of China's transformation since then. China's villages are too diverse and far too complex to allow that. Each Chinese community will have a somewhat different story to tell. But precisely because of the complexity of all of these stories of rural change, we are convinced that grassroots politics and the intricate patterns of development and change in China's villages can most fully be understood and appreciated through microstudies like this.

Our Sources of Information

Our initial study began through chance encounters. We had become socially acquainted with several young emigrants from Chen Village while we were engaged in other research in Hong Kong in 1975. They told us some intriguing anecdotes about their village, which whetted our interest. We began to interview them systematically about their experiences, and we asked to be introduced to former neighbors and friends. These in turn introduced us to still other former village residents. Many of these interviews were conducted in 1975 and 1976, but two of us returned to Hong Kong in the spring of 1978 for four more months to round off the interviewing, and returned again for two months in early 1982 to bring the village's story further up to date. By then, we had met and interviewed twenty-six former Chen Village residents who had moved to Hong Kong.

From 1988 to 1990, two of the authors, Chan and Unger, undertook yet further rounds of interview research in Hong Kong and for the first time were able to visit Chen Village to talk with residents in their homes. The interviewing and visits provided the information for two and a half new chapters for the second edition. Visits to Chen Village in 2006 by Madsen, Chan, and Unger and renewed fieldwork there by Chan and Unger in late 2006 and early 2007 form the basis for the final three chapters about Chen Village in an age of industrial development and globalization.

At the time that the three of us began to conduct research in the mid-1970s, it was not possible for Western researchers to live in a Chinese village in order to observe firsthand the daily patterns of village life. The only way to do a study of a Chinese village was through interviews with émigrés.[2] There were shortcomings to such interviewing, to be sure, but there was also one distinct advantage. The modern history of China has been turbulent, and it abounds with politically sensitive topics. The residents of any Chinese village would have had to worry about saying things to a foreigner that might offend their neighbors or local officials. Our interviewees in Hong Kong generally did not have these same worries, and we were able to discuss with them the informal and behind-the-scenes political

---

[2.] Until China "opened up" in the 1980s, Western scholars of China conducted a considerable amount of research through such interviews with Chinese emigrants. For a discussion of this kind of research and a detailed appraisal of its opportunities and dangers, see William L. Parish and Martin K. Whyte, *Village and Family in Contemporary China* (Chicago: University of Chicago Press, 1978), pp. 344–351, and Jonathan Unger, "The Hong Kong Connection: The Advantages of China Research from the Room Next Door," *China Information* 2, no. 1 (Summer 1987): 27–35.

A Main Square, 1971, Closely Resembling
That of Chen Village

considerations, social networks, and personal feuds that shaped village decisions and the conduct of campaigns.

The émigrés we interviewed in the 1970s quite obviously had their own biases about what occurred in their village. How could the three of us, sitting in Hong Kong, discern and filter out those biases? We came away from our interviewing convinced that we were largely able to do so. This conviction is based, in part, on our opportunity to carefully cross-check each interviewee's account. We repeatedly asked our interviewees to speak about various aspects of the village's recent history in detail, and the informants, independently, were in agreement about most of these details. For example, one of our most frequent interviewees in the 1970s, a young woman named Ao, had served during the Cleansing of the Class Ranks campaign as the public prosecutor of another interviewee, Wang, who had been a leader of Chen Village's Rebel Red Guards during the Cultural Revolution. Wang was made to pay the price through imprisonment during the Cleansing of the Class Ranks. Naturally, Ao and Wang offered us quite different opinions of the campaign. But the descriptions of the campaign that they presented to us during many hours of separate interviewing were largely similar.

We discovered that if properly handled, the differing opinions and attitudes of interviewees could, in fact, help us to comprehend better the conflicting forces and sectoral interests at work in the village. Interviewees such as Ao and Wang very often had retained the perspectives of their own particular social and political positions in the village. Similarly, different types of former village cadres usually recounted events from the vantage point of their former posts, and members of different production teams still seemed to hold to their own team's perspectives on the controversial economic and political issues that divided the village. We will present these different perceptions, and from them will build our own description of a complex grassroots reality during the period of Mao's rule.

Our interviews in Hong Kong in the 1970s and early 1980s were conducted under a wide variety of circumstances, both formal and informal. Sometimes we met with interviewees in our offices at an academic institute; other times we met in coffeehouses, restaurants, in our homes, or in the interviewees' homes. Some of the interviewees from Chen Village met with us for just a couple of sessions of one to three hours apiece; others came for dozens of sessions.

About two-thirds of the three hundred–odd interviews that we gathered on Chen Village during the 1970s and early 1980s were taped and then transcribed verbatim. The rest were recorded through on-the-spot note taking. All three authors conducted interviews in Chinese without interpreters. Usually the sessions were one-on-one, but occasionally several Chen Villagers met as a group with one or more of us. At such times, we would bring up a topic for conversation and then retreat into the background as passive observers. As the villagers reminisced together, we were able to obtain a better grasp of the nuances of social and political relationships in the village.

About half of our interviewees from Chen Village were born and raised in the village. The remaining fourteen respondents, and a very important source of information for events in the village up through the 1970s, were high school graduates from the city of Canton (Guangzhou)—five young women and nine young men. Most of them had settled in Chen Village in 1964 as teenagers and lived in the village as regular laboring peasants for a decade or more. While there, about half of them rose into various low-level political or economic posts within the village. Their knowledge of the village—its institutions and customs, its gossip, policy debates, and production techniques—was both intimate and extensive.

In more than one respect, though, these fourteen interviewees were still outsiders. They were not members of the village lineage—they were not Chens. Most of them had developed an obvious degree of respect and affection for the villagers and had held a positive regard for life in the village. But many of them also had felt that their urban education and culture made them too good to spend the rest of their lives working as ordinary peasants. Thus, their perspectives on village life were likely to be uniformly colored by the attitudes they shared. But through our many interviews with a number of Chens—"insiders" from Chen Village—we were able to cross-check testimony in this respect, too.

We did, of course, also face one final major problem with this initial group of interviewees, urban-born and village-born alike. They had shared a dissatisfaction with their personal lot in Chen Village that was sufficient to drive them to Hong Kong in the years between 1972 and 1981. Four had come as legal emigrants, and the other twenty-two had illegally made the dangerous swim from China to Hong Kong.

They had come for a variety of reasons. For all of the young Chens whom we interviewed, Hong Kong had provided their only means to enter the higher-paid job market of a big city, and some of these earnings were then remitted to their families back in the village. Among the fourteen urban-born young people, all of whom had left for Hong Kong in the early to mid-1970s, five other reasons for emigrating stood out as most important:

· Many of them, as single youths, had encountered severe financial difficulties in the Chinese countryside. On their own, without village families to back them up, they could not save sufficient money to get married or, in some cases, even to support themselves. As they entered their mid-twenties, they began to see no prospects for a better future.

· Some of them had gotten into trouble in the Cultural Revolution and felt this had irretrievably damaged their standing in the village.

· Several of them felt that they were no longer needed or wanted by the peasantry. The village-born youths had recently received enough education to begin to take over their posts and responsibilities. The urban-born youths were being shunted aside by the villagers' preference for their own children.

• Some of the interviewees—Chens and urban youths alike—also shared an important complaint about the Chinese Communist system. They came largely from family backgrounds that the Chinese government had defined as politically unreliable. They felt that because of their official class labels, which they had inherited from their families, they were being condemned to "second-class citizenship." Some of them had once felt they could overcome the disadvantage of their class backgrounds through personal revolutionary zeal. They felt betrayed when they perceived this would be impossible during Mao's lifetime. We shall observe their frustrations as our chronicle of Chen Village's recent history unfolds.

• The faith of many of the young people in Mao and the party gradually had been sapped by the Cultural Revolution upheaval of 1966–68, the launching of a severe "struggle campaign" in its wake, Lin Biao's downfall in 1971, and the subsequent political infighting among the nation's leaders. When we interviewed them in the 1970s, many of them remained convinced that socialist agriculture was preferable to private ownership, and few of them felt hostile toward the Communist government. But a number of them had felt confused, disturbed, and disheartened by the political events of the seventies. We now know from more recent reports from China that a great many young people throughout the People's Republic had felt similarly perturbed by the same sets of issues during those years.

Part of Chapter 10 and all of Chapters 11 and 12 are based on renewed research a decade and a half after we began our initial rounds of interviewing. These chapters derive in part from interviews in the late 1980s with some of the same Chen émigrés whom we had met and interviewed in the 1970s. Although they lived in Hong Kong, all of them were regular visitors back to Chen Village, often spending weekends there because their parents and/or wives and children continued to live in the village. Our information for the 1980s no longer derived from "refugees," but rather, as it were, from dual Hong Kong–Chen Village residents.

With the opening up of China in the 1980s, foreigners were now allowed to travel through this southern region of China almost at will, and so, for the first time, we also paid several visits to the village between 1987 and 1990. But we deliberately did not formally apply to the Chinese government to conduct an extended on-site follow-up study of the village. Faithful to a promise made to our informants a decade and a half earlier that we would retain the village's anonymity, we did not wish to reveal the identity of "Chen Village" to government authorities or to the villagers. Under such a constraint, we made only day trips to Chen Village as friends of the former villagers who had become Hong Kong residents. We visited the homes of some of their relatives on a social basis, wandered through the village lanes, and tried to strike up informal conversations with anyone we chanced upon (including, several times, the village's Communist party secretary). Of course, such trips are nothing like staying in a community for extensive research. Nonetheless, these encounters helped us to fill in our mental images of the village and to double-check the information and impressions of our Hong Kong–based interviewees.

In 2006 and 2007, we returned again to Chen Village. This time, we stayed in hotels in the nearby town that had once served as the commune headquarters. We kept up with our old contacts, visited them in their homes, and spent a considerable amount of time with two families in particular. We also sat around with the several dozen old people who congregate every day to sip tea and exchange community gossip. For a number of days and evenings we wandered around on our own, striking up conversations with other residents and with some of the storekeepers and workers who have moved to Chen Village in very large numbers during the past decade. Chen Village had been an isolated village when we began our research in the 1970s, but today the community sits in the middle of one of the most rapidly industrializing regions of the world. Much of the merchandise that crowds department stores around the globe is manufactured in the region embracing the Pearl River Delta, and Chen Village and the surrounding villages are each today the sites of hundreds of large factories.

To place the dramatic events that have transformed Chen Village into a broader context, we have made an effort to gain a sense of what has occurred in other nearby communities during the past half century. During the mid- to late 1970s we interviewed émigrés from a dozen other villages in Guangdong Province about life in those villages from the 1960s onward. There was considerable diversity among these communities but, as mentioned earlier, all of the political campaigns that Chen Village had experienced up through the late 1970s were carried out in these other villages, and much of the same turmoil, progress, and problems also occurred there. For this book's second edition, émigrés from a further half-dozen Guangdong villages were interviewed in the late 1980s in order to chart the social, economic, and political changes of the period of Deng Xiaoping's rule. To place Chen Village into context for this updated third edition, interviews were carried out in two neighboring villages in 2006 and in the neighboring township (formerly classified as a "commune") in early 2007.

Down to the Countryside

Our book's four-and-a-half-decade saga of Chen Village's journey through revolutionary radicalism and subsequent capitalist industrialization and globalization commences in 1964, before the Cultural Revolution. In the spring of 1964, our group of urban-born interviewees had just graduated, variously, from junior or senior high school in the city of Canton, the capital of Guangdong Province. Though some of these young people had failed to get into higher levels of education, they could have stayed in Canton and reapplied to enter a school the following year. But they declined to do so. A number of them felt inspired by the ideals they had been taught at school and did not want to look "selfish." As one of them reminisced to us in the mid-1970s:

> We had been educated to put the country's and the people's interests first; and had been taught that we shouldn't be afraid of suffering; should become revolutionary successors; and shouldn't just want to stay in the comfortable life of the cities. We had learned [from the first year of junior high school onward] that we should go to the countryside to temper ourselves, so as to be people who could take hardship and have stronger class feelings, and thus be able to become revolutionary successors. Also [we felt] the countryside needed us very much, we who had education and self-confidence. . . . At that time, many people thought that to live in the countryside was no good—too backward. . . . In the previous years very few young people had gone. We would be a frontline unit. We would open up a road to the rural areas.

Thus, when it came time to graduate, this young urban woman—at that time only sixteen years old—had made a public resolution of "one red heart and two types of preparation." The two types of preparation meant that if she passed the exams for senior high school, she would continue her education; if not, she would go to the countryside. Almost all of Canton's graduating students had made similar formal declarations of their intentions to go to the countryside if the nation wanted them to. They were, in fact, under pressure from school authorities to announce such "pledges of determination." It was a nonbinding declaration, but to declare it publicly and then renege left a young person vulnerable to accusations of hypocrisy from classmates who did volunteer. No one was literally forced to go, however, and most students ultimately declined. In 1964 only a small minority of the students had gotten into a senior high school or university, yet only some 6 percent of all of Canton's graduating junior and senior high school students embarked for the countryside.[3] Our interviewees, as part of that small minority, were among the more politically committed members of their generation.

Several of these urban-born interviewees had been exceptionally determined. They had been accepted into higher schools but had had "one red heart and *one* type of preparation." They had *insisted* on the sacrifice and "tempering" of a tough life in the countryside. One of them recalls, "I took the senior high entrance exams only to prove that I could do well in my studies and that I was willing to go, not for having failed, but because I was very red." Several others were going because they were of bad-class origins (their fathers had been capitalists before Liberation), and they felt there was therefore little future for themselves in the cities. By going to the countryside, they thought, they would disprove others' doubts about their political rectitude. But they also came to Chen Village to pursue positive challenges—as one of them has said, "to improve and strengthen my political ideology." Practically all the interviewees had been similarly idealistic—and many of them in addition had high personal ambitions. They wanted to "work for the countryside on the one hand and on the other attain some great achievements for myself," as one of them told us.

---

[3] Jonathan Unger, *Education Under Mao: Class and Competition in Canton Schools* (New York: Columbia University Press, 1982), p. 45.

To go, they had to get their parents' signed permission. An interviewee recalls: "It wasn't an easy task. Twenty of us from my school went to each others' families in groups to persuade each others' parents. We consoled them, 'It doesn't matter. We're all going together and we promise to look after each other.' But most of the parents refused to let their children go." In the end, only a dozen students from the school received their parents' grudging approval.

In all, fifty teenagers were organized as a group to go settle together in one village. Thirty-five of them were enthusiastic students from this and a second school. The remaining fifteen were "street youths"—that is, unemployed teenagers. These latter youths had only a primary school education. They had been looking for jobs for some time, with diminishing hopes of ever finding any in Canton's steadily tightening job market. Their families faced great difficulty supporting them.

The contingent of fifty young people was given a choice of two counties to settle in. One of their options was a county near Canton. The county was known to be relatively prosperous, and they would be able to return home for visits with relative ease. The second county was considerably further away. Though not in one of the poorest parts of Guangdong, the work there would be tougher and the living standards would be lower. At a meeting, the whole group was carried along by the idealistic feelings of the recent high school graduates and opted for the tougher location.

They set out from their schools and neighborhoods amid the enthusiastic banging of gongs and drums. The junior high school graduates were only fifteen and sixteen years old. In a photograph we have of their ostensibly joyous departure, they appear vulnerable, young, and a bit apprehensive. But by the time their transport pulled into the rural county capital and officials of the commune to which they had been assigned questioned them again about their resolve to go to a poor village, their spirits had revived. If they wanted, they were told, they could work in a reforestation farm near the commune market town—or they could go to Chen Village, which was jokingly referred to as the commune's Siberia. They all said, "the further the better."

Thus with their baggage piled atop wheelbarrows, they started off in ninety-degree heat on the two-hour trek from the commune market town. They were soon exhausted: "You see, we students from the city were used to taking buses." At long last, they came to a very run-down village. Thin pigs and scrawny chickens rooted and scrabbled in the lanes. The tired young people set down their wheelbarrows of belongings. "This," their guide corrected them, "is Chen Village's neighbor. You're headed for the poorer place down the road another mile."

They would be spending the next decade in that "poorer place down the road," and they would come of age there.

□ 1 □
Chen Village and
Its Leaders

The Village Setting

A large rushing stream marks off Chen Village's fields from a delta plain that stretches a dozen miles to the ocean. As the young people from Canton forded the stream (there was no bridge nearby), they thought Chen Village strikingly picturesque. The village pressed up against a range of craggy mountains as in a Chinese painting, surrounded on its nearer sides by fish ponds set amid a golden patchwork of fields of ripening grain.

At close range, however, the village no longer seemed at all inviting. In the wake of the late summer rains, the lanes were awash and slippery with garbage and animal manure. The narrow, steep-peaked houses were built mostly of plastered mud, with only small sections of their foundation walls boasting any real brick. They were dilapidated, dank, and reeked of the sows and poultry that shared the quarters with their owners.

The whole village had come out to greet the young newcomers with gongs and drums. The peasants were all barefoot, and the young people found out later that many did not even own a pair of sandals. Men and women alike were dressed in the traditional Guangdong peasant style of black-dyed shirts and baggy black pants—and these were threadbare, heavily patched, and soiled.

The poverty was even more obvious at mealtimes. The peas-

ants often had to make do with a concoction half of sweet potatoes and half of rice, since Chen Village could not raise enough
rice to support its population of just under one thousand. To
make the rice go even further and to vary their meals, they sometimes boiled the rice up as a watery gruel, for breakfasts and
dinners alike. The monotony of their starch diet was lightened
only by bits of tiny salt-dried fish, pickles, fermented bean curd,
and fermented black beans, the kind of strong tasting condiments
that in small amounts could go a long way on rice or in gruel.
Vegetables were eaten only irregularly. (Villagers believed vegetables upset the stomach unless cooked with a bit of oil; and Chen
Village grew so few peanuts that each peasant could be allotted
only four ounces of cooking oil per year!) An egg, or a fish caught
in the stream, was an occasional indulgence. Meat was reserved
for special celebrations and festivals.

Their yields were low and their work exhausting because the
village had only about five hundred acres of arable lands—and 60
percent of these lay up in small mountain valleys and hollows that
suffered from acidity and thin top soils. To get to some of these
hill plots required a three-hour uphill walk.

It was known in the villages roundabout that the Chens had
to toil for longer hours and less reward than most other peasants
in the district. For that reason, the village had always had difficulty finding brides from the neighboring villages for its own
young men; and it was traditionally considered taboo for a man to
marry a woman from within the village. Women who had had the
ill-fortune to be married into the village had a saying: "When
dead, most horrifying is the devil underground; when alive, most
horrifying are the fields of Chen Village." One of the village
women came up to the girls from the city in puzzlement: "If we
had to come into such a bad village there were reasons for it; but
why did you people stumble into such a place?"

Few Chen Villagers had ever ventured beyond the nearby
county towns. This was particularly true of the women, some of
whom knew only Chen Village, the market town about six miles
away, and the nearby village they had been born into. The men
themselves had stayed so close to the soil that they spoke an
accent of Cantonese that differed slightly from all the other
villages around. One Chen woman curiously asked one of the

Village Lane, 1981

new arrivals that first day: "Eh, so you're from Canton? Where's Canton? Is it in China or in America? Is it as big as Chen Village?"

Less than a decade later, Chen Village would produce more than enough rice. Every day the village households would be able to afford a small dish of meat with their dinners (variously of duck, goose, pork, chicken, eggs, or fresh fish), along with a rich variety of vegetable dishes. They would be building their homes of solid brick, with solid concrete floors rather than the traditional packed earth. By the early 1970s the young women would be wearing flower-patterned blouses. The Chen Villagers' political horizons would be far broader and their knowledge of the outside world far greater. Some of the younger ones would even be taking occasional outings to Canton. In the course of this book, we shall see how these extraordinary changes in the standard of living were accomplished. But in 1964 the village world that the young people from Canton entered was still one of severe poverty and very limited horizons.

On the second day that the young people were in the village, they were given a lesson in "class education." Chen Village's "four-bad types" were summoned by the village's party branch to line up in front of the new arrivals. The four-bad types were the former landlords, the pre-Liberation rich peasants, and anyone officially labeled a "counterrevolutionary" or "bad element" because of serious political, criminal, or social offenses. In all, there were about one and a half dozen such people in the village: two former landlords, several former rich peasants, two "bad elements," and all their wives. The newly arrived youths were to know exactly who these "class enemies" were so that they could be on their guard. They had heard a lot about sinister four-bad types, but few ever had had the chance of scrutinizing any at close range. One of the youths recalls, "When I got to the village and saw these landlords and counterrevolutionaries, I felt that deep in their hearts they still wanted to overthrow everything and kill all of us. In movies, they had awful faces. And in the village, when I saw them I feared them and thought they were repulsive to look at. I guess ugliness is a psychological thing. I felt they were somehow actually ugly."

Tales of the Chen Lineage

That same day, the young people were also briefed on the history of the village. They were told how, before the Liberation of 1949, the village had been oppressed and bullied by neighboring villages; how a great many of the men had had to hire themselves out at starvation wages to big landowners in neighboring richer villages; how other families had been reduced to wandering as beggars when times were bad; how the parents of several households had died on the road; how some of these desperate wandering households had had to sell their children into servitude to keep them alive. The village had been scourged by bandits, by Chiang Kai-shek's Guomindang government, and by the Japanese invaders. Exploited and starved, both by outside intruders and local landlords, the village's population had been in precipitous decline in the decades preceding Liberation. Its population had been cut in half. One of the young people from the city recounts: "The village was almost emptied out. If Liberation had come one year later, there wouldn't have been any village! . . . So when people compared the present with the past, they had a lot to be grateful for to the party."

That, at least, was the history the young city people were told. A very different tale was told to us in Hong Kong by three elderly Chens, all of poor-peasant background, who had emigrated from Chen Village in the mid-1940s. They told us of the bravado of the Chen Villagers; how they were feared by neighboring villagers; how in the 1930s the village's celebrations and festivals were of an opulence and grandeur that was the envy of many of the other villages in the district.

It appears memories play tricks. Reminiscences are embroidered with the images and stories that people want to weave of their own pasts. The old-timers, sitting in Hong Kong and employing the traditional measures of village status, wanted to picture to themselves a native village of sound reputation. The more prosperous and self-assertive their village, the better. But those in Chen Village wanted to paint their village history in the contours and colors of the *new* rural status system. When talking to the youths from Canton, they emphasized (and probably exaggerated) the poverty and wretchedness of the village's past—precisely those qualities that made it worthy of honor in China's revolutionary present. But however much the two sets of reminiscences differ, the testimony of old émigrés and Chen Villagers in the 1960s was alike in the sense that both groups strongly felt that their own status was linked to the status of their native community.

Their sense of identity had been reinforced by the fact that Chen Village is a single-lineage community, all the males of which are descended on their father's side from a single common ancestor. The village was settled some four hundred or more years ago by colonists from an overcrowded lineage village in a neighboring county. According to stories told both by the old Chens and younger emigrants, the village's founders had originally laid claim not just to what today constitutes Chen Village but to rich stretches of land on the far side of the stream that marks the present boundary of the village. But skirmishes broke out between the Chens and neighboring lineage villages; and in that early period the Chens lost, were forced off much of the contested land, and had to turn to tilling the thinner soil in the mountains.

To honor their ancestors and affirm their common roots in the past, the Chens eventually built a large brick ancestral hall (until the 1970s it was by far the largest structure in the village) within which they kept the sacred tablets and records containing the genealogies of their lineage. Villagers who claimed descent from particular illustrious sons or grandsons of the lineage founder also built smaller ancestral halls to celebrate their ancestry. There were five of these smaller halls scattered throughout the village, corresponding to the five "branches" of the Chen lineage. But only the most populous branch, the Lotus branch, had paid any great attention to its own branch's ritual life. This may have been because the Lotus members held common material interests: the communal lands owned and rented out by the Lotus Hall (to support its branch rites and to divide among its own members) were greater than those of the other branch halls. But even the Lotus members largely celebrated their ties with the past, and their sense of solidarity, through the rituals that centered on the main village-wide lineage hall. This stress upon community-level solidarity probably was necessary to protect the village from its slightly larger and stronger neighbors. An old man may well have been right when he told us, "In my time it would've been impossible for other villages to go around bullying us because we people of Chen Village had such a strong collective spirit." That spirit remains strong today—stronger, perhaps, than for most Chinese communities. Even in the 1970s the Chen Village leaders would be able to appeal to these feelings of village allegiance to check the independence of the village's various neighborhoods.[1]

The range of mountains behind Chen Village had always provided a safe refuge and lair for bandits. In the 1940s these mountains became the home also for Communist guerrillas fighting first the Japanese and then the Guomindang. The old Chens

---

[1.] Our small sample of villages suggests that under socialism, production brigade (i.e., village) leaderships are considerably weaker in localities where, traditionally, village-level organization and cohesion were weaker: for example, in villages where loyalties used to be centered more on the various lineage branches (or different lineages) within the village.

now in Hong Kong have distasteful memories of the Guomindang. The Guomindang militia stationed in a nearby market town used to come by at harvest time to raid the village's crops. But the Communist guerrillas, on the contrary, were disciplined. Recalls an old man, "Those guerrillas never took anything, and wouldn't even accept food if offered any. I wonder where they did get their food. They were peasants like ourselves. We sometimes met up with them when we were out working our mountain plots. Sometimes they even stayed the night in the village."

About half a dozen of Chen Village's men joined up with the guerrilla bands. They were the type of young, poor, self-assertive men who in earlier decades might have associated themselves with bands of brigands when times were bad. Now instead, still only half-understanding the messages brought by the Communist party, they became affiliated to a movement that would alter profoundly their village's economy, social life, and politics. Their activities in the mountains would earn them the trust of the Communist government in the new era and enviable reputations among their fellow Chens.

The 1950s in Chen Village

The new order did not come to Chen Village, though, through the small guerrilla bands in the mountains. It was achieved through the victories of the Communist armies in north China. About a year after Lin Biao's triumphant march southward in 1949 into Guangdong Province, a small "workteam" of Communist cadres was dispatched to Chen Village by the new Communist government.[2] It had come to carry out a land reform in the village.

The Communist workteam's mission was twofold. It had been instructed not just to redistribute landholdings in the village but also to demolish the power and influence of the rural elite. To accomplish this, it needed to bring the anger and resentment of the poor families to the surface. The poorer Chens themselves

---

2. *Cadre* is the term used by the Chinese to denote any and all officials.

would have to set aside the traditional notion of lineage solidarity. They would have to be convinced to join with outsiders in attacks against kinsmen. They would have to learn to express themselves in terms of "class hatred."

But many of the village households held back initially from cooperating with this Communist workteam. The peasants were traditionally suspicious of outsiders. And the poorest peasants, who had the most to gain from a land reform, were reportedly intimidated by the power the wealthy families customarily had been able to exert over them.

The Communist workteam needed assistance from within the village to reach these poorer households. The local guerrilla movement provided this link. In particular, the Communist organizers could depend upon Chen Sumei. Sumei had not been born a Chen; but he had been adopted (i.e., sold) into the village as a child. He had survived as a young man by scavenging wood in the mountains to sell in the delta villages for use as fuel. He had begun to work underground for the Communists, delivering secret messages as he climbed up and down with his wood. According to the story that has been handed down about Chen Sumei,

> When land reform came to this area, no one dared to move against the landlords. . . . But Chen Sumei knew who were the poorest and who could be organized to do what. He got together some poor peasants who'd speak out, who dared to do things, and he got them to organize against the landlords, to struggle against them. . . . He helped lead the peasants to be masters of their society. Gained quite a reputation!

In emotional "struggle sessions," angry poor peasants led by the workteam and Sumei finally had humiliated the village landlords and stripped them of all but a few parcels of their land, just enough for the landlord families to feed themselves.

Chen Village had only two landlords, and neither of them had had very extensive landholdings. One came from a long-established landlord family. He had been well versed in the classics (and wrote elegant calligraphy) and had augmented his influence by taking on the duties of village judge. The other landlord was nouveau riche. He had, not long before Liberation, developed a profitable trade as a rural pharmacist and had plowed his proceeds into land.

In addition to these two landlords, there were five "rich peasant" households in the village. Three of these were part of the same family—a father and his two married sons. A rich peasant was one who worked part of his fields himself, but possessed so much land that he needed to hire field hands or to rent out much of it. The family of this particular rich peasant actually owned more land than either of the two landlords; but the family members did not share the rural elite's traditional disdain for manual labor and had vigorously worked most of their lands themselves with the aid of hired help. Under the land reform regulations of the early 1950s, rich peasants were not to have the bulk of their lands expropriated nor were they to be attacked harshly like the landlords. For the time being, the high agricultural productivity of such households could contribute to China's economic development. The father in this rich peasant family was able to retain enough land that he still had to hire field hands. Fortunately, too, for this man, he had always been comparatively decent to his hands and thus retained a residual respect among Chen Village's poorer families. According to one of his sons, whom we interviewed in Hong Kong, the landlords had gained quite different reputations: "Those landlords were fierce; they'd beaten people who hadn't paid all their rents."

The relative good fortune of Chen Village's rich peasant households was only temporary. Land reform gave each family in the village a class label, which remained with the family. These labels became inheritable in the male line. The former landlord and rich peasant households officially belonged to "bad" untrustworthy classes, and they would be systematically discriminated against and harassed throughout the years to come.

Villagers who prior to the land reform had had just enough land to support their families were labeled by the cadre workteam as "middle peasants," a category further subdivided into upper-middle, middle, and lower-middle. Upper-middle and middle peasants were not considered politically suspect, but they were officially defined as being less trustworthy than the poor peasants (who had owned very little or no land) and the lower-middle peasants (who had owned some land but had had to supplement this by renting land as tenants or doing field labor for richer families). The former poor and lower-middle peasants belonged to the "red classes." Whenever possible in the coming decades, the government would prefer that members of the red classes be the village officials.

In Chen Village the former poor and lower-middle peasants comprised some 80 to 85 percent of the population. But in the early 1950s, there were not many men from the poorest classes with the necessary abilities to lead Chen Village into the new era. The poor were almost entirely illiterate. Few had ever held positions of responsibility. They had less experience in planning agriculture than the self-reliant middle peasantry. Chen Sumei might have been capable enough to serve as the village's new leader, but he and the few other former guerrillas who had helped carry out the land reform did not remain in Chen Village very long. The Communists had great need for capable men of that sort, and they rose quickly into posts outside the village. Chen Sumei eventually became head of the county's agricultural implements factory, that is, until he fell from political grace in the late 1960s for the sin of philandering and was exiled back to Chen Village.

When the land reform workteam of the early 1950s left Chen Village, the village leadership thus did not pass into the hands of the young, self-assertive poor peasants who had become guerrillas, nor into the hands of the unassertive poor peasants who had remained in the village. Instead, an articulate middle peasant who had been active in the land reform became Chen Village's leader, its party secretary. This man, Chen Feihan, apparently had prestige among his fellow villagers as a capable farmer; but more important, he was literate and would be able to read party directives.

Collectivization

The land reform workteam had already begun processes of change in Chen Village. It would be Feihan's duty to push them forward. The workteam had dismantled the lineage organizations and redistributed to the poor peasants all the lands owned by the lineage and lineage-branch halls. The annual rites were no longer to be practiced. The halls were converted into warehouses. But the land reform had not equalized the peasantry's landholdings. The former poor peasants still had fewer strips of land than the middle peasants, and they had not been able to receive enough tools or draft animals to work efficiently the new land they acquired.

The workteam had tried to make up for this by persuading small clusters of families who were friends of long standing, poor and middle peasants alike, to begin cooperating in what were called mutual-aid teams. It had been traditional to exchange labor, tools, and animals during the busy seasons, but the workteam pushed this mutual aid concept further than had ever been practiced before. The policy worked. Soon even the more recalcitrant villagers were obliged by the pressures of community sentiment to join in mutual aid.

Feihan, the new party secretary, in 1954 organized a more complicated scheme. He started Chen Village's first cooperative. He apparently did so before such cooperatives had appeared in most other villages in Guangdong. Rather than just helping out in each others' fields, the participants would pool their fields and draft animals for the entire year. The advantage was that the members' tiny plots could be combined into larger fields that could be plowed and irrigated more efficiently. At the end of the year, the member families would divide up the profits, some shares going for the amount of labor each had contributed and some shares for the use of the members' various fields and animals. Each family had previously faced the risk that an infestation or flooding of the family's own small plots might wipe out the family financially. The co-op promised more security.

The idea appealed most to the poorest families, whose assets were fewest and whose circumstances were most precarious. The small plots they had received in the land reform may not have been enough to support them. At first, reportedly, just poor-peasant families joined up with Feihan in the new venture. "But the co-ops got bigger and bigger," one of the Chens recounts. "The richer families didn't want to join, but they were isolated and forced in. The co-ops wouldn't cooperate with them on irrigation—pretty much cut off their access to water—to force them in." Before long, most of the peasants of Chen Village had been organized into two co-ops. But the peasants had little experience as yet in managing large amounts of land or organizing sizable squads of laborers. The new system proved too unwieldy; and within the year, many of the families had split once more into mutual-aid teams.

In mid-1956, however, a national campaign to inaugurate even more "advanced" co-ops had been started under Mao's prodding.[3] China's regional party organizations competed to get the new collectives organized. Under the new system, only a family's labor inputs would be counted; annual compensation would no longer be offered for the use of land or draft animals. Through this, the poorer households in Chen Village would be getting a better break at the expense of the former middle peasant and rich peasant households. Once again they found the new proposals in their own interest.

The Great Leap Forward

Before the peasants had time to get accustomed to the new collective arrangements, an even more radical social experiment was launched from on high. A utopian mood was gathering momentum in the party. China's leading party officials believed that the bigger the units of rural production, the more advanced in socialism they would be. The collectives were thus to be consolidated with other collectives to form huge "people's communes." Public canteens were to be set up so that the peasants would not have to spend time procuring and preparing their own food. These canteens were to be free, allowing peasants to be fed "each according to his needs" rather than "each according to his work." The extra time gained from this was to go into extra labor: to carry out massive irrigation projects; to plow deeper and plant more closely; and to establish rural industrial schemes like the smelting of crude steel. National party leaders promised that all this would leapfrog China into an era of abundance and true communism.

[3.] See the "Draft Program for Agricultural Development in the People's Republic of China, 1956–1967 (January 1956)," in Robert R. Bowie and John K. Fairbank, eds., *Communist China 1955–1959: Policy Documents with Analysis* (Cambridge Mass.: Harvard University Press, 1962).

The bulk of the peasantry of Chen Village had retained their faith in a party that had brought them peace, land reform, and mutual aid. They believed the exuberant promises:

> They still have sweet memories of the beginning of communization. "We all worked together, moving from place to place. We ate wherever we happened to be; ah, in the beginning we were all so fat! We could eat any time we liked at the canteens." . . . They really believed that that was communism, that you can have free food wherever you go.

But their enthusiasm quickly soured. The Great Leap Forward degenerated into bureaucratic blundering and organizational chaos. The entire local marketing district of some twenty thousand people had been designated a commune. The cadres stationed at the market town headquarters began issuing a flow of confused, imperious commands. "The whole thing was a mess," an interviewee recalls.

> They pushed a system of planting called "Sky Full of Stars" where a field would be so overplanted the seedlings starved each other out. . . . The peasants knew it was useless, but there was simply no way to oppose anything, because the orders came from so high above. And if one of our Chen Village cadres protested at commune meetings, he laid himself open to criticisms: "a rightist, against the revolution." . . . The peasants were ordered to smash their water jars to make them into fertilizer. They said it was stupid, that the jars were just sterile clay, but they had to smash the jars nonetheless. What a mess! Cut rice was left overnight in the fields [and mildewed] while exhausted villagers were ordered off to do other things. The period was called the "Eat-It-All-Up Period" because people were eating five and six times daily—but there was no harvest that year. Everything had been given to the collective. Nothing was left in the houses. No grain had been stored. People were so hungry they had difficulty sleeping. . . . Some people became ill, and some of the elderly died. Our village became quiet, as if the people were dead.

The villagers had no reason to plant for the next season. With the commune level in charge, most of what they produced would be siphoned off to fill a common pot with eight other villages; and with no likelihood that the peasants of the other villages would be willing to work, Chen Villagers strongly doubted they would get anything back in return. So the Chen Village peasants let their fields go wild, while they scavenged on the hillsides or sat indoors conserving their energy and nursing their hunger.

Chen Village Production Brigade and Its New Leaders

Production was at a standstill; organization and morale were shattered. It was not until 1961 that the government developed a comprehensive set of policies to repair the damage caused by the Great Leap Forward. In accordance with the new dispensation,[4] Chen Village was divided into five production teams, each composed of about forty neighboring families. Each of these teams received property rights over a fifth of the village's lands. This new system was designed to encourage the peasants to produce. If a team produced more, its households ate more. Each team member would be paid in grain and cash only in accordance with how much labor he or she contributed. Small private plots and private handicraft production, moreover, would be permitted again, and the produce could be sold privately at newly reopened rural markets.

Each of these production teams was managed by an elected committee, its members chosen more for their managerial abilities than for their political "redness." Most of them were not in fact members of the Communist party. These production team committees, located so close to the grass roots, could manage the collective labor of peasants much more effectively than the distant leaders who had tried to supervise the gigantic communes of the Great Leap Forward.

The new programs and new forms of economic organization worked with dramatic effect. Villagers began once more to work

---

[4.] The new "Regulations on the Work of the Rural People's Communes," also known as the "Sixty Articles," were published in a final form in September 1962. See *Documents of the Chinese Communist Party Central Committee, September 1956– April 1969* (Hong Kong: Union Research Institute, 1971), 1: 719-722.

hard and in orderly fashion; and by the end of 1961, the village's famine was ended.

Feihan was not in charge of this new chapter in Chen Village's affairs. Two younger men of stronger character and abilities had supplanted him during the Great Leap Forward. For the next quarter century these two men, Chen Qingfa and Chen Longyong, would dominate Chen Village's politics. Both of these men held key brigade posts. Chen Village as a whole had now been titled a "production brigade," and its government consisted of a party branch committee and a brigade management committee. This management committee handled daily administrative affairs and oversaw village-wide projects such as irrigation systems, which were beyond the scope of any of the individual teams.[5] But the seven-man (no women) party branch committee was more important. It made the major decisions, supervised the management committee's work, kept close tabs on the five new production teams to ensure that they acted according to official regulations, and took responsibility in the village for carrying out the national party's political campaigns. Chen Qingfa was the party secretary and Chen Longyong the brigade management chief under him. In 1961 both were not quite thirty years old. The clashes between them would be central to Chen Village's history during the next two decades.

Chen Qingfa

Chen Qingfa's class background had been of considerable help to him in his rise to the top leadership post. He had been one of the poorest of Chen Village's poor peasants at the time of land reform. But his origins were "complicated," for he was related to the village's older landlord family. His great grandfather had served as a minor official in Canton and had secured enough bribes to retire to Chen Village as its major landowner. Qingfa's

---

[5.] Chen Village's management committee originally consisted of a brigade chief, two deputy chiefs in charge of economic management, a militia head, a public security chief, and a man who combined the jobs of accountant and secretarial clerk.

own uncle was the landlord with the elegant calligraphy. But Qingfa's father had been the family's black sheep. He had been a heavy gambler and drug addict who had quickly dissipated his inheritance. He died while Qingfa was still a young boy, followed shortly by Qingfa's mother. Qingfa had had to resort to begging for a while, before being taken in and fed by a childless widow in the village. (To provide for her old age, it had been, and still is today, the custom for such a woman to show kindness to an orphan; Qingfa, true to the implicit bargain, in the 1960s and 1970s helped to support the old woman financially.)

As a teenager Qingfa had tended cattle for his uncle, the landlord, under conditions he considered degrading. When the opportunity arose, he left to join the guerrillas. But life in the mountains proved too difficult for him, and after half a year he had returned to tend his uncle's cows. During the land reform, Qingfa exacted vengeance for his uncle's maltreatment of him. The workteam used his denunciations of the older man to provide Chen Villagers with an example of how class struggle should take precedence over kinship.

Qingfa not only entered the Communist Youth League during the land reform; he soon propelled himself into the leading post in that organization. He took an early and notable role in the new cooperatives, and Feihan in gratitude sponsored his admission to the Communist party. Barely twenty, Qingfa was already moving toward the top.

In the Great Leap Forward he caught the attention of the new commune leadership, as head of a shock brigade of Chen Village youths that came out best in a frantic competition between villages to help construct a county reservoir. The party normally looks for its new grass roots cadres during the heat of major campaigns; and the commune leaders had been ordered to be on the watch for young men who "dare to think, dare to speak, dare to act." Qingfa clearly fit that bill; and Feihan, the party secretary, handicapped by his "unclean" class origins and his slower and less aggressive ways, was eased aside. But Feihan seems not to have minded particularly. Qingfa was his own protégé; and Feihan himself had grown tired and lazier with the years. He retired to the post of deputy party secretary of the village, and in the years to come contentedly spent his days avoiding both decision-making and physical labor.

Under Qingfa, Chen Village reorganized after the disasters of the Great Leap Forward more quickly than the nearby villages. Qingfa encouraged the production teams to take advantage of the village's soil, which was especially suitable for growing sweet potatoes. The village was soon awash with them. In fact, it was through these sweet potatoes that many of the young Chen men secured wives. Families in other villages accepted marriage offers from Chen Village so that the brides would be able to carry sacks of potatoes home to their own kin to tide them over the bad period. Well into the 1970s, when lamenting the hard work in Chen Village, some of these women would complain, "If it hadn't been for your sweet potatoes we wouldn't have had to marry into this place."

Qingfa himself took advantage of Chen Village's brief good fortune in 1961 and hired a matchmaker. The bride was homely and not particularly intelligent, but the matchmaker had reported correctly (matchmakers often were notorious liars) that she was a strong and energetic worker, a very competent housekeeper, and had "good class" origins. She possessed the qualities that a Chinese villager considered most important in a bride.

Qingfa was slightly shorter than most of the men in Chen Village. But he was muscular, agile, and had formidable stamina in field labor. People in the village closely judged men in terms of two crucial tasks—the speed at which a man could cut grain and the weight a man could lift and carry on a shoulder pole—and by these standards Qingfa was the third or fourth best laborer in Chen Village. All of Chen Village's other leading cadres are also very capable workers, for as an interviewee notes: "In our village, if your labor power isn't passable you can't lead anybody. Your words won't have any power." Qingfa's outstanding physical abilities considerably bolstered his authority.

So too did Qingfa's articulateness and his decisiveness. He had never been to school and was entirely illiterate. But he had a memory that astonished the urban young people the first time that they heard him speak. He could attend a meeting of several days at the market town or county capital and on his return recount to the peasants, in an accurate, clear, and convincing style, the major issues that had been discussed and the series of new complicated directives that were being handed down. Moreover, according to one of our interviewees, "he wasn't a 'mouth' doer, the type of fellow who speaks about getting a lot done but never gets to it. When Qingfa said something had to be accomplished he'd move on it the next day by the latest. . . . He had a brisk decisive work-style like that of an army man."

Qingfa exercised a formidable temper to get what he wanted. He purposely let his temper flare at strategic moments to intimidate subordinates into going along with him. Qingfa was supposed to share decisions with the other members of the village's party leadership committee, but he would violently curse and bang the table to dominate every decision.

In Chen Village other cadres used the same type of explosive leadership style to secure compliance from their own subordinates. But Qingfa's temper went beyond that of other cadres; sometimes his temper got the best of him. He even angrily smacked children when he caught them at mischief, knowing that their parents would not dare to protest against a party secretary. He could make life uncomfortable for any household that stood against him.

Qingfa could be gregarious and charming as well as domineering. He enjoyed evenings of relaxed talk with old friends. He felt loyal to old acquaintances and kinfolk. He even remained on good terms with the old bandit-turned-guerrilla who had introduced Qingfa into the mountain band of Communist guerrillas. After Liberation the man had been rewarded with a customs job, but he was caught taking bribes, wounded his superior in a scuffle, and was sent back to Chen Village in disgrace, officially labeled as a "bad element." He was thus now among the four-bad types. But instead of behaving submissively as a four-bad type should, he had continued to put on superior airs and to insult other villagers. Yet Qingfa loyally protected him whenever he obstreperously got himself into trouble. Qingfa did so in the face of the party's strict policy that such a man be treated as a political and social pariah.

Playing Politics with Teams

Qingfa also showed particular loyalty to some of his kin. He was from the Lotus branch of the Chen lineage, the branch that had maintained the greatest sense of identity before the Liberation. Most of the members of the Lotus branch lived in the same neighborhood at roughly the geographical center of the village. In contrast, the memberships of other lineage branches tended to be scattered among the various village neighborhoods, as a consequence of their weaker sense of identity.

Qingfa went out of his way to be helpful to his relatives and neighbors when it was his responsibility as party secretary in 1961 to set up the village's production teams. Membership in the teams was to be based roughly on the various neighborhoods. Qingfa carved out the No. 1 team from the northeast corner of the village, a neighborhood consisting largely of middle peasants. He established the No. 2 team in the northeast neighborhood, which was occupied almost entirely by former poor peasants. He split the western side of the village into two numerically equal teams: No. 4 and No. 5. And he gerrymandered the boundaries of the No. 3 team, where his own house was located, so as to include in it primarily families of the Lotus branch (see Figure 1, p. 32).

Once the team memberships had been designated, all the village lands had to be divided among the teams. The village fields were of a number of different grades, ranging from the nearby fertile paddy lands to only marginally arable plots in mountain pockets far from the village. Qingfa carefully divided each grade of land into five roughly equivalent portions. Because of the complex topography, it was not possible to devise portions of exactly equal size, quality, or distance; so to ensure fairness, representatives from each of the new teams picked straws. Qingfa operated the lottery, and according to what his confederates later confided to a member of Qingfa's own team, Qingfa cheated. He contrived that each time the straws were picked, the team of his own kinsmen and neighbors received plots that were slightly better and closer to the village.

A year later, Qingfa was instructed by the government to divide each of these five new production teams in half, as it was believed that teams with smaller memberships would find it easier

Figure 1.   The Production Teams Formed from
Neighborhoods, 1961

to organize their own work. There would now be ten teams of about twenty to twenty-five households apiece. Again Qingfa quietly performed his manipulations. When he split his own neighborhood, he made sure that all the kinsmen to whom he felt closest were grouped together in the same team, and he again rigged the straw lottery to ensure that they received the marginally better plots.

Qingfa's manipulations were in no way blatant. He could not afford to alienate the rest of the village. The lands of the new No. 6 team, Qingfa's team, were only slightly better than those of the other nine teams. But his discreet show of loyalty to his kinsmen and neighbors was to set the tone for his political operations during the next several years.

However, it cannot be said that the Lotus branch was being kept alive as a body of kin whose loyalties to one another superseded the newer political or economic arrangements. Qingfa and his fellow good-class team members did not, for example, transgress the new "class line." Though Qingfa's landlord uncle and two former rich peasant families were included in the No. 6 production team, they were treated as social outcasts. Moreover, once the livelihoods of the peasants were tied to cooperation with

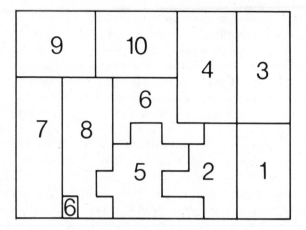

Figure 2. The Production Teams after Division, 1962

fellow *team* members, the families of the Lotus branch who had ended up in team No. 6 realized they had little to gain by continuing to show loyalty toward Lotus branch members who lived beyond the boundaries of their team.[6]

Qingfa initially had played favorites toward his home production team in part because, against official Communist doctrine, he held onto traditional kinship loyalties. But it was also useful to him, both as an individual and as a brigade official. He could expect gratitude and loyal cooperation in return for his patronage.

As brigade party secretary, Qingfa ultimately was responsible to his party superiors at the commune seat[7] for maintaining law

---

[6] Martin K. Whyte has found this to be true of other Guangdong villages, too: "the central economic dependence of peasants on their families and teams, and secondarily on their brigades, creates solidarity and vested interests in these basic level units, and rivalry with other nearby units, even when these are composed of kinsmen as well" ("Family Change in China," *Issues and Studies,* July 1979, p. 56).

[7] The word *commune* had been retained for the administrative district of nine villages that surrounded the local market town. But the commune level retained little of the power that it had held during the Great Leap Forward. It ran the shops and tiny local industries that were situated in the market town; it organized the flood-control and road-building projects that were bigger than any single village could handle; and its party committee, which had its headquarters in the market

and order in his village; for assuring that each team paid all its taxes and planted and sold an annual quota of grain, peanuts, and sugar to the state at the low prices set by the state; and for laying the foundations for the community's future economic development. But Qingfa had been provided with only modest political leverage to carry out these responsibilities. Beyond its quota requirements, each team was economically self-sufficient. Each production team's leadership controlled the distribution of its profits. Though the brigade administration operated some village-level enterprises, these included only a flock of ducks and geese, a small brick kiln, an orchard, and half-grown stands of pines that had been planted on some of the mountainsides. The salaries of the brigade cadres, including Qingfa's, had to be funded largely through small levies on the teams, and these had to be negotiated annually at a meeting between all the team heads and brigade cadres. For any new village-level projects, separate negotiations with the team heads had to be held to raise the funds and manpower. The weakness of the brigade administration's financial base undermined Qingfa's capacity to dominate the brigade as he would have liked.

In such circumstances, Qingfa could turn to his own No. 6 production team to back him up. But he needed a broader base of support. It became necessary to extend his patronage politics to a few other teams. For instance, he built goodwill and incurred special debts from the No. 1 team, a team that had been carved out of the neighborhood of middle peasants on Chen Village's northeast flank. It was of extreme importance to any team that its team head be a very capable agricultural planner whose daily orders would command his team members' respect. Team No. 1 had a problem here. A team head was supposed to be chosen from among the former poor or lower-middle peasants, the "politically reliable" classes. But in the No. 1 team, "the [several] team members whose class origins were good didn't have the ability, and those with ability couldn't be cadres" because of their class ori-

---

town, was the next higher link in the party chain that connected Chen Village with national political programs. Commune level officials intruded into village affairs only sporadically, mostly to check that planting quotas were being met. From the perspective of the Chen Village peasants, the commune was an administrative level of far less importance than either their teams (neighborhoods) or brigade (village).

gins. Qingfa cut through the dilemma by approving the election of an upper-middle peasant as team head. But it remained difficult for this team head to get team members of better class origins to follow his directions. Qingfa provided him with the higher-level backing he needed, and in return he provided support for Qingfa. Subsequently the No. 1 team, too, got a slightly bigger slice of whatever largesse Qingfa had the power to disburse. And to strengthen his hand, when recruiting new people for the party or for new brigade-level party posts, Qingfa tended to look toward the teams with which he had established special relationships.

The various teams that did not benefit from Qingfa's favoritism were resentful for good reasons. The most disgruntled were teams No. 3 and No. 4, which had been carved out of the southeastern neighborhood of former poor peasants. They had, by chance, received slightly worse lands than any other teams in the lottery. Moreover, they had no effective agricultural planners who were willing to be team heads. The net effect was that the incomes from the collective fields of the No. 3 and No. 4 teams were little more than half that of the No. 6 team. To compensate for their poor collective performance, they devoted more time and effort to their private plots and their private raising of pigs. So successful were they at this that their members' total incomes almost matched those of team No. 6. But their suspicions that Qingfa had rigged the original lottery festered as a point of conflict. They squabbled with the No. 6 team and resisted Qingfa more often than the other teams.

Chen Longyong

Qingfa had problems also with his immediate subordinate, Chen Longyong, the head of the brigade management committee. Whereas Qingfa's party branch committee supervised Chen Village's affairs, Longyong oversaw day-to-day administrative duties. Longyong also sat on the party committee, where by force of personality he was, second to Qingfa, its most influential member.

As leading brigade cadres, both Qingfa and Longyong shared an interest in strengthening the brigade level of management and developing the brigade-wide economy. But they were uneasy allies. Longyong was a decisive and stubborn man and one of the most talented agricultural planners in the village. He preferred his own opinions to those of Qingfa; and whenever possible he pursued his own course. Longyong's leadership abilities and strength of personality were on a par with Qingfa's. He was not as smooth a talker, but he was an effective public speaker nonetheless, with almost as keen a memory. (Longyong, too, was totally illiterate.) While Qingfa ranked among the best laborers in Chen Village, Longyong, a powerful man some six feet tall, was perhaps the village's single strongest worker. When he had the time to help a production team with its labor, or when he led a corps of Chen Village's young people to work on a commune irrigation project, Longyong would work at a ferocious pace, pulling his co-workers forward beyond their own normal speed. He had a raw, domineering style of command similar to Qingfa's, and he inspired the same respectful fear among ordinary peasants. But Longyong, unlike Qingfa, had learned to unleash his temper only when it was strategically to his benefit. In the long term, as we shall see, his astute use of this self-control would provide him with political advantages over Qingfa.

As boys, Qingfa and Longyong had "worn the same pants"— that is, they had been inseparably close friends. Qingfa had been Longyong's sponsor to the party, and when Qingfa had taken over the brigade's leadership in the Great Leap Forward, Longyong had stepped into Qingfa's role as head of the shock brigade of Chen Village youths. But their relations had soured in office partly because they were so similar in their capabilities and aggressive natures. Longyong chafed at having to yield to Qingfa's final word at party branch meetings; Qingfa was repeatedly infuriated by Longyong's stubborn resistance.

They had disagreements also over Longyong's sense of self-righteousness. Qingfa did not pass up opportunities to receive small gifts of poultry and other foodstuffs from villagers or to snack with friends at brigade expense. But not Longyong. A hard-driving, unsociable man, he disdained such affairs. He usually was as strict with himself as with others. Whereas Qingfa found the time in the late afternoon or early evening to tend to his private plot, Longyong, in counterpoint, poured almost all of his energies and time into his public duties. He neglected his private plot, and his family ate the worse for it. It is possible, from what we know of Longyong's character, that he was consciously putting himself forward publicly as the more righteous of the two men. More importantly, the two leaders apparently came into repeated small conflicts over Qingfa's favors to the No. 6 and No. 1 teams. Longyong was from one of the western neighborhood's former poor peasant families, a member of a small, disorganized lineage branch that to most intents and purposes had ceased to exist. Having no special feelings of identity with any fellow branch members, his loyalties to Chen Village were undivided. "Longyong's base was in the brigade, not the team. You couldn't say the people [in the team where he lived] were his 'own people.' Not like Qingfa who had his foundations a bit in the team, a bit in the brigade." If given the choice, the sectors of Chen Village that had been shortchanged under Qingfa's patronage practices would have preferred a man like Longyong as the village's "local emperor."

Whatever the two men's conflicts, Qingfa appreciated Longyong's abilities as brigade chief and wanted to continue using him; but he apparently felt that Longyong posed a danger to him as a rival. The government's decision in 1963 to carry out a Four Cleanups campaign[8] in the countryside presented Qingfa with an opportunity to check Longyong's ambitions. He could use the campaign, in the words of one interviewee, to "put Longyong firmly back in his place, to show Longyong what Qingfa could do if he wanted, so that Longyong would be obedient in the future and not dare to challenge him."

The Small Four Cleanups

The Four Cleanups campaign had been organized by the party leadership in Peking to "clean up" the corrupt practices of local rural officials during the "three lean years" of economic setbacks after the collapse of the Great Leap Forward. This was to

---

8. On the Chinese party central committee's announcement of the Four Cleanups drive, see Richard Baum, *Prelude to Revolution: Mao, the Party and the Peasant Question, 1962–66* (New York: Columbia University Press, 1975), pp. 23-28.

be the first step in a series of major efforts that were being planned for the countryside: to repurify the local party organizations; to bolster the peasants' morale after the catastrophes of the Great Leap; and to improve the workings of the rural economy. As a first step, in what the villagers would later recall as the "Small" Four Cleanups, the Chen Village party branch received official directives in 1964 to carry out a drive to stamp out any signs of corruption, great or small, among the village's officers. This drive was to be organized and controlled by the village party secretary, Qingfa.

Qingfa's major targets were team-level cadres, in particular warehousemen, cashiers, and accountants. These were posts that provided few official rewards. Unlike brigade cadres, the team cadres got little in the way of supplementary income for their efforts, and they had to engage in as much manual labor as an ordinary team member. But their jobs did provide them with small illicit perquisites. For example, a warehouseman in charge of overseeing his team's granaries and the distribution of grain rations to all the team's households found it relatively easy to appropriate a little extra rice for himself and his family and to weigh out slightly bigger portions to close friends and relatives. Several of these team cadres whose peculations had been blatant now had to make public self-examinations. A few were relieved of their posts. Qingfa was intent upon showing his own party superiors that he meant business in carrying through the campaign. But only one brigade-level cadre was touched by a charge of corruption, and that was Chen Longyong.

At the end of the Great Leap Forward, some lumber had been left over from the building of a large wall-less shed that served as the village meeting hall. Longyong had asked Qingfa if he could buy some of the surplus lumber to erect a small kitchen for his house. Since lumber was, and still is, in very short supply in Guangdong Province, access to it, even for purchase, is a privilege of some substance. To use one's political position to obtain such priorities was exceedingly common, and at the time few people would have criticized Longyong for making the request. His house was small and run down, and his standard of living below average for Chen Village. According to one interviewee, Qingfa had not only been sympathetic to Longyong's request; he had insisted that Longyong take the lumber free of charge.

Qingfa may have felt that by thus putting Longyong in his debt, he could expect a certain amount of deference in return. But Longyong was not the type to give this. He did not abide by what Qingfa probably considered a tacit bargain between the two men over the lumber; and he still put on an annoyingly righteous front.

Now, during the Small Four Cleanups campaign, Qingfa brought up Longyong's appropriation of the lumber as the basis for attacking him, as if Longyong had furtively stolen it. Longyong was obliged to get up before a mass meeting of the whole brigade to deliver a self-confession. It is normal practice in such a campaign for the accused person to protect himself and seek a lighter penalty not by protesting innocence or turning against the people who control the campaign but by going along with the tide. In a low-key way, Longyong confessed to his use of the wood. He probably expected that he would only be asked to pay for the lumber. But after Longyong had made his confession, an interviewee recalls, the next person to get up was Qingfa:

> He said, "The brigade chief is right in what he said about misusing his authority, but what he's done is even worse than he's said. Do you agree?" And the whole crowd yelled out, "We agree!" The people in the crowd didn't have much choice; no way to say they disagreed. Some of them certainly had sympathy with Longyong, but would have been afraid to say anything for fear of getting into trouble themselves.

Because Qingfa painted the incident as a flagrant example of cadre corruption, an appropriately exaggerated version of Longyong's transgressions was dispatched to the commune headquarters. An interviewee from the No. 6 team recalls that years later Qingfa privately "admitted he'd gotten Longyong unfairly."

Qingfa had not fully realized that the commune-level party committee was under pressure to show its own strict rectitude in the campaign. The commune committee took the case more seriously than Qingfa had expected it would. It indicated that it would expel Longyong from the party, putting Longyong permanently under a political cloud. Qingfa still had need of Longyong's strong abilities as a cadre and production planner, and he found himself belatedly having to intervene in Longyong's behalf.

In the meantime, Longyong had felt devastated by the accusation of corruption and by his sudden fall from political grace. He had not cared much for material possessions, but he loved power and very much wanted to be respected and honored for his work on behalf of the village. He wanted "face," and now he had none. He went home and made an ineffectual effort to hang himself. Fortunately, as an interviewee sympathetic to Longyong recalls, "his wife came in and saw him and stopped him. His wife didn't sleep for a couple of days. She stayed awake watching him, for fear he would commit suicide. He had been so fierce and powerful before. Now he'd lost everything all of a sudden and was being condemned."

In future years, Longyong would make a public issue of the ordeal he had been put through, reminding villagers how Qingfa's betrayal and their own ingratitude had almost caused his death. "You elected me to be a cadre," he would tell them, "and I worked as hard as I could for you; but then you turned against me, and if it weren't for my wife, I would have killed myself." In the long term, Longyong astutely would be able to transform the incident of the lumber into part of his own political capital.

In the short term, however, the Small Four Cleanups campaign had been twisted in Chen Village to serve Qingfa's personal political purposes. Qingfa presumed he would be able to retain control of events in Chen Village and that the campaign had, if anything, strengthened his hand. As one interviewee remembers, "Longyong was withdrawn. . . . I remember remarking to a friend one day when we saw Longyong and Qingfa at a distance that Longyong looked like a mouse in front of a cat. [During that period] Longyong seemed obedient." But Longyong was also not a man who would forget or forgive.

The contingent of fifty urban youths had entered Chen Village from Canton just as the struggle meetings against Longyong were getting under way. It was the young people's introduction to village politics. Within several more months they would be witnessing dramatic new twists in Chen Village's political history. The state would intervene directly in Chen Village's affairs to carry out what became known as the "Big" Four Cleanups. It was the beginning of an eventful two years that would dramatically reshape the village's institutions and economic programs, the concerns of its peasants, and the struggles between its leaders.

· 2 ·

The Big Four Cleanups

The Workteam

In the winter cold of early February 1965, a contingent of thirteen cadres entered Chen Village. They announced that they were a Four Cleanups workteam that had come to "squat" at the brigade. For the first time since land reform, outside cadres had come in to take over control of the entire village's affairs.

The peasants were soon aware that this cadre workteam was only a branch of a larger team that had set up headquarters in the commune seat. They soon knew also that of the thirteen workteam members in Chen Village, three of them—the workteam leader, the political director, and the clerk—made up the leadership core. But no one in the village knew who any of the thirteen cadres were, where they were from, or what posts they had held before. No, the villagers were not supposed to know, they were told: "Things that should not be asked, you shouldn't ask; things that should not be seen, you shouldn't see; things that should not be heard, you shouldn't hear." Thus, the peasants were simply to address the workteam cadres by the title "Comrade" plus their surnames. In urban areas this term of address often bears a connotation of fraternal equality; but the peasants of Chen Village normally had used the title exclusively for outside officials whom they regarded with distant respect.

In insisting on anonymity, the workteam members were following standard operating procedures for workteams throughout the country. Although we were not able to interview any of the members of the workteam that came to Chen Village, we did interview a former member of a Four Cleanups workteam in north China; and we can use his insider's understanding of the procedures followed by such workteams to complement the impressions recalled by the residents of Chen Village.[1] According to this north China interviewee, he and his colleagues had been given three major reasons for insisting on their anonymity. First, it was supposed to convey to the peasants the image of a workteam composed not of fallible individuals but of sacrosanct representatives of the Communist party. Second, the anonymity could help the workteam members present a united front to the peasants and local cadres. The less that the villagers knew of them the fewer chances a troublemaker would have to foment splits within the workteam's ranks. Finally, since most of a workteam's members were from nearby counties and communes, anonymity would render them less vulnerable to rumor mongering while the campaign was in progress or even after it had ended. As we shall see, the workteam members in Chen Village would later have reason to appreciate these precautionary measures.

As the workteam settled into Chen Village and the peasants got to know them better, the approximate backgrounds of these cadres gradually emerged, if not their exact identities. About a third of them, including the workteam head, were middle-aged officials at the commune or county levels. They did not have much schooling, but enough to be able to write Chinese characters. Another third of the workteam was composed of university students or educated urban cadres. (Among them was the

---

[1] Even though this former workteam member's experiences in north China occurred a year earlier than the campaign in Chen Village, many of the incidents, the sequence of phases of the Four Cleanups campaign and its internal logic, as described by this interviewee, were remarkably similar to what occurred in Chen Village. It is significant that the intervening controversy among China's leaders over the direction of the campaign, and the Twenty-three Articles which Mao had just pushed through in January 1965, did not noticeably alter the methods used by the workteam that entered Chen Village. (On the Four Cleanups documents, see Richard Baum and Frederick Teiwes, *Ssu-Ch'ing: The Socialist Education Movement of 1962–1966* [Berkeley: Center for Chinese Studies, 1968]).

only woman in the workteam, a young university graduate.) The final third were politically promising young peasants in their twenties. The admixture of backgrounds served several functions: the middle-aged rural cadres and the young peasant activists provided the workteam with personnel who were familiar with rural conditions and agriculture; the university students and urban cadres provided the skills needed to interpret the upper-level documents on the campaign, to collect dossiers on the village, and to compile reports; and finally the younger members of the workteam, of both urban and rural origins, would have an excellent opportunity to learn the arts needed for handling future grass roots political campaigns.

From the moment the workteam cadres entered Chen Village, they conducted themselves as they had been instructed at prior training sessions: they were "neither cold nor warm" toward the local cadres; were friendly toward the ordinary peasants, especially the former poor and lower-middle peasants; and were positively icy toward the four-bad types. One workteam member almost immediately learned the hard way to abide by these instructions. Before Liberation, he had fought beside the former guerrilla who was now a "bad element." Sighting his old comrade-in-arms, he had assumed the man still was in good standing politically and had rushed forward to greet him. Belatedly told that he had been friendly toward a four-bad type, the embarrassed workteam cadre had to issue a public self-criticism for having inadvertently failed to "draw a clear class line." In the Four Cleanups, class labels would be more strictly taken into account than ever before in the short history of the People's Republic.

Sinking Roots

Within a day of entering the village, the cadres had embarked on the first stage of the new campaign: the "sinking roots and linking up" phase. To gain the respect and trust of the good-class peasants, the workteam cadres were to make every effort to practice the "three togethers"—living together, eating together, and working together with the poor and lower-middle peasants. Each workteam member joined a different production team and immediately sought out a household with which to room and board. These lodgings were to be chosen with great care, since such households were to be cultivated to become "backbone elements" for the upcoming investigations. The families were not only to have an official poor and lower-middle peasant status but also were supposed to be genuinely impoverished. It was felt by the Four Cleanups leadership that homes in particularly stringent financial straits would be more likely to have grievances against the village establishment.

A Peasant Bedroom.   Chen villagers could not afford such mosquito netting until the mid-1970s.

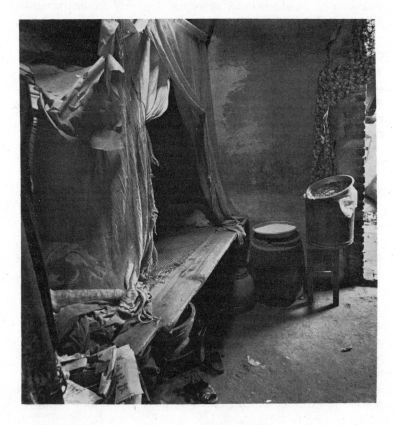

Our English idea of room and board does not perhaps convey an accurate image of the workteam cadres' housing arrangements. Some of the families with whom they boarded lived in little more than shacks, into which they had crammed all their belongings, several months' worth of grain reserves, a few poultry, and perhaps a pig. In the smallest homes, there was not even room for an

Living Room, 1981. Note grain stored below the table and winnowing baskets hung on the wall.

extra makeshift bed. In two of the teams, the workteam cadres moved into single-member households and slept in the same cramped bed as their bachelor host. In a couple of multimember households that were too congested to squeeze in a visitor, the workteam cadres slept in abandoned sheds near the family's house and became one with the household by eating all their meals there. But they paid the family for everything they consumed. In a society where the diet is meager, a cadre who does not take advantage of his position by helping himself to others' food earns respect.

Living Room.   Note tools and pig-feed.

Several days after the workteam arrived in Chen Village, it convened a mass meeting for all the peasants except the four-bad types, who as political pariahs were strictly excluded from all forms of political participation in the community. The peasants were to be told what the campaign was all about. The workteam read out to them the documents of the Central Committee concerning the Four Cleanups and stressed how Chairman Mao had warned, "Never forget class struggle!" Since so many years had passed since Liberation, since landlords and rich peasants had lost their property, and since counterrevolutionaries were kept under strict control, many people had mistakenly assumed, the workteam's spokesmen said, that the class struggle was over. The political consciousness of many people had been deadened. But these bad classes were still around, and their way of thinking still influenced others' behavior. The most concrete manifestation of this was in the performance of the cadres. If China's cadres changed for the worse, then the dictatorship of the proletariat would collapse from within. China and Chen Village would become like they were in the old days. Peasants would be swindled and suffer. Production would deteriorate. People would eat more poorly and dress in rags. Did the peasants want that to happen? Cadres were becoming afraid of hard work, greedy—only wanting pleasure. They wanted to become big shots, ignored the opinions of the peasants, no longer worked for the public good, enjoyed special privileges, ate meals at team and brigade expense, stole public funds. Beating people, cursing people, arbitrarily taking advantage of people—they were doing all sorts of bad things. This was evil and feudalistic. So now there was going to be a campaign to correct the cadres, to teach them to follow the revolutionary line of Mao Zedong. If a cadre had done anything wrong, the masses should make it known. And the cadres themselves would be expected to make self-confessions.

But the peasants remained silent. They did not air their grievances, still less expose any corrupt practices. One of the young settlers from Canton explains,

> Most of the masses were afraid. The cadres were like emperors: brigade emperors and team emperors. If you complained about them, they might want to take revenge, something

very frightful. Because a peasant has no way of leaving a village. A cadre's revenge could take the form of assigning them heavy work for years to come.

The workteam had expected this reticence. In accordance with instructions from above, it had already worked out various methods to persuade peasants to speak up, and each of these methods was embodied in a succinct catchphrase: not just "sink roots and link up," but also "visit the poor and ask about their past bitterness," and "investigate and do research." By expressing sympathy with the past sufferings of some of the poor peasants, the workteam was demonstrating its "class stand." The workteam hoped that this would help rekindle the gratitude that these poor peasants had felt toward the Communist party during the land reform and thus help win their active support for this newer campaign. By "sinking roots" in one family, a cadre won the family's confidence and began obtaining from it the facts about the village. Then, with this initial information, the cadres moved on to neighboring poor peasant households to collect more. All the while they tried to assuage the peasants' worry, trying to convince them that they would be protected in the future from the cadres' revenge. Slowly, a bit here and a bit there, a comprehensive picture of the intricate social affairs of the village began to emerge. The workteam acquired an idea of the power relationships in the village, of the factionalism, who was whose enemy or ally, who were the corrupt cadres, whose style of command was particularly unpopular, and so on—all from the perspective of the poor peasant sector of the village population.

To gain greater acceptance by the peasants, the workteam cadres also had to try to demonstrate their willingness and ability to labor well, since this was one of the criteria by which the peasants evaluated a person's worth. The Chinese Communist party was well aware of this. Working together had been made one of the "three togethers," and strictly so. Every day the workteam members spent the mornings holding internal meetings or pursuing their investigations. But in the afternoons they would go out into the fields to labor with the peasants, and while doing so further familiarize themselves with the villagers and village affairs. With this spadework accomplished, the workteam felt prepared to ferret out cases of cadre corruption. Informal complaints and reports from poor peasants provided the initial clues for meticulous auditing of the team and brigade accounts. Using the revised Sixty Articles[2] as its guideline, the workteam checked with the greatest care exactly how many workpoints each cadre should have been entitled to in the past few years. According to the rules, the brigade and production team cadres ought to have engaged in physical labor for at least 120 days each year. Their income from this labor should have been assessed on the same basis as the ordinary peasants. The supplementary allowances they were permitted to claim cumulatively should not have exceeded 1 to 2 percent of the total income of the collective unit. On paper this seemed simple and clear-cut. But the cadres, by virtue of their supervisory roles, sometimes had to spend time going to meetings even when they were supposed to be laboring. Lazy cadres took advantage of this. The peasants in case after case began charging cadres for claiming workpoints they were not entitled to. To arrive at the exact numbers of workpoints that had been overclaimed, especially over a period of several years, would be almost impossible. Yet this was the precise figure the workteam purportedly was trying to compute, shuttling ceaselessly between workpoint ledgers and the information provided by cooperative peasants.

The workteam also checked for irregularities in the work of warehousemen, accountants, and cashiers. The warehousemen were responsible for supervising the team granaries, the accountants for computing the amount of income realized by each production team and the earnings of each peasant, and the cashiers for disbursing cash to the team members. Invariably, irregularities were discovered. But, as with irregularities in the workpoints given to village cadres, it was difficult to determine how much was the result of corruption and how much the result of the inevitably sloppy bookkeeping of semiliterate and untrained village officers. For example, one team's accountant had simply jotted his figures down on slips of paper and thrown them into a big basket. When the workteam audited his accounts they were in

---

[2.] "Regulations on the Work of the Rural People's Communes (Revised Draft)," in *Documents of the Chinese Communist Party Central Committee* (Hong Kong: Union Research Institute, 1971), 1: 719–722.

utter confusion: sometimes his "records" suggested there should have been money left over, but perhaps a thousand *yuan* (Chinese dollars)[3] would be missing; sometimes there was supposed to be a debit, but there would still be money in the team's till. The chaos—and the temptation to pilfer—was compounded when at times the cashier, warehouseman, and accountant were one and the same person (sometimes the teams had not been able to find enough literate peasants of trustworthy class backgrounds to fill all the posts). Often even the cadre charged with corruption did not himself know the exact amount of cash and goods he had pocketed.

To a certain extent, both cadres and peasants took it as natural that a cadre should enjoy some of the advantages that accrued to a post. "They accepted this kind of thing," observes one former villager. "After all, who would have wanted to be a cadre if you couldn't gain something extra out of the trouble?" But even when the amounts were small, quiet resentments sometimes accompanied the peasantry's tacit willingness to look the other way. The workteam's job was to articulate these resentments and to encourage them to surface. The workteam's ultimate goal was to lay the groundwork in Chen Village for a new strict code for cadre conduct.

Though it was well nigh impossible for the workteam to compute in cash the exact amounts of corruption, precision was not really what the workteam's meticulous investigations were striving for. Their concern was to get the peasants to participate publicly in accusations, be they petty or serious. But the peasants so far had only been willing to impart information confidentially. Having succeeded in "sinking roots" in the village, the workteam now had to organize them into a force for attack.

Linking Up

As an opening wedge, the workteam had already begun in earnest to cultivate activists. Activists in China do not hold any

---

[3.] At the official exchange rate, one thousand *yuan* in 1964 amounted to $400, U.S. currency.

official post but gain informal power and status by loyally cooperating with officials to carry out political campaigns or implement government policies. In this particular campaign, activists could help the workteam in two main ways. One was in the collection of research materials on the village, a task that could best be fulfilled by Chen Village's sent-down urban youths. They were educated and could efficiently take notes, prepare reports, and help audit account books and workpoints; and as outsiders to the village who had not yet had time to get entangled in village politics, they could be trusted to dig impartially into the affairs of the local cadres.

The second important function activists could play was to help set a spirited atmosphere in criticism and struggle meetings. The urban-born youths could play this role, but local peasant activists would carry more influence with their neighbors. Generally, the workteam was able to convince three types of good-class villagers to overcome their fears: older people with very solid reputations within the community who felt relatively immune to subsequent cadre reprisals; young local peasants with strong political ambitions, who were prepared to run the risk of angering local leaders; and peasants who so resented the way they had been treated in the village that they were willing recklessly to confront the powers-that-be.

To get these peasants to testify against their cadres, a better structure for organizing the peasants was needed, and so too a means to assure that cadres would not later be able to take revenge. Party documents provided a solution. In each village, a Poor and Lower-Middle Peasants Association was to be permanently established. Such peasant associations had been used in the land reform period, and thus they would lend an aura of historical legitimacy to the peasants' prosecution of cadres. After the campaign was over and the workteam gone, the new peasant association was to supervise and provide a check upon the cadres' use of power. But while the workteam was still in the village, the association was to operate under the workteam's control.

All former poor and lower-middle peasants who did not have problematic histories in their dossiers were automatically made members of this association. The workteam also selected a brigade-level committee of eleven: one representative from each of the ten production teams plus a chairman. Official party instructions stipulated that these committee members should not be cadres, that they should be currently poor (with economic circumstances at least below average), and that they should have shown themselves comparatively willing to speak up against cadre corruption.[4] As it turned out, most of them came from the families with whom the workteam members were boarding.

It had been more than a decade since Liberation and since the revolutionary redistribution of wealth and the means of production. Why were these former poor peasant households still more impoverished than their neighbors? The reasons were several. Many of the former poor peasants had had few private possessions and meager housing at the time of Liberation. Though some of them had acquired houses from richer peasants during land reform, these had tended to be in poor condition, since the peasants of other class origins were allowed to keep their main dwellings while having their run–down annexes and storage huts expropriated. Moreover, many of the older poor peasants were not physically fit, a legacy of pre-Liberation malnutrition. Their previous straits as hired laborers had also left some of them without the expertise to plan their own farming well. They thus were not always shrewd in the use they made of their private plots, which provided a major source (more than a quarter) of most peasants' income. Some others, though, were still poor simply because they were caught at the stage of a peasant family cycle when there were more mouths to feed than hands to earn incomes in the fields. Until the children were old enough to lend a hand, a family was apt to be strapped for cash.

The former poor peasants in Chen Village who were the brightest and most capable had had a chance to distinguish themselves after the arrival of the Communists. Like Qingfa or Longyong, they had risen into the ranks of the brigade and team cadres. In fact, with so many brigade and team committee posts

[4.] Directives also suggested that this village-wide committee should consist mainly of older former poor peasants, a couple of activist good-class peasants, and at least one woman to fulfill a quota for females. For further details on the setting up of the Poor and Lower-Middle Peasants Association, see Richard Baum and Frederick Teiwes, *Ssu-Ch'ing,* pp. 95-101.

to be filled, fully a third of all the adult male peasants (and a higher proportion of the former poor and lower-middle peasant men) had become cadres of one sort or another. So when looking specifically for genuinely impoverished poor peasants who were not at the same time cadres, the workteam's choices were relatively limited. Those available tended to be both less competent and less physically capable than the average peasant. In fact, several of the new poor peasant representatives were considered by teammates as nothing but weak whiners.

Two of the poor peasant representatives, moreover, came from "wanderer" families, which did not belong to the Chen lineage but had migrated into the village in the 1940s and had never been totally accepted by the other villagers. But the workteam was not particularly concerned with the prestige of these poor peasant representatives. It was looking for candidates willing to speak up against cadres; and the more vocal the better. In fact, several of these poor peasant representatives were so ready to tell other people off even when they themselves were unable to carry through anything successfully that they soon were nicknamed "mouth revolutionaries." But as their status rose with the backing of the workteam, the other peasants had to be more civil toward them.

To counterbalance the drawbacks of these representatives, the workteam turned to a very prestigious old poor peasant. This person was in his mid-sixties, which the Chen peasants considered long past the age for active leadership. He was no longer at all influential in village politics. When he had to talk publicly, moreover, he spoke so inaudibly that he had acquired the nickname of Uncle Mumbler. But he was an "old revolutionary," one of the village's earliest party members and the head of the land reform's Peasants Association. He was also, by coincidence, the symbolic head of Chen Village's lineage—the last living member of the most senior generation, the generation closest in descent to the village's founding fathers. For these two facts alone he enjoyed high status among the peasants and the village cadres. But beyond this, he was a kind and approachable man, not the sort who went about criticizing and embarrassing other people or "eating other people's food." Nor was he one to shirk work, even though his laboring ability was declining. When the workteam arrived in

Chen Village, he was still serving as a production team head but was gradually, with dignity, being eased aside.

He was the only cadre in the village who was not criticized in the Four Cleanups campaign. Instead he was elevated to the chairmanship of the Poor and Lower-Middle Peasants Association. But he would not have to actively denounce other cadres in the campaign. His role was to give respectability to the association.

Lighting the Fire

Three months after their arrival, having collected enough evidence and organized a core of activists—having "sunk roots and linked up"—the workteam was ready to push on to the next stage of the campaign: "lighting the fire." The workteam summarily gathered together close to a hundred people—all of the brigade and production team cadres and all the poor peasant representatives, plus two sent-down urban youths who were acting as aides to the workteam—to go to the commune headquarters for sessions that would last three weeks. It was time to begin the painful process of "cleansing the cadres hand and foot." Every cadre was to be confronted. Longyong, who was still smarting from Qingfa's betrayal of him in the Small Four Cleanups, remarked to a colleague that he liked this new turn of events. "Okay," he reportedly said, "Now we'll have the chance to see who's the worst!"

There were about a thousand people at the first meeting: cadres, poor peasant representatives, and workteam members from all the brigades in the commune. To provide an idea of what was to be expected from all the parties concerned, the workteam headquarters scheduled a prototype session for the assemblage. One of the brigades in the commune had been chosen as the commune's "test spot," and the local cadres from that brigade were dragged out and subjected to humiliating denunciations at the hands of their brigade's poor peasant representatives. These "test spot" cadres then responded with appropriate confessions.

Immediately afterward, the conference split up into its constituent brigades. In what were called back-to-back proceedings, the poor peasant representatives of each brigade slept and ate sepa-

rately from their village's cadres. For days they were systematically reinterrogated by the workteam about cadre malpractices,
while the two sent-down youths carefully took down all of their
remarks for the public record. Meanwhile, in a different room,
other members of the workteam were relentlessly putting pressure
on the brigade and production team cadres. As one of the two
sent-down youth aides remembers:

> The workteam again and again had to explain the policies to
> the cadres, telling them not to be scared, that they should
> confess. But the cadres were of course scared and wouldn't
> talk. So the workteam kept on "guiding" them to talk, that
> they should make a clean breast of it, etc. In the other room
> the workteam had to keep telling the poor peasant represen-
> tatives not to be afraid of later revenge. That is to say, the
> workteam mobilized both sides: one side to do the others in,
> and the other side to be done in.

The whole process lasted about two weeks. By the time the
workteam had compiled enough written accusations to lay
charges against the cadres, the cadres were frightened, and completely exhausted. "They were thinner by more than a dozen
pounds. No appetites. We could see the rice going into their room
in big baskets and going out again in big baskets. People like
Qingfa could barely eat, only a bowl or so. Thinking about it
now, those cadres really looked pathetic."

The scene had been set for the face-to-face struggle sessions.
One by one the cadres were confronted with "concrete" charges
by the poor peasant representatives. As each cadre took his turn as
target, the rest of the Chen Village cadres had to join in with the
poor peasant representatives and workteam members in hurling
accusations at him. Surprisingly, the village cadres showed no
reluctance to participate. Our interviewee, who once was a member of a Four Cleanups workteam in north China, offers some
interesting observations from his own experience:

> Among the cadres themselves "contradictions" began pop-
> ping up all over. For example, when it came to dealing with
> the brigade accountant, *all* the cadres from the production
> teams and brigade bombarded him with accusations! . . . The
> general psychology of most peasants was that they must at all

cost show their activism; they'd even walk up to give him one or two slaps in the face. . . . Whoever had problems, whomever the workteam had evidence on, had to go through [these accusations and grillings] as if going through a sieve. One by one, one by one. Today you were being dealt with by others; tomorrow you'd be dealing with the others and you yourself would be very active. Especially those who had been falsely accused would think that by showing activism they could wash away their own problems. This formed the emotional underpinnings for struggle. That's why the Communist party used this method to divide and demoralize.

The Chen Village cadres had to face marathon interrogation sessions lasting through the night—if necessary continuing almost nonstop for several days. Fresh groups of questioners would be brought in every few hours to continue the browbeating. There would be continual shouts of "Confess! Confess!" Gradually the exhausted target would give in to the pressures and admit guilt on one or another point. But as a sent-down youth who observed these proceedings remarked: "Of course the workteam cadres yelled it wasn't enough. No reason why it should be enough, because the workteam and the poor peasant representatives had already decided beforehand who would pass through after only one session, who should be struggled against several times, who should be dealt with severely and who more leniently." Nothing more than the circumstantial evidence produced by the peasants was necessary to make a charge against the cadres. Nor were any attempts made to examine the final confessions for any hard evidence. When, out of exhaustion, the cadres finally had admitted what their interrogators wanted them to admit, that *became* the final proof of their wrongdoing.

To use this method of investigation in China is known as "giving credence to extorted confessions" and is expressly forbidden by the party in campaigns or trials. Despite this, the extortion of confessions was frequent—though unlike in some other villages, no physical force was used in the heat of the grilling.

The question remains: why did the workteam override very basic party disciplinary regulations? The experiences of the workteam cadre from north China provide a possible explanation for the excesses. There, the provincial workteam command post had put out a work progress newsletter for all the workteams in villages thoughout the province. The commended workteams were invariably those that had uncovered grave malpractices and corruption. The impression was given that the more corruption and wrongdoing that could be ferreted out, the greater the achievements of a workteam. A group interest developed among the workteam cadres to inflate the charges.[5] They reckoned that if they did not, they would be reprimanded by their superiors as lax—and that if they did inflate the charges, they might gain commendations in the personnel dossiers that followed them throughout their careers.

Expose and Denounce

When the peasants saw the Chen Village cadres returning to the village utterly wan and dejected, some of them thought the workteam had gone too far. But the ordeal was far from over for the village cadres. It was time for the "expose and denounce" phase of the campaign. The cadres would now have to "go into the water," that is, face the peasant masses in struggle meetings. As one interviewee puts it, "The idea was to instigate the peasants to 'speak bitterness' against the cadres just as during the land reform they'd spoken bitterness against the landlords." At the commune seat the brigade cadres had been interrogated by a limited number of people, but now they would have to face hundreds, many of whom they had been accustomed to ordering around every day.

Again, the workteam carefully controlled all the sessions. Before each mass meeting they gathered together a group of the peasant activists whom they had cultivated. The interviewee who

[5.] In this and many other respects, the pressures of the Four Cleanups paralleled the cadre rectification campaign of 1948, described by William Hinton in *Fanshen: A Documentary of Revolution in a Chinese Village* (New York: Vintage, 1968). Despite the passage of two decades, the top party leadership was setting a strikingly similar scenario for the new campaign, as if in purposeful imitation of that earlier use of workteams; and in the process, as seen here and in the pages that follow, the party was pushing the Four Cleanups toward some of the very same extremes.

had been a member of a Four Cleanups workteam in north China describes how this worked:

> When I got together with the activists, I told them about the content of the upcoming meeting, the kind of problems that would arise, how we should solve them, even assign who would speak first and who should speak last. It was all very tightly organized, though it didn't take more than 20 minutes to prearrange it with those activists. Basically nothing could go beyond what we'd planned. Our people had prepared, were united, and so we were bound to carry the meeting. Ha! And after every meeting the activists would stay behind for about half an hour to "synthesize" the experience, to discuss what we'd learned from the mass meeting.

Young people from the Chen Village militia were among the most vocal and aggressive of these activists. Practically all the young men and women from former poor and lower-middle peasant families had been recruited into Chen Village's basic militia when they were about fourteen years old and remained in it until they married.[6] It was considered normal for such youths, especially men, to be somewhat reckless and brash. In their own social circles they influenced one another, sought to impress each other, and competed to prove their bravado. They were encouraged to channel this collective brashness in ways helpful to the authorities. Recalls a Chen villager:

> During any big struggle meeting you had to rely on these militiamen to push things forward. Old people or middle-aged persons don't like to struggle against people. They're afraid to hurt people's feelings. But young people aren't afraid to do these things. They don't know anything about these close personal relationships, and during the struggle meetings they'll struggle and attack with all their might. When they come home, their parents are liable to yell at them: "Bastard! What the hell do you think you're trying to do—minding so much of other people's business!"

[6.] Within the basic militia there was an elite corps of about twenty armed militia, who were entrusted with carrying weapons. The armed militia were chosen from among the most physically fit and politically reliable young men of the village.

But such attacks were ultimately to these young people's advantage. It was a distinct mark of political activism, and as rewards some of the most able and vociferous of the youths eventually would be elevated by the workteam into junior positions of authority in the village. The cadres under attack, moreover, did not tend to take the young people's charges personally and only rarely sought reprisals in later years. As an interviewee puts it, it was considered a "custom" that young people would take the lead in criticizing people during political campaigns. After all, "the older cadres themselves had criticized others in their own time to get their start."

Night after night, the peasants had to attend the struggle sessions. After finishing their dinners, they would assemble at their own production team's headquarters and march as a group with stools, chairs, and mats in hand to take their seats before the makeshift stage that had been erected in front of the brigade headquarters. Each production team's members would sit together, the men grouped on one side and the women on the other, as traditional propriety dictated. Members of the militia sat in front, where they could better influence the mood of the audience.

Workteam cadres would open these sessions with emotional speeches. To overcome the ordinary villagers' reticence to participate, activists in the audience would interrupt periodically from the floor with shouts of denunciation notable more for their ferocity than accuracy of content. Amid this noise and chanting and excitement, the rest of the audience's emotions would begin to run high. Gradually, some would shed their initial inhibitions and hesitantly join in. The "struggling atmosphere" having been properly established, the accused would be led out onto the stage, head bowed, with a placard hanging from his neck stating his crime. He was expected to say a few words acknowledging his guilt and pleading for forgiveness from the masses. Invariably, the activist-led crowd would cry out, "Insincere!" Then one by one, the various preselected activists would get up and yell out charges against him. Others in the audience (especially young people) spontaneously would jump up from their seats and add more detail to the charges. At last, vilified and humiliated, the accused was led off the stage.

On the opening nights the brigade militia head was "struggled against" on numerous counts of indiscriminately cursing and humiliating people, and the public security head for pocketing jewelry handed in by the peasants to the commune at the time of the Great Leap Forward. Some cadres got off with only one of these sessions. But for any cadre whose crimes were considered particularly onerous or who had refused to admit complete responsibility for his purported offenses or had not assumed a sufficiently contrite pose, the struggle sessions would resume for several evenings. Only then was he allowed to "pass the gate" and "get out of the water."

The ferocity of the outbursts against particular cadres did not always result from the type of resentments for which the cadres were *supposed* to be attacked. The attackers, according to one of the sent-down urban youths, included

> those who'd been ill or in some other hardship of one sort or another, who'd approached a cadre for help and hadn't gotten all they'd hoped for; or those who had asked permission to build a house and had had the chosen site rejected; or . . . because some cadre favored some other peasant and was better to the other fellow; or even feuds going back three generations. All these were personal selfish reasons, not at all like Mao's "class struggle" reasons.

Some of these peasants also adopted a strategy of overkill. As one interviewee puts it: "The feeling was that if you're going to get a cadre in a campaign, you should get him good; make sure he'll never be able to make a comeback. Otherwise he might cause you all sorts of trouble." As a struggle meeting reached this stage of spontaneous and wildly exaggerated charges, the workteam's artfully prestaged efforts to control the meeting slipped away. "It took the workteam a long time to stir up the people to speak, but once things started to come out, they came pouring out and nothing could stop them." From the workteam member's opening address of lofty political rhetoric, the accusations degenerated into a pandemonium of petty personal grievances. Though this was not what the workteam cadres would have liked to see, they realized they were able to attain a heated meeting precisely because they had been playing upon such personal resentments. The best means to surmount the remaining problems would be to raise all these accusations, be they serious or petty, to the "level of ideological principles." If the peasants were not yet familiar with ideological concepts and terminology, they would now be given lessons on how to unite practice with theory. The peasants soon would know when to yell, "you've acted in a feudalistic way!" or "your thinking is revisionist!"

The cadre who most clearly could be charged with the newly learned phrase "political degeneracy" was Feihan, the deputy party secretary who had been party secretary before Qingfa. Feihan had gotten into the habit of shirking almost all labor and had become overindulgent in his consumption of publicly owned foodstuffs. When he went to the commune seat for meetings, he had indulged in affairs with various women. His peculations, flaunted laziness, and moral laxness made him ripe for village-wide abuse.

Longyong was criticized for his overbearing and harsh style of command. But the workteam had found relatively little new evidence of economic corruption in his case. The criticism directed against him was milder than for most other cadres. Longyong could take private satisfaction in that.

Getting Qingfa

It was Qingfa who received the most thorough and harshest grillings, precisely because he had so recently been Chen Village's "local emperor." The workteam had specially cultivated a number of peasants who harbored strong resentments against him to take the lead. Among the most vocal of these activists was a young peasant from Qingfa's own production team who was not a member of Qingfa's lineage branch. Since most of the Lotus members of the No. 6 team composed a tight-knit circle that dominated the team socially, this peasant must have felt isolated and resentful. Other accusations against Qingfa stemmed, by no coincidence, largely from teams No. 3 and 4, which had blamed Qingfa for the poor quality of the lands distributed to them. Members of these two teams had been less docile toward Qingfa than most other villagers, and consequently they more often had been the victims of Qingfa's tempestuous outbursts. In particular, two teenagers from the No. 3 team who had been harshly slapped by Qingfa for having played with a brigade cart now came forward as political activists to lambaste him. The workteam had the incident phrased in dramatic political terms: Even the landlords never beat people themselves, yet Qingfa dared beat up the poor and lower-middle peasants! A big crime indeed! The team heads of several of the teams that had been disadvantaged under Qingfa were encouraged to step forward to support such charges.

The workteam leaders also openly played upon Qingfa's favoritism toward the members of his own lineage branch. They used Qingfa's abuses of patronage as a means to inculcate new ways of thinking among the peasants. One of the sent-down youths recalls:

> The masses, once their thought was raised by the party, wouldn't stand for that type of clannish thinking. Before the Four Cleanups the peasants in Chen Village were still backward. Many thought people naturally behaved that way. . . . But things changed in the Four Cleanups. Really did. Before, of course, folks were dissatisfied with Qingfa. . . . But the workteam used this dissatisfaction to say that lineage feelings *generally* are bad. They got the masses also to speak up in this way.

Qingfa came under angry scrutiny also for having enjoyed the good life. In a rural society where the diet consisted mainly of carbohydrates and where meat was a luxury, the most common form of cadre privilege had been, as the Chinese put it, "drinking big and eating big." Qingfa had often used his authority to arrange for after-meeting snacks of chicken or duck with other brigade cadres and friends, or even meals at the expense of the brigade. Or he would take his entourage to the brigade's orchard to have their fill of any fresh fruits that happened to be in season. Peasants cynically called such cadres members of the "Eating Big Association," but they had been too intimidated by the power of the cadres to speak up publicly. Now the workteam was coaxing them to denounce this "rotten and degenerate lifestyle." It was charged that Qingfa had been so concerned with living comfortably that he had had his door front paved with concrete (and brigade concrete at that) "so smooth even a blind man passing by couldn't have stumbled."

Even Qingfa's readiness to accept invitations to dinners was laid as a charge against him. To it was appended a more serious accusation: that he had betrayed the class line. "It didn't matter whether people weren't of good class origins, so long as they asked him to go to eat, he would eat. We criticized him for losing his class stand in eating. Some people said he was bribed." For having accepted a gold chain and two earrings in return for issuing a former rich peasant household an exit visa to Hong Kong in 1962 (when border controls between China and Hong Kong were relatively relaxed), he was accused of having betrayed the proletariat. In reference to Qingfa's reluctance to discriminate against his old crony the ex-guerrilla, it was said that Qingfa was happy to maintain a cordial relationship with a "class enemy" while being all too eager to bully his "class brothers," the poor and lower-middle peasants.

But the peasants were milder in these condemnations than many of the workteam members would have liked. One of the urban youths recalls:

> They yelled at Qingfa: you ought to have served us poor and lower-middle peasants. You cheated us. . . . But while the peasants on the one hand cursed him, on the other they only wanted to teach him a lesson. They weren't as extreme as we urban youths. These people knew that he had come from really impoverished class origins. They knew that his thinking had changed while in office. They used to call out to him in these struggle sessions: "Remember how you were a little beggar, running around? Have you forgotten that so quickly?" At that time I thought, how could the poor and lower-middle peasants make him out to be their own kind of person? I thought they were too soft on him. . . . We shouldn't have treated him like the workteam did—like an enemy.

There was one sense, though, in which the peasants did feel Qingfa inexcusably had betrayed the interests of the poor and lower-middle peasants. Qingfa was guilty in their eyes of too much obedience to his party superiors at the village's expense.

They were particularly incensed that when the county had established a commercial forest in the mountains behind Chen Village in 1960, Qingfa had acceded to requests that Chen Village contribute three square miles of terrain that had been credited to the village during the land reform. The peasants were convinced that Qingfa could have avoided handing over the land. They could point to the village next door, where the party secretary had fought successfully to retain its lands and had had his village plant its own forests. That village would soon be reaping an income from its trees. "The feeling was that Qingfa had been selfish, thinking only of serving his personal interests through compliance with the upper levels. This was actually one of the major reasons folks wanted to 'get' him in the Four Cleanups." But that was exactly the facet of Qingfa's performance that the Four Cleanups workteam would have found praiseworthy, and so the peasants avoided raising the issue openly in any struggle session.

Interspersed with the brigade-wide struggle sessions were smaller production team sessions to criticize most of the team cadres. But in most cases these were not as fierce as they had been for the brigade cadres. In particular, team heads got away relatively lightly. If their ordeals were made too harsh, it would have become extremely difficult to find suitable, competent replacements. So some merely endured "denunciation sessions." That is, they were not dragged out from behind the stage to face the masses but only had to walk up to the stage voluntarily from a seat in the audience to recite a self-confession. Normally this would be accepted as basically sincere, and the team officer would not be required to bow his head in abject subjugation. The audience, led by the activists, nonetheless would make prepared statements about the seriousness of his offenses and would conclude with the hope that he would truly repent. The accused would dutifully proclaim how grateful he was for the lesson he had been taught by the masses and would resolve to mend his ways. After that, he would be allowed to step back into the audience. Despite the relatively mild and formalistic nature of a denunciation session, it still was a humiliation a team head would not easily forget.

Putting Policy on a Solid Footing

Campaigns in China often are permitted to swing too far toward extremes in order to let momentum build up at the grass roots. One of the sent-down youth activists explains:

> The workteam had said we should let the masses freely expose. Even though there might be personal vengeance in it, it didn't matter. Just let them speak out. . . . If the workteam had tied up the masses' legs like women with bound feet, then they couldn't have mobilized the masses. If the masses had been required to present proof before they said anything, then the campaign couldn't have gotten off the ground. We understood this. . . . The most important thing was to observe the performance of the cadres when receiving the masses' attack. And then in the very end, during a "putting the policy on a solid footing" [luoshi zhengce] phase, only the accusations for which there was solid evidence were used when finally deciding the cases.

During this fourth and final "solid footing" phase of the Four Cleanups campaign, the peasants were to put the cadres' errors into a more moderate context. The prior exaggerations were now supposed to be viewed simply as constructive efforts to teach the cadres a lesson. There was a shortage of capable personnel in the Chinese countryside, and most of the deposed village cadres would be needed to continue in village management; they ought not to be permanently tainted. Thus, whereas the workteam had earlier tried to win merit for itself by exposing large amounts of corruption, now that most of the cadres had gone through their baptisms of "struggle" the workteam was instructed by its superiors to be scrupulous. Accordingly, the brigade accountant/clerk who had been accused of embezzling 2,000 yuan was now said to have taken only 100 yuan. Seeing this new leniency, the public security head, who under pressure at the interrogation meetings had admitted to stealing a cache of jewelry, retracted his confession, claiming only minor infractions. When someone yelled at him: "Are you trying to swindle us poor and lower-middle peasants?" he claimed he had falsely confessed only because he had been exhausted by his long interrogation. "The party tells us to be honest," he said. "If I continue to pretend that I was telling the truth, I wouldn't be honest. My crime would be all the greater." Since the evidence was not conclusive, he was asked only to make a small reparation.

But even when the charges had been scaled down considerably, it was still not easy for cadres to pay back things they had already consumed or money long ago spent. Therefore, on the grounds that their personal property was derived from ill-gotten gains, these cadres were ordered by the workteam to have their possessions laid out in public for auctioning. On display would be rare and expensive items like watches, a bicycle, medicine sent from Hong Kong. The peasants would come by to see what they could afford to buy, or at least marvel at the way the party had rooted out cadres who had cheated them. It was to be the campaign's final penalty against errant cadres. Qingfa in particular had to undergo the humiliation of having his "home cleansed," his most treasured personal possessions expropriated and publicly displayed.

The workteam cadres had taken over completely the running of the brigade and production teams' affairs, but long-term arrangements had to be made now to provide again for indigenous leadership organs. In particular, with the autumn crop planting season in late July approaching, capable team cadres had to be mustered to take care of production. It was time for the "rectification of cadre ranks."

Elections

Each of the workteam cadres began organizing an election for the production team in which he or she was boarding. The peasants always viewed team elections with the utmost seriousness, knowing that their "rice bowls" depended upon good team leadership. To the ordinary Chen Villager, a good production team head was more important than a good brigade party secretary. On its side, the workteam realized that the opinions of the "masses" had to be respected; otherwise production would suffer.

Thus the workteam members began privately soliciting the views of the peasants, especially the older and more experienced ones, on who the best candidates might be. A meeting was then called of the team's poor peasant representatives, its activists, and several of the peasants known for their agricultural experience. Under the guidance of the workteam cadre, these dozen or so people, about a quarter of the team's able-bodied peasants, drew up an initial slate of seven candidates. The production team management committee would consist of one team head, two deputy team heads, one accountant, one cashier, one warehouseman, and a woman's representative. However, the list of recommended nominees that was handed down to the rest of the peasants for discussion did not specify which of the proposed candidates should hold which post; that decision was to be left to the team committee itself after the election. But from the particular mix of nominees, the peasants would understand. The experienced peasant in his thirties or early forties most likely would be the team head, and the up-and-coming young men in their twenties would serve as deputy heads. The somewhat educated nominees were to become the team accountant or cashier, and the only woman candidate invariably would become the woman's representative.

For a week or more, the impending team elections would become a topic of earnest discussion among the peasants. They would talk about it as they worked in the fields. The women would discuss it, food bowls in hand, as they visited with neighbors while their husbands and older children ate dinner.[7] The men would talk about it as they squatted together under a shady tree after dinner smoking their pipes. Last year did so and so direct production well enough? Was he officious? Lazy? Did he find excuses to go off to too many meetings? Should they elect someone else or reselect the same team cadres as before? The activists would try to "sell" the nominated slate; but if a particular proposed candidate encountered serious resistance from the peasants, in a second meeting between the activists and the workteam member, the name might be dropped and substituted with a more popular choice.

---

[7] Women often did not eat with their husbands, but used dinner time as the chance to make the rounds of the neighborhood to socialize with other women. Whereas after dinner the husbands could relax with male friends (unless there was a political meeting), the women had to work most evenings to finish the housework.

Dinner Time

Trying to convince the peasants to adopt a slate was only one side to the story of team elections, however. The workteam members also had to try to get the proposed candidates to accept their nominations. This was no easy task since most of the proposed candidates were none other than the recently criticized cadres. There were simply too few other capable peasants of good enough class background who would be willing to shoulder responsibility for the livelihoods of some twenty-five families. But many of the cadres were far too angry to consent readily to take up their posts again: "They said that after this their children, grandchildren, and great-grandchildren would never want to be cadres. They felt they'd been rejected, treated like lepers. Their kids in school also had had a hard time of it; no one had talked to them."

The reluctance of team cadres, particularly the team heads, to continue in office was not, however, a new phenomenon. It was, and would continue to be, an annual problem. A team head's job was both difficult and thankless. It involved daily squabbling with peasants over job assignments. It invariably meant criticism from team members for implementing unpopular government policies (for instance, policies curtailing the amount of time that peasants could spend on private plots and private sidelines) and criticism from brigade cadres for not pushing these same policies hard enough. Moreover, the post of team head demanded a great number of extra nightly meetings that took away from the time the cadre could spend on his own private plots. The extra pay in workpoints did not usually make up for this lost private income. For all of these headaches and pressures, a team head received few rewards. If he succeeded in raising the income of the production team, he was awarded the respect and gratitude of his neighbors; but if he failed, he would incur their scorn. Before the Four Cleanups he might have enjoyed a few officially illicit but customarily accepted perquisites: the opportunity, say, to maneuver a relative into a favored job or quietly to give himself priority in the purchase of a scarce consumer item like a bicycle or sewing machine. But in the immediate aftermath of the Four Cleanups, even these marginal advantages had temporarily vanished.

In general, brigade leaders and worried teammates every year had to expend a lot of energy persuading team leaders to continue in their posts. The single most effective weapon was to appeal to their sense of responsibility, pointing out to them that there was no one else as capable of fulfilling the duties and arguing that *someone* had to do it. Needless to say, in late 1965 the workteam was finding it especially difficult to convince the recently disgraced team cadres that their services were still indispensable to the masses. But most of them finally would consent. "What else can they do?" remarks one still ideologically committed interviewee. "Are the poor and lower-middle peasants all going to refuse such posts? Are they willing to give over the reins of such positions to the landlords?"

Once the resistance of most of the nominees was exhausted, the date for the team elections was announced. On that day all members of the team who worked full time in the fields (as young as fourteen years of age) had a right to vote, with the exception of the four-bad types. These elections put a formal stamp of approval upon what had already become the consensus. For the first time ever, the voting this year was by secret ballot, but the results usually were near unanimous.

There were hitches, however, in one of the production teams: a symptom of the fear and bitterness that remained among local cadres over the conduct of the Four Cleanups campaign.

> The election for our team head was not very exciting because the members were one-sidedly in favor of the former team head. But after he was elected, he refused to say what all incoming team leaders would normally say. . . . Right after an election the team leader should stand up to say a few polite words like: "You have chosen me, but I really don't have the ability. I hope that you all will help me in the future. If I make any mistakes, please point them out to me." . . . But he just sat there and said: "I do not want to be team leader. I told you not to elect me. I don't want it." It took the workteam cadre a week to persuade him. . . . He finally gave in.

Six of the ten team heads stepped back into their posts. All were from the western and central neighborhoods, where the collective production had been progressing satisfactorily. The workteam had refused to sanction only the reappointment of the No. 1 team's head on the "class" grounds that he was of upper-middle peasant origins. In his place, the workteam secured the election of the eldest of the urban sent-down youths.

Throughout the village, as usual, the minor team posts were shuffled around more than the top team leaders, and in several teams genuine contests emerged. Different clusters of relatives and friends, for reasons that were probably less than public spirited, discreetly pushed forward newly educated peasant youths who were their own kith and kin for the posts of team cashier, warehouseman, or accountant. In several cases, the ballot counts were close. But in most teams, one or more of these posts were offered to the sent-down youth outsiders. Besides being better able to take care of the paperwork involved, the urban-born youths had no relatives and no dependents; and thus, the peasants reasoned, they would not be so subject to temptations to embezzle funds or unfairly provide favors.

A few months later, after the autumn harvest, the peasants were notified by the workteam that elections for the brigade management committee would now also be held. Again, meetings of activists were convened by the workteam to select a slate of candidates, and the elections were then formally discussed in each production team at a general team meeting. On the day of the election, the peasants all went with their production team to a lychee grove on the western edge of the village. There they sat in a circle under the trees to hear short speeches and then cast their vote by secret ballot. Those who could not read and write were assisted by younger people. In most cases the results were near unanimous. Longyong and all other former brigade cadres, with the exception of the militia chief, were reelected.

After sounding out village opinion, the workteam provisionally reappointed Qingfa as the party branch secretary.[8] Though he had acted too much like a "local emperor" and had succumbed too often to favoritism and the lure of a more comfortable life, his abilities were self-evident and he had in no ways literally been a corrupt cadre. But the workteam dropped Feihan as deputy party secretary, as much for his lethargy as for his wrongdoings.

Directing the Spearhead Downward

Despite the rehabilitation of most of Chen Village's "four unclean" cadres, and the approval of their comeback by the peasants themselves, it was still necessary to restrengthen the cadres' authority and prestige. One means by which the workteam sought to do this was, in China's own terminology, by "directing the spearhead downward." Thus as the struggle meetings against the cadres drew to a close, the workteam launched a new wave of struggle meetings against the four-bad types. The four-bad types in Chen Village were, except for the ex-guerrilla, all "tame," carefully trying always to behave as submissively as they could.

[8.] There are never elections for the posts of brigade party branch secretary and deputy secretary. These are always appointed by the party level above: normally by the commune party committee, but in this instance the Four Cleanups workteam. The rest of the members of the brigade party branch committee are selected by a secret ballot of all of Chen Village's thirty party members. The party branch committee, as the highest political body in the brigade, normally has had enough power to entirely control nominations to the brigade management committee. Thus the ordinary peasant normally has enjoyed far less say in the brigade management elections than in his or her own team's.

But they were now accused of laziness, lack of repentance, and disobedience. The purpose of the exercise was to bring home to the peasants the idea that the "antagonistic contradictions" in socialist China were not between themselves and the cadres, but between themselves and these old "class enemies." The four-bad types needed to be struggled against, the workteam told the villagers, in order to keep such class enemies from having any illusions that the recent struggles against the cadres had at all weakened the dictatorship of the proletariat in China.

Tied to these rituals of class struggle in Chen Village were moves sharply to strengthen the class line. The workteam had aleady systematically begun working toward this by setting up the Poor and Lower-Middle Peasants Association and by carefully reinvestigating the class origins of every family in the village. These reinvestigations were supposed to ensure that no mistakes had been made during the early 1950s when each family's class label had been established. But the underlying purpose of the new checks apparently was to reinforce the notion among the villagers that these class label distinctions were to remain important to Chinese society during the decades to come. At almost every meeting, the workteam members were singing the praises of the poor and lower-middle peasants as an inherently revolutionary group. The good classes were to be made to feel that the revolution had truly been in their behalf and that the revolution would continue to represent their interests. In return, they were being asked to revive and strengthen their gratitude to the Communist party and to trust the party's push for renewed change in the countryside.

The workteam also played an active role in recruiting new members into the village party branch. In normal times, it was the party branch's responsibility to mobilize selected peasants to apply for party memberships. Their applications were then reviewed by the commune party committee. If successful, the candidates had to undergo a year-long probationary period, during which they could attend local party meetings as nonvoting observers. But this time the workteam, not the local party, was doing the recruiting. Seven villagers became probationary members. Because most of them came from the families with whom the workteam cadres were rooming and boarding, these households gained a somewhat disparaging nickname as Chen Village's "Boarding Party."

Several teenagers of poor and lower-middle peasant origins whom the workteam specially favored were not yet old enough for party membership. But they were given formal titles as "revolutionary successors." The idea was that as they came of age, they would accede to positions in the brigade leadership. Several of them, having been coaxed into "activist" aspirations by the workteam, in later years did rise into important brigade-level cadre posts.

Thus the workteam had dismantled the structure of authority in Chen Village, rebuilt it, and even laid down a foundation for its political future. Now it could concentrate on other aspects of village affairs.

▫ 3 ▫

Studying Chairman Mao

Cleansing the rural villages of corruption was not all that the Chinese leadership hoped to achieve during the Four Cleanups campaign. As the movement's other name—the Socialist Education campaign—implied, it was also to be directed at transforming the ideology, social mores, and economy of China's villages.

Introducing the Mao Cult

In the one and one half decades since the Communist party had arrived in Chen Village, the peasants had been exposed to numerous campaigns. But even though time and again they had heard vaguely of the thought of Chairman Mao, their recognition of the Communist ideology remained spotty and fragmented. Now, in the fall of 1965, the workteam received directives that its principal mission was to teach the thought of Mao to the peasants. According to the party headquarters in Peking, studying Mao's thought would produce a "spiritual change" in the peasantry's consciousness that in turn would encourage them to work for social and economic progress. The new Mao study thus was not to be simply a kind of dispassionate intellectual learning. The peasants were to be led not just to understand the basic principles of Mao's teachings but to become morally and emotionally committed to them. Mao's sayings would be imbued with an aura of sacred virtue and power.

A new organization known as the Mao Zedong Thought Counselor Corps was set up by the workteam to take charge of this sacred duty. The best recruits for it were the village's sent-down urban youths. Better than any local peasants, such youths excelled in book learning. They would be able to read Mao's writings and systematically expound them. Moreover, they were idealistically intent upon dedicating their own lives to Maoist principles; they could serve as examples for the peasants to learn from. And because they had not yet developed any close personal ties in the village, they would be in a better position to criticize fellow villagers for failing to live up to Mao's teachings. Their duties initially had no pay attached. These were to be accomplished only after work hours and demanded an enormous amount of energy and time. But the youths felt highly honored to be selected to carry out what they considered a glorious mission.

In the winter of 1965–66, the ten counselors (one from each production team) were sent off to a ten-day training session at the county seat. Together with about a thousand other young counselors from the whole county they were to learn "politics" and "philosophy" and then go back to their own villages to transmit Mao's thought to the masses. Not many of the high school students had read much of Mao's works in the original, less still those of Marx or Lenin, and some of them went to the training session worried that they might not manage to learn Mao's philosophy well enough to teach it. But their apprehensions were soon allayed. The core of their training concentrated on Mao's "three constantly read articles." Each of these articles stressed a different socialist virtue. "Serve the people" taught self-abnegating service to the masses. "In Memory of Norman Bethune" taught international communist brotherhood and sacrifice. "The Foolish Old Man Who Moved the Mountains" taught perseverance in the face of difficulties. These stories were not new to the young people from Canton. They had studied and discussed them many times in school. Now they were told to memorize the essays word by word and also to study manuals instructing them how to present the Maoist classics to the peasants: what were the main points to emphasize; how the points could be made vividly concrete; and how model brigades had organized exceptionally effective programs of Mao study.

As a finale to the training, the new counselors were provided with the chance to visit one such model brigade. They were to see the magical power of Mao Thought in raising the peasants' consiousness, and through that the economic level of the brigade. They were duly impressed by the tour.

> That brigade was situated in barren hills with settlements dispersed all over. . . . I thought: if people so poor could learn Mao's works, why couldn't our village! Completely illiterate peasants talked about how they let Mao's sayings penetrate their actions—they put in their own words what the sayings meant to them. Ah, this campaign had really been effective! In several years they'd achieved a lot!

The enthused young people were then dispatched back to Chen Village to set about applying what they had learned. As a first step, having themselves just learned selections from Mao by heart, they felt it would be of value to the peasants to do the same. One of the counselors recalls:

> We first had the peasants memorize quotations. Then we had every party member, every Communist Youth League member and every Mao Thought Counselor memorize the entire articles. After that all the peasants had to memorize the articles too. But their level of literacy was really too low. The peasants weren't able to memorize the whole thing. In other localities the people had to get up in front of others and recite the articles from memory; or whole families would have to memorize them together; or a whole production team would memorize them together. These sayings of Mao were used like the Holy Scripture!

The new concepts to be memorized were "revolutionary," but the method of transmitting them was traditionally Confucian—the belief that repeated memorization and chanting aloud would, with time, imprint the moral message indelibly in the mind. Yet there was one vital difference. The children in traditional China were not expected to comprehend fully what they had memorized until they were older and more sophisticated. In Chen Village, the peasants were supposed to use the messages expounded in Mao's works in their daily behavior within a very short period of time.

The Mao Thought Training Sessions

Special intensive sessions thus were organized systematically to introduce the peasantry to the Maoist world view. Every able-bodied peasant (again excluding the four-bad types, who were made to attend separate isolated sessions) had to go through this five-day training in Mao's thought. The villagers were divided into five groups of a hundred people each, which were to take the training in turn. Each contingent was a carefully balanced mix of teenagers and elderly, progressive and backward, men and women. For the whole five days they would not have to labor. "Not to labor and still to be given wages was a novelty." What was more, they were to be given "lectures!"—a new experience for most of them. Most of the villagers eagerly awaited their turn to participate.

The first set of training sessions opened immediately after the first winter plowing of early 1966, in the open-sided dirt-floored pavilion that was the brigade's Cultural Hall. The Mao Thought counselors, the workteam cadres, and the brigade cadres (who only recently had been elected back into office) ran these sessions jointly, since few of the young Mao Thought counselors, despite their enthusiasm, would be capable of handling big lecture classes on their own. They were either too shy or not articulate enough. The training sessions were to serve as a training for them as well as for the peasants. In time, some of them would develop into excellent propagandists; but for the time being, the major talks would still be given by the more educated and experienced of the workteam cadres.

Both mornings and afternoons opened with choral singing of revolutionary songs. The very first morning, difficulties were encountered in these opening choruses. Chen Villagers had never sung in unison before. Many were embarrassed to do so, especially the older men. Only the younger ones were ready to try out their voices. But the only songs they had ever known were from the popular Cantonese operas. They found the new tunes and words strange. The counselors, however, were not discouraged. Through daily coaching, the villagers eventually learned to sing passable renditions of songs like "Tilling the Land for the Revolution," "Serve the People," and "The East is Red."

Having warmed up the morning class with singing, the work-team cadres would begin their lectures. The brigade's main Mao study counselor provides a sample of their political teachings.

> They'd say, "Previously the members of our class were like slaves or beasts of burden. The party through tremendous effort and sacrifice has taken power for us. So many people died on the Long March; so many people died for the cause. Now we are the masters of our own house. If we won't put in the effort to protect this political power, that's no good, is it?" They'd also say, "You have to remember, even though we have now turned ourselves around there are many people in the world who have not been liberated, who have not turned themselves around. We must work for their libera-tion. We have to produce a lot of grain; a lot of material things; a lot of money, to make our country strong enough to enable this revolution to be carried out. We are sur-rounded by enemies: the USSR, the USA. . . . So we can't have a false sense of security. We must keep on working, keep on struggling, keep on producing. We must thwart the forces of revisionists and reactionaries. Political power is for us and for other peoples. Although [the younger people here] were not born into the miseries of poverty, we should give our energies for those who suffer. So we want and need to work for the revolution."

The speeches contained other concepts, too, embodied in a politi-cal terminology that was still new to many of the villagers: phrases such as "spontaneous capitalist tendencies" and "bour-geois thought."

After lunch each day, the peasants broke up into five smaller discussion groups of twenty members apiece. Each group was headed by a production team leader and a Mao Thought counse-lor. These sessions functioned along the lines of tutorials and were designed to make sure each peasant understood the morning lec-ture and could relate it to his or her own circumstances. But the peasants were not used to sitting and listening for so many hours, and by this time of day they were easily distracted. The effective-ness of these afternoon sessions depended heavily upon the group leaders' resourcefulness.

As teaching aids, the group leaders could draw illustrative

lessons from special "recall past bitterness" meetings that were being held each night. At these "bitterness" recitations, the cultural hall's kerosene lamps were extinguished to evoke the darkness of the past, and old peasants who had suffered particularly depressing experiences before the Liberation were called upon to speak. One related how his father had died of hunger. Another told how poverty had driven his mother, brother, and himself to wander as beggars from town to town. This man was asked to tell the story for each of the five training sessions; but each time, when he reached the point in his narrative where his mother died of starvation, he stood before them gulping wordlessly in pain, unable to continue. In the darkness, punctuating such reminiscences, people would cry out: "Down with the old society!" or "Down with the Guomindang reactionaries!" or "Down with the landlord class! Long live Chairman Mao!"

On the afternoon following such a "recall past bitterness" meeting, the discussion group leaders would point out "the sweetness of the present": how many new buildings and grain-drying yards had been built, how much the standard of living had risen, how the population had increased. The counselors, using examples less abstract and closer to home than the morning speakers, consistently reminded the villagers that their lives were improving today only because there were revolutionaries like Zhang Shide (the martyr of Mao's essay "Serve the People") who had selflessly struggled in their behalf. The Chens similarly had to be selfless and devote themselves to the collective—or else China might revert to past evils. The peasants were called upon one by one to renounce their own personal acts of selfishness.

One of the exercises of the five-day sessions was to show the peasants how to make these public self-examinations. First the discussion group leaders made their own self-confessions. They cited specific examples of how they themselves had transgressed Chairman Mao's teachings, and vowed to improve in the future. Then one by one everyone in the group had to say, in effect: "We're ungrateful. The present life is so good compared to those old days, yet we're not satisfied and selfishly complain that it's still too hard." Each one was expected to add a couple of concrete examples of his or her own selfishness: how one had been paying too much attention to earning workpoints; or how another when sent to take care of cows had not wanted to go. Initially it was very difficult for the peasants to make such speeches. They were not used to this type of introspection nor accustomed to speaking up publicly. When their turn came, some of them took a long time before they could utter a few words. But a counselor recollects, "We patiently encouraged them. If they said a few words we'd immediately praise them; and they'd get more encouraged and say more. If anyone cracked jokes about the difficulties someone else had in speaking, he'd be soundly criticized for harming the activism of someone studying Mao's works!"

Throughout the five days, the workteam and counselors impressed upon the peasantry that their debt of gratitude was owed specifically and directly to Chairman Mao and that, hereafter, they needed to abide by his teachings. The peasants were always supposed to call appropriate Mao quotes to mind whenever faced with decisions or difficulties of any kind. "Some peasants," recalls a production team head, "did use what they were taught. If some member of my team lazily stopped working, some other peasant might ball him out, 'Hey, you're selfish. Chairman Mao tells us to work selflessly for the collective.' . . . Some peasants patterned themselves on the quotes."

Mao's Preachers

Henceforth, to reinforce such thinking, two or three nights every week the peasants were required to meet with the team or brigade level Mao Thought counselors to learn new revolutionary songs and Mao quotes. At least once a year, usually during the late winter and early spring slack season, the peasants also spent several days in refresher political sessions.

Initially, at least, many peasants welcomed the evening meetings—and especially the teenagers. They were too young to have much standing in the village. But because they had had a primary school education, they often were called on to lead the older generation in the Mao study sessions. In this one area they could claim superiority over their elders—in an activity that bordered on the sacred. As one young peasant (who later on became politically "backward") recalls today,

The youths truly believed in Mao's thought. In their hearts they really felt this Mao Zedong was something, thought every one of the quotations made sense. Everyone felt more progressive and public spirited. [Later], during the Cultural Revolution, we felt proud hearing the rumor that our Chairman Mao was now a leader of the world, that even the foreign visitors praised and worshipped Mao Zedong when they returned to their own countries.

Whenever movies were shown in the village and a red sun (the symbol of Chairman Mao) flashed on the screen, Chen Village peasants would burst into spontaneous applause of admiration and support.

This glorification of Mao legitimized the work of the Mao Thought counselors. A counselor's reproach could not simply be dismissed as criticism from an immature youngster. It had to be taken seriously. The counselors, after all, spoke as official interpreters of Chairman Mao. "Those counselors were really good with their mouths," recounts a former team cadre. "They used Mao quotes as examples; they used them as a means of influencing people's 'face.' "

The counselors' best opportunity to wield this power came in the daily half hour of Mao study that was organized during the peasants' lunch break. Since most of their fields were far from home, the peasants would bring their lunches with them and then would normally either rest under a shady tree or run up into the hills to water private plots or to cut grass.[1] Now, instead, they would have to spend most of that spare time in Mao study. The counselor or a deputy counselor in each labor squad[2] would read the peasants a passage or a quotation from Mao's writings, carefully selected to bring out current problems in the labor squad or the village. For instance, if some peasants were doing their work carelessly, the counselor in a righteous voice could read a quote

---

[1] Mountain grass could be sold as fuel for a tidy sum, and when women at work in the fields in the morning saw grass in the hills above (grass-cutting was largely women's work), "they glued their eyes to the sky and never looked down." They would conserve their energies till the lunch break and exhaust themselves furiously cutting the grass.

[2] A production team was divided into two to three labor squads.

from "In Memory of Norman Bethune": "There are not a few people who are irresponsible in their work, preferring the light and shirking the heavy, passing the burdensome tasks on to others and choosing the easy way for themselves." Then the counselor would lead the workers in a discussion of how "certain people" were being irresponsible and lacking in their devotion to Mao's glorious thought. Even without any names being mentioned, everyone would know who those certain people were. A few activists who had been briefed before the discussion would take the lead in condemning irresponsibility, and everyone else would feel pressured to speak out against laziness, including the laggards themselves.

Besides anonymously criticizing the backward, the counselors would commend—this time by name—those who had worked harder than usual. This technique was particularly effective with "backward elements" who had recently made some progress. The often exaggerated compliments opened them to criticism from teammates if they began to slacken off: "So and so has been getting all that praise, but he's not doing good work at all any more; what a phony!"

The counselors rarely criticized or disagreed with any cadres publicly for fear of stripping them of their authority in the peasants' eyes. The workteam had advised the counselors that the cadres had been hurt enough in the first half of the Four Cleanups, and that it was now appropriate that public praise be used to rebuild their authority. But the counselors discovered how to bring pressures to bear in private. The brigade's chief counselor recollects:

> We could use Mao quotes to try to control events. Even the cadres couldn't oppose a whole rash of Mao quotes that made a certain point. We used the quotes to help them from being too extreme. We even used this to help control the work style of Longyong. You don't criticize him, just mention that Mao says, ". . ." and you quote a saying whose gist is that cadres shouldn't ever be arrogant in their work style.

Peasants and cadres alike did not enjoy being hectored by a band of righteous youngsters. Many of the villagers, moreover, were not enthusiastic about restraining their personal and family interests in favor of the collective's. But no one dared criticize directly the sacred messages of Mao Thought, and the counselors therefore could wrap themselves in Chairman Mao's aura as a means to shield themselves and anyone else who could be linked to Mao. They took this step, for instance, in behalf of the brigade's singing and theater troupe of a dozen local and sent-down youths (entitled the Mao Thought Propaganda Troupe). There were no qualifications for joining the troupe other than youthful enthusiasm, an ability to sing vaguely in tune and dance a few simple steps, and a willingness to write and memorize the lines of political skits. When the counselors overheard some peasants disparaging the mediocre quality of a new troupe production, they lost no time in silencing the ingrates:

> The next day we commended the Propaganda Troupe—said how praiseworthy it was that they had such activism, such enthusiasm, such boundless respect for Chairman Mao. We noted that they sacrificed their free time to struggle to present Mao Zedong's revolutionary truth. We also criticized those people who criticized the Propaganda Troupe—told them exactly what kind of an attitude they should have toward Mao Zedong's thought!

Raising seemingly mundane issues to the level of "political principles" worked. It became inadvisable for any peasant to be critical of anything identified with spreading Mao's gospel.

Unable to attack the preaching, some peasants instead attacked the preachers. One counselor recalls, "They opposed us because we'd denounced revisionism and struggled against individual selfishness. . . . They said that we counselors were 'mouth revolutionaries,' that all we really wanted was to climb up, wanted to become big officials, were faking activism." As Mao study became more regularized the counselors became increasingly vulnerable to this allegation that they did not always practice what they preached. They had had to start taking time off from labor to prepare their lessons; every five days, for instance, they met together to discuss how to use the materials handed down from the commune and county Mao Thought Corps. Some peasants liked to grumble that the counselors labored only half the time and spent the other half (an exaggeration) comfortably rehearsing how to tell others how hard they should work.

Under pressure to demonstrate that they could pass the same test of unstinting labor that they had imposed on others, the Mao Thought counselors had to drive themselves to exhaustion. Peasants worked hard mainly for economic reasons, but these young urban-born counselors labored hard to maintain their reputations and the effectiveness of their political preaching. At every moment he or she was in the fields, a conscientious counselor had to present an image of battling ferociously at the "front line of production."

Unfortunately, not all counselors had the tenacity or strength to keep up this frantic labor. One counselor, for example, contracted severe rheumatism in her legs while working barefoot in the wet paddy fields; and when her pace subsequently slackened, she became the butt of the jokes of "backward elements." They nicknamed her the "Light Work Department Head." Certainly they were aware of the distinction between a poor work record caused by ailments and one due to laziness. But didn't Mao's ideals demand that people courageously surmount all obstacles, even physical handicaps? This was her Achilles heel; to have given her any benefit of the doubt would have meant laying oneself open to her righteous and irritating criticism. She came under intense and unkind scrutiny until she finally gave up her job of counselor. Then and only then did her teammates show any sympathy for her ailments. A large group of them contributed money to buy her a sewing machine so that she could do something constructive besides farm work.

Those who survived as counselors had had the stamina to work as hard or harder than any of the peasants. They won their rights to be preachers through willpower and physical endurance.

Broadcasting the New Order

These counselors had a powerful new medium of communication to help in their proselytizing. This was the production brigade's wired broadcasting system, set up when the village acquired electricity in 1966. The system consisted of thirty loudspeakers positioned throughout the village, with four large ones installed in the village's main meeting places. The volume was tuned loud enough that even while indoors people could hear the announcements.

Ao, a sent-down urban youth who had proven herself an efficient and devoted Mao Thought counselor, had been chosen by the workteam to fill the newly created post of brigade broadcaster. At the time Ao was only seventeen, a small thin girl. But she was more hard driving and ambitious than any of her older male colleagues. A vigorous, enthusiastic laborer, she got more work done than many of the sturdy peasant women. Articulate, bright, a conformist but not exactly a yes-woman, she had been cultivated by the workteam to become a Four Cleanups activist and then a workteam aide. Helping the workteam collect materials on the peasants and cadres had given her an opportunity to accumulate a full store of knowledge on Chen Village's history, its informal power structure, its social networks and feuds. This was the kind of knowledge an astute Mao Thought counselor and broadcaster could use to good effect.

The new broadcasting system altered the peasants' lives in more than one way. Ao became the village's relentless time-keeper. Despite collectivization, the peasants' daily lives had not been regulated by the concept of time necessary to industrial life. In fact, in 1966, only two peasants in all of Chen Village owned watches. In the mornings, it often took an hour before all of a team's members sauntered in to begin work. But with Ao's announcements this changed: "Commune members, comrades, please note that it is now 7:30 A.M. We hope that everyone will go as quickly as possible to your production team's headquarters to study." Rather than show disrespect for Mao's sacred thought, peasants had to be sure they were on time for a few minutes of Mao quotes before the day's labor was assigned.

The hour Ao came on the air in the morning varied from season to season. It could be as late as 6:30 A.M. in the slack seasons and as early as 4:30 A.M. in the summer busy season, when peasants customarily labored hectically in the fields for twelve or more hours a day. The first announcement was to get the women out of bed to allow them ample time to feed the pigs and prepare breakfast before their husbands arose. The broadcasting continued nonstop for two hours until everyone was assembled. When everyone returned home in the late afternoon, the broadcasts resumed for another two hours.

About half of the broadcasting time was given over to music and reports from the provincial radio station, which were transmitted to the village via a hookup with the commune headquarters. The other half was devoted to brigade news and pep talks composed by the brigade broadcaster with the help of the Mao Thought counselors. Ao was devoted to this work. She believed that ideological change was the leading factor in the construction of a socialist countryside and felt the broadcasting system was an effective instrument to bring about this change. Eventually she discovered how best to exploit the new medium so as to prod the whole village in the desired directions.

She kept a very close watch on all the daily goings-on in the village at all levels. The Mao Thought counselors in each production team became her chief sources of information. But, if need be, she got on a bicycle and pedaled from labor squad to labor squad, participating in their work and gathering materials for her reporting. When peasants saw her coming, they would nervously joke: "Better watch out; if you get a little lazy, the next thing you know you're on the loudspeakers." Sure enough, in the evening "certain people" in team No. 2 who had been purposely lagging behind would hear about their selfishness in Ao's clear and determined cadence (which she had carefully developed by imitating the professional radio broadcasters). More often than not, though, Ao fulsomely praised people. In the course of a year she commended (often with exaggeration) about half of the adults in the village.

She commended not just individuals but whole production teams. Particularly during the agricultural busy seasons, she reported on each production team's accomplishments: which team had already transplanted how many acres of rice sprouts; which team had accumulated how many pounds of natural fertilizer. With a few other counselors, she even erected a bulletin board at the center of the village pictorially comparing each team's progress. She persistently played upon the peasants' pride in their team to spur them to race against other teams.

The Mao study, the broadcasts, the contests, praise, and criticism resulted in a greater work discipline. People felt under pressure to conform; but they also believed in the power of Mao's teaching to give them better lives, just so long as they faithfully obeyed his words. During the agricultural slack season, production team heads found it easier to convince members to work on public works projects.

Yet the team heads had mixed feelings about Ao and the counselors. They appreciated the counselors' efforts to mobilize the peasants to labor harder; but there were also conflicts of interest between counselors and team heads. The team cadres were the guardians of their own particular team's interests, and they disliked the counselors' sense of loyalty to higher levels. As disciples of Mao and the party, Ao and most of the other sent-down youth counselors believed in the submission of the individual to the collective and the subordination of the smaller unit to the good of the greater whole. They saw, moreover, that their own future prospects primarily depended upon the brigade's appreciation for their work. In the years to come, whenever the brigade leaders' responsibilities clashed with the teams' interests, the Mao Thought counselors put themselves at the brigade leadership's beck and call. "Our work of influencing public opinion made the brigade cadres' work much easier," Ao says, and she admits that "our broadcasting system was the mouthpiece of the brigade management committee."

The Antisuperstition Drive

Since Liberation, a great many of the traditional institutions and customs had been eradicated or weakened in Chen Village. The younger generations of peasants, for example, cannot recall today ever having attended any lineage rituals. Ancestral halls had become warehouses. Professional geomancers no longer plied their trade of choosing lucky sites for burials and new homes. But rituals at the household level had been able to survive. Indeed, many of the local cadres engaged regularly in such rites.

The urban youths and the workteam were disturbed with what they saw. Each peasant house invariably still contained a little ancestor altar. The villagers burnt joss sticks for the warrior god Guangong and a variety of kitchen gods. A crumbling temple had been allowed to stand outside the village entrance because no one dared to tear it down, for fear of angering the many ghosts it housed. Before all important events, the villagers faithfully consulted the astrological almanac. Most disturbing of all to the urban youths, when villagers were ill they turned to the ministrations of several old women from the village who claimed magical healing powers. Their favorite prescription was a concoction of incense ashes soaked in water. For a fee, the old women also burned strips of red and gold paper bearing the words of magic incantations. They whipped the sleeping mats of their patients to drive away the evil spirits. Falling into trances, they careened around the sickroom speaking in tongues.

One of the final tasks of the Four Cleanups workteam was to discredit such traditional beliefs and practices. The party was convinced that so long as the peasants continued to hold to "feudalistic" values steeped in superstition, they would not be able or willing to accept entirely the thought of Mao and a socialist world view. An antisuperstition drive was on the Four Cleanups agenda.

As in other drives, another locale was to serve as a model. The workteam escorted Chen Village's production team heads and other cadres to the most "progressive" brigade in the commune, where the drive was already under way. There, for the cadres' benefit, a performance was staged. Several pre-Liberation professional fortune tellers were brought out onto a stage and ordered to talk about the tricks they had used to make people believe in them. Some of the old miracle healers and shamans similarly admitted they were quacks. To destroy the myth that the magical powers of jade warded off misfortune, several activist peasant women went onto the stage and dramatically smashed their expensive bracelets, while publicly declaring: "I have to destroy superstition!" When Chen Village's cadres returned home, they were to promote similar lessons.

In order to disprove the protective powers of the Chen Villagers' gods, the workteam and cadres prodded the heads of every family to publicly burn their kitchen gods with their own hands. In pushing this through, persuasion was mixed with coercion. The workteam organized meetings at which preselected poor and lower-middle peasants were urged to the stage to deliver speeches. An interviewee has provided a sample declaration: "Before, the landlords exploited us. There was nothing to eat. Life was hard. Did gods ever protect us? No! But since the party came, after Chairman Mao came, we have things to eat, we have clothing, life is better. So we shouldn't believe in the gods. We should believe in Chairman Mao!"

In short, the power and glory of Mao Zedong's thought was supposed to fill the void left by the destruction of traditional religious practices. The peasants were asked to take down the good-luck sayings on red paper that customarily graced their front doorposts and replace these with similar bright red strips of paper bearing quotes from Chairman Mao. Where the household altars had hung, every family had to paste up a photograph of Chairman Mao. The peasants initially were skeptical and obeyed only passively. It became incumbent on the workteam to demonstrate to them that Mao's thought could bring them far greater security than their gods, their ancestors, or their shamans.

The workteam most easily could dispel the peasants' beliefs in miracle cures. The commune-level Four Cleanups workteam installed a workteam doctor at the commune seat—the first trained physician ever available to the peasantry. Very soon after his clinic opened, a man from Chen Village was rushed there in severe pain. The doctor removed a large tumor from his stomach, and then let him and his kin see and marvel at it. The operation reportedly made overnight converts of many of the peasants. They were happy to follow the workteam's suggestion that Chen Village pay to send two young people to the county seat to take a newly opened course for training rural medical aides—the so-called barefoot doctors. One was to be trained in Western practices, the other in Chinese medicine.

To debunk the gods would be more difficult. A bad crop or any other calamity would confirm the peasantry in their fear that the gods would exact vengeance for their disrespect. Only bumper harvests and rising living standards would allay their worries and ultimately convince them that the gods they had worshipped had been powerless pieces of paper and wood. Only then would they fully believe that the answer to all their problems lay in "arming oneself with Mao Zedong's thought" and that selfless, collective hard work produced the only true miracles. "So at the end of the Four Cleanups," a team cadre remembers, "the workteam concentrated on improving production. The workteam needed to push production in the last phase of the campaign so that the earlier parts of the campaign would turn out successfully."

Learn From Dazhai

Higher production would depend upon harder work. The Mao counselor network and broadcasts had been successful in encouraging a new work ethic and new peer group pressures against malingerers. But to sustain this enthusiasm and these pressures, a new system for evaluating and rewarding work was also necessary.

For the past several years, the peasants had been paid for their labor by a system of piece rates—so many workpoints for finishing so much work. The advantage of this system was that a person's work could be evaluated by fairly clear-cut quantitative measures. In transplanting rice, for example, each woman (rice transplanting was women's work) had been paid simply in accordance with the total length of the rows that she planted in the paddy fields. The disadvantage of this system, however, was that the women were rewarded for being concerned solely with how many feet of seedlings they planted and not with how well they did the planting. To maximize their pay, some would plant the seedlings too far apart and in their hurry not push them in deep enough, so that when the fields were flooded, the seedlings came floating out. When coming near the end of a row, women would anxiously look around to see if good or bad rows were coming up. In the irregularly shaped fields, a bad row was one that was relatively short, since any woman assigned to it would soon have to waste time (and thus lose workpoints) shifting all her materials to yet another row. So if the row coming up were short, a woman would slow down in her work to avoid it. But if the row coming up were long, she would speed up, even at the expense of carelessness, to be able to grab it first.

The new wage system was to eliminate the shoddy work that

such "selfish" attitudes produced. This "Dazhai" system was named after a production brigade in Shanxi province that Mao Zedong was promoting as a model for all of China. Despite its mountainous and arid terrain, the peasants of Dazhai village, it was said, had lifted their brigade up by the bootstraps through total commitment to the virtues preached by Mao—self-sacrificing hard work, self-reliance, and tight collective solidarity. This Maoist commitment was supposed to be exemplified in Dazhai's radically new remuneration system.

The Dazhai wage program was introduced into Chen Village several months after Mao study had begun. Under the Dazhai method, one's labor was evaluated in terms of its overall quality and the attitudes that went into it, not simply in terms of the quantity of work each worker accomplished. At a monthly mutual appraisal meeting, every member of a production team had to declare how many workpoints he thought he deserved for a full day's work; and each of these self-appraisals was then judged by all the teammates.

Strong activist men normally were asked to go first to set the correct tone. One of them would stand up and self-effacingly say something like (in the words of an interviewee):

> In the month since our last appraisal meeting, on such and such occasions I didn't try my hardest. I should study Chairman Mao more, speak up more in meetings, should be quicker to obey my labor assignments, and should become more progressive in my thinking. I shall try to do better in the future. I have not tried my best. I deserve only nine workpoints a day.

Every interviewee agrees that in using this earnest self-deprecating language, these men generally were not just engaging in a formal show of rhetoric. They believed in what they had been taught in Mao study, and many of them genuinely measured their behavior throughout the month to see whether it conformed to the promises they made.

Then came the appraisals by teammates—normally a round of praise for a first-class activist, followed by the most important part of the entire meeting, the evaluation of how many daily workpoints each was worth. Instead of the nine workpoints the activist had modestly asked for, he would be granted ten, the maximum on the workpoint scale. First-rate laborers were well respected, and few would begrudge them the honor or the income. But those members who were lazy or who did not come to every political meeting would be criticized and given low ratings.

In short, the new method was relying on peer group pressures to get people to work as hard as they could and to cooperate as closely as possible with other members of the work unit. The politically enthusiastic dragged along in their work those who remained politically backward. If the latter ever tried slackening off, not only were their incomes reduced; they were publicly humiliated through low workpoint appraisals. A peasant's workpoint rating quickly became a mark of his or her formal standing in the community.

The new Dazhai method had a second important aspect. It carried one step further the egalitarian economic leveling instituted during the land reform and collectivization of the 1950s. As in the fifties, there was a constituency in the village with a particular interest in supporting the new measures: the village's poorer households. Under the piece-rate system, a strong skilled worker had at times earned twice as many workpoints in a day as a weak and clumsy man. That would now change precisely because cooperative attitudes, not just strength and endurance, would be taken into consideration. A weak man who tried his best for the team would receive his due reward. While the best workers earned the full ten points a day, under the new Dazhai method the weak man could count on some 8.5 points.

Indeed, that eventually became the *minimal* rating for male adults, even for those who were weak *and* lazy. A major reason for this unplanned development was, ironically, the steadfast insistence by the men of Chen Village that no man should be allowed to slip below any woman in the scale of prestige defined by the workpoint ratings.[3] In most of the production teams, no

[3.] Under the piece-rate system, a similar inequality had been imposed. Tasks where women predominated, such as transplanting, had been assigned relatively low workpoints for the amount of labor and skill required. All the tasks with which men were associated had earned greater workpoints.

woman under the Dazhai program ever was granted a rating of more than 7.5 points a day.[4]

The narrow wage spread *among* the men and an equally narrow spread among the women (from a low of 6.5 points to the high of 7.5) meant that extra work no longer brought a person any significant extra remuneration. But the new workpoint system's promise was that hard and efficient collective labor would result in better harvests and thus would bring prosperity to every one of a team's households. As a Chinese saying put it: "All boats float higher when the water rises."

To get this collective water to rise, a peasant would not only have to work hard, but would have to ensure that other team members also did their fair share. Peasants had sound economic reasons, therefore, to participate in rigorous praise and criticism of teammates. If they failed to criticize one another vigorously, lazy work habits might creep back in, and this would not even be counteracted (as under the piece-rate system) by the peasants' desires to increase their own personal wages.

This was not immediately a danger, though it would become one in later years. For the time being, during the height of the Mao study campaign, the villagers' spirit of collective concern and their willingness to engage in mutual scrutiny still ran strong, and the Dazhai system was effective in prodding them all forward. More rice shoots survived transplanting; people stayed out after dark to finish their chores; harvests were cut more efficiently and more quickly.

---

[4] Many of the middle-aged wives saw no reason for complaint. Whatever earnings they lost out on, they said, their husbands recouped for the family. But a number of the younger unmarried women, influenced by the young women from Canton, were frustrated and objected. Ao, who championed their cause in her broadcasts, observes, "They felt that here they were putting out a tremendous amount of effort and were transplanting just about as much grain as the men, and yet they'd still be so far behind the men in workpoints. 'We're as good as the best men, and we don't even get as much as the worst men.' The strongest women were really vehement about this matter. The men argued back that only men could do vital work like plowing. The women would respond that this is only because of tradition, that the women could plow just as well if the men taught them—which the men wouldn't. But no matter how the women argued this way and that, they were never able to transform their status."

The Production Drive

Learning from Dazhai also meant heavy investments in labor to transform the collective's natural environment. Chen Village's land in no way was as forbidding as Dazhai's mountain slopes, but to transform it would require hard and persistent work. Potholes as deep as six feet studded some Chen Village fields, and the workteam instructed the peasants to fill these in. This involved emptying loads of soil carried on shoulder poles from the mountains. Wherever fields were too sandy, the villagers now had to mix the soil with clay. Where the soil of the mountain fields was too acidic, deep trenches were dug to leach out the acidity. Work was begun on leveling out the rice paddy fields so that the rice shoots could all be planted in the same depth of water. Irrigation ditches that had been left undug due to conflicting interests between production teams were now put in under the workteam's commands. Paddy fields were flooded and drained on more pre-

Opening Up a New Road

cise schedules, and the water in the fields was changed more often than before.

Customarily, after the backbreaking work of transplanting rice, villagers had worked at a rather leisurely pace until the harvest season drew near. No longer. They cleared hillsides to plant lychee and pear trees and bamboo; and now that the village had electricity, they installed a water-pumping station to irrigate the new groves. At the foot of the hills they introduced new crops that could be sown and harvested during slack seasons—a cash crop of melons, new high-yield varieties of peanuts and sugar cane, and "wood yam," a long tuber that could be ground into a flour and sold at a good profit.

Chen Village's grain yields were low compared to neighboring counties in the Pearl River Delta. Though the workteam members were by no means agricultural experts, some of them were from those counties and were able to introduce the Chen Village cadres to the new techniques being used there. They led the production team heads on tours of inspection and introduced them to the "miracle" rice hybrids that Chinese scientists had begun distributing to south China's richest counties two years earlier.[5] Under conditions of good water control and heavy applications of fertilizers, these new hybrids could produce up to twice as much grain per acre as ordinary rice.

The peasants of Chen Village nursed a healthy reluctance to try out radically new agricultural techniques. People as poor as themselves could not afford to risk their basic food crops in experiments. They had bitterly relearned this lesson during the Great Leap Forward. Had the village not been under the workteam's control, the local cadres might never have sanctioned a headlong plunge into these innovations. But the workteam was

[5] Benedict Stavis, *Making Green Revolution: The Politics of Agricultural Development in China,* Cornell Rural Development Committee Monograph No. 1 (Ithaca, New York: Cornell University Press, 1974) p. 31; and Thomas Wiens, "The Evolution of Policy and Capabilities in China's Agricultural Technology," in *Chinese Economy Post-Mao* (Washington, D.C.: Joint Economic Committee, U.S. Congress, 1978), p. 676. In the Philippines, American scientists independently had developed similar strains of short-stemmed "miracle" rice. Introduced throughout Southeast Asia in the late 1960s and the 1970s, these gave rise to the massive crop increases known to the West as the Green Revolution.

adamant, and the workteam had the power and the prestige. Chen Village joined the Green Revolution.

Since this new "miracle" rice required increased fertilizer, which would have to be applied at just the right times and in just the right amounts, the workteam used manuals to teach the villagers how to use nitrate fertilizers; it taught them what fertilizers to apply to combat alkalinity and acidity and how to employ phosphorous fertilizers with peanuts. But the government would not be able to sell the village enough of the manufactured fertilizers. So the workteam had the teams plant a winter crop of nitrogen-fixing alfalfa and then plow the crop under before the first rice crop was sown. The teams learned also how to grow algae-like plants in the water around the rice shoots as a nitrogenous "green manure." To acquire every available bit of compost for the fields, drives were also organized every two months to clean up all the gutters and piles of garbage in the village (which incidentally led to a noticeable decline in illnesses).

The village had always been short of labor during the height of the harvest periods. Bigger grain harvests would exacerbate these peak-season labor shortages; and the village faced the threat that part of the crop would simply rot in the fields. Under the workteam's direction, Chen Village therefore also took its first small steps toward agricultural mechanization. It bought several rudimentary pedal-driven threshing machines to relieve one of the most time-consuming of the harvesting tasks. Before, grain could be carried in from the fields only by shoulder pole—slow and exhausting work. Now during the slack seasons, the teams began widening the narrow dikes that separated the paddy fields so that new two-wheeled rubber-tired carts (the first carts other than wheelbarrows ever used in Chen Village) could be pulled along the paddy dikes. The carts could haul two to three times as much grain in one load as even the village's strongest men previously had been able to tote on poles. But even with these labor-saving devices, the bigger harvests meant that the harvest workload was heavier than ever before. One interviewee recalls working sixteen or more exhausting hours every day during the two-week peak of the July harvest season. But through this, the teams managed to bring in all of their bumper harvests on time. All the families that year were allotted more grain than they could eat. They could abandon their diets of gruel.

These initial successes in production encouraged villagers to accept the new ways and beliefs as demonstrably superior to the traditional ways. A former team head claims that "even the old generation had to believe because they had eyes and could see that production had increased. The younger people definitely didn't believe in the gods or superstition any more." During the next decade and a half, the kitchen gods never went back up on the walls; and peasants no longer openly put their faith in charms, auguries, or fate.

The economic changes and the new organizations that had been introduced during the Four Cleanups were to alter village life in complex ways. They gave rise not just to new attitudes, but also to new rhythms of daily life, new patterns of social interaction, and new aspirations. They aroused new expectations of what the village leadership should provide.

The Second Fall of Qingfa

A new leadership would have to respond to these expectations. For in the midst of this new campaign to transform the village economy, Qingfa suddenly and dramatically was ousted once more by the Four Cleanups workteam. He had not adequately taken stock of the fact that he had never been restored fully to the good graces of the workteam cadres.

The workteam had its own reasons for disliking Qingfa. When under attack during the earlier phases of the Four Cleanups, he had been silently defiant. Up on stage he had "repented but hadn't seemed repentant." The workteam had wanted the peasants to view its sudden reversals in the "putting policy on a solid footing" phase as a magnanimous gesture toward contrite wrongdoers; but Qingfa's quiet stubbornness had made his restoration look more like he had been vindicated. Worse yet, he injudiciously had begun reverting to his old ways. He let newly cautious peasants drop by his home to return to him free of charge the auctioned goods they had bought when his house had been "cleansed." He once again played the autocrat in all his dealings with subordinates and ordinary peasants. He dropped hints that he still held teams No. 3 and 4 in disfavor.

The final straw came in May of 1966, when a goose belonging to a normally meek peasant from the No. 3 team wandered into Qingfa's courtyard and Qingfa brazenly claimed the bird as his own. The Four Cleanups may not have taught Qingfa any lessons, but it had given this peasant a new courage. Rather than let himself be bullied, he took the matter to the workteam member in charge of the No. 3 team. This was the young woman who was a university graduate. At the next brigade-wide meeting, she sharply attacked Qingfa. But instead of making the appropriate contrite remarks, Qingfa resorted to his ferocious temper to still her criticisms. "Having been restored as party secretary," one observer of the incident muses, "he probably felt the campaign was all over and he could explode as he did." Amid a flow of invective, he belittled the woman cadre's credentials: "When I was staging the revolution you were still nothing!" The refined urban-bred woman burst into tears in front of the assemblage. It was Qingfa's final undoing. The Chen Village workteam reported him to the commune workteam headquarters. He was again stripped of his post; and he was placed on probation as a party member, with warnings that any further missteps would result in irrevocable loss of his party membership.

To take Qingfa's place, the Chen Village workteam promoted a man in his late twenties who had been the Communist Youth League secretary. His name was Chen Jinyi. He, too, was one of the best farm workers in the village. He thus had the physical assets that were a sine qua non for respect in Chen Village. Jinyi's class background was that of a "small rentier": that is, before the Liberation his father had died while Jinyi was still very young, and his widowed mother, unable to till the land herself, had rented it out to get an income to support them. To be a small rentier was deemed essentially nonexploitative. However, such a background was not considered an especially good one. But in the Four Cleanups, Jinyi's family had been one of the only families in the village to have its class label revised upward, perhaps because the workteam had its eye on Jinyi as a potential "revolutionary successor." Jinyi could now claim a politically suitable lower-middle peasant status.

Jinyi was an unusually diligent and dedicated worker, with a reputation for total honesty. He had handled his job as Communist Youth League secretary without reproach. But he was not a forceful or terribly competent person. Two interviewees have separately characterized him, with some disdain, as "simple." Even though he was literate and could take notes, "when he listened to a report at the commune seat and came back to communicate it to the masses, you had no idea what he was talking about. He had no logic at all—just said incoherent things, a sentence here, a sentence there."

Jinyi had not wanted the party secretaryship, but he accepted it out of duty when it was urged upon him. So long as he held the post, he worked at it up to the full level of his limited ability. But he was no match for Longyong.

For the past half decade, second only to Qingfa, Longyong had been the village leader. He possessed the personal probity, the physique and strength of character, the knowledge of agriculture, and the skills in management that attracted the respect of most of the villagers. Hence when the workteam deposed Qingfa, the peasants generally expected that Longyong would succeed Qingfa as the real power in the village. Jinyi, the new party secretary, would *formally* be Chen Village's leader by virtue of his party post. But Jinyi was too junior in prestige, too inexperienced, inarticulate, and indecisive to wield effective power on his own. He would have to turn to Longyong. Jinyi himself realized it; Longyong also realized it. From the very start, even while the Four Cleanups workteam was still in the village, Longyong had emerged as the senior partner in the two men's relationship. It was Longyong who pushed through the final word on any issues he felt strongly about, and who then saw to it in his unrelenting way that the villagers carried out those decisions.

Longyong seemed to like the type of relationship that he had with Jinyi. Because Longyong was not an appointee of the commune party committee or any other body above the village, he was not directly and immediately responsible to the higher authorities for any mistakes he might make. He could be less inhibited in pushing through projects than if he had been the party branch secretary himself. He could at the same time dominate Jinyi without owing him any favors or deference. While the workteam was still in the village, Longyong was somewhat re-strained. But in later years he became Chen Village's local emperor.

Through the Four Cleanups' struggles against cadres and the Mao study campaign, Longyong and the other cadres had learned several lessons about how their power could most safely be wielded. They had learned that the party was not tolerant toward the type of particularistic patronage that had formed so important a part of Qingfa's leadership style; nor was it tolerant of the petty corruption common to village cadres. The village officers had gained a deeper appreciation, too, of the political advantages of a poor or lower-middle peasant class status. It provided "political capital" in one's dealings with outside authorities and could be made use of if one was determined to stay in command or had ambitions to get ahead.

Longyong had learned these particular lessons well. They suited his temperament and many of his own values. In the future he would be righteously severe toward the bad-class families, al-ways reminding them and others that he himself held to a poor peasant's "class stand." He had learned anew the political value of his relatively abstemious lifestyle and of his harsh but impartial leadership style. In the coming years, he would rigidly eschew taking any personal gifts and would flaunt his probity and per-sonal poverty. Other cadres still enjoyed the village custom of late evening snacks with their friends. But Longyong (and Jinyi) would refuse all invitations, even from kin. One of the youths from Canton observes,

> He knew that if he snacked with other families, in a future campaign some peasant might have said "So-and-so's son got a job at a commune factory because that family is in good with Longyong." If Longyong had informal relationships with even the poor and lower middle peasants, if he wasn't cold and didn't keep his distance, people wouldn't be con-vinced he was selflessly upright.

Thus, to ward off pressures both from above and below, he was content to maintain an image of unapproachable and austere recti-tude. A sent-down youth who had frequent run-ins with Long-yong recalls cynically, "Longyong didn't mind people finding him obnoxious, so long as he could avoid others getting a handle on him."

The Four Cleanups workteam had already put Longyong on the grill for being both harsh and manipulative. But the workteam itself had displayed considerable harshness and manipulation. The impression was left that such faults in a cadre's workstyle were not nearly so serious as favoritism or corruption and indeed might be acceptable to higher authorities so long as it was exercised for the right cause. Longyong would himself learn in due time how to manipulate campaigns—and in particular, how to use Maoist rhetoric on these occasions to destroy opponents.

Longyong had learned anew in the Four Cleanups that it was impolitic ever to oppose higher political levels on any issues that were pushed by the national party. To do so left one vulnerable to charges of political heresy. During the next decade, Longyong would pursue all the party's nation-wide campaigns with ostentatious enthusiasm and vigor, even when a campaign was unpopular among the peasantry. But Longyong repeatedly would fight against more locally devised economic policies whenever he thought they impaired the village's economic interests. He had seen in the Four Cleanups how Qingfa had left himself vulnerable to attacks from below by giving up the reservoir acreage. In the years to come, Longyong would consolidate the peasantry's backing by stubbornly blocking the attempts by local higher levels to infringe upon Chen Village's prerogatives. He repeatedly would anger the commune's cadres, well aware that a brigade management chief who had the support of his own village could not easily be ousted from above over nonideological issues.

Longyong championed Chen Village's interests even more than was politically safe or wise, however. He was a village chauvinist. He was always anxious that Chen Village seem better and develop more quickly than all the other villages around, and he was always quick to take personal offense if he thought Chen Village had been slighted or was being taken advantage of.

Longyong knew that economic development was not only the surest way to raise the village's stature vis à vis other villages; he was also aware that expectations of a progressively better life had been aroused in the Four Cleanups, and that the peasantry's willingness to back any leader would depend ultimately upon the fulfillment of those expectations.

Longyong had a solid foundation to build upon. With all of the agricultural innovations of the Four Cleanups, the village's economic prospects in 1966 looked especially promising. A peasant from Chen Village recalls nostalgically, "By the end of the Four Cleanups, production had been grasped well and everything was well managed. For the first time since Liberation, our countryside had really been given a chance to develop steadily. . . . Things would have gone ideally if Chairman Mao hadn't started the Cultural Revolution."

· 4 ·

The Cultural Revolution

By the spring of 1966, the first signals of the Cultural Revolution were emanating from Peking. But few in Chen Village would have surmised that the village would soon be thrown into renewed turmoil. The workteam was in the process of creating a new stability in the village. The peasantry was still enthused with the recently inaugurated Mao study sessions and had only recently embarked on the energetic efforts to build up the village's agricultural infrastructure. The village cadres had only recently been reinstated in their posts and were happy to see the concerns of the Four Cleanups campaign turn toward economic development and renewed political stability.

But there was one group in the village that, within months, would be responding enthusiastically to the stirrings in the world outside—the urban sent-down youths. Many of them harbored an explosive mixture of disappointed idealism and frustrated ambition. This mixture of sentiments needed only the catalyst of national events to spark off a rebellion. To understand why, we must turn back in time and relate the young people's experiences since their arrival in the village.

Hopes and Frustrations Among the Sent-Down Youth

The contingent of fifty urban-born youths who came to Chen Village in 1964 had not initially joined the peasant production teams. Instead they had been organized into their own "Youth Team." Using government funds provided for their initial settlement, the village had renovated its large ancestral temple to serve as a dormitory and dining hall for them. Each of the village's ten production teams gave up about an acre of land so that the young people could raise their own collective crops. Except for some advice on agricultural techniques, they were left on their own. The seven Communist Youth League members among them formed a Youth League branch and served as the leadership hub for the Youth Team.

Most of the urban young people had had mixed motives in volunteering for the countryside. On the one hand, as one of the leaders of the Youth Team idealistically put it:

> We came to the countryside to perform in a revolutionary way, to prove that we obeyed the party, to prove that we were useful to the country. We came because we had this line of thinking. No one forced us to come at that time. Everyone wanted to advance.

But wanting to "advance" as a revolutionary had a careerist as well as an idealistic side. It meant not only to devote one's life in service to the Chinese people but also to move into a position of leadership. Thus, almost from the moment they arrived in Chen Village, they strenuously began to compete with one another. "You wanted to advance and I wanted to advance. The competition among us was keen."

It was particularly keen because they had quickly realized there would not be room for more than a handful of them to rise in the village. A few mechanically minded persons might be needed to help set up new machinery, but the mechanization of the village would only proceed at a slow pace. The village very well might need literate political personnel, but just a few. The young people came under each others' close and jealous scrutiny to see who among them would prove most worthy to succeed.

The Chairman's maxims taught that hard work and abstemious living were two of the characteristics of a good revolutionary. The young people accepted these ideals, but in trying to outdo each other, they pushed themselves to the point of exhaustion. Competing at harvest time to carry heavy loads back from the fields, some of the young men struggled under shoulder-pole burdens of more than 150 pounds. The health of a number of them was soon impaired. But if any of them sought to take a rest, the others disdainfully considered it a retreat from hardship and a weakening of willpower. The full weight of their disapproval was felt in their nightly formal "small group" discussions. In these, the Youth Team members read and reread aloud Mao's essays on the proper attitudes of a true revolutionary and appraised each other's successes and failures in living up to the Maoist ideals.

The young people from Canton cooked only the most meager of rations in their canteen in order to become spiritually steeled like "the old peasantry who'd experienced the exploitation of the old society." Unlike the peasants who used soy sauce with their rice, they insisted on flavoring theirs with salt water. They collected wild vegetables for the Youth Team kitchen, rough fibrous material that the peasants used only as pig feed.

> It wasn't so bad for us girls. We were just able to satisfy ourselves with our share at dinner. But not the boys, who were expending such a lot of energy. They became *so* hungry. They had headaches and stomachaches. . . . But if any of them bought food for themselves outside, we criticized them for not leading a properly hard life. . . . The peasants would tell us to eat a little better . . . but we didn't listen.

The seven members of the Youth Team's Communist Youth League branch spurred on this extreme contest to be purists. As "assistants to the party," they had automatically assumed positions far superior to their teammates from the moment they had arrived at Chen Village. They made all the decisions for the fifty teenagers. The others resented it but had to put up with it. They were trying anxiously to get into the League, a decision that lay in the League members' hands. They thus tried to demonstrate their revolutionary élan and their equality with the League members by out-performing them. The League members in turn struggled to justify their own claims to superiority by acting in an even purer manner than they had demanded of those below them. They all became trapped in an upward spiral of efforts to act as "poor and lower-middle peasants."

In general, it was the high school graduates among the urban-born youth who possessed this mixture of high ideals and high ambitions. The fifteen "street youths," recruits from the urban unemployment lines whose education had ended with primary school, did not nurture any grand hopes of rising to the top. They therefore, according to one of the high school graduates, "neither put great demands on life nor great demands on themselves; so they weren't backbone elements of our group." They had come to the village to find work, not to prove themselves. But they were a fragmented minority in the Youth Team; and when the former high school students that first year zealously competed to be activists, the street youths were swept up by the group's mood and followed suit.

Eleven months after the young people arrived in Chen Village, the Youth Team disbanded. Despite the young people's energetic labor, they were inexperienced and had not produced enough to support themselves. The village production teams wanted their fields back. From now on the youths were to be incorporated into the production teams, five to each team. Once they did not live and work together as a Youth Team, no longer under the vigilance of the Youth Team's Communist Youth League branch, no longer exposed to incessant peer-group pressure, the fervor of many of them lessened noticeably.

The street youth were the quickest to discard the activist zeal. But most of the former high school students, too, gradually dropped out of the contest to look progressive. Among them were those whose health had been impaired; those whose will to achieve was less intense; and those who had never been articulate enough or physically strong enough to stand out in the crowd. Many of them were disheartened by the slimness of their chances of ever making any significant contributions or of carving out a secure niche for themselves in the countryside. They were having difficulties simply supporting themselves. Some even had to rely on stipends from their parents in Canton to make ends meet.

There were, however, still some dozen young people who

hoped to prove themselves and gain official recognition and posts. These still-activist youths desperately resented the special opportunities the Youth League members were enjoying. The League members had been the only ones given a chance to exhibit any leadership capabilities in the Youth Team; and even afterwards, when brigade cadres or the Four Cleanups workteam had needed assistants, they primarily had sought out and used the League members. Nine of the twelve Mao Thought counselors were recruited from among the ten members of the League branch. Quite obviously, to get ahead still meant, first, to get into the League.

Few of the young people were succeeding in this. It was national policy that League recruitment should proceed slowly, but not as slowly as in Chen Village. The sent-down youths began to strongly suspect that the incumbent League members were reluctant to dilute their own power or their chances to rise in Chen Village by letting anyone else into the League branch. In those first two years in the village, despite the heroic efforts of so many of the youths, the League branch admitted only three new members into its ranks. League members were insisting also on monopolizing for themselves every available post, to the point that they literally exhausted themselves and fell behind in their work. Our interviewee Ao, who had been one of the League branch's leaders, still speaks defensively to this point:

> It was our duty to do all that work. The others didn't know how to manage anything. . . . But some of the other kids would complain to me: "You're in charge of the Mao Thought counselors for the village, and the village's cultural center, and you get to do the village's broadcasting, and to be a materials gatherer for the Four Cleanups workteam. And we have nothing to do." They'd become jealous of me. . . . [But] they did have a bit of their own work to do, such as reading the newspapers to the peasants and doing volunteer work as night school tutors. I don't know why, but everyone wanted a post. They still labored okay in the fields, but individually they began complaining.

These dissatisfied young people had also a more serious cause for worry—the fact that the party was increasing its emphasis on the class line. Though they could find ways to vent their feelings against the League members, they were helpless, and unable to protest openly, against the favoritism shown toward the "good classes." Most of these former students were from families that had officially been categorized as petty-bourgeois—"middle class" on the Chinese scale of classes. Some were even from bad-class homes, such as those classified as ex-capitalist. The village initially had been willing to accept the government's declaration that all the urban sent-down youths had committed themselves to the revolution by volunteering to settle in Chen Village. But as the Four Cleanups campaign had heated up, the officialdom and the peasantry increasingly measured people's worth and trustworthiness by the yardstick of class origins. Though there was no clear change in the peasants' friendliness toward the urban youths, and though every one of the sent-down youths was allowed to join the new Poor and Lower-Middle Peasants Association, a pall was being cast over their prospects in the village. The workteam, for example, initially allowed only the good-class urban youths to join the Poor and Lower-Middle Peasants Association; then those who were of middle-class status; and only lastly the bad-class urban youths. Moreover, "the upper levels had begun applying the screws," one of the League members remembers. "League applications had to be passed on to the brigade level, and then to the commune level. They had to make absolutely sure there were no black spots in the family histories." The young people who still held ambitions were disturbed to observe that every one of the three sent-down youths who got into the League was of good-class background.

By the eve of the Cultural Revolution, only half a dozen of the young people could think of themselves as having won out; and of this half-dozen, three were climbing well above any of their peers. One of these three was Ao, whose work as a propagandist during the Four Cleanups had moved her to the center of village attention. The other two were Stocky Wang and Red Cheng: two of the new good-class League members.

During the next couple of years, these two young men would be playing significant parts in Chen Village's history. Both were articulate, hard-driving, ambitious, idealistic young men. Both had been among the most fervent and self-denying of any of the young people during that first year in the Youth Team. But the key factor in their initial rise above their fellows—and the factor that would soon bring them close to the center of power in Chen Village—was their sterling class origins.

Stocky Wang's father had died just before Liberation, and his mother had remarried well. His stepfather had fought in the civil war and Korea and was considered a war hero. Wang's official class status was that of his stepfather, an extremely good status. Bored with his studies, Stocky Wang had volunteered for the countryside after junior high school, rather than continue into a teacher-training vocational school. His reasons for coming to the village were not as idealistic as those of many of his peers, but he had soon gotten caught up in the fervor of the young people's competition. During the Four Cleanups, his origins and abilities had won him a Youth League membership, a strong supporting role in the campaign to cleanse the village cadres, a central place in the Mao Thought campaign, and a post on the village Youth League's governing committee. Of all the urban young people, the Four Cleanups workteam favored Stocky the most.

Red Cheng, too, had come from a family origin that was illustrious compared to most of the sent-down youths. His father was a skilled worker who frequently won citations as a model worker; his older brother was a Communist party member. In junior high school, to his family's dismay, Cheng had been a poor and disorderly student; and he was caught finally in an act of petty theft. His elder brother furiously berated him for not living up to the dignity of his proletarian background; and Cheng, vowing to turn over a new leaf, volunteered for the countryside as proof.

Perhaps because of this, he was one of the most relentlessly uncompromising of the sent-down youths. In the evening discussions among the young people, he insisted more fervently than anyone else on making major ideological issues out of small incidents. While still in the Youth Team, he had climbed only to the second echelon of the sent-down youths' political elite. But when assigned to a production team, recalls Ao, "he was like a fish let loose in the sea." Physically, he broadened and became well muscled and was soon counted among the stronger men in the village. He was adept at learning agricultural techniques and, some said, would soon be the equal of a team head in his knowledge. He impressed the workteam and brigade leadership with his outspoken defense of brigade policies within his production team.

Such espousals sometimes annoyed his new peasant teammates, and some muttered that he was an "immature kid." But there was a genuine quality to Cheng's single-minded passion that the peasants and the team leadership alike respected.

The certainty of Ao, Red Cheng, and Stocky Wang in their own rectitude had been reinforced by their experiences of success. They were the brigade's leaders in Mao study, righteously and sincerely trying to lead the peasantry toward their own and the party leadership's vision. But just as righteously, they insensitively lectured and prodded their less successful peers from the city. Ao observes,

> I looked down on them. I thought, how can you be so backward? . . . We used to have heart-to-heart talks with them. We pointed out things from the papers about the need for self-sacrifice, perseverance, etc. We'd get them together to sing songs. Give them Mao Thought lessons. They didn't like this— didn't like us giving them lessons, teaching them songs, and so forth. They didn't like us to be their commanders.

The ones most angered by such morale boosters were the dozen remaining activists, who had not, in their own opinions, received adequate recognition from the brigade or the Four Cleanups workteam. Most of them had achieved useful spare-time posts in their production teams as team accountants, team cashiers, and junior Mao Thought counselors. But these were nothing compared to the glory and power enjoyed by the sent-down youth "aristocracy." These other activists, too, wanted higher achievements; they did not want to be trapped as just ordinary peasants all their lives. For the most part, they were of middle-class status, the sons and daughters of white-collar workers and professionals. They had never felt discriminated against before. They resented the "class line," but did not feel cowed when it was strengthened. Privately, by 1966, they were becoming sore.

One of them was an interviewee named Li:

> I felt that even though we were more active and brighter than some [of those] kids of good class background, just because of our class origins, we weren't given the opportunities to use our skills. I was very dissatisfied because our futures were being suppressed by our class labels. I saw myself

getting up every morning and taking a hoe and going to dig in the fields. I began to think: does it mean that for the rest of my life I'll be working like this? I looked around, and this place was so backward. When I looked down from the hills above, there was just a little patchwork of fields. It wasn't that I shunned difficulties, but I found my efforts meaningless. So when the first summer harvests [of 1966] had been gathered and there was a slack-season break, I took the opportunity to go back to Canton for awhile to see my family and enjoy myself a bit.

When he returned to Chen Village in the autumn of 1966, Li brought with him the Cultural Revolution.

The Rebel Red Guards

Even before Li had gone to Canton in August 1966, he and his friends had, of course, been aware of the Cultural Revolution. Throughout the spring of 1966, they had known of the rumblings in the national press about the "poisonous weeds" in Peking's literary circles. By late spring the campaign had widened into published attacks against the Peking municipal party committee and attacks against "bourgeois" academics. The young people had been curious about the gathering national political storm, but they had few inklings as to what the issues might be and what relevance these had to their own conditions. The Four Cleanups workteam in Chen Village sporadically held meetings to denounce dutifully whatever culprits came under attack in Peking. But the workteam members had no better understanding than the sentdown youths of the faraway events, still less the peasants.

By the summer, news was coming through to Chen Village that in Canton the students were attacking bad-class teachers. The commune-level workteam headquarters prudently responded to the new events by organizing the students at the commune market-town high school to "struggle" against some of the local teachers who had "historical" problems. Except for such ritual shows of support, it seemed the bewildering events in Peking and Canton would never reach the countryside. All seemed well in the rural districts. The Four Cleanups was in the midst of being drawn tidily and successfully to a close; the prestige and effective-ness of the village cadres were being reestablished; the drive to spur agricultural production was in full steam.

When Li pedaled off to Canton on his bicycle in late August, he visited his old school and found that the good-class students at the school had taken command of the student body and were preoccupied with attacking the school principal. The major com-plaint against the hapless principal was that he had attended devot-edly to his mother, an elderly woman of bad-class background. Li was perturbed by the charge. The harsh class line that it signified cast a shadow over anyone such as Li who was not strictly of the "red" classes. But Li nevertheless found the raucousness of the unfolding campaign exciting. With several of his former class-mates he set out on an "exchange of revolutionary experiences" to other parts of Guangdong Province.

By the time Li and his friends had returned to Canton from their hike, the Cultural Revolution in Canton's schools had been transformed. Canton's middle-class students had been quiescent but unhappy onlookers during the preceding weeks when it had seemed Mao supported the "struggles" against the bad-class teachers and principals. But the Chairman, through some of his top supporters in Peking, had just let it be known in the first week of October 1966 that the campaign in the schools had to change direction. The middle-class students quickly had picked up on the refrain that "capitalist roaders in the party" were to be targets for attack. Glad for the chance to push the campaign away from the class-based struggles, they began bombarding local party commit-tees with whatever criticisms they could dream up.[1]

Li read these students' wall posters avidly and hurried back to Chen Village. He entered into animated discussions with a group of about ten other sent-down youths.

> Our understanding was that the Cultural Revolution should
> be a movement from the bottom upward, not from the top
> downward and not lukewarm, as the commune was handling

---

[1] The background to these events is explained in Anita Chan, Stanley Rosen, and Jonathan Unger, "Students and Class Warfare: The Social Roots of the Cul-tural Revolution in Guangzhou (Canton)," *China Quarterly* 83 (Autumn 1980).

it. . . . We discussed among ourselves why the Cultural Revolution was only erupting in the cities and not the countryside. . . . The atmosphere in the commune seat was so dull at that point, like the calm before a storm.

Li's little group was composed of frustrated activists like himself. They now saw an opportunity to express their activist devotion. They felt no personal qualms about criticizing the workteam members and brigade officers who had slighted them. Through such criticisms they could show that they themselves, and not the workteams or the cadres or their more successful peers, were the true followers of Chairman Mao.

The most excited of the friends was a young man of capitalist origins named Gao. Gao had always been enthusiastically activist, so much so that he had risen to be a brigade-level Mao Thought counselor despite his bad-class credentials. Gao and Li composed a wall poster in behalf of the group and stuck it up in the market town near the commune headquarters building. It was the first of its kind in the commune.

> We were young, only 18 years old, so we didn't think carefully about the possible consequences. I wasn't afraid of anything at that time. I was affected by a sentence Chairman Mao had said: "Are you concerned with the affairs of the country? Have you participated in the Great Proletarian Cultural Revolution?" In our poster we asked the workteam and the commune what the hell they were doing. We said they were pointing the spearhead in the wrong direction, only spearing little shrimps and little fish . . . like the commune school principal . . . and we accused the lower level cadres of only taking care of production and not paying any attention to the Cultural Revolution. That poster was really something!

They signed their poster: "The Maoism Red Guards."

The poster was tacked up while the brigade cadres, workteams, and Mao Thought leaders from all over the commune were meeting at the commune seat to discuss the new economic production drive. When the cadres emerged from their sessions and were faced with the poster, their immediate reaction was scorn for what they considered the naiveté of the young people and anger at the challenge to their own positions. But the commune-level workteam, unclear about the political complexities of the agitation in Canton, did not want to commit any political errors in handling the incident. It was best to react with caution. Li recalls:

> When the cadres of other brigades left the commune head-quarters, Chen Village's cadres had to stay behind. They were instructed by the commune-level workteam heads to go back and educate us. They were told we were a bunch of kids, not knowing what we were doing, that we were messing around but were not reactionary, and so we should be reeducated. The commune's public security head ran all the way out to the brigade, took me to one side and asked me why I wrote this big-character poster, under whose order was it. I said, "no one asked me to, I did it on my own initiative." I also said, "if you think this is something special, you should go outside, to Canton, to have a look and you'd understand." He said, "I'm not saying that you were wrong, I only want to know who asked you to do it."

After this incident, the relationship between these rebellious youths on the one side and the brigade cadres and the workteam on the other grew tense. The workteam members held a talk with the youths. "In the talk we accused the workteam of suppressing the masses. We told them they should let the masses carry out their own Cultural Revolution. They scolded us for knowing nothing. We replied, 'How much do you know? We know more than you do!' So we pressed them—and they knew nothing."

The ordinary peasants were almost as nervous as the commune cadres and the workteam about any antiestablishment agitation. A young peasant from Chen Village recalls, "We were already a bit disturbed and scared by all the stories we were hearing about Red Guard behavior, how the Red Guards in the cities were going around burning and breaking things." Unable to ignite much sympathy or support from within the village, the band of sent-down youths wrote to Zhao Ziyang, the party secretary of Guangdong Province, asking him what they should do to bring the Cultural Revolution to Chen Village. A note came back from Zhao Ziyang's office acknowledging receipt of the letter, but offering absolutely no advice. All that anyone in the village knew, however, was that the youths had sent a letter of unknown contents to Zhao and had received a reply. The brigade cadres and workteam members grew more apprehensive and increasingly hostile toward the urban youths.

The only real success of the Maoism Red Guards lay in the active support they gained from five of the local young peasant men. Most of these five had been to high school. They were almost the only peasants in Chen Village to have done so, and they were also among the only peasants who regularly read the newspapers. They came from poor and lower-middle peasant households and so had little fear that they might end up in trouble. They were greatly enjoying the sent-down youths' impassioned discussions of the confusing and tumultuous national events.

The rebellious sent-down youths were very careful, however, to keep at a distance any young peasant who was not of good-class background. Although the Chen Village peasantry and local cadres had not cared much about the urban youths' class labels, the villagers were very sensitive to any local peasant's class origins. The sent-down youths of middle- or bad-class origin were determined not to sully their own standing in the Poor and Lower-Middle Peasants Association by associating with villagers of lesser status.

Despite the young people's confused, strident calls for revolutionary disorder, the Chen Village workteam did not directly move to squelch the troublemakers. To do so would only provide solid evidence for the young people's charges that the workteam was trying to constrain Cultural Revolutionary activities. The workteam instead called a meeting of its own protégés in the sent-down Youth League branch and suggested to them that their rebellious peers were undermining the socialist cause. Separately, the workteam cadres got out the dissidents' dossiers and asked Stocky Wang, their favorite, to go speak privately with several of the rebels who seemed most vulnerable to pressure: in particular their spokesman Gao. Wang obediently pulled Gao aside and pointed out to him that his father had been executed in the 1950s as a counterrevolutionary and that Gao was in no position to act foolishly. The warning had the intended sobering effect. Gao retired from the leadership of the Maoism Red Guards and began quietly patching his fences with the brigade cadres and workteam members.

The middle-class members of the small band were not so easy to intimidate, however. They chose as their new leader an older and more pugnacious advocate of their cause, nicknamed Overseas Deng. Deng had been born and partially raised in Indonesia. His parents were wealthy but loyal to the motherland. They had sent him as a child back to Canton to be educated. After high school, rather than apply to a university, Deng had decided to "temper" himself by heeding Mao's call to go to the countryside. Already a League member, he had been one of the most enthusiastic and politically zealous members of the Youth Team. He had also revealed himself as the most mechanically talented of the young people, and in 1965 had been instrumental in installing the village's electrical system. But he was an extremely stubborn person who would defer to no one, and the workteam had decided not to let him become a Mao Thought counselor or gain access to any other desirable posts. Assigned instead to set up the machinery for the village's new rice mill, he inevitably had a serious run-in with Longyong, a man as intensely stubborn as he. With no future in Chen Village either in the political establishment or as a technician under Longyong, Overseas Deng was in a rebellious mood. Recalls one of the Maoism Red Guards, "When he argued in our behalf against the workteam he stood his ground. He was really good at that, banging tables and chairs. So he became our leader."

The orders filtering down from above indicated that any Red Guard group should be allowed to have its say. So the workteam felt obliged to permit almost daily confrontations with the young people at evening meetings that all the peasants had to attend. The cadres would read out Cultural Revolution documents from the newspaper and end with appeals to the peasants to "grasp revolution and speed up production"—with the emphasis on speeding up production. Then the spokesmen for the young people would come forward to reinterpret the Cultural Revolution documents in ways more favorable to themselves. Always they returned to the same argument: that all the rural officials were suppressing the Cultural Revolution, and that the rural capitalist roaders should be brought to justice. (The young people today admit that they had not known at the time what the term *capitalist roaders* meant or to whom it might apply.) The peasants were annoyed by the tumult.

Li admits: "They thought we were confronting the cadres too much. They thought the cadres had already had their fair share of punishment and shouldn't be hassled."

The Good-Class Red Guards

A little more than two weeks after Gao and Li had stuck up their wall poster, the workteam came up with a means to put the young rebels firmly back in place. Further documents had arrived from above directing that Red Guard groups were to be officially organized in each village—and the directives stipulated that these Red Guard units were to be controlled by young people of impeccably "red" class backgrounds.[2] The workteam quickly moved to put together a new Red Guard corps to supplant the luckless Maoism Red Guards. Under the leadership of Stocky Wang and Red Cheng, only local young poor and lower-middle peasants with records of political activism would be permitted to participate. The new organization was named the Mao Thought Red Guards, and it was ushered in at a solemn ceremony attended by all of the Chen Village peasant militia.

The group's first act was to post an order that the Maoism Red Guards disband. Their decree stated that the Maoism Red Guards, not being of China's "five red classes," could not be allowed to play a leading role in the Cultural Revolution. As a bystander recalls, "The Mao Thought Red Guards came along like a wind and blew the Maoism Red Guards away."

The new Red Guards also "blew away" the village's Communist Youth League branch. As Stocky Wang observes, "We replaced the League, and took over its status. The purpose of our Red Guards was to protect the special rights of the red classes. The League contained a number of members of non-red origin, so its leadership role had to be removed; ours had to be higher."

Ao and the few other successful middle-class activists were at first perturbed at having their own status lowered. They tried

---

[2.] "Circular of the Party Central Committee on the Great Proletarian Cultural Revolution in the Rural Districts" (Dec. 15, 1966), in *Current Background* [U.S. Government], no. 852 (May 1968), p. 31.

recouping by forming their own little group, "for those of us who couldn't enter the Mao Thought Red Guards but wanted to help them carry out the Cultural Revolution." They recruited for their group a dozen local middle-peasant youths who actively wanted to show their own support for the new official order.

The Red Guards of Stocky Wang and Red Cheng, followed tamely by these impure-class adherents, quickly embarked on a series of dramatic activities that turned the Cultural Revolution in Chen Village sharply away from attacks upon the workteam. Under direct instructions from the commune-level workteam, the Mao Thought Red Guards set out on a new Destroy the Four Olds campaign. Young people would be given free rein to be militantly progressive, as opposed to being rebellious. Showing how truly red they could be, the Mao Thought Red Guards ordered girls and women to cut off their long pigtails and wear their hair short; they forced peasant households to bring out their ancestor tablets and smash them; they broke the housewives' "feudal" molds that were used for imprinting rice cakes with traditional good luck symbols; they searched for and burned "feudalistic" books like the *Romance of the Three Kingdoms,* the *Water Margin,* and old Chinese medical texts.

The young zealots did an especially thorough job of ransacking the homes of the four-bad types for evidence of subversion. When the villagers were all asleep one night, Chen Village's emergency siren called out the militia for lightning raids against every bad-class house. By morning the homes of the former landlords had been cleared of furniture, clothes, cash, and odds and ends of jewelry. Among the belongings of one of the landlords, they found a poem by a Tang Dynasty poet which lamented the hard lives of China's peasants, written in the landlord's elegant calligraphy. The excited discoverers subjected the miscreant to an emotional struggle session: "Before you exploited us; now you have to work a bit and you complain!" (Slap!) They had heard a rumor that the other landlord had hidden away guns at the time of the Liberation. To no avail, they interrogated him for several days nonstop at the old Ancestral Hall. In search of the rumored weapons, they dug up the packed-earth floor of the old man's bedroom; frustrated, they dug into his ancestral graves.

The charges and struggle sessions and searches for signs of a hidden counterrevolution focused the villagers' attention on the easily scapegoated bad-class elements and away from criticisms of the brigade cadres. Even the members of the Maoism Red Guards felt a need to show their support by tagging along behind the Mao Thought corps, contributing to the campaign as best they were allowed.

Since the Maoism Red Guards had recently accused the workteam of not turning sufficient attention to attacking capitalist roaders, the workteam now suggested that the Mao Thought Red Guards drag out Qingfa and accuse him—dramatically—of having been a capitalist roader. "Because it was a campaign," recalls Stocky Wang, "we definitely needed such a target." Old charges were dredged up and reinterpreted as vicious instances of capitalist roading. Qingfa had an older sister who had been married to a poor peasant who used to beat her, and just before the Liberation she had run off to Hong Kong and remarried. Occasionally she sent back small gifts and money to Qingfa and his family, and this Hong Kong connection gave the phrase "capitalist roading" a tangible context to local ears. Qingfa was now denounced in horrified tones as "a party member receiving foreign capitalist goods!" He was obviously a man who politically "steps on two boats at the same time." Qingfa's feet became swollen from standing rigidly to attention at struggle sessions. But finally, having grown bored with their own rhetorical extravagances, the Mao Thought Red Guards quietly let Qingfa go back to his own team.

A few weeks earlier, the gadflies in the Maoism Red Guards had presented themselves as the true followers of Chairman Mao. The Mao Thought Red Guards were now equally determined to show their own deep love for China's "Great Helmsman." The Maoism Red Guards earlier had belittled the local cadres' concentration upon raising production, yelling that they were doing so at the expense of inattention to Chairman Mao's new campaign. The brigade management committee was eager to disprove this criticism. Pursuing a suggestion from the commune, it was more than happy to provide funding for the Mao Thought Red Guards to paint the village red, the color symbolizing Chairman Mao's revolutionary line. Under Red Cheng's direction, can upon can of paint was expended to remake Chen Village into a "red ocean."[3] Carried away by the Mao Thought high tide, the new Red Guards went a step further. They bought a large stencil of the Chairman's head and painted in his portrait *everywhere* (though Stocky Wang prudently raised objections when the Mao Thought Red Guards began brushing in the portrait on the walls of the outhouses).

The rush of activity under the Mao Thought Red Guards had catapulted Stocky Wang and Red Cheng into prominence in Chen Village's political structure. As Stocky Wang recalls, "We Red Guards really had power then. The workteam was shrewd and let us wield the power. We took the workteam's role, and the workteam became our advisors. Even Jinyi, the new party secretary, had to come to us for everything. Production was handled by the old cadres; politics was in the hands of the Red Guards."

But their power ultimately lay in the workteam's backing; and this backing folded in mid-December when a national directive suggested ominously that many of China's workteams might be handed the blame for excessively rough handling of village cadres during the Four Cleanups.[4] The Chen Village workteam received orders from above to pull out; it packed its belongings and slipped out of the village. It left so quietly and hastily that its members did not even say goodbye to the peasants.

The small band of Maoism Red Guards felt vindicated by this new turn of events and sprang back into action with renewed barrages of criticisms against the departed workteam. For once, they found some of the village officers openly in agreement with them. Several local cadres even suggested that the workteam be brought back to face criticism for its earlier harshness toward Chen Village's officeholders.

[3.] This political fad had originated in the cities, as a tactic to make all walls politically sacred and therefore off limits to rebellious wall posters. In late December 1966, the Communist Party Central Committee officially denounced the "red ocean" brush-work as "a wicked act against wall posters and the Great Proletarian Cultural Revolution." (See the "Circular of the Party Central Committee and State Council Prohibiting the Extensive Promotion of the So-called 'Red Ocean,' " in *Current Background*, no. 852 [May 1968], p. 33.)

[4.] Richard Baum, *Prelude to Revolution: Mao, the Party and the Peasant Question, 1962–66* (New York: Columbia University Press, 1975), p. 151.

Boiling A Riceless Porridge

Events in the world outside seemed to be spinning totally out of control. Amidst the turmoil in Canton in the middle of January 1967, an alliance of young Red Guards and more experienced cadres who called themselves "Revolutionary Rebels" temporarily "seized power" from the politically paralyzed leaders of the Guangdong provincial government. They called for similar seizures of power from all lower officials in the province.

The teenagers of the Maoism Red Guards of Chen Village responded exuberantly to this "seize power wind." They once more could proudly proclaim themselves devoted rebels. Without much forethought, they marched over to the brigade headquarters one evening while the cadres were holding an after-dinner meeting. A member of the group recalls:

> We suddenly broke in, and Overseas Deng said: "We have come to seize power!" The brigade secretarial clerk said: "If you want it, then here it is!" He brought out the brigade's official seal [which was used to validate all official correspondence] and said, "Well, who wants to take it?" But none of us dared to. It came as a surprise. Actually we'd no real idea of what it meant to seize power. Suddenly it occurred to us that if we took the seal, the next morning when people came to ask for this and that we'd have to decide whether to give the stamp of approval. We'd also have to take the lead in planning production. But we'd have no idea how to do any of it. We were inexperienced. So the seizure of power ended in nothing. No one dared to take that official seal.

Having backed off from seizing power, the Maoism Red Guards turned to writing wall posters. They belligerently brought up the same kind of complaints as had been aired during the Four Cleanups campaign: cadres had engaged in petty corruption and were overly harsh on the masses. Since most of the peasants could not read, the posters were little noticed. Moreover, the Maoism Red Guards quickly ran out of things to say against the cadres. "After all," Li admits today, "there weren't really many instances of capitalist roading in the village." The irritated peasants let them know just how much they were wasting their time. "Go ahead and run around boiling up riceless porridge"—that is, a porridge composed only of water—one of them scornfully told the young people. "We'll just worry about taking care of our private plots." The young people began to grow tired in the face of the peasants' indifference and the hopelessness and confusion of their cause.

They also began to become worried about their own circumstances. Almost everyone in China has a dossier, which follows one through life. One evening the dozen Maoism Red Guards cycled to the commune seat and demanded to see all of the "black materials" the workteam might have gathered on them. Some fierce banging on tables and yelling again worked wonders. The commune's organization was in disarray, and as one of the young rebels recalls, "the atmosphere at the time was that we Red Guards could do anything we liked." Two representatives of the Maoism Red Guards were led upstairs to the commune's dossier office. They cut the tape with which the workteams had earlier sealed the dossier cabinets, and rummaged for the incriminating evidence. They discovered that the comments on each of the fifty sent-down youths were generally fair, even when acerbically critical. But they discovered also that much of the handwriting was Red Cheng's. During the Four Cleanups he had secretly been given this power over their dossiers! And they discovered, too, that the workteam had been "cultivating" Red Cheng to enter the Communist party. One of the youths recollects, "It was then that we fully realized how great [all along] the 'contradiction' had been among us sent-down youths."

Thus far, the young rebels had been trying to prove the superiority of their political devotion. But increasingly during the early spring of 1967, their personal discontents and frustrations began to surface in their internal discussions. They dwelled on the alleged mistreatment they had borne: that they had been given poor housing and inadequate help in adjusting to rural life. They complained among themselves that the local peasants really looked down on them for being of impure class origins.

Throughout China, many of the sent-down youths were leaving their villages and returning to the cities to form their own urban-based Red Guard organizations.[5] They were claiming that the policy of sending urban youths to the countryside was part of Liu Shaoqi's "black line." In the weeks following the incident of the dossiers, almost two-thirds of the urban youths began to gather around the leadership of the Maoism Red Guards to debate whether to leave Chen Village and go back to Canton. Bitter arguments broke out between these dissatisfied urban youths and their more successful colleagues in the village: the triumvirate of Red Cheng, Stocky Wang, and Ao (who had become aide-de-camp to the first two). This trio argued that the youths' revolutionary dedication would be placed seriously in doubt if they left.

And then, suddenly, Stocky Wang switched sides. He, too, had been invited the prior autumn to apply for party membership, but a closer investigation of his background had revealed that his biological father, whom Stocky had never seen, had been a Guomindang official. To the peasants, and even to the Four Cleanups workteam, the literal ties of blood counted for a lot. His application was rejected.

After the Four Cleanups workteam had left, Stocky's difficulties were compounded. He allowed himself to get ensnared in factional infighting within his own production team. Several team cadres were trying to oust the team head, who was prone to nepotism and had reverted to his old ways soon after the workteam's departure. This, however, was not the real reason for their hostility toward the team head. It had developed from a wholly unrelated feud between the wife of the team head and their own wives. But Stocky Wang, as his production team's Mao Thought counselor, took a righteously incensed stance on the nepotism charge when prodded by the other cadres. During the Cultural Revolution, Mao study had intensified and had become increasingly overlaid with ritual; the peasants, for example, were lined up to recite a Mao quote before and after every work day, much like an opening and closing prayer. One day, in pursuit of the team head, Stocky selected a Mao quote that he thought apposite

[5] Stanley Rosen, *The Role of the Sent-Down Youth in the Chinese Cultural Revolution: The Case of Guangzhou* (Berkeley: University of California, Institute of East Asian Studies, 1981).

for the circumstances. He had all the team members recite in unison as their parting quote: "All freaks and demons and poisonous weeds should be denounced!" Furious at the implication, the team head peremptorily resigned.

What had counted to Stocky, as a politically enthused sentdown urban teenager, was the incorruptibility of a cadre. But Stocky's priorities and those of the peasants did not coincide. Their team head happened to be one of the two or three best agricultural planners in the village; and what mattered most to a peasant household was a good harvest. After repeated persuasion, the team head "reluctantly" acceded to the team members' pleas that he continue; but he demanded new team elections. In these, he defeated the candidate Stocky was backing, the less competent deputy team head, forty votes to a dozen. With Stocky's class origin in doubt, his poor political judgment self-evident, and his team head a new-found enemy, Stocky was politically on the skids. Many of the peasants in his production team were pleased. Stocky had captured so many of the posts that had been open to the sent-down youths that he was always preoccupied with meetings, rarely laboring. His very success became his final undoing. He had been derisively labeled by the peasants as a "meeting specialist," the Chinese term for a person who adroitly uses meetings to avoid work. He was becoming a political encumbrance, and the brigade leaders decided to ease Stocky aside. They informed him that he no longer would receive any wages from his team for the time he spent in meetings or at his Mao Thought Red Guard activities. Bitterly insulted, Stocky Wang changed sides.

Stocky was an able speaker. He not only switched sides, he let himself be drafted as a spokesman for the Maoism Red Guards. By now, the dissatisfied young people had built up a network of contacts with the sent-down youths from other villages, and Stocky and his new comrades spent their days pedaling through the countryside to "investigate" their new friends' circumstances. They discovered that most of the sent-down youths in the district were unlike the group in Chen Village. Almost all were poorly educated working-class youths who had not been able to find jobs in Canton and had come to the countryside as a last resort to scratch out a living. While still in Canton, some of them had been promised that if they labored in the countryside for several years, they would be allowed back to the cities and given permanent urban employment. Many of them had bickered with the peasants over the workpoints they were allotted; some had stolen off from work whenever they could; had pilfered foodstuffs from the collective fields; had made off now and then with a private chicken. Some of these young men and women even bedded down together. Unlike Chen Village, where the peasantry had generally been decent to the sent-down youths, in most of these other villages the peasants had looked down upon and resented the urban contingents as nuisances. In some villages the team heads had retaliated, by cheating the young people in their end-of-harvest pay or had vindictively assigned them to the most onerous tasks.

The Chen Village youths wanted to think of themselves as idealistic even when they turned their attention to their own problems. Thus, rather than complaining publicly about their own conditions, they began championing the cause of these less fortunate youths from the other villages. Stocky Wang had made contact with a large group of like-minded former students from two communes away, and one day in midsummer a couple of dozen of these former students pedaled their bicycles over to Chen Village to compare notes on their common cause. Other urban young people from brigades nearby began drifting in to join the discussions. The peasants became alarmed. A young peasant militiaman recalls, "We'd heard a rumor that at one village the sent-down youths had put poison in the wells. And we'd also heard that at a state farm in the district they'd invited in truckloads of Canton students to start a violent struggle." So when the village leadership saw dozens of young men converging on Chen Village, says Stocky, "they took these youths as troublemakers coming over to stir up trouble; they didn't like us linking into large groups and behaving secretively." The Chen Village leaders marched into the building where the young people were meeting and angrily ordered them to disband. The young people refused. Our interviewee Li remembers:

> We argued we should have our freedom of speech. But the cadres were so angry they blew the emergency siren to assemble all the armed militia. So the whole village rushed out to see what the hell it was about, and the militia came running up with their rifles and surrounded us. They accused us

of holding a "black meeting" and said our words were counter-revolutionary. We said they were wrong, that the militia was a tool; they were not really pointing their spearhead toward real class enemies but instead were just coming after us. They in turn yelled we were going around insulting the poor and lower-middle peasants [by complaining about the treatment of urban young people in the countryside]. . . . Longyong exploded at us: "How dare you people say bad things about the poor and lower-middle peasants! When did the poor and lower-middle peasants ever do you any harm? . . ." We wouldn't budge. So in the end they telephoned the commune seat to send some army people down. The army men came but refused to take sides, just separated us. . . . After that, we felt it would be difficult to stay any longer in the village.

Within days, Stocky Wang was helping to lead two-thirds of the urban-born youths back to Canton, furious and low-spirited. Most of them would end up spending the Cultural Revolution idly at home with their parents. A minority, still activist, briefly would try "rebelling" in Canton against Liu Shaoqi's down-to-the-countryside black line. It was a hopeless cause—and some of them already realized it would be. In the end, they would be forced back to Chen Village.

The Collapse of Brigade Leadership

When the workteam had suddenly departed in December 1966, the village leaders had found themselves very much on their own. In place of the tight controls that had been exercised over Chen Village during the Four Cleanups, the chains of command that linked Chen Village with the national state were rupturing. The political institutions above the village had rapidly disinte-grated, first in Canton, then at the county and commune seats. The brigade-level cadres could no longer rely upon the backing of the state's power to enforce the brigade's decisions vis à vis its constituent teams.

At the same time, and just as serious, by January 1967 the various village-wide organizations were beginning to fold. During more normal times, the Chen Village leadership had been able to mobilize the village's party and League members to build support for its policies. It could have used the militia to develop and coordinate the enthusiasm of young activists in support of the brigade-level projects. It could have used the public security committee to threaten those who resisted the brigade officers' interpretations of law and order. And it could have counted on the Mao Thought network of counselors to praise and criticize teams and villagers in accordance with the Maoist ethos and brigade-level programs. But now, as the county and commune party organs suspended activities, the brigade's own party branch no longer received directives regularly and no longer gathered in twice-monthly meetings. The militia, cut adrift from higher levels, halted its political and para-military training sessions. The public-security committee eased off its regular meetings. Many of the village's Mao Thought counselors had deserted their jobs and were beginning to contemplate a return to Canton. The brigade's capacity to impose sanctions and its mechanisms for persuasion and mass mobilization had dissolved. Any production team that wanted to ignore brigade-level requests could do so with impunity.[6]

Qingfa perceived here an opportunity to further weaken the new brigade leadership and perhaps regain a measure of power for himself. The members of his own team had dutifully gone through the motions of struggling against him on the command of the workteam, but their loyalty to him remained essentially intact. The head of Qingfa's production team, No. 6, was Qingfa's brother-in-law: their wives were sisters from another village. The brother-in-law and the rest of the No. 6 team natur-

---

[6.] An interviewee from a different part of Guangdong Province reports that in his native village actual bloodshed between teams resulted. There, each team was a separate hamlet. "In the Cultural Revolution all sorts of 'contradictions' emerged among the teams over natural resources and timber stands. Each of the teams mobilized its militia unit and even dared to use arms. For example, our team and the team next door had a long-standing dispute over a woods of bamboo—that was ours. Our team was bigger and fiercer, and so we used guns. If the other side tried to get any bamboo we'd let off a gun. And we quarreled with them over the possession of hills. These were the very same conflicts we'd had before the Liberation. In fact, my father had been stabbed back before the Liberation in just this sort of quarrel."

ally preferred to see Longyong, Jinyi, and their colleagues "fall from the political stage" and to see Qingfa back in the seat of power. The brother-in-law also had his own personal reasons. He was a strong-willed man who was proud of his own abilities as an agricultural planner. As a result, he had often had disagreements over policy with the equally strong-willed Longyong, in Longyong's capacity as brigade production chief. He had no qualms now about defying Longyong, and when Qingfa returned to the production team the brother-in-law was happy to listen to Qingfa's counsels.

Hence, soon after the workteam had left Chen Village, the No. 6 team had begun to ignore the authority of Longyong and the new inarticulate party secretary, Jinyi. When Longyong and the brigade management committee tried to get the various production teams of the village to improve the road that ran by the brigade, to dig new irrigation ditches of eventual benefit to the community as a whole, or to carry out other such projects, the No. 6 production team declined to do its share. When this production team resisted, the other teams also balked. The authority of Longyong and his colleagues on the brigade management committee, already weakened, deteriorated further. Though Longyong inveighed against the No. 6 team and Qingfa, he could not follow up his threats with any concrete action.

The brigade officers were becoming utterly frustrated in their work. They had felt abused in the Four Cleanups campaign, and now, having agreed little more than half a year earlier to come back to their posts, they found themselves faced with insubordination from the teams and from the Maoism Red Guards. Thus when the latter stormed in on the brigade officers' after-dinner counsels in mid-January 1967, the brigade clerk may not have been entirely facetious when he had offered them the seal of responsibility. The brigade cadres were in a mood to quit and go back to being ordinary peasants in their own production teams. The last straw was provided when the Maoism Red Guards, having backed off from "seizing power," began plastering the village with wall posters rehashing the old charges of the Four Cleanups campaign. Enough was enough. It was sufficiently hard trying to help lead Chen Village without being buffeted, abused, and left powerless by one campaign after another. First singly and then en masse, Chen

Village's cadres abandoned their duties and went back to tilling the fields and their own private plots. Longyong was left alone at the management committee's helm. Furious, he berated them: "If you're all going to treat me like this I don't give a damn. We all worked together; but now you're taking all the responsibility and laying it all on me! I won't be a cadre any more either! I'll just go back to my production team." By the close of January 1967, the brigade management committee had ceased to exist.

Only Jinyi, the new party branch secretary, remained at his post. Having only recently assumed his position, he had not felt as frustrated or as irate as the brigade cadres who had experienced the Four Cleanups. A stolid, hard-working person with a strong sense of duty, he tried in his steady but unimaginative way to assume the responsiblity for leading the village through its troubled times. But he was hampered by a weak personality and by a lack of any institutional mechanisms through which to carry out his leadership. He was a party secretary without a functioning party apparatus.

When the village's major political institutions disintegrated in early 1967, the most serious and immediate concern was to find a way to assure the stable functioning of the village economic order. The spring planting was rapidly approaching, and the harvests would be badly affected if the planting were not properly organized. All of the team heads and their team committees had loyally stayed at their posts, since, in Ao's words, "they knew if they didn't work their team members wouldn't have anything to eat." But the plans of all the teams had to be coordinated. The flow of water between teams had to be properly regulated. Under the Dazhai workpoint system, the "shock troops" of young labor activists from the ranks of the militia would have to be marshaled to set the pace both in planting and harvesting. The village urgently needed a new governing body.

The Cultural Revolution Leadership Small Group

In early 1967, units of the People's Liberation Army (PLA) were being dispatched into the countryside of Guangdong to assure the preservation of economic and political order. A corps of several junior officers took control of the administration of the commune, and a few of them temporarily entered Chen Village with orders to set up a new village administration, to be called a Cultural Revolution Leadership Small Group. As stipulated in a directive from the party central committee, it was to be fashioned from the Poor and Lower-Middle Peasants Association founded in the Four Cleanups.[7] But unlike the association, the small group was not established to lead mass struggles against any of the cadres. Its task was to assure social stability and agricultural productivity amid the Cultural Revolution turmoil.

When asked to elect members of the Poor and Lower-Middle Peasants Association to sit on Chen Village's Cultural Revolution Leadership Small Group, however, the production teams simply sent the same poor peasant representatives who had been selected in the Four Cleanups campaign. Though these were by no means the most competent people, the peasants' concern was just to have some operating organ at village level to hold things together. Ao recalls, "It was done casually and by consensus. The masses felt it wasn't any big deal; they were much more serious if it came to electing a team head, because that was directly tied to the question of eating."

Only two of the members selected for the small group had not served previously as poor peasant representatives; but they were precisely the two who would end up playing important roles in the village during the Cultural Revolution. One of them was a thirty-year-old army veteran named Chen Sunwang. Though the PLA unit occupying the village had not intervened in the other team selections, in the No. 8 team it did push Sunwang forward to enter the small group, which in turn elected him its director. The visiting soldiers had liked Sunwang's military background and his local reputation for tough-minded efficiency. A hard worker with a strong, severe personality, Sunwang was in many respects like Longyong. He was, additionally, semiliterate. He

[7] The Directive of the Party Central Committee on the Great Proletarian Cultural Revolution in Rural Districts declared: "The authoritative organs leading the Cultural Revolution in the rural areas shall be Cultural Revolution committees of poor and lower-middle peasants, to be democratically elected by poor and lower-middle peasant congresses" (*Current Background,* No. 842, pp. 31-32).

had been taught to read in the army; and, says one former villager, because "he had left the village for the army and had learned something about the outside world he could analyze things better than most of the other peasants. So he was respected by the others." His class origin also was impeccable; in fact he and his mother had drifted into the village in the 1940s as poverty-stricken refugees. In the early 1960s, soon after his discharge from the army, Sunwang had agreed to head the brigade's militia.[8] But he had given up that post after a few years because he had disliked having to argue constantly with Longyong. He felt that the high prestige that he enjoyed as a returned army man was sufficient. He felt no need to bolster it with a formal post. He had remained satisfied to influence the village in informal ways, by speaking out at public gatherings and by pressing his opinions in closed meetings of the party committee. When the leadership vacuum arose in the village, however, he allowed himself to be persuaded by the PLA officers to step in temporarily: "He felt it dangerous to have a situation in which no one held power."

Red Cheng was elected to the small group because the poor peasant representative from the No. 3 team had gotten sick. He had made a very good impression upon the peasants. Unlike Stocky Wang, his class pedigree was unblemished. Even more importantly, and again unlike Stocky Wang, Red Cheng had made up for the time he spent at meetings and political work by laboring at an unstinting, near fanatical pace. The villagers resented "mouth revolutionaries," but Cheng lived up to what he preached. And though his Mao Thought Red Guards had been a nuisance with their zealous smashing of rice-cookie molds, Cheng had stood in defense of social order against the unpopular provocations of the Maoism Red Guards. He had, it was felt, identified his interests with those of Chen Village. Literate and persuasive, Red Cheng became the vice-director of the small group.

[8.] An interviewee, a sent-down youth, believes still in the official perspective regarding such a post: "To be the head of the militia company was considered an important position. Only [trustworthy] people, people with a very sad past, could take up such a post. These were people who would really believe in Mao. Whenever there were campaigns, they were bound to be on the front line. I'd great respect for such people for the way they love and trust the Chairman."

Almost immediately after these elections, the PLA soldiers left Chen Village. The small group was left largely on its own. It had been given enough "outside" legitimacy to sustain itself as the village's leadership organ. But as with the preceding brigade management committee, the new leadership organ's effective authority was weak partly because the Chinese state was in disarray. And the small group was doubly weak because the poor peasant representatives on it were generally inarticulate, incompetent people who could not command much respect. Sunwang and Red Cheng therefore almost automatically held most of the power. But they in turn had to rely heavily upon the real sources of informal authority in the village. The key person—especially to assure economic order—was Longyong.

Longyong was content for the time being to remain officially only an ordinary peasant. He did not want to be held accountable for any errors that might be committed. He told a confidant that after the Four Cleanups and all the succeeding troubles, "I'm not going to do anything that people can look at." But Longyong's resignation as brigade production chief had created a vacuum, and he probably had realized all along that the brigade informally would have to seek him out again.

Sunwang, Jinyi, Red Cheng, and Ao had begun going frequently to his house to ask his advice on running the brigade and to obtain his backing for their actions. Gradually their informal meetings became the regular means for coordinating the activities of Chen Village; and they became the village's ruling quintumvirate. They acknowledged the formal leadership of the poor peasant representatives in the Cultural Revolution Leadership Small Group, but they bypassed them. Jinyi and Sunwang kept frequent contact with some of the older party members to assure that adequate production plans were being implemented in the production teams. Sunwang turned to the revived militia to assure order and to set a fast pace in farm labor. Red Cheng called upon the Mao Thought Red Guards to provide activist voices to whip up the proper atmosphere at brigade-wide meetings. Ao threw herself into her task of broadcasting the glory of Mao's thought over the loudspeakers. Gao, having restored his standing with the Chen Village cadres, had remained in the village, and in company with Ao he helped rekindle the Mao study network, which incessantly urged team members to heed Mao's thought by selflessly "getting a firm hold on production." Longyong called upon his former subordinates in the brigade management committee to pitch in when help was needed in coordinating brigade activities. Later in the Cultural Revolution, when the party central committee directed that each village establish a full-time Production Small Group to assure local economic stability, he and the other brigade cadres took up their duties more formally again. But even before then, at crucial moments Longyong would step in from the wings to impose his quintumvirate's decisions upon village meetings.

The new system of administration worked—at least in organizing the economy. The village was able to take advantage of the new irrigation and drainage works and the agricultural innovations introduced by the Four Cleanups workteam. The year 1967 was blessed by good weather; and the peasantry were pushed to work diligently by Mao slogans and by the pace-setting militia and Mao Thought Red Guards. The peasants' income from the summer and autumn harvests rose to double what it had been when the Big Four Cleanups began in 1964: from half a *yuan* a day to a full *yuan*. The Mao Thought counselors impressed upon the villagers that the teachings of Chairman Mao (above all else, the lessons of diligence, perseverance, and energetic concern for the collective's welfare) paid off in near miraculous economic development.

Reemergence of Old Rivalries

The new village leadership had less success handling Chen Village's relations with the world outside. Before the Liberation of 1949, neighboring villages in Chen Village's district sometimes had been hostile armed camps. Those conflicts had ended under the peace and order imposed by the Communist government. But now the Cultural Revolution had thrown the organs of state power into a dangerous paralysis: dangerous because the enmities of previous generations, though dying out, died slowly and could easily be rekindled. Chen Villagers still pointed to fields that now belong to other brigades as "lands that were stolen from our village many generations ago." The children from different villages would taunt each other and get into fights. The adults still shouted out disparaging jokes when people from other villages passed by Chen Village's fields on their way into the mountains. With the breakdown of state order in the Cultural Revolution, the lingering historically rooted tensions could provide the grist for renewed troubles.

In the autumn of 1967, the waters of the small river that borders Chen Village had risen dangerously in the wake of heavy rains. Chen Village had repaired and raised the height of its own dikes during the previous few years and safely watched as the floodwaters threatened to spill over the opposite banks into the fields of a village in the neighboring commune. It was a larger village than Chen Village, one that before Liberation had once tried to raid Chen Village in a feud. There was no love lost between the two communities. The disorder of the Cultural Revolution now allowed the people of that village to try to turn the disaster away from their own doors by breaking the dike on Chen Village's side of the river. They were sighted crossing the river with sledgehammers and picks. Sunwang and a few others hurried out to negotiate their departure. To be fair, he argued, things should be left to fate. But he was tied up at gunpoint, and the destruction of Chen Village's dikes began. In Chen Village a crowd of furious villagers was soon preparing to advance on the dikes. The village militiamen grabbed all the weaponry that was stored in the village: twenty-odd rifles and an antiquated machine gun. Others brandished clubs and farm tools. Among the most excited was Longyong, who tended to become overheated at any challenges to Chen Village's pride or interests. Ao and Red Cheng and a few other sent-down youths tried desperately to calm down the Chen Village cadres. But in the midst of the emotional tumult no one listened.

Fortunately, by the autumn of 1967, a rudimentary administrative structure had been patched together under military supervision at the commune level. Fortunately, too, one of the newly appointed leaders was on a visit to Chen Village, and—coincidentally—he was Sunwang's father-in-law. Because of this the villagers trusted him; and because he was a superior official, it seemed prudent to hear him out. He was able to persuade and browbeat the armed crowd to hold back, and to threaten the dike wreckers into halting their work. Then he hurried off to negotiate with the leaders of the neighboring commune. A favorable decision soon came back: Chen Village's dike would be spared. Narrowly, order had been restored to intervillage relations. Nature took its course, and the river flowed over the opposite bank.

Qingfa's Mischief

The Chen Village leadership was troubled by internal weakness as well as by such external disorders. Though most of the peasants had been happy to accept the new leadership's formal and informal authority in matters related to their own economic interests, some of them balked when asked to subordinate their immediate interests to the entire village's future development and to the demands of the Chinese government. Playing on these feelings, Qingfa had room to continue resisting the "upstarts" who had taken over his posts and power.

Whatever Qingfa's flaws, he had been a capable and forceful leader of the village. It had been under his regime that electricity had been installed and the first steps taken toward the village's present prosperity. He had been disliked for his favoritism, but he still commanded grudging respect for his quick mind, persuasive powers, energy, strength, and experience. Qingfa and his friends now spread the opinion that the new brigade cadres were inept compared to himself. At informal after-dinner get-togethers with old friends and former subordinates among the village's party members, he made much of Longyong's abrasiveness. What he said struck responsive chords. Qingfa's team, moreover, continued to resist the brigade level with impunity. Refusing to provide labor for various brigade projects, it made effective use of the time and energy it saved to benefit the team's own economy. Its prosperity increased even faster than other teams'.

Qingfa went further. He had his team engage in illegal trade and profiteering. In the hilly regions, it was comparatively inexpensive to raise oxen on the mountain grasses. Qingfa arranged for his team to buy oxen there at low prices in order to resell the animals for much higher prices in the rich delta counties. Trading of oxen across county lines was against the rules, but Qingfa made good use of the connections he had acquired during his tenure as party branch secretary. The extra income helped cement even further the No. 6 team's loyalty to Qingfa. The peasants of the other teams, seeing Qingfa's success at this, considered doing this sort of thing too.

The government that year set the grain quota for Chen Village at some fifteen tons of rice. Since Qingfa's No. 6 team was better off than most of the village teams, the brigade, as was normal practice, requested from it slightly larger deliveries. But the No. 6 team refused. Instead, the team sold its surplus grain on the free market for several times the quota price.

The county stipulated that each team was to plant nine acres of sugar cane. But a team could not make much money on sugar. So the No. 6 team planted only three and a half acres in sugar. When it was clear that the brigade could not make Qingfa's team come to terms, other teams followed suit. The No. 4 team planted higher-priced peanuts on the fields zoned for sugar cane. Longyong fulminated at the No. 4 team leader, only to be brushed off with the reply: "Just let those upper-level officials come down and try to be team heads and then they'll know what should be done." Despite Longyong's gradually expanding hold in village politics, without the power of the state to back him up, he still could not thoroughly control the brigade's affairs or unequivocally subdue his old rival Qingfa.

Qingfa now began working behind the scenes to win back his share of power in Chen Village. He had been set aside by the cadre workteam in May of 1966, when the Cultural Revolution was already beginning. In the autumn of 1967, the Communist party central committee in Peking announced that the "verdicts" against cadres who had fallen during the Four Cleanups should stand, but that cadres who had been accused by workteams after the inauguration of the Cultural Revolution could seek redress.[9] Seeing this, Qingfa had his friends mount a word-of-mouth campaign stressing that Qingfa had fallen during the Cultural Revolution and not during the Four Cleanups campaign. They wanted to fan up sentiments in the village to have Qingfa's name officially cleared. They particularly wanted his probationary suspension

---

[9.] See Richard Baum, *Prelude to Revolution*, pp. 151-156. The Party Central Committee retroactively and almost arbitrarily fixed May 16, 1966, as the dividing line between the Four Cleanups campaign and the Cultural Revolution.

from the party to be removed so that when the Cultural Revolution ended, he could be a brigade cadre once more. It was obvious, they said, that the brigade's affairs could not be run smoothly without Qingfa's participation and cooperation. The argument won adherents, and not just in Qingfa's own team. One of its supporters, the village's new Communist Youth League secretary, remembers he had felt Longyong and Qingfa should be persuaded to work in tandem; that the enervating splits in the brigade had to be ended. "I thought Jinyi was too weak. Longyong had Longyong's strong points; Qingfa had his. Both of them should come out to be cadres." Some of the older peasants in Chen Village, who remembered Qingfa in his better days, felt likewise. So too did the cadres of the No. 1 team and Qingfa's "buddies": those people who, in the words of the Communist Youth League secretary, "thought they could get some advantages from the brigade if Qingfa were a cadre."

However, the particular maneuvers that Qingfa had adopted to stymie the new brigade leaders and to force his own return were, if anything, counterproductive. Though Qingfa undoubtedly viewed his actions as furthering his hold on the No. 6 team and as aggravating the brigade's relations with the other teams, the main consequence of his actions had been to regenerate the other teams' dissatisfaction with him. When Qingfa's team did not provide the manpower for urgently needed projects or did not sell its fair share of quota grain, these other teams, after all, had had to make up the deficiencies in labor and grain. In the short run, Longyong and the other brigade cadres were being weakened; in the long run, Qingfa himself was providing Longyong with the political leverage to crush him.

We cannot know at what point such a plan began taking shape in Longyong's mind. But in late 1967 and early 1968 he already seems to have begun moving his props strategically into place. As a first step, Longyong would want to make sure that people favorable to himself sat on the brigade's public security committee, Chen Village's prosecutory body. One obstacle here would be an aggressive young man nicknamed Shorty. Shorty had been "cultivated" by the Four Cleanups workteam to spearhead attacks on Longyong and had been awarded the post of poor peasant representative of the No. 8 team, Longyong's own team.

Longyong and he had remained on very brittle terms from that time on. Fortunately for Longyong, Shorty had not been elevated into the Cultural Revolution Small Group; for the No. 8 team, Sunwang had been the PLA officers' choice. But Shorty remained the team's poor peasant representative and its delegate on the public security committee. He remained an irritant and a potential danger to any plans Longyong might pursue. Shorty had to be driven from his post if Longyong was to have full control over the public security committee.

The Persecution of Shorty

The decline during the Cultural Revolution of social order in Chen Village provided Longyong with the pretext. Wandering chickens and ducks were being stolen as never before. There were rumors of a peeping tom prowling the village at night. Worse yet, stories circulated of adulterous sex in the hills. Many villagers agreed that private property, personal security, and public morality were all endangered. Something needed to be done. The times were ripe to make a public example of Shorty, Longyong decided.

Shorty had a bad reputation as a woman chaser, but he had recently married. His bride, Maiyen, was a bright, hardworking, argumentative widow of about 30. One day the rumor reached Maiyen that Lilou, the most infamous woman in the village, was having an affair with Shorty. Maiyen, affronted and enraged, loudly let it be known throughout the village that she was out for revenge against both her husband and his rumored paramour.

The alleged adulteress, Lilou, was an exceptionally intelligent and capable woman who had been married into Chen Village in 1949. She had never laid eyes on her husband until the wedding ceremony, and she discovered herself wedded to a dull-witted, irritable, half-blind man. Desperately disappointed, she had petitioned the land reform workteam for a divorce, but the cadres had refused. If divorced, they feared, her husband would never be able to find another woman. Her repeated requests over the next two decades were always denied on the same grounds by the brigade's male officers. Once she ran away but was caught by a village search party.

Despite the party cadres' insensitivity to her wishes, she had been unstinting in her collective labor and a decisive speaker in behalf of Communist party programs. As a result, in 1958 she was admitted into the party. But Lilou compensated for her ill-starred marriage by turning to a succession of lovers. She was an ugly woman, but coquettish. Each of her six children, gossips said, resembled a different man in the village. Lilou's flouting of official Communist moral standards so outraged the Four Cleanups workteam cadres that they had her expelled from the party. Her new liaison with Shorty made her a timely target for a campaign against loose morals.

Longyong approached the brigade's public security committee. He claimed histrionically that the reputation of all of Chen Village was being affected by a messy scandal. Something drastic had to be done for the sake of the village's reputation, for the sake of revolutionizing the village. Ao, who was secretary of the public security committee, recalls, "When Longyong went on in this way, you couldn't dare oppose him."

The public security director called all of the village to a denunciation meeting. But when Shorty ascended the stage, he upset the meeting's schedule. Rather than launch into a contrite confession of adultery, he began discoursing explicitly on his wife's frigidity. In the recollections of an interviewee, Shorty shouted: "Every time I wanted to do things with her, she said she was bleeding." Maiyen, furious, reportedly screamed back, "You're talking a lot of bunk! When you go to bed, you just go to sleep." She proceeded to disparage his potency in intimate detail, with withering asides about Lilou. Lilou leaped angrily to her feet, and she and Maiyen began trading ribald sexual insults.

Some of the urban youths had been organized to provide short political speeches and shouts of condemnation from the audience. But they sat in flustered and astonished silence. "We had never heard anything like this before, and we were all blushing. . . . We were over twenty years old and we didn't know what they were talking about!" Most of the village men just sat back and enjoyed the show. They were sympathetic to Shorty and had no intention of meddling in his affairs. The public security director alone tried vainly to restore a semblance of order. But he could not handle the quarreling trio on the stage, and he gave up with a shrug.

Longyong had stayed out of sight on the sidelines, as if he had had no connection with this meeting. He had been afraid that if he took any part people would gossip that he was trying to exact vengeance against Shorty. But the meeting was unraveling in ways embarrassing to brigade authority, so Longyong stepped out onto the stage and spoke up. Shorty ought to be ashamed, he shouted: "If a cow doesn't want to drink, you push its head into the water." It was all Shorty's fault for not forcing himself on his wife. But Longyong's intervention only worsened the tumult. His denunciation session was collapsing around his ears, and he was now caught on stage. Emotionally out of control, Maiyen, Lilou, and Shorty were hurling insults with unabated frenzy. As a fitting climax to a preposterous evening, Maiyen traded blows with her husband on stage and chased him off into the night.

The meeting had descended into farce. But Shorty's moral probity had been formally, even if farcically, called into question. He was not officially dismissed from the public security committee, but the other public security members simply no longer invited him to attend their meetings. The brigade speedily granted a divorce to his wife, Maiyen; and after a decent interval, Maiyen was asked to sit in Shorty's vacant seat on the committee.

Though Longyong's first effort to conduct a "struggle" meeting seemed an embarrassing failure, he had set the stage for more effective and terrifying crackdowns on his adversaries and on Chen Village's least popular and most vulnerable peasants. The Cleansing of the Class Ranks campaign was on the horizon.

· 5 ·

The Cleansing of the Class Ranks

A New Village Government

The Cultural Revolution had been raging for two years. Mao had seen his political opponents fall; and it was time for stability again.

As a preliminary step, the villagers were directed to hold elections to establish a new governing body to lead Chen Village into the post-Cultural Revolution era. Thus, in May of 1968 the brigade and team cadres and leading activists were assembled to draw up a slate of nine recommended candidates for nine committee positions (the same number as had sat on the old brigade management committee). Additional nominations could be made at production team meetings; but with the weight of the village leadership marshaled in favor of the nine preselected candidates, anyone else would be hard put to win. Qingfa did make a lame effort to muster support. According to Ao, he even tried to "buy" votes by telling village party members and team heads that if they backed him, he would help them secure privileges when elected. But he soon sensed the futility of his efforts, and in the end he did not put his name to the test. Longyong, making full use of the prestige he had gained in holding the village together during the Cultural Revolution, effectively dominated the nominating committee—and the slate he controlled swept the elections uncontested.

Chen Sunwang, the army veteran who headed the Cultural Revolution Leadership Small Group, had refused an offer to be on the slate. He said that he simply did not want the constant strain of arguments with Longyong. Red Cheng's name was absent, too; he recently had been inducted into the army—another step up for him on his career ladder. Ao and Gao, the other two urban youths who had shown potential as cadres during the Cultural Revolution, were nominated and elected through Longyong's good graces. When, however, the names of the village's newly elected officials were passed up to commune authorities for pro forma approval, the commune vetoed the appointments of both youths. Ao recalls her rejection:

> The commune secretary and two important cadres came to see us two. . . . They began praising us, how we were supported by the poor and lower-middle peasants, etc. . . . Oh I thought we'd gotten it! We were so red, and in the elections we'd gotten as many votes as the reddest and the most trustworthy of the brigade cadres. . . . But then they went on to say that they'd just been to Canton to look into our class backgrounds and that it was better for us to wait a while, let us become more mature before joining the leadership ranks. I was shocked! It was all because my father had worked under the Guomindang as a physician in the army medical corps! . . . I went home to cry; and several important village cadres (Longyong among them) came to comfort me and sat by my bedside.

Two local youths of poor peasant extraction took Ao and Gao's places.

The least popular of those elected to the new committee was a man in his early forties nicknamed Baldy. He was Meiyan's elder brother, and another of Longyong's personal choices. Years earlier, Baldy had served as a brigade cadre, and villagers remembered that he had been "unjust." He therefore made an embarrassingly poor showing in the elections; in protest against him, a sizable number of peasants simply abstained from casting their ninth ballot. Longyong, however, disregarded this expression of disapproval, and when the new village committee met to decide among themselves who would occupy what duties, he pressed successfully for Baldy to become the public security head.

In the forthcoming campaign, Longyong would be making

astute use of Baldy. As Stocky Wang, one of Longyong's detractors, put it, "Baldy was a puppet dancing around out front. . . . He played the bad guy so that Longyong could remain the good guy. . . . He played the role of being 'hard' so that Longyong could keep a 'soft' profile."

Bolting the Latch

The political whirlwinds for which Longyong was preparing were not long in coming. The government in Peking wanted to put a quick end to the Cultural Revolution's residual turmoil. Once more it wanted law and order; it wanted reestablishment of the local political structure and hierarchy; it wanted peasants and workers to obey cadres; it wanted lower-level officials to obey their superiors. The government was willing to countenance a new "struggle campaign" to achieve these ends.

Ao recalls this new swing in the national political climate:

> Originally the door latch had been let loose in the Cultural Revolution, and people were allowed to rebel. What a mess! . . . But now the latch was bolted again very quickly, the peasants said. As the new campaign went from stage to stage, at each stage the situation became clearer, and every one of the bad elements was cleansed away. Mao Zedong used the masses' power to enforce a dictatorship over the bad elements. Fierce! I didn't think the latch could have been bolted up again so quickly. It had been such chaos!

The orders to "bolt the latch," as Ao phrased it, arrived in the summer of 1968 in the shape of a national party document entitled Six Points for Public Security. It was necessary, this document declared, to cleanse from the good classes the evil influence spread by six kinds of miscreants:

1. Those who were opposed to Chairman Mao Zedong

2. Those who opposed Vice-Chairman Lin Biao

3. "Bad" Cultural Revolution leaders (in practice these were the heads of organizations which had been defeated in the struggles) and "black hands" (those from

the losing side who had manipulated events from behind the scenes)

4. "Hidden counterrevolutionaries" (bad-class people
who had moved at the time of the Liberation to districts where they were not known and had passed
themselves off as members of the good classes)

5. Criminals (guilty in the Cultural Revolution of such
crimes as arson, murder, or rape)

6. Four-bad types who had not reformed themselves
properly

When the peasants were informed of the impending campaign, many greeted the news with apprehension. The son of an
upper-middle peasant recalls: "A number 12 typhoon signal was
up . . . a political typhoon signal. . . . No one dared to breathe.
Anything could happen." The wording of the Six Points was so
overwrought and the six categories so vaguely limned that it was
not very clear to any of the listeners exactly who might be an
enemy of the people deserving to be purged from the "class
ranks." There was ample room here to settle personal vendettas.

A workteam of several party cadres arrived to help get the
campaign rolling. But they went about their business desultor-
ily—like "sparrows pecking at rice." Probably they had not for-
gotten the unenviable fate of workteams two years earlier at the
very end of the Four Cleanups campaign. This hesitant new
workteam stayed in the village only a short while and then was
recalled. Fresh directives from above said that the campaign was
to be a mass campaign and that the masses themselves should
handle it unhindered by outside workteams. In reality this meant
the campaign was left in the hands of the Chen Village leaders.

The commune called them to a series of exhortatory sessions.
Each village would be expected to prove its political devotion in
an eruption of grass roots militancy against the types of criminals
named in the Six Points. They were to treat the campaign as a
holy crusade; as Ao observes, "the more extreme the better."
Reports on communities which were considered models in the
campaign implied that village cadres would not be doing their job
properly if they did not uncover damnable misdeeds among at
least 3 percent of their adult population. The campaign's demand

for wide-ranging "struggles" would have to be met. That was just fine with Longyong, Baldy, and the others. It suited their own local purposes.

To ferret out and prosecute people who had contaminated the "class ranks," they first needed to expand the village's public security committee. In ordinary times, this committee consisted of eleven members—one representative chosen from each of the ten production teams plus a brigade cadre (in this case Baldy) as committee head. The committee normally handled cases of petty theft (mostly chickens and ducks), mediated private disputes, discouraged sexual misbehavior, and kept a wary eye on the local four-bad types. The committee head normally worked full time at his job, but previously the committee as a whole usually met only about once a month, after work. Now it would have to meet almost every day. It would also need the assistance of several full time staff aides—to help interrogate suspects, compile dossiers, write up formal accusations, transcribe what was said at all of the struggle sessions, and compose final reports to be read at higher government levels. To accomplish all of these tasks, a special cases small group, headed by Ao, was set up under the public security committee.

The Ordeal of the Four-Bad Types

The first villagers to be targeted by the public security committee, to no one's surprise, were the four-bad types. The Six Points, after all, had specified that unreformed four-bad types were to be punished, and to Longyong and his colleagues (and perhaps most peasants) *all* four-bad types were unreformed. Even though most of the four-bad types had long been anxious to stay out of trouble, the prejudiced eyes of village opinion easily discerned evidence of their lack of genuine repentance even in the smallest remembered incidents. One of the sent-down youths observes: "Everybody felt that . . . if, like everyone else, a landlord grumbled that this year's crops weren't as plentiful as last year's, . . . then this indicated the landlord might really be trying to oppose Chairman Mao."

Now, with the Cleansing of the Class Ranks campaign in particular, the peasants *wanted* to hold to such suspicions. They realized that so long as the campaign centered on the evils of the four-bad types, ordinary villagers like themselves would remain safely out of the spotlight.

The cadres had separate reasons for starting with the four-bad types. "Class struggle" against China's bad classes, as the revolution's original and still-present enemies, conveniently reaffirmed the cadres' own legitimacy after the anti-party confusion of the Cultural Revolution. Accordingly, just as in similar struggle sessions at the end of the Four Cleanups, the heads of Chen Village's four-bad households were dragged out one by one onto the village stage and subjected to a furious torrent of abuse. Most of the half dozen accepted their fate meekly. They had been through all this before and knew that resistance would only worsen their plight. As required, they confessed that their hidden attitudes were wickedly unregenerate.

But the "bad element" who was a former guerrilla would submit to none of this. He had never been properly cowed by his bad element status. When the militia came to his house to arrest him, he met them with cleaver in hand, and before the frightened militiamen could apprehend him, he retreated into the hills. His escape gave added credence to the peasants' fears of "class enemies." People kept to their houses at night, and the militia itself did not risk going into the hills to hunt him down. He was captured only after several days, when hunger obliged him to sneak back home for food.

When dragged before a struggle session he was, one interviewee recalls, still "hard-mouthed." He defiantly refused to bow his head or admit to any wrongdoings. That was the final straw. "There was a feeling of mass hatred against him. . . . And when he was beaten, he still glared at people, as if he were picking out whom to get revenge on in the future." Fear added to the anger. The beating continued, but the lights were turned off so that he would not be able to identify any of his assailants in the darkness.

Punishing the Rebel Youth Leaders

Everyone was aware that the attacks against the four-bad types were intended only as the opening scene of a major campaign. The public security committee had already begun openly to gather evidence against the most prominent and active of the youths who had gone back to Canton at the height of the Cultural Revolution.

There was scant liking for them in the village. The cadres disliked them for having condemned all of the local leadership during the first year of the Cultural Revolution. And as far as the peasants were concerned, the youths had behaved with inexcusable arrogance and unruliness. First, during the heyday of the movement to study Mao's works, they had dared to criticize peasants for being selfish and politically backward; and then these very same youths had pirouetted 180 degrees, had disobeyed any authority that did not accord with their own self-centered inclinations, and had then deserted the village entirely. To the peasants, they seemed hypocrites of the worst kind— "fake activists."

Worse yet, having returned to Canton (where, the villagers heard, the youngsters were complaining that the countryside was an unfit place for them to live), they had even mustered the nerve to return to Chen Village after each of the harvests to claim their "basic grain" ration.[1] The Chens could not easily forgive people who tried to get something out of the village for nothing. And they identified the young people with the turmoil in Canton about which they had heard so many startling rumors.

In reality, very few of the thirty-odd youths who had followed Stocky Wang and Overseas Deng back to Canton in mid-1967 had played any role in the urban Red Guards' violence. Even Stocky Wang had participated only briefly in the activities of a militant Red Guard group composed of sent-down youths. He had withdrawn in distaste after a month, when members of the group set fire to a school occupied by their opponents. As the year passed, the Cultural Revolution's disorder and political convulsions had increasingly perturbed Stocky and his cohorts in Canton. Says Stocky:

---

[1] Since the young people were back in Canton illegally, they had not been able to buy rations of grain there. They therefore had reappeared in the village periodically during the Cultural Revolution to buy the cheap rice guaranteed to every production team member.

> I still believed in Chairman Mao. But no longer Lin Biao, nor anyone below Mao. We saw that the Cultural Revolution didn't solve any problems. Instead a lot of people died, and public order degenerated. Among the student Red Guards there was even a lot of sex! We heard stories about that. . . . It was really chaotic. So I just read novels and went swimming.

The peasants back in Chen Village had been even more alarmed than Stocky at the stories circulating about Red Guard violence and "immorality." They were ready to see the young people's leaders pay the penalty.

By midsummer of 1968, notices were being posted up throughout Canton commanding all sent-down youths to return to the countryside. Neighborhood committees went from door to door to ferret out illegal residents. The young people knew that if they lingered on in Canton they would get their families in trouble. But they also sensed there might be serious political trouble awaiting them back in the village. So before setting out again for the countryside, Stocky Wang and several of his friends pledged in sworn brotherhood, as in the traditional Chinese stories, that they would "be united in offense and defense."

Other young people had already begun drifting back to Chen Village. Among them was a "street youth" named Liang. He foolishly brought with him a hand grenade somehow acquired in Canton; and in a juvenile show of bravado he exploded this in the river as a demonstration of how to catch fish. The village cadres were alarmed at this recklessness and felt doubly convinced that the sent-down youths had been up to violent activities in the city. Liang became a chief target for interrogation.

Threatened, browbeaten, and promised leniency if he would reveal the misdeeds of people like Stocky Wang, Liang implicated Wang as a Rebel Red Guard ringleader. He insisted Wang had masterminded the looting of a thousand watches and had ordered the burning of that school. For these cooperative allegations, Liang was granted the promised leniency. He was released and was asked to work with the public security committee as an informant.

The first of the former leaders of the Maoism Red Guards to arrive back in the village was Zhao, one of Stocky's daily companions that past year. He was approached almost immediately by Liang and another youth, who warned him that the public security committee was "digging up dirt" on the sent-down youths and that Zhao ought to make the best of a bad situation.

> They suggested I be smart this time. They said I shouldn't take too much responsibility on my back, and that I should let Stocky Wang carry the burden. . . . Of course, I felt that this kind of talk lacked any standpoint. We'd done no wrong, after all. . . . We'd all gone back to Canton together. We'd only put Wang up as our leader, and he hadn't done anything wrong throughout the Cultural Revolution. . . . So I said: "We shouldn't throw stones at people who've fallen into a well."

Liang promptly went to report Zhao's obduracy to the public security committee.

The struggle meetings against the four-bad types were in full swing, and Zhao was smart enough to take the conversation with Liang seriously. But he did so in his own way. He and a good friend developed a scheme to help each other out in case either of them fell into trouble. They knew they would not be allowed to defend themselves publicly, nor, once apprehended, would they even have time to arrange for a friend to come to their aid. As a peasant remembers,

> During the campaign no one even knew who'd be the target each evening. So some of the audience would sit there shaking. The militia would stand at the back with ropes in hand, and when it was announced who the victim was, the militia would move up from behind to tie the fellow up.

If this should befall either Zhao or his friend, the other one would immediately yell "Correctly handle contradictions among the people!" Their idea was to preempt any attempt by the public security committee to classify their case as "a contradiction between the enemy and the people."

Four days after Zhao's return, Stocky Wang himself arrived back in Chen Village. The moment he entered the village, the militia came for him. They tied his two arms tightly behind him and dragged him to the special cases small group for interrogation. That very evening he was struggled against.

Stocky Wang was accused of having participated in "beating, killing, and looting" in Canton and of being a "black hand" of the

Cultural Revolution, that is, one who manipulated others to do evil things in his behalf. Several sent-down youths stood up to testify against him, Liang the most vocal among them. The team head whom Wang had tried to topple during the Cultural Revolution then mounted the stage to charge vehemently that Wang had stirred up factionalism in the team in order to harm agricultural production. He even took the opportunity to slap Wang hard once or twice in the face. Stocky, like all other struggle targets, was obliged to accept such abuse passively, bent over fully at the waist, arms and head down, unable to shift position for the full, aching duration of the struggle session.

When the accusations against Stocky had been recounted and dramatized to exhaustion, Longyong rose to his feet and, according to an interviewee's recollections, yelled: "There are also people here who want to protect this rotten Wang, who want to obstruct the revolution! . . . They are active counterrevolutionaries! . . . Don't you think we should do something about it?" At these words two members of the militia grabbed hold of Zhao and dragged him up onto the stage. Zhao would be a warning to others not to be recalcitrant about informing on political subversives. Amid the shouted condemnations, Zhao with some comfort heard his friend, true to his promise, yelling most loudly of all: "Correctly handle contradictions among the people!" Some of the peasants, taking this to be part of the official litany, began to chorus: "Contradictions among the people!" Militiamen had to wade into the crowd and bodily cart away the dissident cheerleader. "Luckily," Zhao observes, "they couldn't find any 'weapons in his luggage,' and so in the end he was left alone. . . . You know, sometimes I felt those cadres really were leading the peasants by the nose."

That evening was the first of many nights Stocky Wang and Zhao spent in the village "cowshed." A "cowshed" was a makeshift jail of a type that had sprung up all over China during the Cultural Revolution to lock up "cow ghosts and snake demons" (a traditional epithet used to denote the supernaturally sinister forces of evil). According to normal government policy, wrongdoers could only be placed in a prison after their cases had been reviewed at both the commune and county levels. But the Chinese legal system had disintegrated, and for the duration of the

Cleansing of the Class Ranks, cowsheds were to be used as kangaroo jails for the kangaroo courts.

The Chen Village cowshed was none other than the dressing room that had been built behind the village stage for the song-and-dance Propaganda Troupe. Here both men and women prisoners slept crowded together on the hundred-square-foot floor. When Wang and Zhao entered, they were chagrined to see, huddled asleep, all the four-bad types who had been struggled against in the previous days. It did not bode well for the two youths. They had been thrown together with the village's bad-class pariahs.

Ten days later, Overseas Deng arrived back in the village and immediately joined them in the cowshed. The village leadership had been determined to nail him, for Deng had gone out of his way to antagonize them. He particularly had made an enemy of Longyong, when Deng had served as the brigade's electrician before the Cultural Revolution. As one of Deng's friends recalls,

> When Longyong hadn't understood some piece of machinery and would tell Deng to do such-and-such, Deng would refuse, simply not listen. A lot of folks got to know about these run-ins, and Longyong probably was sore that Deng had damaged his prestige—a mere youth not even pretending to listen to the brigade management chief.

Deng and Ao had been on even more icy terms. As an "expert" good with machines, Deng had let it be widely known that he considered a "red" such as Ao to be an incompetent careerist, a "mouth revolutionary" of little value to the village. Now Ao would have the opportunity to show him how competent a "red" she really was.

In many ways, Deng made a far easier campaign target than Wang or Zhao. He was, after all, a Chinese from Indonesia, not native born. Moreover, since his father was a wealthy merchant, Deng had had access to an unusual amount of money by Chinese standards. Deng might have assuaged the peasants' mistrust by downplaying his foreignness and by being discreet about his wealth. But he was not. After the Youth Team had been disbanded in 1965, he gradually had abandoned his activist asceticism and had made a point of flouting village convention. He had bought an expensive shortwave radio and tape recorder and listened to Indonesian music and foreign-language broadcasts. He dressed in loudly colored batik shirts rather than the somber colors of a Chinese village. He had seemed "bourgeois" in his lifestyle. While others went barefoot, he had not been embarrassed to walk around in shoes. He had not even had to work in the fields like everyone else, but had had it all too easy as the brigade's electrician. Says one peasant from the village, "He'd been just sitting there playing with his own legs and still getting his two meals; and so we felt, 'you were allowed to lead such an easy life, and even then you attacked the brigade cadres!'"

When Deng had left for Canton during the Cultural Revolution, he had circled the city every day to read the wall posters. When the public security committee interrogated his friends to build a case against him, they reported his uncanny knowledge of Canton's affairs. Worse yet, since Deng did not have a family in the city like other urban youths, he had never met his friends at home. His friends confessed they did not even know his address. The Chen Village peasants, who had never been to a city and had lived all their lives in a small enclosed world, could not imagine how this could be possible. Anyone so knowledgeable about the ins and outs of Canton's turmoil and so secretive about where he lived *must* be a spy. And his fancy radio equipment must have been obtained to monitor reactionary foreign broadcasts and receive directives. Aggravating his case, one of Deng's best friends admitted under interrogation that Deng had reported coming across several beggars in Canton and had also related details about shortages during the Cultural Revolution in the city's supply of food. Though these were no more than plain statements of fact made casually in conversation, the special cases small group concluded that Deng was spreading malicious rumors that socialism did not work well in China. Charged with being a "black hand," a spy, and a propagandist for counterrevolution, Deng joined Wang and Zhao on the cowshed floor.

In the Cowshed

Despite their precarious situation, the three youths came into the cowshed in a mood of almost lighthearted defiance.

They were not particularly frightened by the accusations against them. They had not, after all, been involved in any "fighting, killing, and looting," in any spying, or in any of the other transparently absurd charges that had been pasted together against them. They felt certain that when all the facts were finally in and reviewed by a higher level of the party, they would be vindicated. Thus, they were very careful to distance themselves both physically and psychologically from the four-bad types all round them in the cowshed. All the while that the struggle meeting audiences were denouncing them in extravagantly inflated terms, they inwardly still felt themselves very much members of the "people" in the Chinese political system, in no way akin to the "class enemies."

On October 1, China's National Day, the trio celebrated by cutting out a red-papered silhouette of Chairman Mao and tacking up revolutionary couplets alongside it "to show," as Zhao puts it, "that we, too, were loyal, even though we were locked up here together with these four-bad types." Stocky Wang adds: "We faced our cutout of Chairman Mao feeling like big heroes and martyrs. We were so sure of ourselves, as if we were struggling against the forces of evil. I even dared to play the flute. . . . We really made the cadres mad."

The most self-confident of the three was Overseas Deng, even though his case, on paper at least, appeared the most serious and complicated. When the special cases small group wanted to collect his tape recorder and radio from Canton as evidence against him, they asked him for the address; he loudly and righteously questioned whether they had a search warrant, citing rules and regulations, trying to show that in every way he would stand upon his rights. Throughout those first days, he repeatedly let his inquisitors know that he had only disdain for them and their campaign.

The old four-bad types adopted an entirely different approach to their plight. They barely communicated even with one another. Fear and mistrust had taught them the wisdom of keeping silently to oneself. Any mistaken attempt to seek understanding from another prisoner only made one vulnerable to informants—and under the pressures of the campaign, everyone was a potential informant. The incongruously activist behavior of the three urban youths in the grim little room only served to remind their cellmates of the need to remain always guarded and close-mouthed.

The optimism, activist bravado, and disdain of the three sent-down youths did not last long. Within weeks, it was crushed under the weight of interrogations, cross-examinations, and the damaging testimony of fellow sent-down youths. Every time the special cases small group got hold of new "evidence," each of the three youths was subjected to another round of pressure to "confess." Being literate, they were required to hand in written "confessions." They were made to write, point by point, about anything and everything they had done that the special cases small group might have interpreted as counterrevolutionary, describing in detail the time, place, the other people present, and so forth. Writing these "confessions" was a great psychological strain. How much should I now reveal about myself and others? Has someone else already mentioned this particular incident? If I write such-and-such will I somehow inadvertently betray any friends? Does their description of an incident differ from what I'm writing? As feelings of uncertainty and anxiety grew, their will to resist declined apace. Aggravating their psychic exhaustion was the repeated rejection of their confessions. Every time they wrote one, it was rejected as incomplete and insincere—and they would have to start all over again in yet greater detail. Each day, the special cases small group sifted through these reams of writings, carefully searching for inconsistencies between the different suspects' accounts and for information that would generate new cases and draw in additional suspects.

While they wrote, a 24-hour guard was mounted inside the door of the cowshed to ensure that the three imprisoned youths did not speak even a word to each other. Ao, who was in charge, explains:

> We purposely kept the suspects isolated so they wouldn't know from each other what the campaign was really about. They wouldn't know what was serious and what wasn't, and wouldn't know what they could safely confess to and what they couldn't. And during questioning they'd be isolated from each other so that we could use the different stories and confessions to get further evidence and confessions. We let

suspects know that their friends were talking, and got them
mad at their friends so that they'd in turn tell.

Ao learned to master these various techniques. A dozen or so
additional sent-down youths who had made the mistake of desert-
ing the village for Canton were subjected to lengthy interrogations in which they were accused of complicity in the crimes of
their three unfortunate colleagues in the cow-shed and threatened
with imprisonment. Through coaxing, threats, and incessant reit-
erations of the slogan of all Chinese legal proceedings—"leniency
toward those who are frank, severity toward those who resist"—
an ever growing number of these sent-down youths came under
an ever greater strain to "confess." When they finally admitted to
some alleged wrong (there was, in the end, no alternative), Ao
would use this initial admission as leverage to extract more damn-
ing information. The best way to protect oneself was to admit
complete guilt promptly and contritely to what one hoped was a
minor offense, and then to cooperate by similarly incriminating
others.

Ao had the power to initiate interrogations and to extend
them for as long as she wished. All who faced her remember her
as "fierce." Without her, remarks one of the former rebels, "the
brigade government couldn't have gotten nearly so much material
against us." With an escort, she would sail into the cowshed or
some house, even in the small hours of the morning, order someone out of bed (or in the cowshed, off the sleeping mats), and take
the suspect away to be grilled.

Li was among those who were called in like this, and he still
speaks with anger in his voice when recollecting Ao's zealous
pursuit of her quarry:

> I myself didn't have to go into the cowshed, but I did have to
> undergo prolonged questioning. For two days they didn't let
> me out of the brigade headquarters. . . . Baldy and Ao kept
> on ordering me, "Confess! Confess!" I really didn't know
> what to confess. . . . Finally, they gave me a sheet of paper.
> On it were written a whole lot of things I was supposed to
> have said and done. This was all supposed to be evidence that
> the others had given against me. . . . But I couldn't remem-
> ber where exactly I had said those things or to whom. And
> they were such ordinary things. But heavens! Ao had raised

them all to the level of "political principle and political line"! She really made it sound so serious! Everything was written by her. She was in charge of collecting materials, and whether it sounded minor or serious lay in her hands. How could she write about me: "has *always* been dissatisfied with the party and Chairman Mao. A black hand of the Cultural Revolution." She just said: "Look, look at the report! See whether you agree to it or not." What could I say? How could she say that! We came from the same school. She knew me. How could she say "*has always been*"! . . . She knew how important this kind of thing was for anyone's future in China. How could she have done that!

Yet Ao did believe in what she was doing. Even her detractors admit as much. During the Cultural Revolution she had been even more hostile than the peasants toward the sent-down youth rebels. Ao had been working hard and religiously as the village broadcaster and Mao Thought leader to invoke the thought of the Chairman against anyone who deviated from orthodoxy and local order. She had not reflected on Mao's thought; she had proclaimed it. When, on the basis of Cultural Revolution directives, her rebellious urban colleagues had started to assert that Mao's thought provided a justification for *dis*order rather than order, Ao had been genuinely horrified. Such thinking threatened the foundations of everything most meaningful to her. Bitter arguments with the rebels had, on one occasion, degenerated into a fist fight.

Ao was not just out for petty personal vengeance now. She was sincerely convinced that Stocky Wang and the others had become counterrevolutionaries. She saw herself in noble terms as a mainstay of the village in defense of the revolution. She argues even today that she, Longyong, Baldy, and the other cadres were objective in their accusations during the Cleansing of the Class Ranks.

Within just a week or two of grueling interrogations, "hard" evidence against the trio in the cowshed began to fall solidly into place, as if in vindication of Ao's relentless pursuit. First one sent-down youth, then another, and then yet another cracked and confessed that Wang, Deng, and Zhao had made blasphemous remarks in Canton about Chairman Mao and Vice-Chairman Lin Biao. Wang had told friends privately that even though Mao Zedong was a heroic figure, he was now "old and blinded" by unscrupulous subordinates. Moreover, in Stocky's own recollected words, Mao had been made into "a religious idol to worship, and his thought had become like a Chinese herbal medicine store—people could come to pick from it whatever they wanted." Worse yet, in the last phases of the Cultural Revolution, when Lin Biao's closest followers in the army were disarming and repressing Canton's rebel faction, Deng had passed word to his friends that fortune-tellers throughout Canton were saying that Lin Biao's photographs revealed the face of a crafty fox. Many Chinese believe that people's characters and fates can be analyzed through facial features, much as many Westerners believe in palm-reading; and Deng's gossip suggested that Mao had better be on his guard, lest his chosen successor betray him.

Finally, even though all of them still held the Chairman in high esteem, Stocky, Deng, Zhao, and their friends daringly and jokingly had referred to Mao as "Old Fatso!" The term was popular among young people in Canton, and had they stayed in Canton it would have done them no harm. But Chen Village was not Canton. The peasants never even said "Mao Zedong," but only the more respectful "Chairman Mao."

They were shocked to learn that some of the rebellious youths had actually questioned Chairman Mao's wisdom and had even gone about making grossly disrespectful jokes about him and scandalous slurs against the vice chairman. A zealously devout Mao Thought leader like Ao looked upon such remarks as reprehensible and blasphemous heresies, a chilling revelation of the ideological depths to which the accused youths had sunk. To Ao, these remarks were positive proof that the young people were treasonously anti-Mao and anti-Lin Biao, as itemized in two of the six points for which suspects could be punished in the Cleansing of the Class Ranks.

During the first week of his confinement, Deng had not had to face a full-fledged struggle meeting, and he had remained stubbornly and irritatingly cocky. But Ao had been busily preparing the groundwork against him. Stocky Wang recalls the crushing effect of the first struggle meeting Deng endured:

> Deng never guessed other people could expose so much about him. Perhaps he couldn't even remember what he'd

said about Mao and about Lin Biao, and about Jiang Qing being a "stinking woman." The brigade was shrewd the way it used other sent-down youths to get him. When he was brought back from the struggle meeting to the cowshed, he was talking about committing suicide. . . . So when he went on talking in such a way that evening, all our razors, nail-clippers, and scissors were taken away. He was crying. I think he was scared—scared and regretful. But after he calmed down, he was all right. His real concern then was only about the length of his sentence. Not any more stuff about whether we were innocent or not.

Zhao, too, was frightened when some of his half-forgotten indiscreet comments were revealed to him, and when one after another of his increasingly detailed "confessions" were rejected. His interrogators liberally dropped hints that 95 percent of the people were good, and that only 2 or 3 percent were evil politically and warranted sustained attack. "I was so young and if I became one of the 3 percent I'd be scarred for the rest of my life; in all future campaigns I'd end up as part of the 3 percent." They talked to Zhao about sentencing: for this he could be given so many years, for that another number of years. "I found that they were pressing me into a corner as a counterrevolutionary. It was then that I gave up and let them do whatever they liked with me." He confessed to whatever he was accused of.

Stocky, too, recalls how his confidence had given way to fear and self-doubt and finally to confused feelings of guilt: "I still believed in Mao Zedong. So I was afraid that perhaps my own thoughts were wrong. . . . There was a psychology of repentence. I thought it might do good to be frank, wrong to be adamant . . . I truly felt ashamed of my faults."

Attacking Qingfa

Just one day after Deng's disastrous struggle session, Qingfa was plucked out of the audience by the militia and hustled onto the village stage. Qingfa and his friends must not have been altogether surprised; indeed, they had already taken precautionary measures. When the special cases small group secretly had begun to compile evidence against Qingfa, it discovered that a young peasant in the small group who was a member of Qingfa's lineage branch already had burnt the Four Cleanups dossier on Qingfa's "old crimes."

Despite this loss (indeed, perhaps aided by the dossier's destruction), the small group devised a case for Qingfa's arrest. Since any party cadre who had been deposed in the Four Cleanups prior to May 16, 1966 (the official starting date for the Cultural Revolution) was not permitted to "reverse the verdict," it could now be claimed that during the Cultural Revolution, Qingfa had been trying to climb back to power illegally. True, with Qingfa's dossier missing, one could no longer verify when Qingfa had been deposed by the workteam; but no matter. Qingfa later confided to his fellow inmates in the cowshed that he himself could not precisely recall the date of the verdict; how could anyone be expected to remember any specific calendar date so long after the event? But the leaders of the Cleansing of the Class Ranks insisted that they *could* recall—it had definitely been before May 16, 1966. And since they held the power, their word prevailed. "You'd already fallen in the Four Cleanups," they charged in that first struggle session, "yet you dared to try to grab votes when the new village committee was being organized!"

The public security committee faced a real problem, however. Even though a charge of "reversing a Four Cleanups verdict" technically gave them a handle on Qingfa, it could not very easily be portrayed as an act which pointed to a counterrevolutionary consciousness that warranted "struggles" against him. Qingfa's reputation, after all, was altogether different from the four-bad types. Because of their class origins, the latter were presumed to be opposed to the revolution from the core of their being. Any small missteps, any expressions of insolence could be taken as evidence of their hatred for all that Mao Zedong and the revolution stood for. But Qingfa not only possessed a poor peasant class status; he had been a long-time member of the village's Communist party branch and an effective village leader.

Qingfa's accusers therefore had to maneuver to raise his errors "to the level of principle and line"—to present charges that Qingfa purposely had undermined the revolution. As a prelude, it was necessary to cast doubt on Qingfa's poor peasant credentials.

He had been a destitute orphan for years before Liberation, so officially his poor peasant status was as valid as any of the other poor peasants of Chen Village. But his father and grandfather had, after all, been landlords. To discredit him, the special cases small group concocted a short jingle: "The nature of a fruit depends on its root; From his class roots you can tell the nature of a man." Ao recalls:

> We also dug up his old dirt. . . . He was called a "landlord's son" and we pointed out that the foul smell of his old class had come to the surface. That's why, before, he'd been so fierce toward the poor and lower-middle peasants. . . . He was a descendant of the exploiting class who hated socialism and who had tried [in the Cultural Revolution] to ruin the collective economy!

Though Longyong was the commanding figure of the campaign in Chen Village, he tried to stay in the background throughout these sessions. Since Qingfa had treated him shoddily four years earlier during the Small Four Cleanups, Longyong knew that if he were to assume any open role it would smack of personal vengeance. Thus it was Baldy who ran the show against Qingfa; and in keeping with Baldy's penchant for harshness, he put the former party secretary through a painful ordeal. Qingfa was not struggled against only once, but every two or three days for a couple of weeks. During these sessions he had to stand before his adversaries for several hours at a time, hunched forward defenselessly. After each session he would be dragged back to the cowshed, his face puffy from slaps.

To build public support and a sizable constituency for these attacks, Baldy had to rely on more than just the young activists in the militia. He sought out most of the brigade and team cadres, who still were sore at Qingfa's repeated stratagems to undermine brigade-level cooperation throughout the preceding year and a half. Once Baldy had enlisted the aid of some of these cadres, some of the ordinary peasants were happy to join in: "Their old bottled-up resentments against Qingfa . . . exploded in these slappings." But the majority of the Chens did not relish struggling against the old party secretary. They retained mixed feelings about him. Nonetheless they, too, passively joined the chorus with the attitude that "when a wall is falling anyway, everyone might as well push it." Even some of Qingfa's friends were organized to step forward to expose him. No matter what they may have thought of the proceedings, to refuse to take part would only focus attention upon themselves.

Qingfa accepted the accusations and the abuse with an outward show of submission. As one interviewee remarks: "People like him who'd gone through so many campaigns in the past—after all, he'd been in trouble in the Four Cleanups—knew what to do, how he should perform." He confessed to almost all the charges against him—he had done the evil things he had been accused of during the Four Cleanups, and he had established "illicit links" with his brother-in-law and other friends to reverse his verdict. He denied only the allegation that he had intended to escape to Hong Kong. He was adamant on this point—and for that he was pummeled and battered.

The commune level was supposed to make sure that Qingfa, as a prominent former cadre, was not simply being framed by village rivals. A commune official therefore sat in on some of the small groups' interrogations. But he lent his approval to their operations. The situation boded ill for Qingfa.

His illiteracy left him especially vulnerable to the efforts of the public security committee to submit a strong case against him to the higher levels of the party. The committee's final report included not only what others had said against him but also what he himself allegedly had admitted. The document was full of exaggerations and embellishments. But it was read out loud to him so rapidly that he had no time to grasp the implications of all of the wording; and he affixed his thumbprint in approval. Qingfa later confided to Stocky that he felt as if he had been "cheated into crimes."

Qingfa had far more to worry him than any of the three sent-down youths. He had a family of several small children who needed financial support. Making matters even more depressing for him, his wife, to protect the family, publicly repudiated him. One day when the militia escorted Qingfa from the cowshed to take a bath in the river, he passed by her, but she lowered her head and refused to greet him. Qingfa felt alone, abandoned, and scared. In the cowshed, he broke down a couple of times and cried.

Neither the confessions he had volunteered in the threatening climate of the struggle sessions nor the report written by the small group could be counted officially as conclusive evidence against him. For the judicial record, he was expected to write his own self-confession in the calm of the cowshed. Since he was illiterate, the three educated youths transcribed this for him. In detail, he went through his life history and all those incidents for which he had been charged, but in addition asked the youths to record precisely every occasion he could recollect when he had been arrogant, selfish, or bureaucratic. He carefully noted how he had looked down on the masses, how he had cheated them. He himself "raised all questions to the level of high political principles." In short, he made a skillfully self-effacing confession, entirely appropriate to someone who faced the risk of heavy punishment and who wanted to show to the authorities at higher levels a contrite willingness to turn over a new leaf.

As for whether he was truly repentant or not, Stocky Wang observes, "He was probably a bit regretful, but as a peasant, to the very end he'd say privately that it was due to fate, that his fate at birth had been no good. . . . He'd learned a lesson from all this, but at the same time he didn't really feel he was very much in the wrong."

Several of Qingfa's main supporters suffered for their allegiance to him. The young man who had burned Qingfa's Four Cleanups dossier was made to face a brigade-wide struggle meeting, and he, too, briefly occupied the cowshed. Other friends of Qingfa—his brother-in-law and the old team head of the No. 1 production team—were spared full-fledged struggle sessions, but were forced to dictate "self-examinations" and to face smaller-scale public criticisms in front of their own production teams. The No. 6 team, seeing the writing on the wall, drove the brother-in-law from his post as team head.

Persecuting the Unpopular

If the village cadres wanted to seem appropriately "red" in this campaign, they had to target far more people than the four-bad types, the three urban youths, Qingfa, and their closest cohorts. Altogether, these targets came to barely more than a dozen, nowhere near the 3 percent cited for model villages. Interspersed with the struggle sessions against the sent-down youths and Qingfa, therefore, the brigade had begun meeting almost nightly to target other campaign enemies. Like the religious Puritans of early America, Longyong, Ao, and the others had no qualms about witch-hunting. Since the campaign was supposed to entail class struggle, it had seemed logical to them to move on, in their self-righteous intolerance, to various social outcasts in the village whose class backgrounds seemed contaminated.

Before Liberation, when the Guomindang had formed "mutual responsibility groups" in each village to suppress Communism and ensure civil order, a security headman had been imposed over every hundred households. He had been held responsible for repressing anything illegal that occurred in his group. Since few peasants wanted the onerous task, the Guomindang sometimes had simply forced it upon some peasant. Recognizing this fact, the Communist party had not taken any reprisals against such men. But many peasants retained a lingering suspicion of them as tainted somehow by the hated policy they had enforced for the Guomindang. They were considered to have "complicated political histories" and "sullied class natures." Thus, one of them was pulled out now as an example of a degenerate character. In his own right, he was an offensive, terribly quarrelsome old codger who allegedly used to peek in on his daughter-in-law while she was taking a bath. It was relatively easy to mobilize the villagers against a licentious old troublemaker like him.

Indeed, since the campaign was supposed to be a "mass campaign," with the ordinary masses playing a major role in exposing the evils among them, free play was given now to such suspicions and prejudices. The Chen Villagers were practically invited to point the finger at those of their neighbors who were vulnerable and whom they liked the least.

In short order, more than half a dozen unpopular villagers who were kin to the four-bad types were attacked. At least half of these were argumentative widows: among them a middle-aged daughter of a landlord, whose rich peasant husband had hanged himself in the midst of the land reform. After his suicide, her personal financial affairs had been investigated, and she had been classified as a poor peasant in accordance with the letter of the law at that time. But many of the villagers thought she should have been classed a rich peasant. What made her truly vulnerable, though, was that her behavior persistently got on people's nerves. She was an arrogant woman, and those who disliked her felt that in view of her problematic class background, she should have been a little more humble in her relationships with "pure" poor and lower-middle peasants. Moreover, as a neighbor recalls, "Because she had money sent to her from relations in Hong Kong, she hadn't felt any need to go out to labor. Others envied her, that her life should be so good. And though she wasn't exactly acid-tongued, she was always around the village during the day, and gossiped too much. . . . Over the years, through that, she'd tread on a lot of people's toes."

Four adolescent girls had lived in her house since puberty. It was a tradition in many villages within the region for teenagers to sleep away from home in groups in what were called "youth houses."[2] Interviewees say that their family's homes otherwise would have been too cramped to allow their parents privacy in sexual relations. Girls usually slept in the households of widows, and boys set up sleeping quarters with their friends in abandoned houses or in makeshift dormitories, such as the one over the brigade militia headquarters.

The widow had taught sewing and other wifely arts to the four teenagers lodging with her. As was the custom, she had also related traditional stories about sex, from a motherly concern to provide "her" girls with a premarital education. Though parents half-expected a woman in her position to convey such information, during the Cleansing of the Class Ranks it was claimed that she had recounted salacious tales for the wrong reasons. Ao explains, in a voice still indignant:

[2] This old custom seems to be prevalent only in certain parts of Guangdong Province, mainly in the Pearl River Delta region. See William L. Parish and Martin K. Whyte, *Village and Family in Contemporary China* (Chicago: University of Chicago Press, 1978), pp. 231–232; and Robert Spencer and S. A. Barrett, "Notes on a Bachelor House in the South China Area," *American Anthropologist* 50 (1948): 463–478.

These girls were very young, only about 16. When the public security committee spoke with them, it was like a big
revelation to them. They didn't know how they could have
been so muddled before; didn't know how bad her class origins were; hadn't known what a bad thing it had been for
that old woman always to be filling their heads with these
old vulgar stories. . . . When it was explained to them how
class enemies corroded the thinking of young people, they
felt they had been corrupted.

The girls publicly spoke out against the widow and were duly
lionized by the brigade's broadcasting apparatus. The widow
moved into the cowshed.

The stress of being under attack unhinged another woman.
She was the widow of a "poor peasant bully" who had been in the
employ of both the Guomindang and landlords. The widow herself
had gained a reputation for being an ill-tempered shrew toward her
children and neighbors alike, and therefore the struggle sessions
against her were particularly vehement. Zhao recollects her behavior in the cowshed after she had been badly manhandled and frightened in one such session: "Her hair was all disheveled. . . . and she
began mumbling to herself. Her nerves were all muddled up and in
the end she couldn't control her bowels. . . . So that was it. She
was sent home and eight or ten weeks later she died."

She was the sole fatality of the campaign. But her incident
illustrates the campaign's brutality—and the rationality that imbued it. The old woman had become a target for attack because
(her personal quarrelsomeness aside) she had been wed years before to an "enemy of the masses." We asked Ao how it could be
fair to attack the wives of bad elements when their marriages had
been arranged by their parents, not of their own free will? But Ao
still justifies the attacks. She notes that the widow did, after all,
share in the loot her husband had brought home. She had benefited from his having been a "bully," she had never shown any
penitence, and so why shouldn't she now have to pay the penalty
for all those past sins? Besides, Ao pointedly added, whether the
woman had chosen her marriage herself or had had it thrust upon
her was an irrelevant issue: "Weren't landlords' children inferior
because they'd been born into bad-class households? Hadn't I
myself lost out because my father had a record?"

Ao's point was that every person inevitably is part of a family unit and *should* be identified as such. The other leaders of the Cleansing of the Class Ranks campaign in Chen Village undoubtedly believed the same. In traditional China, the government in extreme cases would hold an entire lineage to account for what one of its members did; and more recently the Guomindang on occasion had punished whole extended families for the transgressions of a single Communist member. The Chen Villagers were simply operating within this tradition of attributing shared responsibility for the crimes committed by one individual.

Guilt, in short, could be personal or merely by association. And even personal guilt did not necessitate an evil act. You could be guilty of holding to a wrong attitude or of inadvertently possessing a corrupting influence. A string of casual comments, when carefully analyzed by the public security committee, might reveal a hidden and dangerously discontented political mentality. Thus, even a "pure" poor peasant, to his own surprise one evening, was hoisted onto the struggle stage, since he had been heard to remark repeatedly over the years that he ate more eggs under the landlords than under the Chairman. The public security committee declared this a ludicrous and scurrilous falsehood that demonstrated a deep-seated enmity toward the new China.

This arbitrary targeting (even a pure poor peasant could be attacked) helped generate a gnawing climate of fear within the village. Some inadvertent mistake in either word or deed might land *anyone* on the stage in front of a hostile crowd. In a vicious circle, the fears deepened the villagers' mutual suspicions, encouraging further searches for evildoers beyond their own sphere of family and friends, further arbitrary outbursts of violence in the heat of the struggle sessions, and yet greater fear.

This climate of fear led to the revelation by the village's barefoot doctor of the one genuine criminal act uncovered during the campaign. This young barefoot doctor had been selected by Qingfa at the end of the Four Cleanups to receive his paramedical training. Shortly thereafter, he had been one of the few peasant youths who had associated with the rebellious Maoism Red Guards; and the year following, he had supported the aborted moves to "reverse the verdict" for Qingfa. Not surprisingly, Longyong urged that the public security committee interview him and check his medical account books for signs of petty larceny. The investigations were singularly unsuccessful, but when faced during his interrogation with the stock warning of "leniency to the frank, severity to those who resist," the young man panicked. He confessed that, about a year previously, he had sexually molested a twelve-year-old patient while she was under anesthesia. Not even the girl herself had been aware of the incident. In the struggle sessions that followed, the child rapist was punched and kicked by the enraged villagers more than anyone else who had had to "face the masses."

Narrowing the Circle

The struggle sessions had coincided with the two-month autumn slack season. The busy harvest season of November was now approaching. At one time or another during the previous two months, some twenty villagers had been forced into the cowshed.[3] Some had been struggled against once or twice and

[3] Interviews with people from other villages indicate that the ferocity and scope of the Cleansing of the Class Ranks varied considerably from place to place. According to an interviewee from the community next door to Chen Village, for instance, the campaign there was similar to Chen Village's: there were no sentdown youths in that village, but "several tens" of people with bad-class backgrounds or "muddied histories" were struggled against and imprisoned in a "cowshed." Yet an interviewee from another region of Guangdong reports that in her own relatively isolated mountain hamlet, the campaign had almost no impact. She never even attended a struggle session.

A former county-level official from a third district reports that there, the Cultural Revolution had not yet been resolved. During the latter half of 1968, the local militia units had been issued weapons to destroy the still-active rebel groups, and hundreds of the county's rebels were killed. Only when the province dispatched an army unit to seize control of the county in early 1969 was the Ranks campaign formally launched. During it, some of the four-bad types and their like were struggled against; but, more memorably, the army arrested the militia heads and the county and commune officials who had been responsible for the recent mass killings.

A 1974 manifesto by the Li Yizhe group of dissidents in Canton claimed that altogether in Guangdong province (population fifty million) almost 40,000 died and one million were struggled against during the Cleansing of the Class Ranks. If this unofficial reckoning by the Li Yizhe writing-group of former rebels is at all released after a few days; others, such as Qingfa, Deng, Stocky, and the barefoot doctor, had been made to endure multiple struggle meetings. By the latter part of October the cadres in charge, and even the nightly audiences, were physically and emotionally drained.

It was time to begin "narrowing the circle." The campaign leaders were supposed to focus on the most egregious cases, and the rest were to be released. Gradually the cowshed emptied. The four-bad types, with the exception of the obstinate ex-guerrilla, returned home. A week later, after six weeks in the cowshed, Zhao, too, was let go. The night of his release the brigade called a mass meeting.

> They told me to go out and confess. Actually I said the same things that I'd said before; but then out came Longyong, who said to the masses: "His explanation this time is better than his previous ones! Do you think he's being frank?" And the peasants, looking at Longyong's face and hearing what he said, knew his decision already. So they yelled: "Frank!" Then Longyong said: "Should we release him?" "Yes, release him!" With that I was released. . . . [Laughs] It was like directing people to act in a play.

The circle of those in the cowshed had narrowed down to five: the ex-guerrilla, the barefoot doctor, Stocky Wang, Overseas Deng, and Qingfa. Their offenses were considered too serious to be handled at the brigade level alone. The reports and other evidence detailing their crimes had been sent to the commune for review, and a directive had not yet come back. Their cases were left in limbo. While awaiting verdicts, they remained in captivity under a tight guard.

---

valid, then Chen Village's record (some twenty villagers struggled against and one fatality out of a population of a thousand) would have been about average for the province. (See Li Yizhe, "Socialist Democracy and the Legal System," *Chinese Law and Government* [Autumn 1977], p. 23 [in English].)

□ 6 □

A Leftward Lurch and a Solid Footing

Even while the struggle meetings were still in progress, a new drive was gathering steam in Chen Village. Throughout China, party directives had been calling for heightened adoration of Chairman Mao. The Chairman had destroyed the enemies of the revolution in the Cultural Revolution; he was China's savior; whatever he said or wanted was absolutely correct. The entire country was to pledge its allegiance to the "three loyalties"— loyalty to Mao, to Mao's thought, and to his revolutionary line. Once the late autumn busy season was over, Chen Village dutifully responded with a frenzy of devotion.

Celebrating the Three Loyalties

To show their loyalty, the Chen Villagers now marched with big wooden placards bearing Mao's portrait to their evening political meetings. There, before the session opened, they joined hands in a circle and clumsily danced Loyalty Dances—something like a Virginia Reel—to the tune of "Sailing the Seas Depends on the Helmsman, Making Revolution Depends on Mao Zedong's Thought." Dancing is not part of the southern Chinese culture, and many of the peasants, especially older ones, felt awkward and embarrassed to traipse around publicly like this.

Each peasant, whether literate or illiterate, brought along to all meetings a private copy of the Little Red Book and vigorously waved these on cue during all the speeches and discussions. At home, moreover, most families prominently displayed the four volumes of Mao's collected works. Some households even had multiple sets, since many team members now received free extra copies as awards for diligent labor. It did not matter that most of the owners of the books could not read. The sets were sacred ritual paraphernalia, the Word made tangible.

Before every meal, in imitation of the army (where the Mao rituals were reaching extraordinary proportions), Chen Village families began performing services to Mao. Led by the family head, they bowed to a portrait of Mao; intoned in unison a selection of Mao quotations; sang "The East Is Red"; and as they sat to eat, they recited a Maoist grace. The following was the most common in the village:

> We respectfully wish a long life to the reddest red sun in our hearts, the great leader Chairman Mao. And to Vice Chairman Lin Biao's health: may he forever be healthy. Having been liberated by the land reform we will never forget the Communist Party, and in revolution we will forever follow Chairman Mao!

Middle-aged former poor peasants tended to be the most fervent supporters of this Mao cult. "They'd suffered a lot in the past," Ao explains, "and they'd seen great improvements in their lives because of Mao. I myself [very actively] took part, but it was because I wanted to do everything the party told me." Most of the younger peasants, being more educated than their elders, found the rituals silly. But it was impolitic to say so. On the heels of the Cleansing of the Class Ranks campaign, there were very strong pressures to conform.

Understandably, in this climate of devotion and political anxiety, few objected publicly when the district[1] party headquarters sent down directives that the ritual displays of loyalty to Mao should be accompanied by radical shifts in economic policv Ao, who supported the new moves, explains: "The new cam-

---

[1] Fourteen counties make up the district (*zhuan qu*) that contains Chen Village.

paign wanted to raise people's thinking, that they should listen to Mao's thought and discard their private economic activities." Some of the cadres in Chen Village had misgivings about this. But in the immediate aftermath of the Cleansing of the Class Ranks, and in the very midst of the Mao cult, they, too, did not dare resist higher authority on a matter of ideology.

Fruit trees and stands of bamboo had been allotted to all the households during the land reform. Now the peasants were asked to donate all of these to the teams. There was no overt opposition, but on the evening of the announcement, families clambered up the hillsides to chop off the bamboo stalks that were good for weaving baskets. In the morning they had only bamboo stumps left to donate. The cadres picked out one of the landlords' sons who tried this. He was summarily consigned to the cowshed for a month for sabotage. Other villagers got the message.

In line with the suggestions of the higher party levels, the brigade next asked the peasants to give up their fishing nets. Many peasants supplemented their diets by fishing in the nearby river after work. They handed in the nets obediently, but many of them tried to retain the valuable lead weights. The brigade proclaimed that they were not being loyal. The weights were handed in.

As the campaign gathered momentum, the Chens were also granted the opportunity to give up their private plots. "The idea," one of the young people from Canton observes, "was that the existence of the private plots led us to be negligent about the team's production. . . . The cadres asked a couple of activists to show their dedication by giving up their plots: to be models for the others to follow. These particular fellows in our team wanted to show off their activism. Then anyone else who held back could be accused of being politically backward."

When the Chen Villagers all followed along, the village cadres also grabbed the opportunity, without any directives from higher levels, to prohibit all after-work grass cutting. The cadres had found it irritating that so many peasants had tried to conserve energy during work time in order to be able to chop grass vigorously after hours. Instead, grass cutting now would be conducted as one of the collective sideline enterprises of a production team.

The peasants next were invited to hand in their breeding sows to the teams. Chen Village had long specialized in raising piglets for sale to other villages. The village had a natural advantage. Mountain grass was readily available for cooking pig feed; and piglets required cooked food if they were to remain healthy. Delta villages short of fuel paid good money to buy the Chen peasants' half-grown piglets.[2] But without grass or private plots on which to grow the pig feed, the Chens had no option but to hand over their breeding sows.

They could see that in other villages, even in other counties, the peasants were being asked to make similar sacrifices against "selfishness." They told each other the new campaign was like bad weather; it could not be averted. They consoled themselves that at least everyone was in the same boat.

The villagers would later refer to this as the period of "eating ding dong rice." Without private endeavors to pursue, they could all quit their day's work together at the sound of a bell and go home immediately to eat. It was comfortable, but many of them were worried. Their private endeavors had given the families more than a quarter of their total income, and few believed that the collective sector would now be able to make that up by taking on the same enterprises. "Some peasants with lots of kids said that if their various sideline activities were restricted in this way," Ao remembers, "there was no realistic way for them to survive financially and raise their families."

Even more disconcerting to some of them, as the campaign reached its climax, land ownership and the accounting of wages were removed suddenly from the hands of the teams and given over to the brigade level. In one fell swoop, the teams disappeared. The peasants were to continue to labor under their team heads, but only as work squads subordinate to the brigade's commands.

Most of the brigade cadres were skeptical that this new arrangement would work out. But at the same time they were relieved that the various policies had been pushed through without too much difficulty. They had been under pressure from

---

[2] Eighty percent of the Chen households owned at least one sow, and each could produce three broods of piglets in two years. The sale of just one such brood—some ten half-grown piglets—provided a family with almost as much income as the husband could earn in half a year's work in the collective fields. The Chens jokingly referred to the sows as their "piggy banks."

above, and they felt trapped in a competition with other villages to prove Chen Village's activist superiority. Now Chen Village looked good. The cadres were able to report to higher levels that the brigade had "rid itself of selfish people." But as one villager recalls, "whatever the praise from the leaders above, the ordinary peasants were unhappy and felt it was a weird period of time."

Almost alone among the cadres, Longyong seemed genuinely happy about combining all the teams. According to Ao, "he liked new things and felt it was interesting, like it's interesting to move into a new house." But Longyong's vociferous support for the amalgamation of the teams quite obviously was grounded in more than just an uncommon penchant for change. He knew it would greatly increase his own authority and powers of initiative. He argued, moreover, that there would be economic and managerial advantages. With the brigade serving as the accounting unit now, and responsible for all wages, there no longer would be quarrels between different teams over such matters as whether proposed irrigation systems would be to their own teams' immediate benefit or not. As a slogan of the time put it, the brigade would become a "single beehive."

Ao and a few of the other urban Mao counselors supported any move that propelled the village closer to communism. But the peasants balked at the new measure. The richer teams in particular were disturbed. They felt it largely was through their own hard and efficient work that they had obtained higher living standards than the other teams. They resented suddenly having to put their fields and investment capital into a common pool.[3]

The poorest team had the most to gain economically from the amalgamations (a full day's work there had earned only some 60 percent of what the same labor earned in the richest team). But even it was unhappy with the new arrangements. As a junior

---

[3] Similar objections by prosperous teams in other parts of China are reported in Jack Chen: *A Year in Upper Felicity* (London: Harrup, 1973), p. 364; in *Philosophy Is No Mystery* (Beijing: Foreign Languages Press, 1972), p. 70; Heilongjiang Provincial Radio, in *Foreign Broadcast Information Service: China Daily Report* [U.S. Government] (November 2, 1971), pp. G1-4; and Victor Nee, "Post-Mao Changes in a South China Production Brigade," *Bulletin of Concerned Asian Scholars* 13, no. 2 (April 1981):32–33.

cadre from this team explains, "It wasn't so much a financial question; it's a personal thing, whether you want to have to work alongside and cooperate with certain other people. We'd had individual animosities and group disagreements with other teams." They did not want to abandon their own team loyalty; they did not want to be part of a larger group to which they did not feel any close personal identity.

There was no outright resistance, but the pace of work slowed. As Ao laments,

> Much less field work got done. No one felt they had responsibility for any particular fields in the brigade. A group would get out to the fields no earlier than their late-starting neighbors and would quit in the evening when they observed other groups were quitting. They saw that extra effort wouldn't be of any benefit to themselves. Where normally a group would have completed [a certain task in a given time], they now only finished a mere portion of it.

This same dispirited performance disrupted production in other villages, too. Within about a month, higher levels in the party were sounding a retreat in the face of this peasant disaffection, back to team ownership. The Mao worship and the coercive momentum of the Cleansing of Class Ranks campaign had been of little use when confronted with the peasantry's steadfast reluctance to abandon team ownership and private endeavors. The peasants won. Team ownership was restored. A couple of months afterward, in the final phase of the Cleansing of the Class Ranks campaign, the Chen Village peasants would receive back their private plots, pigs, and trees and resume all of their private sideline activities.

Several years later, party pronouncements retrospectively blamed Lin Biao for the various excesses of this aborted Three Loyalties campaign. Several interviewees think the accusation justified. The exaggerated displays of loyalty to Chairman Mao, the economic ultraleftism attached to that loyalty, and the phraseology employed throughout the Three Loyalties movement—all seemed to them to smack of Lin Biao. Ao, who had supported every measure in the campaign, now has her own interpretation of it: "This was all Lin Biao's line to make people hate Mao Zedong!"

Sentencing the Prisoners

For the five in the cowshed, life had settled down into a daily routine once the "struggles" had ceased and the Three Loyalties occupied center stage. Every morning they had to bow to a portrait of Mao and ritually "beg forgiveness three times." Then they were marched out to the fields under guard of the armed militia. During the first month, they had worked the entire day with placards clumsily hanging from their necks, inscribed variously with the slogans: "Diehard Supporter of Liu Shaoqi," "Cultural Revolution Black Hand," "Counterrevolutionary." (After the novelty of the placards wore off, they were removed.) No one passing by would speak to the five. They were given the heaviest and dirtiest tasks, the kind normally assigned to the four-bad types. At dusk they trooped back to the cowshed and incarceration.

They could look forward only to their three meals a day. Qingfa, the barefoot doctor, and the old guerrilla had these brought over by their families. (Qingfa's wife, to distance herself, never came in person; she sent the youngest daughter in her stead.) Since all of them received their normal grain rations, the two urban-born youths did not face any problems of hunger, but Stocky and Deng were expected to depend upon the generosity of friends for all nongrain foodstuffs. Not so long ago, however, these same friends had been forced to denounce them in struggle meetings, and they were not willing now to seem openly sympathetic to "cow ghosts and snake demons." None came forward to cook for them.

An old half-blind poor peasant widow whom Overseas Deng had helped out financially during his first years in the village eventually started bringing Deng meals on her own initiative. Her venerable age, unassailably pure class status, and fragile physical condition made her invulnerable to any charge of being too soft on a "cow ghost." Deng gave her enough money to buy meat for his dinner, and he ate well. Stocky Wang, in contrast, was hard up. He had to cook his own meals of plain rice, ironically in a real cowshed on the stove used for heating up cow feed. Occasionally he stole leaves of leftover cabbage from the drying ground to break the monotony of this diet. Several peasants once caught Wang at this, but they kindly looked the other way. At long last a second old poor peasant woman on welfare mustered the courage to feed him; and in later years Stocky repaid the kindness.

Though all of the other peasants continued to keep their distance, the animosity shown toward the prisoners receded noticeably once the initial feverish contagion of the "struggles" had abated. The detainees gradually became accustomed to their labor regimen: "once we let things go and felt 'do whatever you like with us,' we even had good appetites and gained weight; no worries, you see." Except perhaps for Qingfa. During these months in detention, his hair turned entirely grey.

As the Three Loyalties sputtered to a close, word on the disposition of their cases at long last came down from the commune. The masses, in a demonstration of China's mass-line policy, should advise on what punishments the prisoners deserved. In final public confessions, four of the five agreed to every one of the accusations against them. But Overseas Deng, while admitting his blasphemies, still denied adamantly the charges that he had listened to counterrevolutionary foreign broadcasts or had been a spy.

The public security committee rose to the occasion. It instructed the villagers that the sentencing should follow national "lenient-strict" guidelines, which stipulated short sentences for the repentant and long sentences for those who obstinately refused to show contrition. To demonstrate how to implement this policy, the brigade chose the barefoot doctor as a case that could be treated leniently, since he had come forward with his own astonishing confession of rape. Overseas Deng, on the other hand, provided the example of someone who clearly deserved to be dealt with strictly.

The two cases were brought up for discussion in each of the production teams. Once again a team member, Zhao participated in these deliberations. As best as he can recall, the Mao Thought counselor's short opening sermon went as follows:

> Deng's resistance to rehabilitation is obvious despite the lessons of the cowshed. He still doesn't admit his guilt. Even if he hasn't killed anybody, the things he said could have caused thousands of heads to fall! . . . Deng had made some of us think of reviving capitalism! Compared to him, the barefoot doctor's crime was trivial. He only endangered one person, not the whole society.

Deng deserved twenty years at hard labor. The child molester deserved two. The question was thrown open to the floor.

Some women objected:

> No, the worst thing in the world is this kind of rape. How could we let a sex monster go? He must have ten years! . . . Then see whether he dares to do it again! Setting such a bad example! But that Deng, he only really operated with his mouth. Two years. That'll give him a chance to understand things better!

Seeing this opposition, it was the job of the Mao Thought counselor to "guide the opinion of the masses" until the peasants arrived at a consensus similar to what had been predetermined by the brigade—two years for the barefoot doctor and twenty for Deng. In the end, the audience acquiesced, with one proviso. A peasant raised the question: "Isn't the heaviest sentence, except for the death penalty or life imprisonment, twenty years? So twenty years would be too much. Fifteen years sounds more appropriate." Others fell in with this compromise: "Well, perhaps you're right. Ah, yes, rebelling against the party, a counterrevolutionary, yes, maybe deserves fifteen years. Who told him to be against the party?" That was the consensus in most of the other team meetings.

It was agreed that both Qingfa and the ex-guerrilla deserved eight years and that Wang should be sentenced to five. Having "collected the opinions of the masses," the brigade transmitted these recommendations upward to the commune. The severity of these proposed sentences appears to have been the brigade leadership's way of making a final public issue of the prisoners' iniquities and the masses' wrath.

Luckily for Qingfa and the urban-born youths, however, the national and provincial press had begun to carry articles hinting that the Ranks campaign had caught far too many people in its net and had handled cases too severely.[4] Reading between the lines, it

---

[4] In January 1969, there had been a spate of such editorials in Canton's *Southern Daily*. Several of these quoted Chairman Mao himself: "The target of attack must be narrowed and more people must be helped through education. The stress must be on the weight of evidence and on investigation and study. It is strictly forbidden to extort confessions and then accept such confessions. As for good people who

seemed probable that the "crimes" of most of the people who were still under attack might not, in the final analysis, be deemed crimes.

Sure enough, within two weeks of the brigade's harsh sentencing, word came back from the commune that most of the crimes cited against the five were not, after all, proven criminal acts. In Deng's case, the only substantiated offense punishable under the Six Points was that slur about Lin Biao's treasonous face. The brigade should await further instructions. The five prisoners continued to mark time in the quiet of their daily labor routine.

Putting Policy on a Solid Footing

The political and economic extremism of the Cleansing of the Class Ranks and Three Loyalties had left peasants confused and emotionally exhausted. At the height of those campaigns, attendance at political meetings had been punctual (who, after all, would have dared to be a laggard?). But now villagers straggled in later and later. In the late winter of 1969, when Ao announced once in her broadcast that there would not be any meeting at all that evening, "People rushed out of their houses yelling, 'Hey, no meeting tonight, no meeting tonight!' " They wanted a rest and the peace and quiet of their own homes. Ao herself cut down on her broadcasting, being content to relay more music and news directly from Canton.

---

have made mistakes, we must help to educate them. When they are awakened, we must liberate them without delay."

An editorial of January 12 explained: "We must take into account both the mistakes and the past achievements . . . of good people who have made mistakes, . . . and must not confine our judgment to a short period or a single incident in a cadre's life. We should consider his life and work as a whole. We must not lay siege to the weak point, still less attack one point to the neglect of others or elevate problems limitlessly to the plane of class struggle."

By these criteria, Qingfa and the two urban-born youths might be viewed by higher authorities as victims of the Ranks' excesses (see the U.S. government translation series, *Survey of the Chinese Mainland Press* [*Supplement*], no. 242, for the *Southern Daily* editorials of January 4, 7, and 12, 1969).

Whereas most villagers were anxious simply to have life return to normal, the brigade leaders were worried about what might occur in the final phase of the Cleansing of the Class Ranks. It had begun to appear, as it had at the end of the Four Cleanups struggles, that policies would be "put on a solid footing." Might the village leadership then be blamed for having targeted people who had only made minor mistakes and for having extorted overblown confessions from them (much as the Four Cleanups workteams had come under official attack during the Cultural Revolution)?

When the higher-level cadres made their first moves in 1969, the fears of the village cadres grew. Around the beginning of March, a workteam of three party cadres entered Chen Village. But it departed in disarray before it had time even to call a general meeting. Perhaps the higher authorities were uncertain about how to conclude the campaign, or perhaps there was infighting among the higher-ups—which meant anything could happen. Within a couple of weeks, sure enough, a new workteam of a half-dozen retired army men arrived, and they were from a unit that had leaned toward the rebels in the Cultural Revolution. They declined even to respond to the greetings of the brigade cadres. Within two days of its arrival, this new workteam was applying pressure on individual cadres, in a very mild version of the tactics used by the village's special cases small group during the Cleansing of the Class Ranks. Ao was informed that she had been wrong to cooperate in encouraging exaggerated attacks against the urban-born youths and Qingfa, and she was urged to make a public statement that the person ultimately responsible for these mistakes was Longyong.

> I was overawed by such workteams: felt they must be sent by Chairman Mao. I didn't know what was going on. So I made a self-confession, and declared, too, that Longyong had been too extreme and so had harmed the morale of the masses. Longyong was furious. . . . He said I just went with the wind, that when there were advantages to working with him I went all out; but then when there weren't advantages I went against him. . . . Perhaps I shouldn't have said that *he* had overdone things, only that *I* had overdone things.

After only one week in Chen Village, to the complete mystification of Ao, Longyong, and the villagers, this new workteam abruptly packed up and left, never to be seen again. Regional politics seemed totally in flux. The confusion of the peasantry and the edginess of the cadres deepened.

In early May of 1969 a third workteam consisting of only two cadres walked into the village and without much fanfare announced that it had come to bring the Cleansing of the Class Ranks to a close. And in a gesture reassuring to the leadership, the two men chose to live in the houses of activists whom the cadres reported to be reliable.

This two-man workteam called for a mass meeting to explain its program. The meeting was scheduled to begin at 9:00 A.M., but it was not until 11:00 A.M. that most of the villagers had finally drifted into the village hall. Good friends sat together to share snacks. Many tried to sit as far toward the rear as possible, so as to slip away at the earliest opportunity.

When the workteam's spokesman finally rose to speak, however, it was not in the bombastic manner adopted by so many other workteam cadres, but in reassuring, soft-spoken tones. The workteam's tasks, he began, were multiple. He and his comrade were going to reexamine the Cleansing of the Class Ranks to see if the "contradictions" that had consigned the five targets to the cowshed were, in Mao's terminology, "antagonistic contradictions between the enemy and ourselves" or merely "nonantagonistic contradictions among the people." The workteam would also "investigate and rectify" the local party branch, but would do so fairly and reasonably and would correct, without retribution, any lapses of discipline that might be uncovered. It would help the local party absorb new young members and, to symbolize a new beginning for the village, would oversee new elections for the brigade management committee (henceforth to be called a Revolutionary Committee). To the astonishment of his listeners, he said all this in only about ten minutes. Impressed most of all by his brevity, peasants commented to each other, "This guy has some ability."

The workteam took pains to start its inquiries, politely and cordially, with the village leaders. In interviewing disgruntled villagers, including those still in the cowshed, the workteam projected an equally sympathetic attitude. The prisoners were asked if everything in their dossiers was accurate; and then the workteam reassured Qingfa and the two urban-born youths that their cases were just a matter of "good people making mistakes"—nonantagonistic contradictions.

Release and Repentance

Within days, the county sentenced the barefoot doctor to two years in a labor reform camp, and one by one the remaining four prisoners were set free. Qingfa was the first, and his final confession at a mass meeting was an emotionally moving, virtuoso performance. As Ao recalls, "He said that when he'd fallen in the Four Cleanups he'd been very discontented and had wanted to harm other people, so that he would have a chance to 'ascend the political stage' again. He expressed his ashamed apologies to the poor and lower-middle peasants, to the Communist party and to Chairman Mao." In a voice close to tears, he recounted that the most painful lesson had been his wife's refusal even to look at him. It had jarred him into realizing the full extent of his errors. Before the assembled crowd, Qingfa broke down and wept.

The workteam applauded this emotional display of repentance. It decreed that Qingfa should be released to "labor under the masses' surveillance." That is, he was under a kind of probation: the poor and lower-middle peasants were to watch to see if he worked hard and observed Mao Zedong's teachings. If he continued to improve, he would be restored to the full status of a poor and lower-middle peasant.

Over the next few weeks, the workteam took pains to emphasize that class struggle was by no means being abandoned. But without skipping an ideological beat, it proclaimed that to safeguard the power held in the hands of the proletariat, the truly vital task was to increase agricultural production. And to emphasize that struggle targets no longer were to be sought at the village level, the workteam had a straw effigy of Liu Shaoqi constructed and asked villagers to curse and beat the image of this "number one capitalist roader," as if by so doing they could repudiate all that Liu supposedly stood for. Qingfa took an especially spirited part, angrily flailing Liu's effigy for having led him astray.

In the weeks following, Qingfa was unfailingly energetic in

laboring, cordial to the team and brigade cadres, and always one of the first to rush forward during political sessions to shout out appropriate slogans. In the eyes of the workteam, many of the villagers, and the commune authorities, he seemed a paragon of good-spirited repentance.

He was made an official model. There were a lot of other cadres in the county who had gotten into political trouble during the Four Cleanups, the Cultural Revolution, or the Cleansing of the Class Ranks. Many remained bitter and, unlike Qingfa, were reluctant to cooperate with their former persecutors. Qingfa was led on a tour of all the villages in the commune to "influence and enlighten" such cadres by the testimony of his redemption. He provided the example of how they could rectify their own situations. It was even arranged that he proclaim repentance before a mass meeting at the commune center and before another at the county capital, weeping profusely each time. His histrionic displays paid off. When the party authorities reviewed his party membership, he was not expelled but kept on probation, with every prospect that his contrition might eventually earn him again a full membership in good standing.

About two weeks after Qingfa's release, after some ten months of detention, Stocky Wang and Overseas Deng were put through a public confessional, were released, and placed under "surveillance by the masses." They were even given retroactive workpoints for all the time they had spent in the cowshed. But people initially did not dare to associate with them—so long as they were on probation. They were freed but not yet entirely free.

They had a major cause for worry, moreover. The evidence and confessions contained in their dossiers could always be used to target them anew in some future campaign. However, the leadership in Peking realized this, and it soon reacted to prevent the millions who had been targeted from becoming a huge semipermanent group ever fearful of attack and ever resentful of the government. Instructions came down that all materials collected during the Cleansing of the Class Ranks campaign be totally burned in public bonfires.

Longyong, moreover, was called in privately and reprimanded by the workteam head for his lack of moderation, his inflexibility, and his "warlord workstyle." Few things remained secret for long in Chen Village, and the story of these criticisms made the rounds. Longyong understood that gestures of reconciliation and compromise were needed. As a start, when the brigade received an invitation that year to send a young person to the county capital for technical training, Longyong chose Overseas Deng; and to the bemusement of the villagers, he subsequently installed Deng as his technical aide. If Longyong had to show flexibility and conciliation, he was determined to do so with a flourish.

Stocky Wang found it much more difficult to adjust than had his cellmates. For a year and more after his release, he felt edgy and morose:

> I felt my aspirations had been dashed, and I wanted to withdraw into oblivion. . . . At first, because I'd been imprisoned, there was discrimination against me. . . . But even later, perhaps through frustration, I felt very unsociable. I didn't like to associate much with the other sent-down youths.

It was a mood, as we shall later see, that would place Stocky in trouble yet again.

Qingfa's Return

The commune administration kept a close eye on village affairs and gradually paved the way, that following year, for Qingfa and his friends to become involved once more in village affairs. The commune party secretary who had fallen in the Cultural Revolution had returned to his post; and he passed the word to the village's Communist Youth League secretary, who was mildly friendly with Qingfa, that Qingfa would even be allowed to become a village cadre again.

Thus, less than a year after his emergence from the cowshed, through a show of hands by the village's party members, Qingfa's probationary status in the party was lifted. Shortly afterward, the thirty-odd party members were asked to hold a secret ballot to choose a new party branch committee. Many of the older party members—and not just those who had been aided economically or politically by Qingfa in the past—threw their support to him for one of the seven committee seats. He was one of their own, after all, an "old comrade" who had joined the party with them in the fifties. "These were the party members," remarks Ao, "who earlier in their lives had been activists, but younger men had taken their places. . . . They were people who outside of their party memberships had little prestige in the village." Some of them might have been put off by Qingfa's antics in the Cultural Revolution, but Qingfa's repeated downfalls and harsh punishment had won their subsequent sympathy. Ao says:

> The party members who voted for Qingfa felt his mistakes during the Cultural Revolution mainly had been due to his conflict with Longyong. They felt that, to the extent that he was wrong in his behavior, it wasn't really a question of having the wrong class stand [and that it shouldn't have been put into that context]. These old cadres and party members had themselves made mistakes of one sort or another in the past. They felt a leader *always* makes some mistakes; and they knew the taste of being hurt for these. And they knew, too, that Chen Village doesn't have enough cadres of Qingfa's abilities.

They had been alarmed during the Cleansing of the Class Ranks by Longyong's display of vindictiveness and his thirst to hold untrammeled authority in the village. They wanted someone like Qingfa back in a position to balance off Longyong's power. By a narrow majority, Qingfa won a place on the party branch committee.

While Qingfa was climbing back into the village political elite, Baldy was being pushed down. In 1970 the commune authorities conducted an investigation into Baldy's conduct during the Cleansing of the Class Ranks and had him publicly criticized for his excesses—a surrogate, perhaps, for Longyong himself. Soon thereafter, Qingfa was offered a seat on the Revolutionary Committee, and not long afterward was selected to be that year's public security director, replacing Baldy. His vindication was complete.[5]

[5.] Qingfa's wife, incidentally, was accepted into the Communist party at this time, making Qingfa's household one of the very few in which husband and wife were both party members.

Before the leadership struggles of the past half decade could be brought to a close, however, one last act was required—a formal reconciliation between Longyong and Qingfa. In the middle of 1970, soon after Qingfa had assumed his seat on the Revolutionary Committee and in the midst of a nationwide slogan campaign to "unite together to achieve even greater victories," Qingfa and Longyong ascended the village stage at an assembly of all the village. For the occasion, a huge Chinese flag and a vast picture of Chairman Mao draped the stage backdrop. As the centerpiece of the ceremony, Qingfa admitted to Longyong that during the Small Four Cleanups he had gotten Longyong unfairly; for that, he was sorry. Longyong, for his own part, would not deign to admit that he had been exacting vengeance during the Cleansing of the Class Ranks; but he did confess that after the Small Four Cleanups, he had felt like getting a cleaver and chopping Qingfa. The two rivals shook hands and pledged to work together to serve the poor and lower-middle peasants in revolutionary comradeship. Many in the audience were amused by the tableau: Qingfa trying to appear at once high-minded and affable; Longyong aiming to look magnanimous, but seeming decidedly uncomfortable and reluctant in the pose. No matter how uneasily, however, both men would have to learn to coexist.

· 7 ·

The Great Betrothal Dispute

It had been half a decade since the young people from Canton had first come to the village. These had been years of unremitting political tumult. Now, with the end of the Cleansing of the Class Ranks campaign, a period of fewer local upheavals lay on the horizon. But there still was one more major political crisis to come, less than a year after the Cleansing of the Class Ranks. It arose from a bitter dispute over a broken promise of marriage. The difficulties the young Chen men customarily faced trying to acquire wives lay behind this new village crisis.

The Marriage Revolution

Chinese peasants have always considered it extremely important to have sons and grandsons to carry on the family line. To fail in this would have been unconscionably unfilial to their ancestors. Having daughters was of only secondary importance. "A daughter once married," as the saying went, "belongs to someone else." Parents no longer had any claims to a married daughter's labor power or income, and the children she bore would carry on the line of her husband's family, not that of her parents.

The preference for sons was so great that in traditional times, during hard spells, poor families had fed their sons better than

*Family Portrait. In order to have a second son (the baby),
these parents ignored the government's birth-control
campaign of the late 1970s.*

their daughters—and when the situation became desperate, had
sometimes even purposely let the new-born girls die. This poor
peasant strategy apparently persisted even into the 1950s;[1] and
thus well into the 1970s, there was a slight but perceptible imbalance between the numbers of young men and young women in

[1] A 1956 survey of a village in the Yangtze River valley provides a dramatic
illustration of this. The ratio there between the numbers of males and females

the area around Chen Village. The search for brides was accordingly a matter of considerable anxiety.

Like elsewhere in China, in Chen Village it was taboo for a Chen to marry a Chen, no matter how distantly related they might be. Marriage within the lineage was considered tantamount to incest.[2] Thus all daughters had to marry out, and all incoming brides had to be sought from other lineage villages. In the old days this had been of some benefit to each village. The incest taboo and the resulting circulation of women between villages had assured that each lineage community possessed protective marriage alliances with other communities. After the Liberation, traditional marriage customs persevered; and while other villages in the district took all the Chen daughters in marriage, many of the Chens could not find brides for their own sons in return.

This was partly because Chen Village, though not a poor village by national standards, was poorer than most of the neighboring communities. The Chens found it hard to compete against richer households that could afford to pay higher bride prices.[3]

Ironically, Chen Village's problems had been compounded by the land reform. An elderly woman from the village relates that before the land reform almost all the Chens had found wives. After all, even the rich nearby delta villages had contained tenant

---

under the age of five was an astonishing 1.88 (113 male children to 60 female children). Interestingly, this statistical imbalance is more severe than the results of a 1935 survey of the very same village, when the ratio of male to female children had been 1.36. (See William Geddes, *Peasant Life in Communist China,* Society for Applied Anthropology, Monograph No. 6 [Ithaca, N.Y., 1963], p. 16; also Fei Hsiao-t'ung, *Peasant Life in China* [London: Routledge and Kegan Paul, 1939], p. 22.)

[2] Before the revolution, in fact, the Chen lineage laws had stipulated that intercourse with a fellow Chen was to be punished by complete confiscation of properties and belongings and expulsion from the lineage and village.

[3] Before the Liberation, the dowry that accompanied the bride to her new home usually had counterbalanced the bride price paid for her. But after the Liberation, as young women began doing full-time field labor, their economic value increased. The bride price in most parts of Guangdong Province correspondingly rose, and the dowry all but disappeared. (On this, see William L. Parish and Martin K. Whyte, *Village and Family in Contemporary China* [Chicago: University of Chicago Press, 1978], pp. 180-191.)

families as poor or poorer than many of the Chens.[4] But the land reform and the collectivization campaigns had erased the terrible disparities among the households within these wealthier villages and had lifted the living standards of the formerly poor families there above those of Chen Village. Consequently, when the young people from Canton first arrived in Chen Village in 1964, they found that some 20 or 30 Chen men over the age of thirty were still bachelors, with few hopes of ever marrying.

Not only did such men feel anxious that they would die without a son; more pressing, they faced the prospect of a bleak old age. Though production teams were obliged by law to provide food, shelter, clothing, and a coffin for any needy childless elderly, the amount was a pittance, providing only for the barest subsistence. Other team members looked down upon such welfare recipients as a drain on the production team's resources. To grow old without a son's financial support was a humiliating and frightening prospect.

The pressures to obtain wives, and through them sons, readied many Chen Villagers for a marriage revolution—defiance of the taboo against intralineage marriage. A dozen village men had already paved the way during the momentary millenarian fervor of the Great Leap Forward of 1958. Most of them were young cadres and party or League members. With traditional customs everywhere being overturned, they had calculated that the local social sanctions against lineage "incest" could be ignored; and with free food canteens in the Great Leap Forward temporar-

---

[4.] The old woman says, in part: "[Before the revolution] many of Chen Village's brides, including myself, came from the two Li lineage villages [two of the richer villages in the neighborhood]. . . . Generally people got married to their own kind. You know the old saying: 'Bamboo doors to bamboo doors, wooden doors to wooden doors.' . . . Of course, a family couldn't *really* know the wealth of the groom's family. After all, it was all arranged through a matchmaker, who might well lie and often did. It was possible to go visit, of course, but it was easy for the other village to [conspire and] show your family the wrong house and wrong possessions. So unless you had a relative in the other village there was no way to tell. Yes, just about all the men in Chen Village found brides. Even the poor ones did: the poor married the poor. If really poor, you'd marry a wealthy family's slave-girl."

ily leveling the living standards of households, the poverty of their families was no longer a hindrance to finding a wife. A few of these marriages had been love matches between young activists. Others were arranged with parents of young women who saw personal advantages in their daughter's marriage to a rising village cadre. When wealth could no longer be a major criterion in the choice of marriage partners, the man's local political power became an attractive quality.

But when the Great Leap Forward collapsed, traditional beliefs and mores had again predominated, and marriages within the lineage were again shunned. Though the peasants were able to use their sweet potatoes for a few months to acquire wives from other villages still suffering from famine, thereafter the Chens became increasingly hard pressed to pay enough to get brides.

As one of its programs for social change, the Four Cleanups workteam criticized the renewed taboos against intralineage marriages; and by the tail end of the Four Cleanups some of the Chens were responding positively. Their anxiety about finding brides for their sons had overcome their qualms about intralineage "incest." By 1966, some parents with sons of marriageable age were even suggesting that it might be a mark of village patriotism for young women to stay and marry within the community. These families managed to recruit the officers of the village Women's Association to make the rounds of the village to persuade mothers that their daughters "should not evade their duty to build up Chen Village." The Women's Association pointed out that the village would soon be able to provide a comfortable livelihood for the young women. Why should a mother who cared for her daughter prefer to send her off to an alien village and into a household of complete strangers?

The parents who gave in to such arguments soon discovered an additional advantage. A married daughter who lived just down the lane provided parents with one more household to turn to in addition to their married son's. Occasionally she would kill one of her chickens and invite them over to eat; and if her mother were ill, a married daughter would hurry over to help out. To be sure, parents still depended financially on their sons in old age, and they still felt that married sons stayed in the family and that married daughters were lost to someone else's. But within just a few years, as it became evident that having a daughter close at hand promised an extra measure of security for old age, marriage within Chen Village became the *preferred* match, involving some 70-80 percent of the total.[5]

The families of the young men also preferred such matches, because they could pay lower bride prices for local brides. Bride prices in China had always signified a complete transfer to the man's family of control over the bride and her labor.[6] Now that marriage no longer meant so complete a financial loss for the girl's household, the groom's family could bargain reasonably for a lower bride price. For their own part, the bride's parents found it inexpedient to insist upon a high price that might make it embarrassing later to expect aid from their daughter. Before the shift to intravillage betrothals, the bride price had been a thousand *yuan* and up; within just a couple of years, the payments had plummeted to a modest 100-300 *yuan*.

---

[5] This revolution in marriage patterns has been widespread but in no way universal in Guangdong Province. A survey in the mid-1970s of fifty-one villages scattered throughout the province found that only 45 percent of the surveyed villages had abandoned the traditional prohibitions against lineage endogamy (Parish and Whyte, *Village and Family in Contemporary China*, p. 169).

Chen Village had to continue to import some brides partly because there were slightly more men of marriage age than women; but it was also partly because some of the young women in the village continued to marry out into other villages. They did so either to live more comfortably in a more prosperous village or, if of bad-class background, to escape the stigma attached to their family origins.

The men who still looked outside Chen Village for brides generally were those who, due to physical, economic, class, or social drawbacks, had lost out in the local competition for marriage partners. In the early 1970s a few of them married women from Hakka communities on the far side of the county, well beyond the normal distance at which Chen Village previously drew brides. The Hakka are a Chinese ethnic group that inhabits some of the province's poorest hill country, and they and the Cantonese speakers were traditionally hostile. But once these initial marriage links were made, the new Hakka wives began to serve as matchmakers for their friends in the back country, and a steady trickle of such marriages was negotiated. At the very same time that Chen Village turned inward for marriages, thus, it also was reaching out further geographically and socially, abandoning ethnic prejudice in search of brides.

[6] On this, see Parish and Whyte, *Village and Family in Contemporary China*, pp. 180-192.

Romance versus Pragmatism

In the past, young people had had little say in the choice of their marriage partners. Marriages were almost exclusively arranged by parents through matchmakers. Now, however, the possibility of marrying a fellow villager encouraged young people to initiate the engagements themselves. There was as yet nothing resembling casual dating,[7] but a boy and girl[8] who got to know one another through daily contact might feel mutually attracted. After appropriate consultations with his parents, the boy would work through third parties to approach the girl he admired for a "date." (A young Chen man who married a woman from his own production team observes, if "a third party is used and she turns you down, it's not so embarrassing that way.") If a girl accepted the intermediary's request, she was committing herself to a formal courtship. The boy would start to go regularly to the girl's house to spend awkward evenings chaperoned by her mother. (In return visits to the boy's house, *his* mother would shoo the rest of the family out of the house, anxious that the girl should relax in her son's company and help push matters toward wedding negotiations between the two families.) Each successive move in this courtship would come under the interested and often intense scrutiny of the whole neighborhood. "It's no casual thing," says one villager:

> If people see a young man taking a girl on his bicycle to the commune town to see a play, they'll certainly tease him: "Where were you going last night? When are you going to have us over to eat wedding cakes?" [But if the rear of the bike were empty] everyone in the village will be talking about it: "When Chaolou went to the movies today, I didn't see him carrying Meiling on the back of his bike. At New Years we didn't see him bring goodies to her house!" People do an awful lot of talking about this kind of thing!

[7.] In this respect, Chen Village still was old-fashioned compared to the village next door. A former team head from this neighboring village relates that informal dating was becoming commonplace there.

[8.] Young people through their twenties, until they marry, are referred to in Chen Village as girls and boys.

Intrigued though they might be, most of the villagers were not sentimental about these affairs. They considered a betrothal very much of a practical matter aimed at creating a new and economically viable household. Thus some of the young men of a less romantic bent even preferred to dispense with all the troublesome embarrassment and palpitations of a direct courtship, and instead would leave it to their parents to handle the negotiations through a matchmaker. Usually this would be an older woman with experience in such affairs, who would be paid for her services through periodic gifts of food over the years to come. It was the matchmaker's duty to formally approach the girl's parents and to present the boy and his family to them in the best possible light.

Even when the two youths were edging toward a "love match," they almost always secured their parents' permission before proceeding. The common opinion was that life in the countryside was still too hard to let one's heart rule one's head. Though they might flush secretly with excitement in each other's presence, they would still want to calculate carefully the pragmatic advantages and disadvantages of a lifetime commitment; and parents had the greater experience in such appraisals. For the boy, especially, the parents' consent was almost always necessary, since they controlled the purse strings for the wedding expenses.

The young man and his family would carefully evaluate a prospective wife's personal capabilities: was she in good health and a strong and willing worker who would be an economic asset to the household? Did she have a mild personality, unlikely to argue with his parents or draw her husband into disputes with neighbors? Moreover, was her family well respected? And did she have brothers who could support her parents in old age, or was she an only child on whom her elderly parents would necessarily depend?

For their part, the young woman and her parents would judge the qualities of the young man's family every bit as carefully as they appraised the young man himself. They would be concerned, above all, that his family be of good class origins. For with class labels inherited entirely through the male line, the children she would later bear would automatically carry the all-important stigma or protective aura of the husband's class label. The young woman and her parents also would appraise the economic circumstances of his family. Did they have substantial savings to draw upon? Were the parents still comparatively strong and healthy? Could they be expected to earn their own incomes for a long time before retirement, or would they soon be a drain upon the young couple's finances? Were there too many younger sons in his family still needing to be married (a financially ruinous burden for any family)?

The net result of both sides' careful calculations was that young people with the most desirable mix of attributes almost invariably paired off, be it through a matchmaker or a direct love match; and someone with personal or family weaknesses became engaged to a person with an equivalent mix of weaknesses.

As a rule, peasants wanted to marry as early as possible. They realized that if they married late, the man's laboring ability might begin to decline with age before his children were old enough to work. If so, the family would be in a squeeze that spelled poverty. Many of the poorest families in the village were the consequences of late marriages: an exhausted middle-aged couple, young mouths to feed, and elderly chronically ill grandparents to support. The safest insurance against such a future was for a man to marry in his early twenties and hope for quick pregnancies. A young woman's parents, for this same reason, were extremely reluctant to let their daughter marry a man over thirty. As in the past, any bachelor beyond that age held few hopes of ever getting a wife.

To marry off a son, though, a family had to spend a great deal of money, which took years to raise. They not only had to pay a bride price and provide for a wedding feast, but also had to build a house in advance for the newlyweds. The cost of the building materials alone could easily amount to 1000-2000 *yuan*, many years' worth of savings. Having a well-built separate home for the young couple had become crucial; many of the young women in Chen Village no longer would consent to a marriage without one. They did not want to have to live in the same tiny house as their mother-in-law.

Much of the cash needed for the new house and other marriage expenses was raised by concentrating extra energy on the family's private enterprises: rearing pigs and poultry, cutting and selling grass-fuel, and cultivating cash crops of vegetables on the family's small private plots and on thin strips of laboriously cleared wasteland. Sometimes this money was accumulated partly at the expense of the daughter. Her marriage frequently had to be deferred so that she could contribute a few more years of labor and income toward her brother's marriage. Only when the wedding of her brother was impending would she herself be married off, so that the 100-300 *yuan* brideprice received for her could be added to the family's store of savings.

Thus, whereas the urge has been to marry young, the need to accumulate funds often has caused both men and women to marry at an age well beyond what they would have preferred. As of the mid 1970s the average age of a Chen Village groom was about 24 and that of a bride about 20 or 21.

As a precautionary measure, the family of a young man would try to commit the girl's family to a marriage engagement far in advance. To be further on the safe side, the boy and his parents would seek to place the fiancée's household in their moral debt during this period of engagement. He and his family had good reasons to fear seeing the engagement break off. It might take months or years to find and court another fiancée, all the while that the son drew dangerously close to thirty. Thus as one villager observes,

> A boy's family will give a whole lot of things to the girl's family. They'll send over chickens and ducks and geese at New Years. When slaughtering a pig, they send over pork, not only during festivals but even in ordinary times. Sometimes they'll actually *buy* a goose to send over. . . . So there's pressure on the girl's family. If a girl changes her mind and doesn't want to go get married into the boy's family, there'll be a lot of pressure on her to go. It would bring up a lot of quarreling. Sometimes the girl's family, to preserve its reputation, will try to settle up accounts by giving a sum of money to the prospective groom's family. But the family of the boy may well protest: who asked you to give this to me [to buy your way out of the engagement]? Sometimes there are quarrels so big that the brigade public security committee has to intervene.

In former decades, when marriage engagements were betrayed, the two families had been near-strangers living miles apart

in separate communities. There need never be any contact between them again. But now that the wounded party lived practically next door—often in the same production team[9]—the setting
was rife for ongoing feuds. That is precisely what transpired in
1969, when the passions aroused by a broken promise of marriage
became intertwined with the tensions created by the amalgamation of two production teams. The antagonists were the two team
heads. By the time their feuding had abated, the team's agricultural production had been devastated—and the brigade leaders had
been presented with a serious political dilemma.

Setting the Stage: Amalgamating Production Teams

The collapse of the Three Loyalties campaign in early 1969
had paved the way for a restructuring of Chen Village's teams. In
the very midst of the Three Loyalties debacle, the commune level
had decreed that there should now be five teams, not the ten that
had existed since 1962. Each of the teams that had been split in
two in 1962 were to be rejoined. Most of the peasantry did not
particularly mind. As one of the Canton youths recalls, "When all
the ten teams suddenly had been combined into one [in the Three
Loyalties campaign], there'd been such dissatisfaction and confusion [that] when they redivided into five, people were glad, feeling it was a far better state of affairs than brigade ownership."
    Many peasants recognized, too, that the difficulties over
water distribution and land boundaries, which had been most det-
rimental to production, were due precisely to the earlier splitting

---

[9] Once the young people began playing a stronger role in the marriage decisions, engagements between members of the same team became increasingly common; young men and women were becoming attracted to one another while at
work together in the fields. A fair number of the marriages have even been between members of the same lineage branch. Many villagers still considered it
unseemly to marry within the "fifth mourning degree" (that is, to marry someone
paternally related within the great-great-grandfather's generation); yet even here
the barriers were falling. Several marriage engagements in the mid to late 1970s
came within this tabooed circle—and drew murmurs of disapproval from several
of the peasants who had emigrated recently to Hong Kong.

of these teams—for almost everywhere their fields had been divided down the middle in 1962. Many of the team cadres saw also that a remerger would eliminate the need to buy duplicate sets of certain farm machinery. With the village intent on modernizing its agriculture, the new team amalgamations patently made sense.

But two of the teams—No. 7 and No. 8, two comparatively prosperous teams—initially resisted the demands to unite. The No. 7 team distributed slightly higher incomes to its members than the No. 8 team, and its team head cited this as a reason to remain separate. But the reluctance of both teams went beyond economic rationales. As Ao explains,

> After the original team had been broken into two in the early sixties, all sorts of arguments had emerged, because the new teams were both strong teams and thus had felt competitive. Having quarreled so much in the past, they didn't want to combine. So to push them together, we had them condemn Liu Shaoqi—"it was Liu Shaoqi who had wanted us to split up!" [Ao laughs at the cleverness of the ruse.] Who would then dare to say that they didn't favor reuniting the teams?

But this shotgun wedding of No. 7 and No. 8 made for an unstable marriage. It would take only a spark to set the members at odds.

A Tale of Two Team Heads

The two protagonists in the feud which shortly erupted—the former No. 7 and No. 8 team heads—were both men of considerable ability and experience. They had each been team heads ever since their teams had been founded. For them to cooperate in the new larger team would have been difficult under any circumstances.

Of the two, the abler leader was probably Chen Lousun, the head of the former No. 7 team. He was a meticulous planner, supremely good at allocating labor, and adept at pacing and motivating the work crews under him; he had a feel for when to call rest breaks and when to push hard. Lousun's major flaw was that he took offense easily. He had been known to exact petty vengeance long after the fact by assigning onerous work to teammates who crossed him. But he was intrinsically a fair man and had made a conscious effort to curb these streaks in his character. By the time the teams were amalgamated in 1969, he had largely succeeded.

Lousun had risen out of exceptional poverty. His parents had died penniless and landless while Lousun was a child, and of all his many brothers and sisters, only he had survived to adulthood. He had wandered from village to village as a temporary farm hand until the Liberation of 1949. Granted land and a house in the land reform, he was a respected cadre in the co-ops by the mid-fifties. But he had had no chance to amass the savings to marry, and he had been convinced he would die a bachelor.

Already in his early thirties when the Great Leap Forward arrived, Lousun had been one of those willing to break the lineage's marriage taboos. His bride was a high-strung slovenly woman of middle peasant descent. No one else would have considered her a good catch; but Lousun forever after looked upon her consent to the match as a miracle. An orphan, he saw in his wife the family he needed, and despite her many faults he never slackened in his gratitude. He helped her with the housework and cooked the dinners, tasks other husbands almost entirely shunned. His obvious affection extended even to her kin, and especially to her younger brother, Heizhai, whom he showered with kindnesses as if the young man were his son. "Lousun felt the party had given him everything he wanted," observes a friend: "A position, a wife, a family."

But Lousun was not blessed with the one thing he most desperately wanted. Though his wife provided him with seven children and six survived, all of them were daughters. Neighbors joked with him, "Later on there'll be crowds of matchmakers pouring through your door"; but that was scant consolation.

Baby girls were more welcome and better treated than in previous decades. Young couples who would have wanted to give birth only to sons in earlier times now hoped for two or more sons and at least one girl as the best prescription for a secure old age. But six daughters and no son? Lousun entirely ignored the government's call for birth control; and no one in Chen Village ever criticized him for it. "He's suffered enough already," explains one person.

In his mid-forties by 1970, with a house overflowing with young children, Lousun could not feed his family as well as he would have liked. To his embarrassment, he had to go into debt to the production team every year by requesting more grain than his earnings could cover. (As with other families in this fix, these debts to the team would be deducted from the wages of Lousun's family when his daughters became old enough to begin earning incomes in the team.) His economic plight had taught Lousun to be careful with every penny. He even was reluctant to pay the modest tuition (4 *yuan* per year plus book fees) for his daughters to go to school; they were not, after all, sons. When Chen Village's primary school teachers came on visits, he insisted that the girls were needed at home to help with the housework. The teachers had to prod him for a full year before he relented and let his elder daughters attend.

Lousun's surfeit of daughters and lack of an heir were not his only worries. He was the victim of his wife's insufferable public behavior. She was irascible and lazy and engaged persistently in petty theft. In 1964, she had stolen large bundles of team-owned sugarcane, was caught, and had been fined several hundred *yuan,* to the horror of her husband. She was compulsive; she not only continued to pilfer public property, but worse yet, she made off with neighbors' chickens. She came to work late, crept away early, and malingered in between—yet had the temerity to argue incessantly for higher workpoints. Her misconduct caused her husband perpetual headaches. Team members who wanted to disobey his orders could conveniently use the excuse that he was not willing or able to control his own wife.

Lousun had been invited more than once to join the party. He was a man of ambition and would have liked to. But each time he declined. Were he a party member, he and his family would be expected to adhere to rigorous standards of behavior; he would be all the more vulnerable to his teammates' criticism.

Lousun's new rival, the former No. 8 team head, had earned the nickname of Old Tireless through a lifetime of incessant hard-driving work. His ability to labor so hard, even in his fifties, was his greatest pride. He relished being called Old Tireless. But some of his teammates employed the nickname half mockingly. They were annoyed by his prickly obstinacy, his disregard for others' fatigue, and his long-windedness. "He pushed people too hard when they labored, without any letup," remembers a former team member. Another says, "he treated people like machines." When he held team meetings, they went on for two or three hours or more, as if he were intent on testing people's team loyalty by administering an endurance test. But his teammates had reelected him every year because he was a skilled planner. "His team's production was well handled; perhaps not so good as Lousun's team, but very good nonetheless."

New Team Four and Lilou's Schemes

When teams No. 7 and No. 8 were forcibly combined into the new No. 4 team in early 1969, the question arose as to which of the two men should lead the new team. Ao remembers, "Since each of the two teams still wanted to be separate, each said that its own team head was the better leader." To allow the former team heads to share power and thereby appease the team members, Longyong jerry-built a new organizational structure for the teams. As a party member, Old Tireless was named Team Head in Charge of Politics; and Lousun, as arguably the better agricultural planner, became Team Head in Charge of Production. Old Tireless's pride was preserved through the announcement that, since ideology took precedence over economic management, the title of Political Head would rank higher than that of Production Head.

But the new setup did not work. Neither of the men was willing to take a back seat on production decisions. "Previously," Ao observes, "if one of them had said something it was done. But now, whatever they did, they had to discuss it; and the two of them were unhappy about this. . . . Lousun would say Old Tireless was indecisive; Old Tireless thought Lousun was stubborn. . . . Lousun would push his arguments and Old Tireless would lose his temper." The two men tried hard initially to work harmoniously for the sake of keeping production moving smoothly. For half a year they seemed to be succeeding. But then the fragile relationship was shattered by their fight over a prospective bride.

Old Tireless had only one son, and the boy was a worry to him. Already in his mid-twenties, the son was lazy and always complaining of aches and pains: the very antithesis of his father. Old Tireless's anxiety over the marriage potential of such a son, alongside Lousun's fatherly concern for his young brother-in-law Heizhai, supplied dry tinder for the betrothal feud that was about to rock Chen Village.

The match that sparked the conflagration was provided by the younger daughter of an impoverished widow in Old Tireless's team. She was considered an attractive girl: not so much in her physical appearance (photographs show a pudgy face), but in her vivacity and—most attractive of all—her abilities at labor. She had already earned a bit of notoriety as a flirt by smiling invitingly at would-be suitors—only to reject the formal approaches of their matchmakers. Her mother was intent upon cementing a strategic and materially advantageous match with a cadre's family; and thus in 1968, when Old Tireless's son fell in love with the girl and Old Tireless asked a matchmaker to approach the widow, she quickly gave her assent. But within months, both mother and daughter had second thoughts. The boy's family was fine, but the boy himself would not be a good breadwinner once Old Tireless retired. Old Tireless took it badly when the widow and daughter announced they were terminating the engagement. Remembers a team member: "Having only this one son, Old Tireless didn't want to lose this chance, so he went himself to talk with the girl several times. But she wouldn't pay any attention to him. . . . So Old Tireless developed a real hatred for the girl's family."

Only several months afterward, teams No. 7 and No. 8 were joined. Lilou, the ambitious, frustrated, bright woman whose affair with Shorty had been farcically cut short in that "denunciation meeting," now got into the act. Lilou was the widow's sister-in-law, and in this capacity she approached the widow with some friendly advice: Lousun's brother-in-law Heizhai would be an apt match for her daughter. Lousun, after all, was now an important cadre in the widow's own production team; Lousun doted on Heizhai and would feel obligated to the widow if her daughter married Heizhai; and besides, Heizhai himself had admirable qualities. He was a Communist Youth League member, with good prospects for entering the party. He had served as the No. 7

team's warehouseman and had now become the warehouseman for the new unified team, a strategic post. He was strong, bright and, as an extra bonus, even handsome. And having painted the potential match in brilliant colors, Lilou hastened to offer herself as the matchmaker.

Chen Villagers were quick to see Lilou's own gains in the match. She, too, was a member of the new No. 4 team, and her role as matchmaker would put Lousun in her debt. "Lousun's special responsibility was to take care of the allocation of labor, . . . and Lilou hoped that if she developed this very special relationship with Lousun she'd be able to get lighter work to do in the team."

Lilou had not calculated on Old Tireless's feelings, however. Old Tireless furiously concluded that the new tie between the girl's household and Lousun added public insult to personal injury. It was an affront to his dignity. He saw no reason to maintain any further the two leaders' delicate efforts to cooperate. He began openly to argue against all of Lousun's opinions at team committee meetings, and several times he blurted out allusions to the continued pilferings of Lousun's wife. It was obvious to everyone in the team that one or the other of the two leaders would have to resign eventually—whichever of them could not muster a sufficient contingent of supporters.

Lilou knew that her own standing in the team would be jeopardized if Old Tireless triumphed in such a showdown. She began working behind the scenes to pull together a solid bloc of support for Lousun. But few of the various members of the former No. 7 team whom she approached wanted to seem too closely identified with either side in the feud for fear of needlessly antagonizing neighbors and cadres.

Lilou had to turn instead to a network of in-laws, both her own and those of her sister-in-law, the widow. There was, for example, the husband of the widow's eldest daughter, who could be counted on to carry his brother's family into the alliance. Lilou's own daughter Pumi had recently been selected to head the village Women's Association, and despite her personal qualms she, too, let herself be drawn in on her relatives' side. Pumi in turn was affianced to a high school graduate from the same team (one of the only graduates in the village, in fact). He had overcome the encumbrance of a middle peasant label and had risen first to a low-level brigade post and then was accepted by the PLA. While he served out his term of duty, Pumi and her mother Lilou had cultivated close relations with his family.[10] As prospective in-laws, this household too could be counted on.

Such alliance-building on the basis of in-law ties might seem "traditional" to us; but to the Chen Villagers it was unprecedented. In former decades, when intralineage marriage had been taboo, Lilou's daughter Pumi would have married into another village. She would not have been a village cadre to whom her mother could turn, nor would she have been a link to other families. Nor would the widow have had a son-in-law in her own team to turn to. Nor, indeed, would Lilou herself have had any cause to become involved in a marriage feud, for until recently, matchmakers had not had to maneuver between families from the same village. Nor would Lousun have had a young brother-in-law close at hand to worry about; nor Old Tireless a family in his own village whom he could accuse of welching on an engagement. All this was new; and all these new kinship configurations and linkages had inserted into the politics of production teams an increasingly disruptive potential for factionalism.

Outspoken support for Lousun came perhaps most noticeably of all from the wife of Lousun's cousin, likewise a member of the team. Like Lilou, she was a bright, ambitious, frustrated woman who was fervently activist. But she was so loudmouthed that everyone called her the Gong. The Gong had long been a headache to Lousun, for she customarily became entangled in squabbles with one or another member of the team. "She'd pick

[10] This family was an unusual ménage à trois. Before Liberation the mother had convinced the father to buy a second wife to help her with the housework. In accordance with a government policy allowing concubines taken before 1949 to remain in that state if they wished, this bigamous relationship was never challenged by the local Communist authorities. The two women live in adjoining houses and still share the old man between them. Whether this triangular arrangement is rife with tensions or free of them remains a mystery even to neighbors, since both wives loyally insist upon a solid family front toward the world outside. The engagement of Pumi to the elder wife's only son placed Pumi inside the sacred circle of their family, and for this reason alone they were willing to throw caution to the wind in support of her mother Lilou.

on people's mistakes and weaknesses and aim her invective directly at them," recalls a teammate. "People who hated the Gong said that Lousun hadn't tried hard to keep her under control." Lousun had always replied that there was little he could do and would refer to the saying, "It's harder to change a person's character than to move a mountain." But team members had blamed him for partiality and weakness.

When the feud first flared between Old Tireless and Lousun, many of the villagers initially had felt that Lousun, as the better agricultural planner, would be able to ease his rival aside. The majority of the peasants in the team could be expected to throw their support to him in future team elections, since their incomes depended upon good production planning. But as the maneuvering in the feud dragged on, Lousun was increasingly hurt by his identification with "those awful women relatives." Lilou and the Gong were too vociferous in his behalf, too prone to intrigue, too quick to inflate the widening dissension in the team. They turned a couple of initially neutral team cadres against them—and against Lousun.

Old Tireless also gained the support of the poor peasant representative from the No. 7 team. This man's relations with Lousun had always been shaky since he had been awarded the poor peasant post for criticizing Lousun in the Four Cleanups. Another supporter of Old Tireless was Meiyan, the former wife of Lilou's adulterous lover Shorty. A bemused neighbor remembers, "Meiyan said that Lilou had cheated her by getting on so well with Shorty—so Meiyan certainly wanted to go over to the other side." For his part, Shorty was the former No. 8 team's poor peasant representative and had led the Four Cleanups criticisms of Old Tireless. But he went over openly to Lousun's side only after Meiyan took up Old Tireless' cause. As a team member observes, once the team heads' feud had started, "different people joined different sides on the basis of their own personal antagonistic relations."

But both sides hesitated to initiate any hostile actions against the other. Each group knew that more than half the team's membership was steadfastly neutral, was opposed to any infighting, and would look askance at the side that seemed too openly belligerent. Both camps knew also that any charges or countercharges directly concerning the issue of marriage engagements would leave them open to charges from the brigade that they were being "ideologically backward." And the factions were too evenly divided, finally, for either to be certain of winning. Both sides were aware, comments Ao, "that if you're going to have a huge argument, you'd better be well prepared for it. If not, you'd get wiped out in the whirlwinds."

The conflict between the two factions thus did not come to a head until a routine check of the team's granary raised the suspicion that small quantities of rice were missing. Two brothers in the team, both party members, mentioned that on a recent night they had come upon Lousun's young brother-in-law Heizhai carrying a grain sack toward the widow's house. Since Heizhai was the team's warehouseman and had charge over the stored rice, rumormongers were quick to fit together the bits and pieces of circumstantial evidence into a whispered indictment. He was siphoning off rice to the widow, the gossips claimed, in order to improve the "material basis" of his marriage engagement.

But Old Tireless and his allies initially refrained from publicly raising ugly questions. They had no confidence that they could ever make any formal charges stick. Then unexpectedly, Four-Eyes Wu, a youth from Canton who was the team's newly appointed Mao Thought counselor, made the allegations in their behalf. A friend remembers, "Wu figured Heizhai *must* have stolen this grain, since Heizhai's sister [Lousun's wife] was always stealing." Wu considered it his duty as a counselor to uphold socialist morality and the collective's interests; and "since Four-Eyes Wu was from the city, he was good at public speaking. He knew how to use Mao quotes to good effect." The other urban-born youths were aghast at Wu's impolitic intervention, but Wu would not listen. "He was very stupid," comments one of the sent-down youths from the team. "We other sent-down youths were smart. We didn't get involved in such local struggles. . . . We'd all told him, 'It doesn't matter what faction wins out—it won't be good for you.' We all knew this very well. . . . But he was too subjective, too stubborn, and wanted too much to occupy the limelight."

Old Tireless's backers were quick to chorus Wu's charges. Once their accusations started flying, the supporters of the two factions no longer found it necessary to speak civilly to teammates from the opposing camp. Cadres began giving better job assignments to fellow faction members and worse assignments to those who joined the opposite side. The team leadership no longer could coordinate the work. People started coming to work later and leaving earlier. Yields began noticeably to decline. The team's wage payments at the end of the season were down by a quarter; the grain allotment to each household fell 20 percent. The upcoming spring planting for 1971 threatened to be undermined very seriously by the growing confusion and dissension, and further declines in the team's wage payments seemed imminent. Something had to be done.

Longyong Intervenes

Since the mid-sixties, the brigade leaders had been using the No. 7 and No. 8 teams as Chen Village's "model" teams. When a new program such as the Dazhai wage system was introduced, the brigade leadership had come first to these two teams to initiate the innovation. "The other teams would then feel under pressure to fall into line; they wouldn't be able to say 'Sorry, it can't be done.' " The two teams had been adopted as "models" because their productivity had been high, their leaders particularly capable, and their relations with brigade cadres particularly close. Whereas most teams contained only a couple of party members, these two boasted some five party members each. Several of the brigade's leading cadres, including Longyong, came from these two teams. The troubles in the new No. 4 team were particularly worrisome to them.

Longyong had intervened very rarely in the internal affairs of the No. 7 and No. 8 teams. He had learned from Qingfa's problems; it was best not to provide any reason at all for other teams to feel that he held undue influence over or showed favoritism toward his own neighborhood. But he could no longer stand aloof from the team's affairs. "If this model now fell apart," observes Ao, "it would have greatly influenced the whole brigade's [administration]; so the brigade *had* to put pressure on the team to resolve its problems."

Longyong in late 1970 was faced also by a separate dilemma. Nationwide, another struggle campaign had been launched, called the One Hit, Three Anti campaign. Initially an urban effort to stanch bureaucratic corruption and the grass roots factionalism that had carried over from the Cultural Revolution, the campaign had swept outward into the countryside. County and commune authorities were frightened of appearing lax in the struggle against "class enemies" and therefore were particularly anxious to "score some achievements" by pressuring the levels below. Chen Village would not have to make more than a token showing this time, since Longyong and his cohorts had been overeager to jail people in the recent Cleansing of the Class Ranks campaign. But the brigade would have to come up with at least one struggle target; it was an administrative imperative. Chen Village's former Communist Youth League secretary matter-of-factly remarks that "during every struggle campaign *someone* must be gotten. Even if there aren't enough materials on any one person, someone has to be found. True or false, materials have to be dug out."[11]

Longyong saw a way both to meet the One Hit campaign's demands and to frighten the No. 4 team members back into orderly cooperation. The brigade would "kill a chicken to scare the monkeys." It would target for struggle a vulnerable partisan in the feuding. But who should the object lesson be? The bad-class peasants, normally the most handy targets in a team, had all stayed prudently and scrupulously on the sidelines. Surveying the field, Longyong decided that Four-Eyes Wu best fit the bill.

Wu was particularly suitable on several counts. He was deeply embroiled in the dispute, yet was not a respected and valuable cadre like Lousun or Old Tireless. He was an outsider in the village, without protective kin networks. Nor did he have the protection of a "proletarian" class origin. Moreover, he had run off to Canton in the Cultural Revolution and had said and done imprudent things there. He was, in short, eminently gettable. But Longyong decided the brigade leadership should let Wu himself provide extra hanging rope. "Just allow him to continue messing

[11.] A ludicrously contrived frameup in a different peasant village during the One Hit Three Anti campaign is described in Amnesty International, *Political Imprisonment in the People's Republic of China* (London, 1978), pp. 12–13 and pp. 158–162.

around for a bit longer," Longyong reportedly told some fellow cadres. "The more he messes around now, the better." Meanwhile the brigade officers quietly went to work collecting new "materials" against Wu and lining up witnesses.

When all was prepared, several public security committee members, accompanied by a contingent of the armed militia, arrested Wu early one evening at his home. The brigade leaders had calculated that this dramatic show of force—with Wu marched under guard through the busy neighborhood—would present a clear message to Wu's teammates: renewed discipline was expected in the team or else the campaign might embroil them, too.

At the struggle sessions, in the words of a spectator,

> Wu was accused of "setting fires to see them burn"—causing trouble just for the hell of it. By setting the two factions at each others' throats, they charged, he'd harmed the revolution in Chen Village and damaged production. But if these were the only charges against Wu, they couldn't bring him out as a target for a trial by mass struggle. So they brought in things from his past.

Wu had been a member of the small group of initial Red Guards and had helped lead the other young people back to Canton in the Cultural Revolution. In Canton, he had seen a lot of Zhao and Stocky Wang. He was guilty of many of the "crimes" that Zhao and Wang had been accused of in the Cleansing of the Class Ranks campaign. But Wu had been able to escape the fate of his two friends by hiding out with relatives in his ancestral village until the storm of the Ranks campaign had blown over.

When Zhao and Wang had been interrogated by Ao in the Cleansing of the Class Ranks, the pair of them, under pressure, had implicated Wu for having referred to Chairman Mao as Old Fatso and to Lin Biao as a crafty fox. Longyong hoped now to make use of these old charges. But the records of the interrogations had been destroyed at the end of the Ranks campaign. To officially lay these charges of political subversion against Wu would require a fresh outpouring of revelations from Wu's friends.

The most suitable public witness would be Stocky Wang. Stocky was Four-Eyes Wu's best friend. When Stocky had been let out of the cowshed and had had nowhere to turn—initially a political pariah—Wu had risked his own political security by sharing his food and lodgings with Stocky. Now, precisely because they were well known to be best friends, concerted pressure was put on Stocky. The brigade public security committee came to him with the information that in other districts some of the sent-down youths who had been punished during the Class Ranks campaign were being retried and put back in jail. The hint was obvious. Stocky was disturbed and frightened.

Then one evening Longyong and Jinyi knocked on his door. They had come to ask for his "cooperation." "In the end," says Stocky, "there was no way out. I had to struggle against Wu."

It was prearranged that at a struggle meeting attended by all the brigade, each of Wu's intimate friends would be summoned to denounce Wu and reveal his "crimes." This was an acknowledged ritual of any struggle campaign. But on stage, friends could be expected to denounce loudly and passionately only those incidents that were already known to the authorities. That day, though pressed for fresh tidbits of information, Wu's friends played their role properly. One after another they recounted only the old charges.

Then Stocky was called to the front; and out of momentary weakness and fright he made a short, impassioned speech that went considerably beyond the bounds of what even he originally had intended to say. "Wu's grandfather was a landlord," Stocky yelled, "and because he was nurtured by a landlord, Wu voluntarily has stood on the side of the reactionary forces." His listeners— the brigade cadres included—were stunned. The angle about Wu's grandfather had never been pushed by the cadres directing the campaign—and it placed the charges against Wu in a rather more serious light. Ao, who was working with the public security committee in prosecuting the mass trial, recalls the general reaction:

> When Stocky was in the cowshed a lot of people had had a real respect for him. . . . Especially the sent-down youths respected him. They hated us and respected him. In order to uphold the interests of all the sent-down youths, they felt, he'd led them to the city to rebel . . . and had paid a heavy price for them in the Cleansing of the Class Ranks. . . . But after this One Hit Three Anti incident . . . they all felt he had forfeited his claim to anyone's trust. . . .

> People like myself—we could be forgiven. Our position was different. We had been thoroughly educated in party ideology. We didn't understand other people's suffering; couldn't sympathize with others' situations. We were on top. . . . But they couldn't forgive *him*. . . . They felt Stocky had no sense of righteousness. If you had been the victim of a campaign, they felt, you should know how much suffering it entails, and you should have the decency not to bring suffering on a friend.

The sent-down youths were disturbed also by the implications of Stocky's accusations. Almost all of them could count landlords or other "bad-class elements" among one or more of their grandparents or great grandparents. Stocky's rhetoric had appealed to a logic and an emotion that could damage all of them as a group. One of them notes,

> By adding in the problems of Wu's family background, Stocky was stirring up [the idea that] the peasants should—in the words of Chairman Mao—control the "bourgeois" intellectuals. Our lives were already difficult enough. We felt, are you still going to bring up things like this that will exploit and oppress us? Would you do that to your own people? Some of the peasants felt this way, too—not so much the peasants with the best class origins, but those with middling origins.

Stocky was again a social pariah. "It was too late to undo the damage," he says. "I was terribly unhappy. They all said I'd sold out my friends." Two years later, unwilling to remain an outcast, Stocky slipped out of the village and made the long swim to Hong Kong. He brought his troubled memories with him. He once confided to one of us that when unable to fall asleep at night, his thoughts sometimes turn back to that terrible scene when he had betrayed his friend Wu.

The Storm Subsides

When the public struggles against Wu ended, Wu had been confined to the cowshed to await the end of the One Hit campaign. In due time, higher party levels would have to decide whether or not he should be sent off to prison for his slurs against the chairman and vice chairman.

Wu could have taken no consolation in the fact, but the brigade's scheme had worked. As the "chicken," he had paid a very high price so that the production team's "monkeys" would be alarmed by the trial and cease their squabblings. The two team heads shifted back momentarily into an uneasy truce, and the spring planting was completed in time.

The tensions within the team remained unresolved, however. The showdown, everyone agreed, had simply been postponed. But then, unexpectedly, the immediate catalyst for the feud evaporated. Lousun's wife, capricious as ever, got caught up in a furious argument with the widow over workpoint appraisals; and in a huff the widow called off the engagement. The widow apparently had been waiting for precisely such an excuse. The match with young Heizhai had been creating only headaches for her and her family.

At almost the same time as the dissolution of Heizhai's engagement, Old Tireless's son acquired a bride from a neighboring commune. The young woman later explained to one of our interviewees that she had agreed to the marriage when assured that the family had close relatives in Hong Kong who were willing to send back any consumer items that she might desire. Within a year of the wedding, the couple proudly produced a son.

Old Tireless no longer had any personal reason for retaining a grudge against Lousun's family, and so he amiably set about burying the charges that he himself had helped circulate against Heizhai. He now agreed wholeheartedly that there had been no hard proof in the first place that any grain was missing from the warehouse. He and his friends held no objections whatsoever when Heizhai was nominated for, and accepted into, the Communist party.

Nevertheless, the tussle for leadership between Old Tireless and Lousun had not been put entirely to rest. Most of the cadres on the team committee quietly still followed Old Tireless's lead. In frustration, Lousun finally decided to quit; but the brigade leadership dissuaded him from stepping down until a way could be arranged for him to resign with honor. In 1972, the proper moment came. The brigade's enlarged brick factory needed a new full-time manager, and Lousun was elevated to the post. "As you can see, the brigade takes good care of its veteran cadres," Ao comments. "Lousun was very happy to be out of the production team."

The great betrothal feud of team No. 4 had had a series of happy endings. Ultimately the only villagers who were badly hurt by the whole affair were the two sent-down youths: Four-Eyes Wu, who had stumbled naively and stubbornly into the center of the maelstrom, and Stocky, for his moment of weakness.

· 8 ·

Plunging into a
New Decade

The New Economic Era

The brick factory that Lousun took over was relatively new. Before 1968, Chen Village only had had several comparatively small brick kilns, a small crude sugar refining plant, and a few small rice milling machines. The villagers had had to pay a high price elsewhere for most of the bricks they needed—if and when there were bricks for sale. They had had to spend precious time and labor hauling grain to the market town to be husked. When agricultural productivity doubled during the Cultural Revolution, the brigade leadership understandably had laid plans to use some of the new income to build processing plants.

The first major project was the new and larger brickworks. A brickworks was a natural kind of industry for Chen Village. The clay along the river was of excellent quality, and the heavy shrubs and grasses that blanketed the surrounding mountains could provide a cheap fuel. But the brigade administration did not have any capital of its own and did not have the right to commandeer that of the production teams. In 1968, therefore, Longyong called the heads of all the teams together to negotiate the terms of the project. Since it looked like a promising financial venture, every team head agreed to participate. Each team would put up an equal share of the capital and provide free laborers to build the plant. Though the brigade administration would own and manage the brickworks, each team would receive modest dividends from the expected profits. Each of the teams also would be able to select an equal number of team members to go work in the factory. It was understood, in addition, that the larger share of the proceeds, which the brigade kept for itself, would relieve the teams from having to fund all of the brigade's services in future years.

Opening in 1969, the brickworks was an immediate financial success. Other brigades were starting up small factories and were in the market to buy all the building materials they could find. So the Chen Village brickworks progressively added new kilns, branched out into making roof tiles, and soon employed more than thirty full-time workers.

Other brigade enterprises sprang up out of the profits. A two-story building was constructed to house electrically powered rice-milling machinery. A plant for processing peanut oil was built. The facilities for refining sugar were greatly expanded.

The road between the village and the commune market town had been improved by the early 1970s to the point where it had become readily passable by truck. Taking advantage of this, Chen Village turned next to supplying urban industry with semiprocessed agricultural products. In 1971 the brigade erected an annex to the sugar refinery to extract industrial alcohol from the sugar residue and, that same year, built a small factory to grind wood-yams into a powder to be sold as industrial starch.

The village also had plowed some of its agricultural profits back into mechanization, beginning in 1967 with a midget 17-horsepower tractor. Again, though the brigade was to manage it, all of the teams had chipped in to pay for it. The tractor was supposed to plow more deeply and aerate the soil more thoroughly than an ox-drawn plow. But it broke down repeatedly when pitted against the winter-hardened soil. The brigade, exasperated, soon hooked it to a cart and used it instead to haul bricks and grain. To take its place, the brigade managed to buy a 40-horsepower East Is Red brand tractor in 1973 after four long years on a waiting list. But the new larger tractor soon proved only marginally more sturdy than its predecessor, and major spare parts were hard to come by; so it too was consigned largely to transport duties. Nonetheless, the peasants were pleased with the vehicles. They considered it money well spent to be even partially relieved of the bone-jarring chore of carrying huge loads by shoulder pole.

Every step in the village's development spawned a need for yet further innovations and investments. In 1972, in order to service all the new equipment—the tractors, water pumps, factory machinery, threshers, and carts—the brigade had to set up a repair shop. It soon had eight employees, and it added an electric saw to cut boards from the brigade-owned timber stands.

Most of the new factory workshops stood at the village entrance, and it was a source of village pride that visitors coming in on the new road noticed first the village's industrial development. The villagers were proud, too, of the new skyline of "western style" houses that stood directly behind the small factories. Taking advantage of the locally produced building materials and their own rising incomes, families were scrambling to build such houses for their sons and prospective brides wherever bits of space were made available on the village's outskirts. Although to a Western eye these narrow two-story boxes of brick might seem drably unattractive, the villagers considered them a vast improvement over their old, bleak, peak-roofed dwellings. The new structures had genuine glass windows, upstairs bedrooms (affording an unprecedented privacy to husband and wife), and flat roofs where grain and vegetables could be dried and where families could sleep comfortably out-of-doors on hot summer nights. By the mid-seventies, almost a quarter of the buildings in the village were of this new type.

Even the majority who still lived in the old near-windowless adobe housing were enjoying more comfortable living conditions. With enough grain and root crops available for animal feed, it no longer paid to let sows and poultry use up energy and scatter precious manure rooting in the lanes. New brick pens had been built behind each house to keep them from running loose, and they no longer were allowed to bed down in the front parlor. With the animals penned outside, and with cement replacing all the earth flooring, the peasants began to make vigorous efforts to keep their homes, belongings, and selves clean. Soap no longer was a luxury, and most of the Chens soon adopted the habit of daily baths. Villagers who had grown up infested with lice now

*Drying Grain.   Grandmothers normally remain behind in
the village during the day to mind the children and attend to
household chores.*

also washed their clothes regularly, with water carried in from
four deep tube wells operated by electric pumps. No longer did
they drink and wash in the polluted water of shallow wells.

From the profits of agriculture, a new two-story health clinic
was built in 1970, complete with living quarters for the two barefoot doctors and a small central courtyard where Chinese medicinal herbs were cultivated. The new medical care—and, even more
important, the improved diets, sanitation, and personal hygiene—
led to a sharp decline in sickness, a noticeably longer life expec-
tancy, and a dramatic drop in the infant mortality rate. Indeed, to
the near-incredulity of the old people, during the first half of the
seventies not a single baby died in Chen Village. (Miscarriages,
however, remained frequent, since women engaged in strenuous
work even when well advanced in pregnancy.)

Until 1966 the village had had only a three-room school-
house, and the forty-odd pupils who went beyond the third grade
had had to walk a mile to a school in the richer village next door.

As its prosperity grew, Chen Village expanded its own schooling year by year. By 1970, the village school boasted ten teachers and three hundred pupils in seven grades of classes (five of primary school, with a two-year junior high school section attached). Some 80 to 90 percent of all the school-aged children were behind desks.

To cap it all off, Longyong insisted in 1972-73 upon employing the brigade's new-found prosperity to erect an ambitious monument to the glory of Chen Village—a meeting hall grander and larger than any other in the district. In traditional times a community had proclaimed its prestige and wealth through a massive ancestral hall. Now, with an unlimited access to bricks and roof tiles, Chen Village would boast an even more impressive modern edifice. As one of the Chens relates,

> Our hall's exactly like a movie theatre, three stories high, and can seat the whole village. The main hall has a great arched roof at least fifty feet across, with giant hanging lanterns, and a copper-looking arch over the front doors. Really impressive! Behind, there's a make-up room and even a place for visiting actors to spend the night; and there's a brigade conference room upstairs. In the countryside such a hall is really something. People came from all over the district just to see it.

The village's economic advances also brought a new taste for consumer goods. In 1964, Chen Village had had a tiny semiprivate part-time general store, but with the agricultural boom and the radical turns in national policies, the shop's management was taken over entirely by the brigade. It soon moved into roomy quarters in the largest of the old lineage branch halls, with four full-time staff members. Peasants could now afford to shop regularly for spices, dried fish, pork slices, fruits, candies, cigarettes, household odds-and-ends—and even occasionally a major consumer item. When the sent-down youths had first arrived in 1964, there was only a single bicycle in the whole village; by the mid-1970s, more than half the families owned at least one. In 1964, there was one radio in the village (the common property of the No. 1 team); by the mid-1970s, four to five dozen were privately owned. In 1964, the whole brigade had only one old watch, the

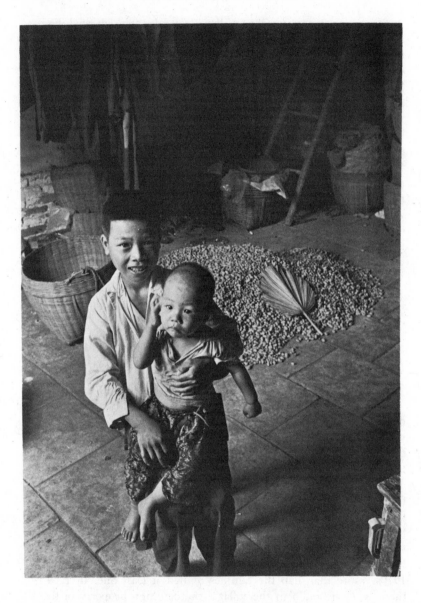

Storage Room.   Children regularly are left in charge
of their younger siblings.

proud possession of the old deputy party secretary, Feihan; by the mid-1970s, a couple of dozen watches could be found in every team. There had not been a single sewing machine in all the village; now a dozen could be counted in a single team.

Such items were exorbitantly expensive, since the state was intent upon making sizable profits on luxury consumer goods. The cheapest bicycle, sewing machine, or watch amounted to more than 100 *yuan,* while a strong man's earnings for a day's work in the collective fields still came to no more than a *yuan.* But there were more families with cash on hand than there were products available. One major reason was that the private endeavors of many of the households were thriving. In particular, the brick factory's voracious appetite for fuel had driven up the price of grass to a *yuan* per hundred pounds, and an energetic woman could chop that much in just several hours.

Bicycles were in especially great demand, since a bike could be loaded up with several hundred pounds of fuel grass each time a peasant returned home from working in the mountain fields. But the village was allotted only about two dozen bicycles a year. If a cadre's family did not yet have one, it was given priority, on the argument that a cadre needed one for official duties. The rest of the families had to depend on their luck in a lottery held once annually.

Despite the growing prosperity, however, a sizable number of the families were still trapped in severe financial difficulties. About a fifth of the households did not even earn enough workpoints to pay for the entire grain ration guaranteed to them under government regulations.[1] These "over-drawn households" were those which, like Lousun's, were caught with too many small children; or consisted of elderly peasants without sons to support them; or had bread winners who were weak or handicapped or

---

[1] This rationed grain could be bought from the teams at the cheap price of 0.196 *yuan* per kilogram. Those who could not pay went into debt to the team. The ration was allocated in line with the calculated consumption requirements of different categories of team members. During a fairly good year in the very early seventies, each working man was allotted 30 kilos (66 pounds) a month, a woman 25 kilos, the retired elderly some 17-20 kilos, and children, depending on their age, some 10-15 kilos.

Village store.

chronically ill. Until they were out of financial debt to their team, they were hard-up for cash.

Even for their better-off neighbors who were indulging in the occasional consumer item, life remained spartan by the standards of China's cities. Almost all of the villagers continued to go bare-foot in winter, until sandals cut from old bicycle tires came into fashion in the mid-seventies. They continued to work 360 days a year, preferring to eke out the extra income rather than have any time off. By the standards of the industrialized West, the Chens still were all dirt poor; but they had come a long way from the malnourished penury of a decade earlier. Exposed now to the better life of the cities, their expectations of what life materially could offer were high and rising fast.

The Enterprise Team and the Consolidation
of Brigade Power

The village's new economic growth had required the brigade to restructure its organization of manpower. Before, the brigade administration had needed relatively few full-time employees. For village-wide projects, Longyong had been able to form temporary work squads that drew laborers from each of the various production teams. The brigade's orchard squad, which in the mid-sixties had cleared the nearby hillsides and opened up several new fruit orchards, had been composed entirely of young people dispatched and paid for by the teams. But such ad hoc arrangements no longer were adequate. Thus a brigade enterprise team, with its own team head and a contingent of foremen, was established in 1969 to incorporate the brigade's rapidly growing manufacturing, service, and sideline endeavors.

Within the next few years, the team's personnel had grown to approximately a hundred full-time workers—about one-sixth of the entire working population of the village.[2] This factory and service work was comfortably near to home, not two hours away like some of the mountain fields; the work—and pay—was assured, come rain or shine, again unlike agricultural labor; and factory personnel earned more than most field workers.[3] So many of the peasants wanted the jobs that a rule had to be laid down to prevent nepotism and resentments. No more than one member in any household was to be hired for an enterprise-team position.

As a result, most of the enterprise employees still had close family and economic ties with an agricultural team. The older factory workers, in particular, continued to identify closely with the teams they had worked in for so long, and most of them continued to attend team meetings to offer advice. But not so the

---

[2] During the agricultural busy seasons most of these workers, though still on the brigade payroll, temporarily were released to go back to their original production teams to help out with the urgent tasks of planting and harvesting.

[3] Each worker was guaranteed as many workpoints per day as he or she would have received in the fields. Thus a strong man who had received a full ten points a day in agriculture got ten in factory work. But the value of each enterprise team workpoint was set as the average value for the three richest agricultural teams.

younger, unmarried brigade workers. They were beginning to see themselves as a separate group with new sets of interests. As one former team cadre noted, "If there's a conflict between brigade programs and team interests, some of them will even side with the brigade." The brigade administration had gained a constituency of its own.

The brigade level's strength was growing in other ways, too. Whereas the brigade management committee earlier had been dependent on the production teams for operating expenses—which sometimes had been only grudgingly offered—it now had discretionary funds of its own. A former brigade employee remarks, "The brigade's power compared to the teams' is determined in good part by its financial strength. If you're poor no one listens to you; our brigade [administration] had more and more of its own money, and so more and more authority."

Longyong gained appreciably from all this. With the Cleansing of the Class Ranks he had increased his political power, irrespective of that campaign's conclusion. The brigade's new-found financial independence consolidated this power, and the village's prosperity bolstered his prestige. Even the interviewees who strongly disliked Longyong grudgingly admitted to us that he was an astute economic manager and a prime mover behind the village's industrialization. He traveled to other brigades and communes to study their economic enterprises, calculated the possibilities for Chen Village, and returned from one trip after another to prod his plans through the brigade party committee.

Longyong commanded even greater respect for his abilities to acquire machinery, spare parts, construction materials, and raw materials through informal channels.[4] There would have been few large buildings and few new industries had Chen Village always waited for allocations through the state's supply bureaus. There was a dearth of almost everything, from small items such as nails and plastic sheets to machine parts and large generators. Many of Longyong's transactions thus were accomplished through private bartering. Stocky Wang recalls, for example, that when "some

---

[4.] For more on this, see Anita Chan and Jonathan Unger, "Grey and Black: The Hidden Economy of Rural China," *Pacific Affairs* 55 (Fall 1982), esp. pp. 460–67.

factory in Canton needed wood, which we could cut from our timber stands, and we needed steel, both sides agreed to exchange." In particular, Longyong reserved the brigade's bricks for sale to customers who could supply commodities that Chen Village wanted. If necessary, Longyong even greased palms. Every time he went on a buying tour, he brought along sugar, peanut oil, and fruit as small "gifts" for the various cadres with whom he would be dealing. This practice had become such a part of life in China that the Chen Villagers never considered it unethical, so long as Longyong did it only in the world outside and for the benefit of the collective.

At the same time, Longyong was careful to maintain an exaggerated persona of austere incorruptibility in everything he touched *inside* Chen Village. When, one day in the early 1970s, the keeper of the village's fish ponds let Longyong's wife buy a couple of pounds of fish as a favor, Longyong loudly stormed after the unfortunate man, flung back the fish with some fanfare, and very publicly chewed the fish seller out. When the brigade cadres in the early 1970s held meetings that spilled over into mealtime, they gradually got back into the habit of ordering up brigade foodstuffs, but Longyong set himself off from them. He never interfered, but he—and Jinyi—ostentatiously abstained from touching even a morsel themselves. "Because of this," admits Stocky Wang, "folks felt that Longyong was better than the other cadres."

Challengers to Longyong

Longyong was riding the crest of his power and prestige. But increasingly he also had to contend with new articulate voices in brigade politics. Among other things, the complexity of running a whole range of small factories meant that the ranks of brigade administrators had to be increased. And the man picked to supervise the manufacturing and to represent the new enterprise team on the brigade revolutionary committee was none other than Chen Sumei.

Chen Sumei, the hero of the 1950 land reform, had risen to become party secretary of the county's agricultural implements factory. But throughout his career, Sumei had given free rein to a dangerous appetite: "Some people like to eat; some like to drink; with Sumei it was sex." While leading the land reform in Chen Village, it was said, he had taken advantage of his authority to rape a landlord's wife. This had been hushed up at the time and in no way had affected Sumei's career. But during his years at the county capital, Sumei engaged in a succession of romantic liaisons; and his sexual escapades finally caught up with him. In the Cultural Revolution he was caught in the act. His political foes publicly savaged him for his philandering, and they even dug up old dirt on the rape case. Sumei was expelled from the party as a moral degenerate and sent back in disgrace to Chen Village to be a peasant again.

Urban youths such as Ao initially looked upon Sumei with fear and disgust: "We thought he was a sex fiend." But to their surprise, most of the Chens considered him a man to respect: "an old revolutionary." Because of his seniority and experience in factory management (and perhaps also because of his personal connections with potential suppliers and buyers throughout the county), he very quickly became the effective head of brigade manufacturing. Inevitably this brought him into sporadic disagreements with Longyong. Unlike ordinary villagers, Sumei was not easily cowed by Longyong's bellowing. Longyong, after all, was so recognizably his junior in age and accomplishment. Nevertheless, Sumei was no longer in the party. Longyong must have felt relieved that Sumei could not disagree with him at the brigade party meetings, where ultimately all the important decisions were made. But here Longyong faced the challenge of a couple of young new party members.

Under the supervision of the two-man workteam of 1969, as part of a new national recruitment drive, half a dozen young peasants had been enrolled in the party branch. Hoping perhaps to counterbalance Longyong's autocratic tendencies, the workteam had quickly elevated two of these recruits—the two who were best educated and most articulate—into the village party committee and even had had them appointed its deputy secretaries. From this party post the brighter and more assertive of the two—a twenty-year-old poor peasant with the nickname of Foolish—soon became Longyong's most persistent and effective critic.

Foolish's mother was a strong-willed widow who had invested all of her hopes in her only son. In the traditional belief that the evil spirits would be tricked into leaving alone a child with a worthless name, she had been the one who nicknamed him Foolish. But foolish he certainly was not; he had proceeded to win a scholarship first to the junior and then the senior high school at the commune seat. At the end of the Cultural Revolution in 1968 his school was disbanded, and, to his mother's severe disappointment, all the students were forced back to their villages. Less than a year thereafter, to his own and his mother's wonderment, Foolish was thrust upward into a leadership post.

Since Jinyi was so inarticulate, Foolish, as deputy secretary, was soon designated Chen Village's representative on the commune party committee. There he quickly developed a network of higher-level party contacts. He henceforth felt that he had nothing to fear from Longyong. Whenever Longyong tried to ram his opinions through the party committee meetings, Foolish stood ready to oppose him. When Longyong angrily reminded him of Longyong's own superior experience, Foolish used his education to thrust the wordings of higher-level directives back in Longyong's face.

They never seemed to see eye to eye. In part it was because they represented the styles of two different generations. Though Foolish had soon adopted the earmarks of a village cadre—overbearing and mandarin-like toward the villagers under him—he remained less autocratic than most of the older cadres. He and his generation were not as willing as their parents to acquiesce passively in "commandism" and bullying. The younger peasants whom we interviewed explained that they and their friends had grown up hearing about the masses being the "masters of society"; and as teenagers in the Four Cleanups and the Cultural Revolution, they had even seen the local and higher level authorities challenged and humiliated. Foolish gained prestige among the younger peasants precisely because he had "that spirit of pulling down the emperor." "He stood up to Longyong and dared to 'nail' him."

But Foolish knew that he was vulnerable to the sarcasm of Longyong and others on two counts. He had little agricultural experience or knowledge; and he had not yet shown that he was a stronger or better laborer than most peasants. "Since he was always going to meetings and didn't labor much, people even began saying things against him to his face. He'd reply, 'How can I do labor when I have no time?' " He was painfully aware that his longer-term prospects as a leader were being undermined by his too-rapid elevation to power without any prior record of activist labor. So Foolish unilaterally withdrew from his tasks as a cadre and returned to his production team to work full-time as a peasant. Longyong apparently felt that this tactic would redound too much to Foolish's advantage, for he complained to the commune party leadership that Foolish had irresponsibly abandoned his duties. The commune concurred, chastised Foolish for a "lack of party discipline," and forced him back to his posts within the week. The final compromise was that Foolish's main duty in the village administration would be to head the militia, a position that, by regulation, would require him to chalk up two hundred days of labor a year. From that post, once he consolidated his credentials, he presumably hoped in future years to advance over Longyong's head to a higher political career.

Ao's Political Disaffection

The rise of Foolish and the several other local "revolutionary successors" foreshadowed a difficult future for Ao and the other urban young people. Now that the peasants' own children were acquiring an education, the urban young people's services no longer seemed indispensable. One after another they were being eased out of the various junior cadre postings they had dominated since the mid-sixties. Ironically, over the years some of them had even gone out of their way to coach activist local youths in public speaking, accounting, and so forth. With some bitterness, Ao later complained, "We were like silkworms spinning cocoons and thus destroying ourselves because of the product we made."

The Chen Villagers, for their part, employed the vocabulary and perspective of the class line as a handy rationale for advancing their own children at the expense of the urban youths. The Mao Thought counselors such as Ao, by eulogizing the innate "revolutionary nature" of the poor and lower-middle peasantry, had been laying out the arguments for their own eventual displacement.

Repeatedly Ao had seen her prospects undermined by her class origins: first in 1968 when the new village committee was elected; then in 1969 when the workteam had selected new party members. And now, as yet younger people gradually came of age, even the posts she already held seemed threatened.

> When I wasn't allowed into the village committee in 1968 I hadn't lost heart. I had thought I should draw the line against my family influence, that I should be able to stand the test. Their explanation was that people like us, of not good origins, should undergo a longer testing period. . . . But slowly I changed. . . . By this time I saw it all very clearly. Our status just got lower and lower.

In her bitterness, Ao conveniently forgot how staunchly she herself had once been in support of a strong class line and of discrimination against bad-class people.

> I felt, "Look, my family background wasn't my own choice. If I'd done wrong then it should be considered my fault, but not otherwise." If your class wasn't good, the party would always question your loyalty, and it would always feel when you did something good that your actions were for personal advancement. They wouldn't cultivate you. I didn't like them dividing people into different levels. . . . With a slightly better class origin, even the most stupid people could put on airs.

The villagers had never taken seriously the frustrated hopes of sent-down youths like Ao, in part because the peasants had never expected that the youths would be spending the rest of their lives in Chen Village. Government policies were always changing, they reasoned; a policy of one period had brought the young people to the village, but a policy of a later period very well might call them back to the city and into urban careers. The peasants liked a number of them and were not particularly anxious that they leave; but the urban youths remained long-term visitors, not Chens. From the very first, the brigade leadership pragmatically had laid its plans with this in mind. The dormitories that the brigade had built for the youths (with funds granted by the government for their settlement in Chen Village) were in the shape of traditional Guangdong granaries. The hope was that once the young people left the village, their lodgings could be put to good use. Little consideration had been taken that they might marry in the village and need family housing.

But the early seventies found the youths still there, and all were in their early and mid-twenties. Without any prospects for upward mobility, they felt stuck in an untenable situation. One of them remarks:

> We felt we were growing older year by year, and were worried. How could we ever hope to get married and have kids? . . . To make a go of it, we'd have to engage in a *lot* of private pig rearing, grass cutting, and work on private plots; we'd always have to work hard from morning to night. We wouldn't be able to endure all that. We wanted a bit of time to read and rest. But then we wouldn't be able to achieve the economic standard necessary for a family.

As a further deterrent to marriage, they knew that under government regulations only single people had ever gotten the chance to transfer back to the city. What if the Chen peasants were right and the state policies changed? Should they remain unmarried just in case?

Already *some* youths were leaving the Chinese countryside for urban posts and universities. For the most part, though, they were the children of party cadres. To the young people who had settled in Chen Village it seemed an outrage—a form of corruption that gave them the feeling that they had been idealistic dupes back in 1964. Complains Ao,

> When those high level cadre kids came to the countryside, they were out again in a flash. . . . Ha! So what did the "glory" of volunteering for the countryside mean? Ha! If they were going back to Canton, then didn't we seem just like garbage being left behind?

In giving vent to her new frustrations and worries, Ao's thinking was influenced by a new contingent of forty urban teenagers who had arrived in the village in the autumn of 1968, at the close of the Cultural Revolution. They were a tiny part of a vast government program that was forcing more than three-quarters of Canton's high school students into the countryside as permanent settlers.[5] Unlike the 1964 contingent, these newcomers were not volunteers; and they had no particular desire to live and labor like peasants. But many of them still held to a youthful idealism, of a kind new to Ao. As students involved in the urban debates of the Cultural Revolution, some of the new arrivals—among them Ao's own younger sister—had developed an independence of mind, a skepticism toward authority, and an eagerness to search out political answers on their own. In wanting a better China, they questioned political premises that Ao had always believed sacrosanct. Ao initially was aghast, but very gradually found herself edging toward this new frame of thought.

> At that time, I still fully believed in the party; and I had an extraordinary respect for Mao Zedong. When my sister [indirectly criticized the top leadership], I said: "If you say that again, I'll report you. I'll get the poor and lower-middle peasants to teach you!" But afterward, I very very slowly began to change. I felt that what she said was factual. . . . My sister had been through the Cultural Revolution, where they feverishly talked about corruption among cadres and so forth. She said that our country wasn't democratic enough, that people had to do exactly what the upper levels said, without thinking.

Some of these younger youths immersed themselves in the Marxist classics and in books that had survived the Destroy the Four Olds campaign. They searched for theoretical foundations that could explain and articulate the problems they saw around them. They organized small informal study groups to discuss new ideas, and even some of the older urban youths joined in. "All my thoughts," Ao says, "now had question marks." Their discussions were not literally antigovernment; they still felt committed to China's revolution and devoted ultimately to the Chairman's leadership. But then, at the very end of 1971, their faith in the Chairman was thrown into confusion and doubt by the Lin Biao affair.

[5] *Southern Daily* (Canton), January 18, 1969. In one fell swoop this new settlement program sought both to disperse the recently warring urban Red Guard factions and to resolve an impending situation of serious urban unemployment.

Lin Biao's Death

Late one night, in the winter cold of December 1971, the party members of Chen Village were roused from bed and rushed to an emergency meeting at the commune headquarters. Two days passed before they returned. They were under orders not to breathe a word of what they had been told, even to their spouses. Every few days a new batch of villagers was called away to the commune seat—first the non-party cadres, then the league members, and then other leading activists. The villagers understood that a major political storm was brewing. In a climate of high drama, they at last were all summoned nervously to a mass meeting at the brigade hall. One of the sent-down urban youths recalls,

> Members of the village militia, with guns at the ready, patrolled the meeting area to keep out the bad elements. You certainly wouldn't want class enemies to hear this news. . . . Foolish read out the document from the party central committee telling how Lin Biao had betrayed Mao and had been killed in a plane crash. . . . The peasants [and ourselves] were of course shocked. . . . They were afraid: "How could someone so close to Mao do something like this? We've got to be really on our guard."

A thick book of documents implicating Lin Biao was handed out to each of the villagers for "study" at the two-day long meeting. All the volumes were scrupulously collected at each session's end and kept under armed guard.

The artificial urgency and secrecy of all of these meetings, first at the commune headquarters and now at the village, lent to the news of Lin Biao's betrayal the aura of a dangerous truth entrusted in strict confidence to a privileged inner circle. Especially to illiterates awed by the weight of printed pages, the thick tomes of documents were supposed to provide tangible evidence of Mao's sagacity and Lin Biao's hidden satanic character. But all the dramatics could not avert a gnawing skepticism. Lin Biao had been almost deified as Mao's bosom comrade-in-arms and designated successor, and then so suddenly he had been declared wicked. "I had felt faithful to Mao," says one young peasant, "but that Lin Biao stuff affected my thinking. Things always seemed to be changing at the top. You couldn't trust everything they said." For many of the sent-down youths, already skeptical, the Lin Biao episode seemed positive proof that the polity from top to bottom was suspect. Says the sent-down youth named Li:

> When Liu Shaoqi was dragged down we'd been very supportive. At that time Mao Zedong was raised very high: he was the red sun and what not. But the Lin Biao affair provided us with a major lesson. We came to see that the leaders up there could say today that something is round; tomorrow, that it's flat. We lost faith in the system.

As evidence of the disjointed swings in the official line, Four-Eyes Wu was languishing in the cowshed. He was still awaiting a higher-level hearing on the charge, billed as the most serious against him, that he had slandered Vice Chairman Lin as an untrustworthy "sly fox." After the revelations of Lin Biao's perfidy, the least embarrassing course was to release him quietly. Wu had already served his function as a target anyway; let him just slip back into village life as if nothing had happened. But the image had to be preserved that party policies were always right. So Jinyi concocted a public statement that the party was showing mercy to Wu despite his multitude of sins, and Wu was called upon to respond with a statement of contrite gratitude. To the sent-down youths, including Ao, it seemed like a sour joke.

Very few were ready any longer to serve as Mao Thought counselors. One of the former counselors, summing up the attitudes of the sent-down youths, says:

> It all seemed so hypocritical. The craze of studying Mao's work was over. Even Lin Biao, the one who had studied Mao the most and who had raised the adoration of Mao to the highest, had already fallen. What was the use for the others to keep on reciting that stuff? Now, in each person's heart, there was this concealed shadow of doubt.

Involuntary Volunteers

Not many months after the Lin Biao revelations, the sent-down youths faced a second shock, of a different kind. Swelling numbers of sent-down youths from throughout the surrounding districts had begun slipping off to Hong Kong; and to stop this the higher-level authorities had decided to transfer most of the urban-born youths in the six border counties to state farms on Hainan. This is the huge jungle-clad island three hundred miles southwest of Canton. During the past few years, the state farms on Hainan had earned unenviable reputations as primitive pioneer settlements run under the iron discipline of the army. Knowing that some of the urban-born youths would try to evade the impending mobilization drive by disappearing back to Canton on visits home, the government opened the campaign by stationing officers at ferries, bus stops, and major road junctions throughout the six counties.

Chen Village received orders from above to enlist a very high quota of "volunteers." Every urban youth was expected to prove his or her "dedication to socialist construction" by signing up to go. But it was tacitly understood that some of them later would be asked to remain in the village: those who were married or already engaged; those demonstrably in ill health; those who were the sole child of a family (Hainan was so far away that visits home to Canton would be limited to one a year); and those who possessed special skills still needed by the village. To be spared, thus, were the barefoot doctor and her fiancé; the youth who handled all the most difficult machinery repairs; the junior high school teachers; and (at the commune's pointed suggestion) a girl from the 1968 contingent whose father was an influential Canton official. Ao, for one, was incensed. Was expertise to be appreciated and family influence rewarded, but a decade of political dedication disregarded? "Even if you raise a dog for ten years," she told her friends, "you don't kick it away like that. Am I more worthless than a dog?" Had this been the sixties, she might have been the first to sign up, eager to set herself up as a model. Now she became the most adamant and the most outspoken resister of all the urban youths.

She even cycled to another brigade to convey her objections to a friend who, like Ao, had gained a reputation as an outstanding activist. But the friend, seeing an opportunity to advance her own interests, telephoned the commune headquarters to report that Ao was "linking up" with other brigades and "inflaming people." At a conference, the commune party secretary singled out the Chen Village cadres and told them, "You've got to get Ao to go. People in other brigades are saying that if she doesn't go, they won't—that if the famous activist won't go, why should they?"

To get the drive against Ao started in Chen Village, the brigade began recruiting "campaign activists." They would be the first to volunteer and then would help isolate and pressure Ao and the others to do likewise. A dozen of the urban youths were willing to play this role. Foremost were those who knew that in the end they would be spared because they were married or had skilled jobs. Stocky Wang, who had recently married a young woman he had met in Canton during the Cultural Revolution (she would soon accompany Wang in fleeing to Hong Kong), and Overseas Deng, who was engaged to a local girl, were enlisted for this "activist" chorus. As if to round out the irony, the brigade Revolutionary Committee recently had put Qingfa in charge of youth affairs, and he was now responsible for orchestrating the pressures. Only three years earlier, Ao had helped send this trio to the cowshed for a year. The times had changed.

Joining these born-again activists were six youths who were genuinely willing to leave Chen Village for Hainan. They had gotten into trouble in the village or could not support themselves financially, and they thought that they had nothing to lose by starting their lives again elsewhere. The very act of volunteering would send them off with a political good deed to their credit. Four-Eyes Wu was the most prominent and articulate of them; and to entice him to sign up as the first genuine volunteer, Jinyi even agreed to get him into the party. Thus, not much more than a quarter year after his release from the cowshed, he became the only urban-born youth ever recruited, as a probationary member, into the Chen Village party. Four-Eyes fulfilled his side of the bargain. He voluntarily went off to Hainan,[6] and before going, gained Ao's admiration for his compassion as an "activist."

> During the high tide of a campaign, people's real personali-
> ties come out clearly. Even though Wu served as their activ-

---

[6.] He later wrote back to friends that the state farm's party committee let his probationary membership lapse; he was, he wrote, "mad as hell."

ist . . . he didn't, to my surprise, use his chance to get revenge. He acted well toward me. In private he sincerely tried
to persuade me that ultimately I had no other choice. But he
wouldn't trample on me or anyone else in public.

A special "study class" was organized for the five most adamant resisters, Ao and her sister among them. For three days
running, from nine in the morning till five in the afternoon, they
had to endure repeated exhortations by a dozen cadres and activists. By the second day of fruitless speechifying and parrying, a
bored poor peasant representative leaned over and whispered,
"*Please,* Ao, sign up. Otherwise we'll just have to keep wasting
our time sitting here." At last, in frustration, the brigade leaders
resorted to veiled threats; it was, they apparently reasoned, Ao's
neck or theirs. "They hinted," Ao recalls, "that I could be gotten
for 'linking up' with other brigades to get them to resist; they
might even look into my past and accuse me of coming from a
family where my father yet again had been politically blackened
[in the Cultural Revolution]. They could say my actions now
revealed my real class nature." Ao had enough experience to calculate the final score. She relented and publicly signed up to go.
But as she affixed her signature, she declared furiously in front of
all the assembled urban youths that she had been forced into it
against her will.

The young people had not been allowed to contact their relatives until they had "volunteered." Now that they had done so,
they were permitted to leave for Canton to say goodbye. Yet once
safely home with their parents, they discovered that they could
resist again. Their parents were prepared to keep them illegally in
the city rather than let them go to a miserable place like Hainan.
Qingfa was delegated to go to Canton to round them up. The
urban neighborhood committees did not want to take on any
added responsibilities, and they dragged their feet when Qingfa
asked for cooperation. Day after frustrating day, Qingfa circulated
on his own from one home to another. Time and again, the
young people would hide in a back room while Qingfa confronted their angry parents at the front door: "We gave our children for you to educate. Why are you trying to send them to
Hainan?" In Canton, Qingfa had no leverage to apply pressure.

"In the city he was like a fish out of water," a peasant out of his element.

The youths remained idly at home for months. Opposition by parents throughout Canton had been so strong that the provincial government felt obliged at last to withdraw its orders. All rusticated youths were to return to the villages to which they initially had been assigned. It was admitted that the young people mistakenly had been "forced" to sign up for Hainan. When Ao and the other youths returned to Chen Village, the brigade cadres sheepishly welcomed them back, explaining apologetically that they only had been carrying out orders. But the rift between the cadres and urban youths was irreparable. Ao's younger sister relates with bitterness: "After we came back to Chen Village we labored less than before. We really felt abused by the village because it had tried to force us to leave. They'd been very unreasonable about it, those cadres."

Increasing numbers of the urban youths in Chen Village became caught up in the "escape to Hong Kong wind," which was already blowing strong in the surrounding communes and brigades. But Ao resisted going for another two years. Capitalist Hong Kong was to her a "decadent city" (she feels so to this day). But in the end, as one sent-down youth after another slipped away to the British colony, she made her choice.

> Life in the village had had value and meaning for me. Now that had changed. Now, I thought, the people and cadres are just out for themselves. : . . So I didn't want to remain in the countryside sacrificing myself. If people there really had a selfless spirit I would have stayed: even living a poor life materially, even being without a family. But the hell with it, I figured. I'll just come to Hong Kong and eat my milk and bread.

In the summer of 1974, Ao made the long and dangerous walk to the coast in the company of Li, one of her former antagonists. They slipped into the water and, sustained by a physical stamina developed in a decade of hard work in Chen Village, swam for a grueling five hours toward new lives abroad.[7]

[7.] For more on Ao and her change of attitudes, see Anita Chan, *Children of Mao* (Seattle: University of Washington Press, 1985), pp. 69–79, 172–82, 199–203.

· 9 ·

The Troubled Seventies

Ao and Li had left behind them a troubled village. By the mid-1970s, the peasants had their own fill of frustrations and complaints. Even as they enjoyed the fruits of the past decade's economic successes, problems and setbacks one after the other had encroached upon production and had begun to sap their earnings and morale.

Undoing the Green Revolution

The Green Revolution of new "miracle" seeds, fertilizers, and better water control, which had so impressively boosted the village's grain production, was stalled. Renewed advances would require improved hybrid seeds, new technologies, and more fertilizers. But the work of the provincial seed research programs had been disrupted first by the Cultural Revolution of 1966-68 and then by the Maoists' new policies with regard to technology. The Maoist leadership had claimed that the "elitist" research institutes were "divorced from the masses," and the agronomists and botanists accordingly had been dispersed to spend most of their time working in the various rural districts.[1] The development of new

[1]. This policy was reversed after Mao's death. The May 7, 1978 issue of *People's Daily* declared: "It is imperative, as soon as possible, to reinstate . . . agricultural

"miracle" hybrids at the province's central research stations had ground to a near halt.

The Pearl Short strain that had transformed the village economy gradually was degenerating. It no longer was immune to stalk rot nor produced such heavy heads of grain. But the peasants themselves were in no ways capable of keeping the seed type pure through selective breeding, let alone improve it through scientific cross-breeding. They could only watch in helpless dismay as the yields declined.

Similarly, Chen Village's Green Revolution had grown dependent upon imported Japanese nitrogen-ammonia fertilizers—and here, too, serious difficulties arose. In the 1970s, supplies to the district and village became dangerously erratic. In line with a national campaign to develop self-reliant local industries, the county government built a small fertilizer plant at the county capital. But the quality of this local product was so poor that the production teams did not want to spend money on it. Yet they were forced into buying the fertilizer because the county-operated factory had to fulfill its sales quota.

To replace "Deng Xiaoping's ivory tower research units," the radicalized party line urged "open-door experiments" within the village itself. Chen Village was asked, for instance, to participate in a research project to concoct the plant-growth hormone gibberellin. Half a dozen young people (mostly sent-down youths, who enjoyed putting their high school science education to use) were sent for a ten-day course, after which they converted a corner of the brigade warehouse into a laboratory. In test tubes, bacteria would be cultivated that excreted gibberellin, and rice shoots would be sprayed with this to obtain quicker maturation and higher yields. A member of the project recalls,

> Our pamphlet told us that American scientists listed gibberellin as detrimental to rice crops—that the growth couldn't be controlled and that the plants would get huge but without

---

scientific research units at all levels, reunite agricultural scientists and technicians who have been scattered, reorganize them and restore normality to agricultural scientific research. . . . Why should working in the rural areas be regarded as labor while working in experimental plots is not?"

full heads of grain. The point was that the imperialists were
doing closed-door research, alienated from the masses, and
that we would outshine them if our experiment worked.

For months, they tried to learn by trial and error how to concoct
the hormone. They embarked on numerous day-long bike trips to
compare notes with the equally bewildered young researchers of
other brigades. Finally, very much to their own surprise, they
managed to cultivate a few successful batches:

> When the plants were about to bear grain, we applied the
> stuff, and within just two days the plants grew a lot. Really
> tall. But at harvest-time, when we compared the grain with
> the yields from ordinary plants, the weight turned out to be
> the same. We hadn't gotten any results!

They tried the gibberellin on melons and vegetables. These grew
prodigiously.

> But strange to say, those vegetables didn't stay fresh for long
> after they were cut. If we'd cut them the night before, by
> tonight they were rotting and shrinking already. . . . There
> was no way we could get to the root of these problems. This
> stuff could only be figured out by specialists.

In two years they attempted half a dozen projects, but
none bore results. They flatly refused to try some of the purportedly successful experiments that had "originated with the
masses, . . . like the one called 702: Feed pigs a formula of
sucrose, eggs, honey, and ginseng in small doses. Of course the
pigs would get fatter! Even people don't eat such good food!
So stupid."

The amateur researchers enjoyed their adventures. However
futile the results, they liked the opportunity to use their initiative. But the other villagers were annoyed. The production
teams' investments in the experiments had come to nought, and
all they could see were "these young people messing around in
their laboratory," getting out of doing a full day's field labor and
enjoying an easy life. By 1973-74 the teams and brigade no
longer would contribute money, and the research squad had to
be dismissed.

Party Commandism

Some experiments and innovations were not voluntary, though. The village was *forced* to pursue a variety of projects resented by both peasantry and cadres. Economic decisions regarding agriculture were being made by the radical top party leadership without regard to economic realities. In particular, with the rationale that north China's agriculture might be jeopardized by a Soviet attack, villages throughout Guangdong were ordered in 1970-71 to cultivate a few patches of cotton and to plant wheat and sorghum as winter crops. Each region of China was to be self-sufficient. "We all said it was crazy"; such crops would never grow well in Guangdong's subtropical climate. But word arrived in Chen Village that in nearby villages, cadres who had refused to cooperate with the program had been subjected to severe criticism sessions. So each Chen Village team planted a few acres in the unwanted crops, with predictable results: the yields were pitiful. Worse yet, nutrients needed for the spring rice crops were sucked out of the soil; and too little time remained before the spring planting to kill off grubs by aerating the soil thoroughly. Yet the "inspired" thinking of the party's higher levels would not be altered by grass roots difficulties. For several years, one failed winter crop after another, the "experiment" continued, not only in Chen Village but in almost all of the Guangdong villages about which we have information.

A nationwide campaign had been launched to emulate Dazhai by leveling mountain slopes to create new fields. Pushed from above to participate, the brigade had the production teams chip in to hire a few large tractors and bulldozers, which filled up several ravines by scraping off the adjoining hillsides. But the excavations and fillings buried the topsoil and exposed an infertile yellow subsoil. For more than a month that winter, the entire village labored to bring in new earth from elsewhere—some three hundred man-days of labor for each team—but they could not muster sufficient manpower to find and fetch more than a small fraction of the new topsoil needed. And even for that small fraction, there were not enough fertilizers available to guarantee worthwhile yields. The newly opened land was uselessly "bald" without a fertile top layer. In the end it could be planted only with tree seedlings, like all the surrounding hills. Whenever they passed the new wasted plateaus, the villagers made sarcastic jokes. "Ha! Good example of learning from Dazhai! Dazhai taught us to level the land to grow trees!"

The provincial, county, and commune party organs had been badly buffeted in the Cultural Revolution; and in the tense political climate of the seventies, they were intent upon playing it safe by adhering militantly and inflexibly to any campaign that came down from above, such as Learning from Dazhai. As the party line shifted, according to interviewees, these party bureaucrats' pressures upon the villages shifted exactly in step. They would suddenly reverse policies when it seemed to them that one or the other of the two factions at the very top of the party echelon had gained the upper hand. They kept a finger cautiously in the air to catch all hints of shifting winds, and whichever way the breezes blew, they mechanically followed.

When a Mao quote was publicized in the national press, proposing that the rural economy be diversified—"Promote agriculture, forestry, and livestock raising, with fisheries as a subsidiary undertaking!"—Chen Village was strongly encouraged from above to branch out into new and potentially profitable ventures. "So we enlarged our fish-breeding ponds," a villager recalls. "But then the line would change and a Mao quote about grain being the mainstay would be pushed, and we'd be forced to convert our new ponds back into rice paddy!" Under that first slogan, the teams expanded their herds of cows and increased vegetable production. But in the next modest lurch leftward in party sloganeering, when that Mao quote about grain taking priority was again blazoned in the newspapers, the middle-level party bureaucracy suddenly declared that raising cows and cultivating vegetables were politically suspect—"running after profits." The animals had to be sold off and the vegetable plots converted back to rice. With half-completed endeavors precipitously abandoned, the labor and capital of the teams were squandered and the productivity of their fields damaged.

In the Four Cleanups the peasantry had discovered that the time-consuming projects demanded by the workteam were in the village's own interest. After the Four Cleanups workteam had left, they had continued to innovate and to engage in labor-intensive projects to improve the agricultural infrastructure. Now, however, they were relearning to distrust all higher-level claims and to resent the imposition of new policies from outside. As of the mid 1970s, most of the Chens just wanted the state to leave their teams alone.

Grain Exactions and a Political Mini-Crisis

They were the most annoyed, if anything, by the state's sporadic campaigns to squeeze more out of Chen Village's stagnating agriculture. Especially in the very early seventies, the party pressed a series of political drives for China's production teams to sell to the state more "surplus" grain: that is, more of the grain left in the team storehouses after all of the households' grain rations were disbursed. These demands for sales of extra grain were couched in ringing phrases about contributing to a higher cause: "Loyalty grain," "Aid Vietnam grain," "Prepare in case of war [with the Soviet Union] grain." But whatever the clarion slogans attached to the grain exactions, the pressures to sell cheaply to the state meant only one thing to the Chen Villagers—that they would have less for themselves and their animals.

Dissatisfaction had been especially keen in the village when the following orders came down from the county in about 1971: To make up for the "surplus" grain emptied from the team warehouses in these campaigns, a tenth of each household's grain ration should not be distributed to the peasants. It was to be stored by the production teams as "reserve grain," to provide the village with a safety net against natural disasters or a Soviet attack. The production teams were asked "voluntarily" to participate; and the peasants, though disgruntled, knew better than to raise any objections.

But then, at a meeting of one of the teams, Sunwang electrified the peasantry by rising single-handedly to challenge the policy. Sunwang had been the chairman of the Cultural Revolution Leadership Small Group; he was an army veteran and party member; he had high prestige among his teammates; and he was furious. He urged his team to resist, in a speech that an interviewee remembers as something like this:

> I'm definitely not opposing any program of Chairman Mao.
> These new demands don't agree with a fundamental policy
> the chairman has set down. No grain that's for distribution
> to households can be touched. You certainly have to give
> people enough to eat! They can play around with the surplus
> grain but not with the grain that's for distribution.

When Sunwang spoke up in this way, the team refused to override him. It reported to the brigade leadership that it could not
arrive at a decision. Other teams followed suit, waiting to see if
Sunwang's team could be forced to comply. The Chen Village
leaders became nervous that higher levels in the party might intervene in the brigade's affairs if they could not keep their own house
in order. So at a meeting of the party branch committee, they
angrily demanded "party discipline" from Sunwang. Peasants
outside the brigade office could overhear the shouting match into
the early hours of the morning. Sunwang, however, could not be
intimidated into retracting his stand, and the brigade reluctantly
had to report to the commune on the teams' recalcitrance and
Sunwang's "bull-headed" resistance.

The commune's own party committee became alarmed that
Sunwang's example might spread to other villages; and so a mass
meeting was duly called at which Sunwang's name was singled
out for criticism. Sunwang would not be swayed. He assured
friends that he was immune to any harsher attack because of the
purity of his political record and class background and the validity
of his Mao citation. But Sunwang had not reckoned on his wife.
Frightened, fearing retribution by the commune, she quarreled
with her husband at a team meeting, arguing that he was en-
dangering the family's future. Enraged by her outburst and the
harm it did to the consensus he had built in the team, Sunwang
stormed across to where the women sat and began beating her.
Several of the women had to pull husband and wife apart.

The resistance sparked by Sunwang disintegrated with the
melee. The panic of Sunwang's wife was contagious. To Sunwang's annoyance and anger, the team gave way to the "request"
for grain, and the brewing mini-crisis in team-brigade-commune
relations evaporated.

Initially the commune leaders thought they had won a point.
Sunwang's defeat suggested the futility of resisting upper level

demands; a team—even close relatives—could not be expected to remain united or to buck the pressures for long. But within a year, Sunwang had the final laugh. In another of those sudden shifts in the winds of party policy, the reserve grain program was retracted, and its initial implementation blamed upon the fallen Lin Biao. The commandeered grain belatedly was distributed to the households. Politically, Sunwang had been right after all. He emerged from the storm a hero of an increasingly frustrated and impatient peasantry.

The Cadres' Worries

As Sunwang's wife had hysterically pointed out, however, Sunwang had been taking a very real risk. In the first half of the seventies, under the slogan "Politics in Command," the party bureaucrats had acquired expanded powers to "get" dissidents, which allowed them to trample upon the legal prerogatives of the lower levels. As Ao recalls,

> Especially in the years after the Cleansing of the Class Ranks, the higher ups could bring real pressures to bear against "local kingdoms"—against units being able just to do whatever they wanted. The levels above us claimed to be Proletarian Headquarters; and they'd use Mao quotes to scare people below them. All this strengthened the county and commune's sway over Chen Village.

The team leaders were more willing to stand up against the commune and higher levels than were the brigade leaders, since the prestige of team heads was more directly related to their management of production to the peasants' satisfaction. If the state made their jobs too frustrating, some of them muttered, they would just quit and return to the less troublesome status of an ordinary peasant. But the brigade cadres felt hopelessly trapped in the middle, sandwiched between the higher levels and the teams. Their party superiors could always threaten to suspend their party memberships if they refused to carry out the unpopular directives of a campaign—and they wanted to retain their brigade careers. Often, therefore, the brigade pressured the teams to comply, as in the reserve grain episode. But the brigade cadres were worried by the peasants' increasing irritation whenever the brigade helped drive them down blind alleys. The cadres began to try to play it both ways.

Longyong had sought to build a reputation as a pugnacious defender of Chen Village's interests, but even he very carefully sniffed the wind to ascertain whether a policy originated with a level high in the party. If a directive that was harmful to Chen Village's interests came from no higher than the commune committee, he made a strong public show of resistance. But if a "request" came from further up, he put on a blustering performance in its behalf, while trying to avoid getting personally involved in its enforcement.

In such circumstances, Longyong and other cadres found it difficult to avoid sounding hypocritical. How could they avoid that image when they repeatedly were obliged to laud policies they and the peasants knew to be unworkable? How could they avoid seeming hypocrites when they fulsomely propagated a certain set of party policies one day and then, as the party line flip-flopped, publicly condemned these same policies the next day? To protect themselves, the brigade cadres had to learn the arts of temporizing—how to moderate the swings in a constantly changing political climate, when to forget conveniently how to take the initiative. A villager recalls,

> Some of them became very clever. . . . They'd do their work a bit at a time, so that they couldn't be blamed from above [for noncompliance]. They could say, "Ha! You people up there can't accuse me of mistakes just because I'm slow at doing things."

Longyong's "Follies"

No matter how Longyong double-talked to his superiors and subordinates, his prestige in Chen Village remained secure so long as his various brigade-level industrial ventures paid off. But with each new project, the profits grew smaller and the risks grew greater. With the brick factory, Chen Village had enjoyed a ready local market and commercial advantages in the village's good clay and convenient sources of grass fuel. With the grain mill and peanut oil press, the profits were only modest, but the extra convenience they provided the villagers was reason enough for establishing them. The small sugar and alcohol refineries and the wood-yam processing plant cut back on the transportation costs to urban markets, and because of this savings they returned small, steady profits. But it was hard to envisage other industrial plants that the village could operate profitably. The peasants of the surrounding district were apparently too poor to provide enough customers for any consumer-product factory; and there remained few other agricultural products that the village could hope to process for urban industrial customers. But Longyong could not accept that. During his initial years of success in industrializing the village, he had become too cocksure about his powers of intuition. He was getting involved in increasingly complex industrial processes and increasingly risky markets, yet he refused to acknowledge the limits imposed on him by the economic circumstances and by his own inexperience and illiteracy. He began to overreach himself.

In 1973, Longyong arrived back from a tour of other villages in high excitement. He began pitching the idea that Chen Village should build a paper-making plant. The commune authorities advised strongly against it. "How can a small agricultural brigade run one," they reportedly argued, "when even the commune town doesn't have [the know-how for] such a factory?" But Longyong dismissed such objections as simply commune-level envy. He also ignored or shouted down all the doubting Thomases in the brigade. These included Foolish, Sumei, and Qingfa. All three publicly expressed apprehension about the new venture—but "not too vehemently, since they didn't want to look overly conservative if it ended up a success; and Longyong, of course, did have a pretty good string of successes at this point."

The new project marked the end of that success. The paper-making machinery was supposed to churn sugarcane pulp and bamboo leaves into a coarse industrial paper fiber; but whereas some other villages had profitably run such enterprises using water-powered mills, Chen Village needed to install and feed an oil-powered generator. It needed to buy expensive chemicals to treat the cane pulp, and it ran into severe headaches coping with the chemical processes. The quality of the end-product was so poor that Longyong had to scramble to find a buyer at any price. After several seasons, even he had to concede the plant was a failure. He let it close. The brigade had lost 20,000 *yuan* at a time when it could ill afford any losses at all. Ao remarks,

> When Longyong's plans had been riding high, he'd been dictatorial. But when that paper factory began failing, he couldn't casually force through his own way any more. . . . Foolish would always say to him something like, "You always think your own ideas are the best, like that paper factory! You wanted it to go through when the rest of us didn't, and just look what a mess you made of it."

This squandering of brigade capital placed another of Longyong's extravaganzas—that large new auditorium—in a new and unflattering light. Only recently, the villagers had been proud of its great size and of the reputation it had gained for the village. But with the collapse of the paper-making venture, snide remarks were heard about how, rather than being reinvested or distributed to the households, so much of the brigade and teams' money and products had gone into the cement, steel, and brick of Longyong's quest for community grandeur. Of what good was such a monumental auditorium when the village's agriculture (and now even its industrial sector) were caught in a downward spiral?

Longyong tried to recoup his prestige by throwing Chen Village's money and manpower into constructing a set of backup dikes to guard against floods. The villages downstream objected that during floods they would be inundated in Chen Village's stead, but Longyong turned a deaf ear. Several of the villages appealed to higher levels, and with the dikes about two thirds completed, the county administration ordered the project halted. Thousands of man-days of the Chen peasants' labor had been wasted by Longyong's failure to gauge how far he could go in ignoring the political influence of other local communities.

Labor Troubles

The peasants in the agricultural teams had another grievance against Longyong's enterprises. The teams were suffering from insufficient labor. The various new unworkable experiments that the state had demanded were severely taxing the teams' labor resources, at the very same time that labor had been drawn away from the fields to man the brigade's new factories. Longyong's dogged pursuit of all those brigade-level endeavors simply meant more agricultural chores for each of the team members who had been left laboring in the fields. They felt at once envious of their colleagues in the factories and peeved that their own harder field labor brought in a declining income.

Because of the setbacks in the agricultural extension programs, the politically inspired failures, labor shortages, Longyong's miscalculations, and the peasantry's own lowered morale, incomes from collective agriculture had plummetted by about a third between 1968 and 1973.[2] This can be seen in a year-by-year accounting of what the best male workers from one of the village's richer teams could earn in a day's work on the team's fields.

1964	Y .50	1971	Y 1.00[3]
1965	Y .80	1972	Y .90
1966	Y .90	1973	Y .80
1967	Y 1.00	1974	Y .80
1968	Y 1.15	1975	Y .45[4]
1969	Y 1.10	1976	Y .80
1970	Y 1.00	1977	Y .70

Other teams exhibited similar declines.

The strongest laborers in each team felt particularly disgruntled. Under the Dazhai wage system, the differences in pay be-

[2] Similar tales from other villages have appeared in the official Chinese press, e.g., *People's Daily,* March 17, 1978.

[3] In 1971, Chen Village's richest team could provide its best workers a daily pay of about Y1.10, while the poorest team could offer only Y .60-.70, a difference greater than the difference in earnings between the highest- and lowest-paid members of the same team.

[4] 1975 was a year of very adverse weather. It was the third wettest year in the 130-year history of Hong Kong, less than 100 miles away, and the winter was Hong Kong's coldest on record.

tween them and their weakest and laziest teammates were rather small—and those in the bottom half were always arguing vociferously for higher personal ratings. The best workers had not particularly minded the narrow wage differentials when the team's total wage pie was expanding every year; but now that the pie was shrinking, it seemed unfair to them. They felt, in the words of the Chinese proverb, "like live frogs dragging along dead frogs." Rather than let themselves be taken advantage of, some of the best laborers slacked off in their work. The labor shortages from which the teams already suffered gradually worsened.

The production team cadres could not find any way to reverse this trend. The political levers that had aided the Dazhai wage system in earlier years—the effectiveness of praising labor activists and shaming laggards—had eroded. The Mao Thought counselors were now largely local youths; and they were not so willing to offend elders and neighbors by chiding them for "backward" behavior or careless work. As much to the point, the Dazhai system depended upon a high morale among the peasants. But neither the counselors nor the peasants any longer put any great faith in Mao's teachings that human spirit and correct attitudes could conjure up economic miracles. The recent reverses in production, beginning about 1970, had badly shaken that faith.

In fact, discouraged by the collective sector's performance and prospects, the peasants were plowing more of their energies into their private economic endeavors. They cleared more hillside wasteland for extra private vegetable plots and raised more piglets and fowls in their spare time. They succeeded, in fact, in greatly softening the financial impact of the collective sector's decline. From their private plots they ate as well as ever. From their sales of vegetables (which are highly priced in China), livestock, and extra fuel grass cut for the brickworks, they accrued enough steady cash to remain frequent customers of the village store.

But all this was of scant help to the production team heads as they tried with much frustration to get the teams' daily work accomplished. They wanted a new system for rewarding labor, a wage system that would get the peasants once again to pay greater attention to their work in the collective fields. Since the Dazhai system no longer provided such incentives, the national authorities—for once awake to the rural cadres' problems—began to hint that villages could, if necessary, revert to a piece-rate wage system. Piece rates could get peasants to work hard for their own interests in a situation where morale was poor and peer-group social pressures weak.

But piece rates had been publicly condemned in previous years as capitalist-roading; and many of the team cadres remained afraid to readopt piece rates unless the authorities officially made it clear that it was ideologically safe to do so. The problem was solved by a new directive, declaring that a revived piece-rate program, whatever its ostensible similarity to the discredited "Liu Shaoqi piece-rate system," would, *mirabile dictu,* be considered a "Mao Zedong piece-rate system." With a few strokes of the party pen, an archrevisionist program of piece rates had been made properly revolutionary. One by one, during the summer of 1973, the team heads in Chen Village steered their teams back toward piece rates.

Longyong was perturbed. Whatever the difficulties in operating the Dazhai program in the seventies, he had less liking for a piece-rate program. Piece rates, he argued, were "bad for people's collective sense"; piece work explicitly encouraged peasants to think only about their own personal material interests, not their team's or village's. Longyong prevailed upon Old Tireless and the other cadres of Longyong's home team—the No. 4 team, the village's official model team—to hang on with Dazhai rather than pitch the team back into piece work. But the lure of renewed incentives for the peasants was too great for the No. 4 team's harrassed cadres to ignore for long. In December of 1973, Longyong's appeals were overridden. The No. 4 team's committee voted to revive piece rates.

Nuisance Campaigns

The peasants of Chen Village were no longer so willing to listen to *any* appeals that were presented in terms of ideology and Maoist ethics. A few years earlier, during the Mao Thought campaign, they had been excited by the Maoist visions of a new moral order based upon altruism, cooperation, and dedication. But their hopes for altruistic cooperation gradually had eroded. Their admi-

ration for the Mao quotes had become edged with discomfort,
once the quotations no longer served just as benign moral maxims
but were wielded as truncheons to batter community scapegoats
and personal enemies. The peasants' ultimate faith even in the
sanctity of Mao and the Maoist credo had been repeatedly challenged: by the Lin Biao affair, by their own stagnating economy,
and by the nonsensical flip-flops in agricultural policies.

They felt increasingly weary of "politics." They were bored
by the high-blown, interminable evening sermons. They wanted
more spare time away from meetings. They worked seven days a
week, and the late afternoons and evenings provided their only
real chance to rest, to attend to their household chores, and to
supplement their incomes through private endeavors. They
groaned every time a new campaign of any sort rolled out of
Peking. They were becoming irritated even with the model films
associated with Mao's wife Jiang Qing. Those same dozen films
had been shown again and again over the years, and as one peasant recalls with annoyance, "if you didn't go to see them, you'd
get criticized the next day at a meeting. They kept saying these
movies were good for you, that it was like studying Chairman
Mao's line. So you got dragged out at night to see them."

Exasperated, the Chen Villagers were already prepared to be
ill-disposed toward the national anti-Lin Biao campaign of late
1972. In this new anti-Lin campaign, for reasons that were clear
only to the top leadership in Peking, everyone throughout China
was required once again to denounce the villain and his policies.
But the villagers discovered that some of these anti-Lin sessions
could be turned, unexpectedly, to their own droll enjoyment. Any
unpopular economic policies that had been promulgated while Lin
Biao was still alive could now righteously be denounced, as if one
and all of those policies had been the fault of that counterrevolutionary scab. For example, the policy of "grain as the mainstay,"
which had been revived yet again since Lin Biao's time, publicly
became the butt of scornful, mock-serious jabs: "Our production
was no good because of Lin Biao! He told us not to plant melon
seeds or other vegetables. He wanted us dead!"

When in 1973 the Anti-Lin campaign was transformed into
the Criticize Lin Biao and Confucius campaign, the pleasure was
lost. The new campaign seemed inscrutable. Even the urban

youths who remained in the village were totally perplexed about the conceivable relevance of denouncing Confucius. They could grasp that the campaign had been turned away from the peasants' aspersions against "ultraleftist" policies. But they could not grasp that a radical leadership camp (the Gang of Four) was now aiming the attacks instead against Zhou Enlai and the moderates in the guise of "Confucianists."

When the cryptic, indigestible essays maligning "Confucianism" were read out at the mass meetings and it was time for audience participation, the cadres and activists obediently stood up to denounce Confucius and to recount how Confucian feudalistic thinking manifested itself in their daily activities. "But," admits one of them, "we couldn't think of anything to say that had much to do with Confucius or much to do with anything." For once, the older peasants who had had some education before the Liberation had an opportunity to steal the show. They were allowed to recite stories from the Confucian classics, supposedly to demonstrate what these despicable writings were like. One of the younger peasants recalls that it was the first time he had ever had direct contact with any of the Confucian writings: "Ah, I felt, so that's what it was like!" But even such meetings stirred only momentary interest. The campaign itself seemed only a final proof to the Chen peasants of how stupifyingly boring "empty politics" could be.

If anything, the Line Education campaign which soon followed (1974–1975) was even less popular. The radical wing of the party still was riding high in Peking; and it believed that the peasants had not sufficiently turned their attention away from private endeavors and back toward their team's agriculture. In Guangdong province alone, 120,000 cadres[5] were dispatched to the countryside in workteams to show that the state meant business. In Chen Village a cadre workteam remeasured the peasants' private plots, and all scraps of plot that exceeded the family's original allotment were confiscated. Some of the peasants were rearing flocks of two dozen ducks or more; they were now restricted to only ten, on pain of confiscation. The number of private chickens that any household could own was likewise cut back

---

[5.] *Far Eastern Economic Review,* October 25, 1974, p. 15.

severely. A fine of five *yuan* was imposed on anyone who took leave during the day to cut grass instead of working in the collective fields.

It was all very annoying. But the villagers had seen party policies shift to and fro too many times already to be at all outraged. They would simply tighten their belts and wait stoically until the political pendulum swung back and again allowed private production to flourish.

The New Generation

Overall, the younger generation was the most dissatisfied of any of the peasantry during the mid-seventies—but for reasons very much their own. Most of the young men in their late teens had received a primary education; and increasing numbers, as the seventies wore on, had even graduated from the village's new junior high school classes. They had different aspirations than those of their parents. The older peasants measured their own and their children's futures, if no longer in terms of miraculous improvements in agriculture, at least in the expectation of incremental advances: "Those older generations of peasants still believe in one thing—that they're today's pioneering oxen. They talk about this being good for the generations to come." Many of their children had begun to repudiate this long-term vision of cumulative, small, hard-wrought contributions from each generation. What was the sense of being educated, they felt, if after graduation there was only the soil to return to? According to one of the sent-down youths,

> The older people aren't so discontented. It's these younger peasants who'd been through several years of schooling. They simply don't want to work in the fields. They find the work hard and feel that such a life is meaningless. They feel their abilities aren't being put to use, because to them farming doesn't need much talent. They dream of working in factories, or shops, or government departments.[6]

6. In a rather sophisticated turn of phrase, one young peasant calls these dashed hopes and the discontent they breed a "negative progress," explaining: "By pro-

Whereas most of their mothers had not yet seen even the county capital, they themselves had accompanied the urban-born youths on visits to Canton. With each such outing, "their thoughts became more complicated and their aspirations to leave agriculture further aroused." To a few of them, at least, Chen Village seemed a backwater in which they were trapped.

They had not experienced any of the difficulties of the pre-Liberation era, and therefore they did not count their blessings as their elders did. The party continued to try to instill a sense of appreciation through periodic "recall past bitterness, think of the present sweetness" sessions, but with little effect. According to one of the sent-down youths,

> Hearing these stories was, for these young people, like watching an unreal movie. They joked about it, smirked and laughed at the old people telling these tales. . . . Most of them didn't believe in it. They'd never experienced it personally and felt it couldn't have been *that* bad. They felt people shouldn't always be looking back like that, shouldn't always compare the old and new society, shouldn't use the past to measure the present.

There was a generation gap even between themselves and their older brothers who had been teenagers during the sixties. A young former deputy team head, still in his late twenties when interviewed, complains: "These students! You tell them to go to weed the fields and you just couldn't imagine how brash they can get. They simply hide away and go to sleep. How dare they do that! My own generation was never that lazy!"

That older cohort of young adults had experienced the Four Cleanups as teenagers. They could recall from the mid-sixties a period that was economically booming and that had seemed to herald a better political future. All of them, even those of bad-class origins whom we interviewed, said they had believed in the party and Mao and had tried to labor hard for the collective. They looked nostalgically back upon their own idealism. But the gen-

---

gress I mean the consciousness of these kids has been raised. . . . Our parents only wanted to be able to fill all our bellies. We young people want more out of life than just that."

eration born in the late fifties and early sixties knew, as teenagers and young adults, only the economic disappointments and confused politics of the seventies. For many of them, the only real heritage of those earlier years of fast growth was the gnawing expectation that things *should* rightfully improve every year. They felt cheated by events.

Many of the young men of this later generation were far more liberal with money than were their parents. They were always asking their parents for more pocket money; and the parents often felt miffed because the sons did not exert themselves either in the collective fields *or* at private endeavors. The elder villagers were even more incensed at the younger generation's dulled sense of right and wrong. Though the incidence of petty theft was relatively low, it was rising. Young peasants were more prone to help themselves to collective foodstuffs in the fields, and some were caught stealing neighbors' chickens and ducks (the most scandalous form of petty crime) to support illicit feasts up in the hills. Most Chen villagers shook their heads sadly and in bewilderment at what had gotten into young people nowadays.

Longyong made it especially plain that he had no liking for this younger generation—and they reciprocated his feelings in kind. One of these young peasants says:

> That fellow Longyong was always in a black mood. He thought himself some sort of savior. Imagine. He wouldn't even let children chew on a piece of sugar cane when they were harvesting the cane. He'd yell at them and fine their parents. When we'd see him coming we preferred to take another path . . . and not have to put up with him.

Among themselves, these young people made cutting jokes about Longyong's imperious airs and his constant annoying efforts to drive other villagers to work as hard as himself. These selfsame aspects of Longyong's behavior had strengthened his hand as a cadre in an earlier period, and still earned him respect among some villagers. According to one of the sent-down youths:

> To the older generation, Longyong's appeals to labor hard have a moral ring. They may drag their feet a bit but they at least agree about the rightness of it. But the younger generation doesn't see labor as having any high value, and so Longyong simply doesn't hold their respect.

If the young people had their way, Longyong would not have been Chen Village's "local emperor."

There were other cadres whom they preferred. They admired Foolish for his senior high school education and his "youthful spirit." They felt that Foolish understood them, that he sympathized with their frustrations and with some of their views. Whereas Longyong always pushed them in his bellicose authoritarian style, Foolish stopped to chat. "He didn't mind us relaxing at times."

Qingfa was another who won their appreciation. His humiliating experiences in the cowshed had softened him. He no longer exhibited any strong ambition to climb back into the driver's seat. In middle age, he seemed satisfied to occupy his own small niche at the fringes of responsibility. A decade earlier, Qingfa had been "fierce as a tiger" but now was "gentle as a lamb." He no longer quarreled with anyone, including Longyong. He was even democratic. When people came to ask him for any decision, he would reply that the entire brigade party committee should discuss the matter first.

He had become more shrewdly attuned to other villagers' feelings, and he joked and "talked backward stuff" with the young people. On Youth Day each year, as the cadre in charge of youth affairs, Qingfa had to make a speech, and he urged the youths (in the recollected words of an interviewee) to celebrate the day by taking it easy rather than working on their family's private plot.

> You young people should go to play basketball. Don't work too hard. If you have more money you'll just be able to buy a better brand of cigarettes; without money you can keep to the cheap brand. If you smoke cigarettes at 20 cents a packet your lungs get black; and if you smoke cigarettes at 50 cents a packet your lungs get equally black. So why work today?

Special Privileges

Qingfa took his own advice about working. He managed to avoid participating in much of the one hundred days of manual labor that was officially required of cadres, by pretending that he always suddenly had other responsibilities to attend to. Those "responsibilities" regularly took him on errands to the commune and county seats and occasionally even to Canton. Since he so assiduously avoided stepping on people's toes and no longer chalked up enemies in the village, he evidently felt he could get away with a decided laxity in personal habits.

Using 2000 *yuan* sent to him by his sister in Hong Kong, he built himself a new house, one of the finest in Chen Village. Qingfa used his "errands" away from the village to secure the materials he needed for the house; he bought sugar and vegetable oil in Chen Village to take with him as sweeteners, to win the good graces of appropriate warehouse personnel.

He still relished feasts and convivial talk among friends and kinfolk, as much as he had in the days when he was Chen Village's "local emperor." He even became daring in his feasting habits. A young peasant of bad-class origins recalls,

> After I was caught trying to escape to Hong Kong, most people didn't dare to come near me. For a few close friends who still dared, I made a dinner of dog meat [a delicacy in the Guangdong countryside], and I invited Qingfa. He came as if nothing had happened! As long as there's food Qingfa would eat with *any*one who asked him.

Qingfa was not alone among the cadres in wanting a pleasant life. Other cadres, too, sought out special privileges as if these were part and parcel of a cadre post. Interviewees complained repeatedly about this. In the past, when the cadres had meetings, they had hurried to get back to working in the fields; but nowadays, says a former cadre, "They'd start late, really meeting for only a couple of hours in the afternoon and making the whole thing into a very relaxed exercise. It's like being on vacation. You get workpoints, free things to eat, a relaxing day."

Some cadres went further. Though not corrupt per se, they edged into that ill-defined territory between perquisites and pilfering. When families tore down an old house to build a new one, for example, the teams and brigade would provide some of the labor to construct the new home, in exchange for the old house's smoke-laden mud walls, which could be pounded into a fertilizer. It became a common practice for cadres to overappraise exorbitantly the value of the walls of their old houses.

The cadres were not overly worried about the peasants' reactions to this petty pursuit of advantages. Partly this was because there was no really effective force within the village with the authority to check on them. The Poor and Lower-Middle Peasants Association had been established by the Four Cleanups workteam to serve as such a watchdog organization, but it never functioned in that capacity. After the workteam had given the poor peasant representatives their posts, no provisions had been established for subsequent grass roots elections of the representatives. The incumbents simply retained the title. In most of the teams, they were granted permission to sit in on the meetings of the team management committee and were allowed to play a minor role in discussions on how to get team members to go along with cadres' plans. Though they served ineffectually in this capacity, they came to perceive themselves as a type of low-level cadre. They, too, enjoyed the meals that accompanied cadre meetings. Thus despite the Four Cleanups' intent, no basis had been provided for any ongoing system of checks and balances.[7]

One might have thought, however, that even in the absence of any independent Poor and Lower-Middle Peasants Association, the Four Cleanups campaign would have taught cadres to stay clear of undue material advantages. The village officers, however, had absorbed a somewhat different lesson from the tribulations of the Four Cleanups. In the long decade since then, the frightening reality of the attacks had softened in their memories. Many of them concluded from the frequent turnabouts of political campaigns that they would be able to survive as cadres—come what may. As one of the urban-born youths observed to us in the mid-1970s,

> The cadres aren't afraid of the masses; and the masses aren't afraid of the cadres. The cadres feel: "Go ahead and get me;

[7] The brigade-level Poor and Lower-Middle Peasants Association, without an independent base, organization, or substantive activities, existed only in name. As required, formal brigade-wide meetings of the association were still held twice a year; but the meetings were presided over by the *party* branch secretary, Jinyi. These were entirely ritualistic sessions celebrating the political superiority of the former poor and lower-middle peasants in the New China, and reminding them of the gratitude they still owed the revolution.

won't I come back to my post just like before?" On the other hand the masses think: "You cheat us, okay, but when a campaign comes along you'll get it." When I first got to the village during the Four Cleanups, everyone was afraid of everyone else. The cadres were afraid of the masses; and the masses were afraid of the cadres taking revenge. But now everyone has experience and they aren't afraid. Everyone's skins gradually have thickened.

Some of the younger cadres were even more daring than their seniors in grabbing perks. Never having suffered in the Four Cleanups, they had no memories at all to caution them. Foolish was among those who openly enjoyed his small advantages. To make more room for his firstborn, for example, he enlarged his house by building into the rear lane. There was a strict brigade prohibition against precisely such encroachments, and in a shouting match at the scene of the crime, Longyong grabbed hold of the chance to point up Foolish's abuse of public trust. But the extension to Foolish's house was already up, and Longyong's righteous fulminations and arm waving in the crowded lane did not embarrass the young deputy party secretary into yielding.

The transgressions of Foolish and the others would have seemed the normal and accepted way of things before the Four Cleanups. But whatever that campaign had taught the cadres, it had taught the peasants not to be so tolerant of party cadres who spouted pious political slogans while eyeing the public trough. The same young peasant interviewees who praised Foolish in one breath would tell biting jokes in the next breath about the various incidents in which Foolish had utilized his posts for personal gain.

The only brigade cadre whom everyone acknowledged had remained steadfastly incorruptible was the incompetent party secretary Jinyi—for Longyong himself, despite his flaunted shows of rectitude, no longer entirely shunned material advantages. Some of the younger peasants were annoyed to see Longyong's son, a junior high school graduate, teaching at the commune high school. Quite naturally, they suspected that he had been selected to attend the two years of teachers' training through the influence of his father. Rumors circulated (correctly) that Longyong had accepted gifts of expensive medicines from Overseas Deng in exchange for Longyong's aid in getting Deng a visa to leave China.

It was rumored, too, that for a new extension to his house, Long-yong acquired lumber at the price set for public buildings, not the legal free-market price. There was nothing particularly reprehensible in this type of illicit lumber purchase. Almost any villager who could have gotten something through official channels at the cheaper public-sector price would have done so without hesitation. But inasmuch as Longyong had always portrayed himself as *the* incorruptible cadre, even such small and commonplace advantage-seeking made him the butt of sour jokes.

The cadres' cheating became an excuse and justification for the peasants' own transgressions. Some of the younger peasants made up a sardonic ditty about the growth of the various licit and illicit cadre perquisites.

> A feast is not mine to eat,
> "Spoils" are not mine to grab.
> Only laboring day in and out,
> Why not go to the fields for a rest?

A few anonymous malcontents went further. They retaliated through minor acts of sabotage against cadres who had crossed them. There have always been such scattered incidents, but the frequency had multiplied of late. Cadres returning one evening from a meeting and meal found briers awaiting their bare feet on the path they had to take. A workpoint recorder who had a fierce quarrel with several peasants found the next morning that the necks of all his ducks had been wrung during the night. Worst yet, Jinyi's pig was found poisoned after he ordered that all hogs in the village be kept locked in their sties for sanitary reasons. Qingfa, who had been publicly pushed by Longyong to take up once more the post of public security head (the least popular cadre position in the village), discovered painfully that thorns had been strewn over his private plot—and he decided to withdraw his name from consideration for the post.

Longyong's Maneuvers

As much as ever, Longyong had little tolerance for disagreement, and to the annoyance of many of the villagers, he persistently maneuvered to weaken or remove from office anyone who dared to be openly critical of him. He seemed, even more openly than before, to relish the role of a village politico—and never more so than when he sought to oust the director of the Women's Association. The incumbent director was Lilou's daughter Pumi. Pumi was perhaps the single most popular and admired woman in the village. Her leadership of the Women's Association had not directly provided her with any appreciable influence in brigade affairs.[8] But it had given her an entrée to the brigade's management committee as the women's representative (the committee's only female member), and she had converted this token membership into a felt presence. The only woman of her generation to have graduated from high school (she was now in her late twenties), she was an articulate, witty speaker who was willing to lock horns with Longyong at committee meetings.

For this very reason, Longyong maneuvered to have Pumi replaced on the committee. He pushed through, as his choice, the youngest daughter of the No. 3 team's head: an inexperienced, immature, unpopular nineteen-year-old. She would provide Longyong with an appropriately pliant and supportive committee member. Just as important, the girl's elder sister was engaged to Longyong's son; and her father just happened to be the new head of Qingfa's old team. As one young peasant observed: "The main point of the matter was that Longyong had never had any kin behind him; and now he was trying to build up that kind of factional base!"

In the guise of doing Foolish a favor, Longyong also quietly lobbied the commune authorities, arguing that the young man was suited for responsibilities of a higher order. It cannot be said whether Longyong's hints and praise played any real part in the

[8.] A woman from the village reports, "The Women's Association has no members, except for its leaders. The brigade level women's committee is just supposed to advise women to participate in family planning programs, and to push the idea that women should study Mao and be concerned about the seed plots. The committee also does a bit of 'secret' stuff, telling girls in a socialist way about sex; and the committee tries to persuade girls to stay in the village and not leave to marry elsewhere. . . . The director of the Women's Association also holds the special responsibility that when cadre meetings are held in the village, she cooks the food and waits on tables."

commune's subsequent decision, but in 1976-77, Foolish moved up to a full-time position in the commune administration. Longyong's most serious rival had been safely elevated out of the running for village leadership.

So, too, Longyong persistently maneuvered to ease Qingfa out of the village. Notwithstanding their awkward conciliatory handshake under Mao's portrait, the two men had remained on sour terms. They barely muttered greetings when they had to squeeze past each other on village paths. Longyong's entreaties in the commune town finally secured Qingfa's transfer into a commune warehousing post. But Qingfa did not seem to mind. A peasant in Qingfa's production team recalls seeing Qingfa sauntering back from his new commune job early one afternoon.

> I called out to him, "How come you're home so early today?" Longyong was standing nearby, and Qingfa shouted back loudly, "My job's very easy and comfortable, only need to work two hours a day." He was really telling Longyong that he'd gotten a good deal despite Longyong's scheme to get rid of him.

After Mao

Even before Mao's death, the villagers had been vaguely aware that the leaders immediately below Chairman Mao were divided into antagonistic factions that were jockeying to assume the leadership. In early 1976, as part of this succession struggle, an airplane, presumably dispatched by disgruntled southern air force officers, had even showered the commune with leaflets denouncing the radical faction (later known as the Gang of Four) and applauding their moderate opponents Zhou Enlai and Deng Xiaoping. When Mao Zedong's death was announced in September of 1976, the villagers understood that, one way or the other, it heralded sharp new turns in Chen Village's affairs.

But not in the short term, despite the arrest of the radical faction a month after Mao's demise. It was not at all certain to the party bureaucracy what Hua Guofeng's rise as chairman portended. A quarter year after Hua's ascension, he presided over the Second National Conference on Learning from Dazhai, and the proceedings retained radical overtones. The bureaucrats reacted to this and to the general uncertainty of the moment by taking the stance to which they had become accustomed: if in doubt, protect yourself by shifting leftward with considerable noise. The year 1977 accordingly brought a new mini-campaign to Chen Village and the surrounding district, accompanied by a barrage of political rhetoric.

It involved sugar. The bureaucracy had suddenly decided that sugar cane had to be planted on a crisis basis.[9] The new campaign's slogan intoned: "Oppose revisionist [Cuban] cane; no imported sugar." Recalls a villager,

> Everyone had to grow cane, even the market towns. Even the commune administration! But since the commune had no land, Chen Village had to lend it some twenty acres. Even paddy fields had to be converted to this stuff. And trees had to be cut down as well. The state had always said trees shouldn't be cut, that the country should be green, yet now they cut the trees! . . . We even had to plant cane at night!

But amid this sugar mini-Leap, there were at least hints of quite different policies to come. In the months following Mao's death, the village store filled up with normally hard-to-get merchandise, including extra bicycles and batches of watches. Urban warehouses apparently were being emptied, to show a disgruntled peasantry that the state henceforth would concern itself more with their material needs.

As the top leadership gravitated into the hands of Deng Xiaoping and his "modernizers" in 1978, material progress increasingly became the watchword: "Economics in Command," no longer "Politics." Floods of political campaigns no longer emanated from Peking; and to the peasants' gratification, nighttime meetings became a rarity. (As if to stress that production drives,

---

[9.] Soon after the fall of the Gang of Four, in a move to the left, the provincial authorities had stopped granting teams the usual 25% bonus for above-quota cane. The acreage voluntarily put into cane in the sugar-producing districts declined immediately. Resorting to administrative muscle, officials presumably mounted this campaign to ensure that provincial sugar deliveries did not unduly suffer. In the spring of 1978, again shifting gears, the authorities reestablished the above-quota bonuses (*Da Gong Bao* [Hong Kong], April 17, 1978).

not continued "class struggles," were to occupy center stage, the four-bad class labels officially were also expunged in early 1979, and the village's former landlords and rich peasants released from their political bondage.)[10] Simultaneously, the state's economic constraints on the peasantry as a whole were relaxed. Peking promulgated directives granting more discretion to the teams and brigades to grow more of what was most profitable to them. Better prices were offered by the state procurement offices in order to secure more farm produce for the urban markets; and the peasantry was actually encouraged to pay attention to private plots and family animals. The provincial government also repeatedly made promises that the teams' manpower and food supplies no longer could be requisitioned through "political" threats by the commune and county. Above all, the teams were promised that the government's rural policies would remain unchanged over the long term.[11]

Longyong and the brigade committee responded quickly to take advantage of these new policies. The Enterprises Team organized new investments to diversify the agricultural economy. It planted new orchards. It purchased colonies of honeybees and soon managed eighty hives. It bought a group of special deer, at a thousand *yuan* apiece, to build up a commercial herd (the antlers

[10] At the end of 1978, the old former landlords and rich peasants in China who still wore "four-bad hats" had numbered more than 4 million. Within a year, this stigma was removed from almost 99 percent of them. Only 50,000 "incorrigibles" retained the bad-class hats (*Beijing Review*, January 21, 1980, p. 14).

[11] See *People's Daily*, May 13, 1978, p. 2 (on Guangdong); also Canton Radio, May 13, 1978, in *Foreign Language Broadcast Information Service: People's Republic of China Daily Report* [U.S. Government] (*FBIS*), May 15, 1978, pp. H1-2. Nevertheless, complaints continued to emerge in the press that the party bureaucracy was disregarding the province's own declared promises. In 1979 the Guangdong provincial party scolded itself (perhaps futilely): "We *must* maintain stability in our policies so as to gain the people's trust. It is forbidden to issue an order in the morning and rescind it in the evening, to change the policies frequently or have simultaneous commands coming from different directions. It is forbidden to change arbitrarily the basic accounting unit [i.e., to change to brigade accounting and ownership]. It is forbidden to shift the burden of economic losses onto the peasants under any pretext. It is forbidden to raise or lower prices arbitrarily. It is forbidden to demand much from the peasants while providing little support for them" (Guangdong Radio, June 16, 1979, in *FBIS*, June 18, 1979, p. P2).

could be sold as a high-priced medicine). Most costly of all, the brigade installed a water-heating facility at the fish pond, so that the Enterprises Team could raise fish in winter as well as summer.

But with this rash of new investments, the brigade was biting off more than the peasants were willing to chew. Many of them were angry at Longyong for financing his new ventures through bank loans, incurring debts that were due in the short term, and then presenting the teams with a fait accompli and a pile of bills. Compounding the peasants' worries, the team cadres simultaneously had plunged into capital investments in new grain warehouses and machinery. The net result was a shortage of cash on hand, and a further downward dip in the peasants' year-end wage payments. Dissatisfied, they continued to shirk their work.

The new reforms had not succeeded in reviving peasant morale. As of 1978, most Chen Villagers were still exhausted by the years of economic setbacks, unhappy with their current circumstances, and pessimistic about the future.

A Sour Inheritance

The dream that Mao Zedong and the party had held out to the peasantry during the 1950s and again during the Four Cleanups had vanished; the opportunity to create a "New China" and a better society had dissipated. One reason, we have seen, lay in the long series of unworkable economic programs that the party leadership had forced upon the peasantry from the late 1960s through the late 1970s till the peasants' goodwill, patience, and credulity had been exhausted. But to understand the fundamental cause of the erosion of faith, it is also necessary to look back to the political struggle campaigns that had shaken the village.

The government had used these struggle campaigns in part as a means of keeping different groups at the lower levels, sometimes cadres and sometimes the masses, dutifully in line out of fears of being targeted. But by a particularly Maoist logic, a campaign also ultimately was supposed to reduce "contradictions" and tensions, paradoxically by increasing those tensions up to and beyond a breaking point. Thus the Four Cleanups initially had tackled cadre corruption by publicly exposing the cadres and exaggerating their wrongdoing, followed by a more conciliatory phase of "putting policy on a solid footing." So, too, other campaigns had lurched toward extremes only to be reined in at the end. The targets of attack were supposed to be "rectified" by their psychic isolation in the face of massed hostility; and the audience was supposed to release and expend its pent-up anger. By the time a campaign had run its course, the catharsis on both sides was supposed to provide a new basis for cooperation and unity.[12]

This Maoist conception of struggle campaigns had been based upon faulty premises. Certainly, in the short term a campaign such as the Four Cleanups did secure most of the cadres' honesty and impartiality—if not always out of community spirit, then out of caution. But the cadres, as well as the ordinary peasants, also clung to old and new grievances; and they had learned from the Four Cleanups campaign how to be politically strategic. Even as the Four Cleanups workteam taught a new moral code, it also tacitly taught villagers how to clothe their motives in the garb of righteousness and, most specifically, how to employ Maoist rhetoric to attack opponents.

Instead of establishing any new unity in the village, thus, the waves of ensuing campaigns had provided an arena for repeated high-pitched infighting, repression, and manipulation. In the attacks launched by the urban-born young people during the Cultural Revolution, the youths had room to fuse their own personal grudges with assertions of high political principles; in the Cleansing of the Class Ranks campaign, Longyong could do likewise—less innocently, far more brutally, and just as righteously; in the One Hit, Three Anti campaign, with the targeting and jailing of naive, hapless Four-Eyes Wu, the righteousness had become blatantly artificial and the attacks purely and strategically manipulative. During the 1970s, in a parallel and similarly disillusioning fashion, the higher levels of the bureaucracy were manipulating Maoist rhetoric and the peasantry's fears of being targeted to force unpopular and patently unfeasible economic policies upon the villages.

[12.] The Maoist ethos and its ramifications in Chen Village are examined and analyzed in considerable detail in Richard Madsen, *Morality and Power in a Chinese Village* (Berkeley: University of California Press, 1984).

In the end, the peasantry had become exhausted with a political rhetoric that all too often had been employed to bludgeon a minority of the villagers and to enforce reticence and conformity among the majority. In the Mao Thought movement of the mid-1960s, they had been taught that self-sacrifice and hard work for the greater good were magic weapons that would improve their lives; but by the mid-1970s they were tired of being pressured into giving up grain for the revolution and skeptical about the credo of a party whose political and economic line kept changing, whose promises of a better life had begun to seem hollow, and whose political pressures were, in fact, retarding the village's economic development. The sour heritage of the late seventies was a climate of cynical mistrust that had not existed even during the depths of the depression of the early sixties.

· 10 ·

The New Era

In December 1978, at an important Central Committee meeting in Peking, Deng Xiaoping and his allies mustered sufficient political muscle to strip Hua Guofeng of his remaining power and to inaugurate plans to steer China dramatically away from the course that had been set by Chairman Mao. The events in Chen Village of the next few years would unfold with a dramatic irony that would have confounded prediction. It was as if Chen Village's tale had been crafted as a work of fiction—as if within the village the Chinese government and the Chen peasants had conspired to write a cynically instructive epilogue to a revolution gone sour. Chen Village would, within a remarkably short period of time, become the embodiment of all that was antithetical to Maoist ideology.

The Exodus

This new act in the drama of Chen Village opened, appropriately enough, with the desertion of its discontented younger generation. In the entire decade since the Cultural Revolution of 1966–68, only some ten people from the village—discounting the urban-born youths—had made the dangerous crossing to Hong Kong. In 1979, however, that trickle to Hong Kong became a sudden flood.

That spring, there had been a riot in the county jail in protest against overcrowded conditions. To alleviate the crowding, the authorities decided to release all those who had been detained merely for trying to escape to Hong Kong. Chen Village and the other villages were immediately swept with the erroneous news that the Chinese government no longer was preventing people from going. That very evening, crowds of young people headed out from Chen Village for the glittering lights and wages of the metropolis. "It was almost like a riot! Everyone was rushing off for Hong Kong."

The same surge toward Hong Kong from villages throughout the border county overwhelmed the guards along the border. Without adequate detention centers, even the small portion whom they caught soon had to be released to try again. With confirmation that escape was easy, the fever spread. One night after another, Chen Village's teenagers, as young as fifteen or sixteen, slipped away from home (often with parental blessings) to join their friends in the British colony. Between May and October of 1979, more than two hundred young people (including a few dozen young women and a couple of dozen married men) had crossed the border.[1] In a few months Chen Village had been deserted by most of its strongest laborers.

Qingfa Triumphant

The flight of Chen Village's young people spelled the defeat of Longyong's economic plans. The village would no longer have sufficient hands to run his brigade-level enterprises—and the newer projects bore heavy debts. That summer, to his embarrassment, the vast auditorium that he had built had to be mortgaged to the state to underwrite the debts due.

The brigade's plunge into insolvency was imminent; and Longyong's authority was dissolving apace. He loudly threatened the families that were abetting their children's flight, but no one listened. He was at his wits' end. When both of his own sons slipped away to Hong Kong, Longyong resigned.

---

[1] The outflow from Chen Village ended when the Hong Kong government, in 1980, clamped down against new immigrants by denying them identity cards and by heavily fining employers who hired anyone without a card.

The ineffectual Jinyi was left at the helm, and the commune leadership understood that a stronger hand was needed. Foolish was one possibility. But he was working as vice-director of the commune's agricultural machinery department and indicated by every means possible that he did not want to return to village life. "Here he had this new job at the commune," explains one of the emigrants, "and if he went back to Chen Village he would have been part of a peasant world again, a move downward."

The commune leadership and the Chen Village party branch looked next toward Qingfa. He had been a capable and forceful leader in his day; he had carefully cultivated amiable relations with other villagers throughout the 1970s; he had renewed and extended his contacts among the commune leadership during his work in charge of commune warehouses; and no one else of any stature seemed willing or able to step into the breach.

When Longyong realized, however, that his long-time opponent might be hoisted back into power, Longyong wanted to fight again for the leadership. But his series of costly failed investments had stripped him of his "political capital." Longyong told an interviewee who revisited Chen Village in 1981 that the commune level had preferred that he, Longyong, get the post; but, he added, he discovered he no longer had enough backing from below.

Most of the Chen Village party members opted for Qingfa, and that swung the contest in his favor. In late 1979 or early 1980, the commune authorities confirmed him as the new party secretary. It had been a decade and a half since Qingfa had lost his power to Longyong, and nearly a dozen years since Qingfa had been excoriated, jailed, and beaten. But the times had turned in his favor; and the top post had fallen into his lap without any real effort on his own part. Politically, Chen Village had come full circle.

Decollectivization

A special irony adhered to the role Qingfa would be fulfilling as party secretary. A dozen years earlier, in the exaggerated, wild rhetoric of the Cultural Revolution, he had been accused of showing insufficient dedication to the socialist cause, of having improper contacts with Hong Kong relatives, of "stepping on two boats [capitalism and socialism] at the same time." Now, directives from the state would be pushing him to follow precisely the path that he had been accused of taking so long before.

A great many villages throughout China in the seventies had experienced the same types of agricultural setbacks and political malaise that had troubled Chen Village.[2] Into the late 1970s, in village after village, production continued to stagnate; team members still slacked off in their work, and team and brigade cadres were finding it difficult to motivate them. Some of the new leaders in Peking were convinced that these problems did not result simply from the harsh radicalism and bureaucratic interference of the immediately preceding years. The difficulties, they felt, had a cause much more far-reaching: too large a dose of socialism had been imposed upon too backward a countryside.

A quarter century earlier, in the mid-1950s, a debate had taken place within the party's top leadership. On the one side were prominent leaders like Liu Shaoqi who argued that collectivization should proceed slowly; so long as modern agricultural machinery was not widely available and farming remained labor-intensive, peasants should work their own relatively small plots of privately owned land. Mao Zedong had been the leading voice on the other side of this debate. He believed that China could not afford to wait till the era of extensive agricultural mechanization. He argued that collectivization should proceed quickly—that collectives would win the peasants' support and that production would climb by means of a more efficient large-scale organization of land and labor. Mao's opinion prevailed, and in 1955–56 a high tide of collectivization had ensued. Now, in the late 1970s and early 1980s, the leadership was implying that the party's basic line since the mid-1950s had been wrong. Moves were under way to roll back two and a half decades of agrarian socialism.

Directives from on high in 1979 advised that China's most impoverished and ill-organized production teams be permitted to adopt a new program, known as a "responsibility system," which would allow the teams to divide production among their house-

---

[2] David Zweig, *Agrarian Radicalism in China, 1968–1981* (Cambridge, Mass.: Harvard University Press, 1989).

holds. The peasant families in such villages would plant and work separate fields and would profit separately from their own crop yields. A team's decision to participate in the program was supposed to be entirely voluntary; but as in so many previous campaigns, Peking simultaneously indicated a decided enthusiasm to see it adopted. Some of the party bureaucrats at county and lower levels who appeared reluctant to implement it found themselves publicly chastised for leftist thinking.[3] Having learned from experience always to tack with the political winds, provincial, county, and commune cadres throughout China soon were endeavoring to show that the leftist tag most certainly did not apply to them. With Peking's blessings, the new drive rolled across growing numbers of districts—with profound implications for China's rural economy.

Qingfa had barely settled into his position as party secretary when his new marching orders arrived in 1980. He was to preside over the de facto decollectivization of Chen Village.

Lots were drawn in each of the production teams to determine which families would be allocated which pieces of land to cultivate. The distribution was to be on a strictly *per capita* basis, with a quarter of an acre of rice land allocated per family member. Since teams still were required to sell grain to the state, each of the households would be responsible for an annual rice-sales quota. But so long as the family handed in its quota, it would be free to plant and sell whatever it wanted to on its allotted fields. Thus, though the teams retained ownership, the Chen Village peasants were again small-scale cultivators, with all of the risks and opportunities for profits that independent entrepreneurship entailed.

The teams had been instructed to distribute not just land but the essential means of production. Farm tools, from shoulder poles to winnowing baskets, were sold off to all of the families. The draft oxen presented a problem. They were too few and too expensive, at a thousand *yuan* apiece, for each family to buy one, yet they were vital for production. So they continued to be owned by the teams, and several families shared one. But almost all of the larger farm equipment—the teams' and brigade's threshers, carts,

---

[3.] See, for example, "Eradicate Leftist Influence, Speed Up Agricultural Development," *Nongye Jingji* (Agricultural Economy), September 1981, pp. 5–6.

and tractors—were auctioned off to the highest bidders (if need be, as with the brigade's large tractor, on credit). The new owners were gambling that they could more than recoup their costs by renting the equipment out to neighbors or by setting up their own transport businesses.

Going a step further, the teams and brigade tendered out to the highest bidders all responsibilities for the village's fruit trees and fish ponds. The new managers would be committed to pay each year the sum they had bid, and in exchange they gained total rights over the yields of the trees and ponds. The village's assets were being parcelled out piece by piece.

Chen Village was among the earlier villages to go this route, but by the close of 1981, up to a third of China's production teams had contracted the land out to their constituent households in much the same fashion. It was not always done voluntarily. Just as the party's policies during the radical era of the seventies had been imposed on villages regardless of local wishes, so, too, the peasants of some villages were now pushed against their will to divide up their team's land and equipment.[4] The policies promoted from on high had swung 180 degrees, but the political system remained unchanged. An imperious leadership and its multilayered bureaucracy were still rigidly dictating to China's peasantry what they must do.[5]

The peasantry of Chen Village, however, had few qualms

---

[4] An interviewee from a village in Xinhui County, Guangdong, relates: "The peasants were literally forced to do it. In fact, one peasant in my team was so angry he refused to go draw lots for the parcels of land he was entitled to. . . . Before, people weren't as worried as they are now; . . . they felt sure of having something to eat in the end. But now [1982], with the land all distributed, they feel financially insecure. . . . Everyone I know in Xinhui County dislikes the new policies. People practically go around saying, 'Down with Deng Xiaoping.' " Another example: the peasantry of a prosperous village in Jiangsu province feared that dividing the large collective fields would play havoc with the irrigation networks they had built up and would be poorly suited to the mechanization they had installed (see David Zweig, "Peasants and New Incentive Systems: Jiangsu Province, 1978–81," in William L. Parish, ed., *Chinese Rural Development: The Great Transformation* [Armonk, NY: M.E. Sharpe, 1985].

[5] On this see Jonathan Unger, "The Decollectivization of the Chinese Countryside: A Survey of Twenty-eight Villages," *Pacific Affairs* 58 (Winter 1985–86): 585–606.

about splitting up the fields. The fervent cooperative spirit of the Mao Thought period of the mid-1960s had been thoroughly eroded by the frustrations of the 1970s. They were now more than willing to go it alone.

In earlier decades, some of them might have feared the new policies. In case of personal illness or a failed crop, a team's pooled land and resources had provided a safety net against starvation. But the Chens felt they no longer needed that type of security. For one thing, most of the Chen families now had a son or daughter in Hong Kong sending back remittances. For another thing, the Chen Village peasants had just been provided with an opportunity to make good money. In that spring of 1980, the county capital had been declared a "special economic zone," where land-short Hong Kong industries would be allowed to expand their operations. As part of this arrangement, the trade barriers between the county and Hong Kong were to be lowered dramatically. All of the villages in the county were given special permission to sell foodstuffs directly to Hong Kong at whatever prices the peasants' produce could command. Chen Village, until recently a rural backwater, was to fall within the economic orbit of a world metropolis.

Indeed, within months the government's procurement office for agricultural produce was closed down in the commune market town, and in its stead wholesalers from Hong Kong were allowed to set up buying stations. They purchased fresh produce at prices several times higher than those previously available from the state. At the same time, in order to allow the peasantry to concentrate on supplying Hong Kong with fresh produce, the state reduced Chen Village's rice quota by 40 percent and entirely eliminated the quotas on peanuts and sugar cane. The Chen families could now put most of their acreage into lucrative vegetable plots. Even more profitably, some of them could convert low-lying rice paddies into commercial fish ponds, to provide fresh carp for Hong Kong's dinner tables. The new crop patterns and marketing opportunities promised the Chens incomes many times higher than they had ever been able to earn before.

Since almost all the able-bodied young males had left for Hong Kong, however, the village faced acute labor shortages that threatened to seriously restrict production and profits. New government policies, though, provided Chen Village with a solution.

Turning yet further from the straight and narrow socialist road, the party leadership had granted permission for the families to hire laborers.[6] The Chens soon were importing farmhands from poorer, more inland counties, especially to help bring in the harvests. These hired hands established a makeshift dormitory in the barn built for the deer (Qingfa had sold the herd to help pay off the brigade's debts), crowded into the teams' empty warehouses (the villagers stored all of their grain at home now), and even moved into the large high-ceilinged brick stalls that the teams had built in the early 1970s under government directives to breed "socialist" pigs (a money-losing proposition now jettisoned).

Some of the Chens stopped working in the fields altogether. Among other things, the industrializing county capital was recruiting peasants from within the county at urban wage scales. Rapidly growing numbers of the young Chen women could obtain jobs there in heavy construction and in the plastics factories established jointly by the Chinese government and Hong Kong capitalists. To take the women's places, their households hired yet more field labor. By 1982, a hundred outsiders were at work in the village on so steady a basis that some had brought along their own families.

Decollectivization in Chen Village went beyond agriculture. In 1980 Qingfa, in accord with a new policy of "contracting out specialized enterprises,"[7] had parceled out the brigade's factories on one-year contracts to the highest bidders. Hiring workers to help them, four Chen families banded together to lease the sugar factory. (As part of the transaction they became responsible for keeping the machinery clean and in repair for the year.) The brick factory was tendered to a total stranger—a newborn Chinese capitalist, as it were—who brought along with him a dozen laborers. Remarkably, it had been only four years since Chairman Mao's death.

Practically all of the endeavors in Chen Village that had been collectively operated were up for grabs. The village store was leased

---

6. This may have been officially permissible only in areas near the "special economic zones." A *People's Daily* article of April 4, 1981, still defined hiring labor as exploitation. Despite this, interviews concerning a few villages in the interior of Guangdong suggest that by early 1982, hired labor was becoming common there, too.

7. See *Southern Daily* (Canton), January 8, 1981, p. 2.

Taking a Live Pig to Market

out to be run privately by a cooperative of four Chen families; and even the village health clinic was put up for bids. It was snapped up for a mere fifty *yuan* a year by the village's barefoot doctor (quite naturally the only applicant), who, true to the prevailing entrepreneurial spirit, alienated patients by raising the fee for any injection to more than a *yuan*. The school remained in public hands, but even here the profit-making fever was felt. Several of the teachers picked up extra money by selling candy in the classrooms, until angry parents forced an end to the practice.

Taking advantage of economic liberalization, some villagers juggled several private enterprises at once. The uncle of one interviewee, using money sent back from his children in Hong Kong, bought a small tractor for several thousand *yuan*, hired a hand to drive it, and went into business transporting construction materials. He bid for several acres of fish ponds and hired a second helper to tend these for him. He opened a small store. All told, he was netting 6,000 *yuan* a year in his varied pursuits, compared to the 2,000 *yuan* earned by the average Chen family still working full time in agriculture. The uncle was so busy managing his business affairs that when the fields were parceled out for a second time in early 1982, he declined to claim any land and left agriculture altogether.

It was tacitly understood that this second allocation of land was to be on a semi-permanent basis, to encourage families to improve the soil quality. Hence, by 1982, Chen Village's fields had become tantamount to private landholdings. Team cadres had few discernible powers any longer, just tasks such as collecting the rice quotas and disbursing agricultural supplies; and it had become difficult to persuade anyone to become a team head. As an emigrant explained, "ordinary peasants, you see, get more time to make money."

Villagers were living well. It was partly that they were earning good money from the high prices paid for produce and from their private ventures. But perhaps equally important to their new lifestyle were the money and consumer items flowing back from Hong Kong. Most of the men who had left in 1979 had found jobs in Hong Kong's construction industry and, dutifully filial, they were remitting savings and were returning on visits home during the Chinese New Year laden down with foreign luxuries. Most families had received electric fans; several possessed electric rice cookers; almost all wore Hong Kong fashions: "Folks no longer sew their own clothes; the sewing machines are going to rust." By 1982, close to half of the village households had obtained gifts of Hitachi color television sets, with special built-in devices to receive both Chinese and Hong Kong programs. Families that only half a decade earlier had been obliged to participate frequently in night-time political meetings now instead spent their evenings glued to TV showings of Hong Kong's soap operas, kungfu movies, and variety shows.[8]

What in previous times would have been considered capitalist roading had become commonplace—the consumerism, the private hiring of labor, the private wheeling and dealing. But the peasants were not particularly worried that their money-making activities or lifestyles might get them into trouble later, even if national policies

---

[8.] Says an emigrant who returned home for a week in early 1982: "Since 1980 the peasants haven't been going to any political meetings. When there's something that has to be related to the village, Qingfa just announces it through the broadcast system. Otherwise, the broadcast system is barely used. Without the political meetings the peasants don't even know the government policies anymore. Only the cadres know what's happening."

Consumerism, 1981

were to shift leftward again. As one of our interviewees explained to us in 1982, "You see, everyone's engaged in all this stuff. Even the village party leaders, even the people in the commune party committee." Why should an ordinary peasant worry about any of his own pursuits when he could see cadres at all levels, from the county leadership down to Qingfa and other members of the party branch, openly and flagrantly taking advantage of their positions to enrich themselves?

The Four Cleanups Nullified

Since 1977 there had been no campaigns, and no signs that any workteams might soon descend on the villages. Government rhetoric spoke of stability; and in addition, there had been a decided relaxation in the party's expectations that villages should conform to rigorous political standards. Qingfa confided to a visitor from Hong Kong: "I'm not afraid there'll be political storms anymore; I'm sitting in a steady boat." He calculated that he could do as he liked henceforth.

He certainly had no desire to pursue the role of the righteous, abstemious, self-sacrificing party cadre of the sort that had been the heroes of official Chinese fiction. Longyong, in his own flawed way, had built his political capital on that model; but it was a model suited to a time gone by. It connoted a dedication to beliefs that neither the peasantry nor the local leaders any longer shared. The leadership style that Qingfa now chose, the style he felt most comfortable with, was more that of the traditional Chinese gentry: oriented toward kinship loyalties and networks of friends and retainers, with the acquiescence of other villagers secured through patronage bestowed and favors traded. It was almost as if the Four Cleanups campaign had never occurred.

The campaigns of the intervening decade and a half had not "purified" Qingfa; like many other party cadres in China, he had emerged more cynical and self-serving than he had been in his youth. He proceeded to milk his new tenure as party secretary for all it was worth, aided by other cadres on the brigade party committee who were willing to connive in mutual back-scratching for their own gain.

As party secretary, Qingfa got the lion's share. There was a large grove of giant bamboo along the river; and rather than put it up for bidding, the committee agreed to let Qingfa take it for ten *yuan*. The grove was worth more than a hundred times that amount. He allocated to himself, free of charge, a hillock of honeysuckle (a Chinese medicinal herb) planted in earlier years for the health clinic. He had the brigade rent bulldozers to relevel the land occupied by Longyong's unfinished dike. Awarding himself the major portion of this land, he hired field hands to till it for him.[9]

[9.] According to Chinese newspaper reports (e.g., *Southern Daily*, January 30, 1982, p. 2), connivance by cadres in parceling out brigade property to themselves occurred in a lot of villages during the decollectivization drive.

Rhetoric about promoting Chen Village's interests went hand in hand with schemes to help those near and dear to him. In 1981, for instance, Qingfa made a trip to Hong Kong to persuade the young Chens who had emigrated to contribute money to the village's economic development. At the wedding banquet of two of the emigrants, attended by most of their generation, Qingfa rose and appealed to their loyalty. "All the other villages around have received trucks and boats," he said, "and our village alone doesn't have any." The emigrants quickly raised HK$60,000 (US$10,000) and bought a secondhand 2½-ton truck and a 50-foot boat, to be used for shipping products to and from Hong Kong. But Qingfa disposed of the new gifts in ways beneficial to old friends from his lineage branch and to the relatives of fellow cadres. Jinyi, the ineffectual former party secretary, was serving now as deputy party secretary, and to put him in Qingfa's debt, Qingfa arranged for Jinyi's son to operate the truck almost like a private business; he would just have to pay the brigade a portion of the profits. Of all rural enterprises, transport is one of the most lucrative, and such an arrangement, said an interviewee, was "like stumbling upon gold." The seven villagers who were appointed to operate the boat, again as a profit-sharing endeavor, were all the relatives of people close to or important to Qingfa.

With the dispersal of the brigade's property, a party secretary had far fewer responsibilities than in previous times. But Qingfa still had a certain measure of power over the peasants. He controlled access to permits of all sorts; and local prosecutorial powers were still effectively in his hands. Qingfa let it be known that villagers could curry his favor by plying him with gifts.[10] "Whenever we return to Chen Village," one of the young emigrants observes, "we, too, would drop by his house to pay our respects. Last time I gave him several packs of foreign cigarettes. All these gifts add up, you know." Qingfa could afford to buy the village's first refrigerator.

[10] Qingfa was not alone in this practice. An interviewee from another village observed, "Nowadays the cadres don't even have to ask, and things like fresh fish will be presented to them. The peasants do so in the hope the cadres will return the favors. My uncle, who's a cadre, tells me he only has to suggest it, and there'll be people coming to volunteer their labor free to work his land. . . . Sometimes the peasants mockingly refer to cadres behind their backs as 'Boss.' "

He flaunted his new wealth. Unhappy with his old cramped family home, he had a new one built and, as money continued to flow his way, quickly decided to erect a third and even larger house. Scouting for a prestigious site, he chose the open space alongside the giant community hall, where the village's outdoor stage once stood—precisely the spot where Qingfa had been "struggled" against a dozen years earlier. No one dared to object to his purchase of the prime site, and on it he constructed a three-story gold-and-white-tiled building grander than anything Chen Villagers had envisaged up to that time. The going rate for construction work was five *yuan* a day, and that was what the Chen Villagers whom he employed expected, but Qingfa in the end insisted upon paying them only three *yuan,* and there was nothing they could do about it.

In the exhausted, sour political climate of the early eighties, corruption had become entrenched at every level of the political system.[11] Most of the Chen peasants felt that so long as they were generally doing well financially, it was best to accede to Qingfa's impositions and to continue to ply him with gifts to stay on his good side. They were convinced that "the commune level doesn't care, just considers it the brigade's own affairs." But more than that, some of the villagers were not particularly perturbed either by Qingfa's appropriations of property or his gift taking. A number of them felt they would do likewise if they were in his shoes. Qingfa's abuses seemed in keeping with a widely shared mood of cynical privatism and advantage seeking.

Even Longyong had accommodated himself to the climate of the times. He no longer put forward a persona of rectitude to challenge Qingfa, as he had in the early 1960s. Like other villagers, Longyong now only concerned himself with his own family and sought to enrich himself as best he could, by hook or by crook. He had leased the grain processing plant and hired two laborers to run it for him, and he spent much of his time away from the village, buying cattle in poor districts and reselling them at a high profit in

---

[11.] In early 1982, Peking announced a major campaign to staunch the spreading corruption. The national drive began with fanfare, but quietly burned itself out in the countryside before it had targeted many transgressors.

richer districts. To do so was still illegal, but Longyong used the official contacts he had developed as a cadre to smooth his way. Even Jinyi had abandoned his earlier stance of incorruptibility. Trying to make extra money, he tagged along on some of Longyong's illicit trips.

Other Chen Village peasants were involved in illegal activities of their own. A dozen years earlier, when faith in Chairman Mao's teachings and in the political system still had a hold on the peasantry, there had been a decided puritanical streak to their values; but in the early 1980s, by contrast, "the winds of gambling and stealing are blowing very strong." When the county mounted a drive to clamp down on organized gambling, the night-time gambling sessions in the village (which drew a clientele from throughout the surrounding district) simply moved into public buildings to avoid getting homeowners in trouble during police raids.

In the mid-seventies, the theft of wandering chickens had been a topic for scandalized conversation. Since then, petty theft had become commonplace. The worry now, for the first time since the Liberation, was for the safety of homes and livestock. Several unattended houses were burglarized (by outside gangs, the villagers preferred to believe), and thieves (this time obviously outsiders) even dared to cart off two oxen by truck. An appeal to the police in this latter case fell on deaf ears, however. In keeping with the times, the concern of the police was to turn a profit: "They're more interested in getting the gamblers than catching thieves because they get a bonus from the county for every gambling party they smash."[12]

The degeneration of public spirit perhaps could be seen most vividly in the filthy state of village lanes. These had been kept clean from the Four Cleanups through the late 1970s. But now they had become rank with garbage again. In the heat of summer, in 1981, a mild stench hung over the community.

Needless to say, interviewees from the village were perturbed by the rapid decay in public morality, but they also were generally

[12.] An interviewee from a village farther inland reported that the decline of social order "has become one of the peasants' major dissatisfactions. Nowadays even brigade militias have been known to go stealing things in other villages. No one in authority cares to do anything about it. It's because there are no campaigns any more. The cadres themselves are corrupt. No one can control the situation."

relieved that the all-too-tight village morality and shows of righteousness of the Maoist era had disintegrated. Whatever the corruption and political malaise of the early eighties, villagers were no longer subjected to the tensions of struggle campaigns; the more politically vulnerable households in the village were no longer periodically being publicly scapegoated; there was no longer any prospect of old women being viciously beaten, as had occurred during the Cleansing of the Class Ranks. The good-class majority no longer needed to persecute others to play up its own "revolutionary nature." Interviewees of all class backgrounds in the early eighties were glad that their village was out from under the "class line" and the political manipulation it had entailed.

Once the government removed its policy of sanctions against the old bad classes, in fact, discrimination against them in the village quickly evaporated. The few young men from such homes who had remained in the community found that class origins no longer counted even in arranging marriages; what instead had become of prime importance was the wealth and income potential of a man's family. Even the old landlords, now retired, could, for the first time since the land reform of the fifties, mingle casually with other villagers: "Old Landlord Mou now sits outside the store every day, reading *Southern Daily* to other villagers and discussing world and national politics!"

Even the old guerrilla-turned-bad-class element was presented with a belated fresh start. Through old acquaintances at the customs office and with Qingfa's help, he was taken back into the customs service; and his son, no longer suffering the burden of a bad-class family label, was appointed team head by his production team. Within the space of a year, though, the father was despondently back in the village, having been caught red-handed at his customs post trying to steal goods. The old man had been too carelessly eager to take advantage of the new lax times.

Heaven's Revenge

It soon transpired that the old guerrilla's old-time patron, Qingfa, similarly had been too careless in his pursuit of wealth. Given the power of his position and the corruption of most of his

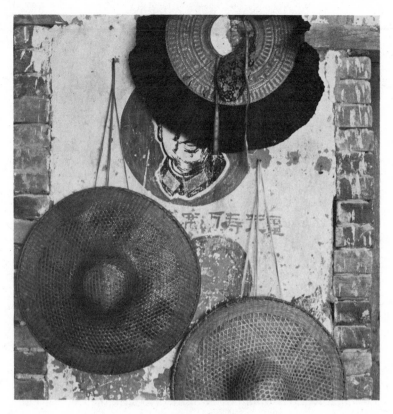

De-Maoification

fellow officials, he had felt he could flaunt his corruptibility. He had not reckoned on Longyong.

Throughout the eighties, during the sporadic anti-corruption campaigns ordered by the top party leadership in Peking, work-teams no longer descended on villages to carry out across-the-board investigations. During these newer campaigns, party officials at the county and former commune seats felt under at least mild pressure to show results, but they were prone to act only when complaints against a particularly corrupt cadre were handed up from below.

In 1983 Peking had announced an Anti-Spiritual Pollution campaign to weed out corrosive Western "bourgeois liberal" ideas, and to give the effort a popular veneer the government harnessed an anti-corruption drive to this larger campaign. Perceiving an opening to bring down Qingfa, Longyong quietly sought out Sunwang, the former Cultural Revolution small-group head. As former cadres, the two men knew how to go about lodging a complaint of abuse of power, and knew how to bring leverage to bear through old comrades at the commune seat. The commune party secretary personally came to Chen Village to investigate the accusations and, having verified them, a public denunciation meeting was organized one evening. A sizable number of villagers came forward to charge that on such and such occasions they had been forced to pay out bribes to Qingfa. Foolish, in his capacity as a commune official, sat at the side recording the torrent of accusations, and compiled them into a legal report. Qingfa was fined some four to five thousand *yuan* and was ordered to hand back the bamboo grove and some of the other brigade property that he had appropriated. He was summarily ousted from his post as party secretary and, as a final blow, stripped of his party membership, a penalty that he had never before incurred.

Qingfa was not broken by this multiple setback. Despite the fines and confiscations, he had been left with substantial capital, and once no longer a cadre he earnestly put his attention to new money-making endeavors. He contracted out large stretches of hillside to grow pineapples and sweet potatoes and to establish an orchard, and hired workers from poorer districts to farm the land for him. Within the space of just a couple of years, he was well on his way to building a small private fortune to replace the public trough that he had previously controlled. And then, as the villagers would put it, fate intervened.

In 1986, Qingfa was invited to attend the wedding of one of his workers. It was in a county a few hours' distance away, and the drunken driver of the minibus carrying Qingfa and other celebrants crashed the van on the way back. Qingfa died in the wreckage.

Some villagers reckoned an unnatural death befit Qingfa's life. One of the Chens recalls that "When he died, people in the village felt he deserved it. They said he craved good food too much, to go so far for a free feast. That it served him right, to have been such a glutton." The Chinese have traditionally believed in fate, and that the mode of one's death is meaningfully intertwined with one's life.

In line with this, even a former deputy team head of Qingfa's team who expresses regret for Qingfa's death—"He did, after all, help out our team from way back, subtly manipulating things so that we'd get the best deals"—nonetheless seconds the view that Qingfa had gotten the end that was coming to him: "If I were superstitious, I would say it was Heaven's revenge."

In villagers' eyes, Qingfa had been destroyed by his own excesses. But in the villagers' eyes, too, the failings that Qingfa had come to represent seemed triumphant: his flaws seemed little more than the village's failings personified. The desire for "free feasts" and the "gluttony" that Qingfa in the end had come to symbolize, and to which his death was attributed, would outlive him. As shall be observed, a hunger for "free meals" aptly represented the prevailing mentality of the ordinary Chen Villager during the second half of the eighties.

A "Revolutionary Successor"

When Qingfa fell in 1983, he was succeeded in office by Sunwang. But the former Cultural Revolution small-group head, albeit honest, was deemed a man of the past. New party regulations had decreed that rural leaders should be educated, and Sunwang was only semiliterate. Directives called for a lowering in the average age of village leaders, and he was already fifty. Moreover, he did not seem forceful or decisive enough in the way he handled his new duties. By 1985, before he had entrenched himself in office, the commune party set him aside in favor of a man of a newer generation.

The new party secretary, a short broad-shouldered 35-year-old named Baodai, had attended one or two years of junior high school, unlike most of the men older than himself. Even as a teenager he had been an able speaker, and in the Four Cleanups campaign the cadre workteam had chosen him as a Mao Thought counselor and as the youngest of the local "revolutionary successors" who were to be groomed for leadership positions. Despite that show of favor, at the beginning of the Cultural Revolution, attracted by the excitement, he had been one of the five local good-class youths who had initially sided with the sent-down youths'

Rebel Red Guard group. But he had quickly and pragmatically seen the foolishness of his ways, switched sides, and in 1968 had been selected to sit on the Cultural Revolution leadership small group as a representative of "youth." Flushed with enthusiasm, during the Cleansing of the Class Ranks campaign he was memorably active in ferreting out counter-revolutionary suspects as a member of Ao's investigative team.

Baodai was duly awarded with a brigade post as Communist Youth League secretary and, some years later, as the village's militia head and then in turn the public-security head. In between these latter postings, to consolidate his credentials as a man of leadership caliber, he had served a stint as a production team leader. He was paying his dues and moving steadily toward the top.

He had held the added advantage of not having any blood kin in the village. His father, as a child, had wandered into the village as a refugee and had been adopted by a childless couple. One might have thought that having no blood relatives would have been a severe handicap in a lineage village, but most of the Chens reasoned that someone like Qingfa, enmeshed in a circle of kin relations, was bound to show undue favoritism to relations. It was considered by villagers somewhat less than coincidental that first Chen Sumei, the village's first party leader in the 1950s, and then Chen Sunwang, the Cultural Revolution leadership small group head, and now Chen Baodai—all of them adopted into the village—had been able to rise to the top politically. They were, after all, men who might be expected to show somewhat greater impartiality in their relations with villagers.

Baodai had yet an additional advantage in the wake of Qingfa's fall. Though he had served under Qingfa during the early eighties he had not been Qingfa's man. He was, in fact, from the old No. 4 team, the neighborhood that had had conflicts with Qingfa ever since Qingfa rigged the land allocations in 1961–62 in ways that disfavored that team. Baodai had, in fact, been considered more "Longyong's man"; and now, with the repudiation of Qingfa's corruption and Baodai's rise into the top leadership post, Longyong and those who preferred him could take satisfaction.

During the following years, Baodai fulfilled those hopes. He was considered relatively uncorrupt as the village party secretary—despite a clear willingness to accept private gifts and cash from his constituents. The Chen Villagers had adopted a relaxed and markedly realistic perspective on corruption that allowed Baodai to get away with such behavior and still retain a decent reputation. Villagers reasoned that a man with the qualifications and connections to be a party secretary would, were he to resign, be able to make an excellent living in the private sector. The post of party secretary paid Baodai only 1,500 *yuan* a year, far less than the income of the average family, so it was deemed acceptable that he should see to his own interests and make up the difference through private donations. A livelihood on a par with that of the village's most successful entrepreneurs was almost considered his due. Many of the cadres in other villages were far more greedy, in the pattern of Qingfa, reaching well beyond such an income in their demands for bribes and payoffs. Corruption is defined in the countryside as grossly overstepping the informally acceptable levels of payoffs—not the generous but routine private donations that Baodai was accepting.

Baodai's "take" was similar in spirit to what the Chinese official-dom of imperial times regularly practiced. Underpaid by the imperial court, a county magistrate under the emperors was half expected to supplement his income in the form of gifts and money from impor-tuning citizens. The Chinese government in the 1980s, caught in budgetary squeezes at all levels, seemed tacitly to have reverted to this tradition: setting low salaries for officials and then looking the other way when officials augmented these as best they could.

It was the practice even with the county's police, and Chen Villagers complained that they wanted far more than their due share in bribes. Even worse was their chaotic approach to bribe-taking. A Chen Village family, using remittances from a son who had left for Hong Kong, bought a secondhand minibus and began running a transport service along the county's main through road, but police from each of the commune towns along the way lay in wait to extract fines and bribes from them and others on the road. The random, uncoordinated, escalating demands for money soon drove the family out of business. Corruption, villagers agreed, was out of hand in the mid-1980s. It was felt the police in particular needed to better coor-dinate their exactions and bring them down to a more tolerable level. But it took several more years before the various police units finally got their act together.

· 11 ·

The Midas Touch

By the close of the eighties, the majority of Hong Kong's industry had moved across the border into the neighboring counties of China, lured by cheap labor. The once-sleepy Chinese border town of Shenzhen had grown into a skyscraper city populated by immigrants from throughout Guangdong and the interior of China, who labored to produce electronic goods and garments that still often bore the label "Made in Hong Kong." The labels were not entirely inappropriate. Economically, the border between Hong Kong and China had, as it were, moved northward into China.

Seeking yet cheaper rents and even cheaper labor, Hong Kong entrepreneurs had begun looking beyond Shenzhen, and by 1989–90 much of the two-hour journey from Shenzhen to Chen Village, on a road vastly overburdened with truck traffic, passed through a scene of frenetic construction. New factory buildings and their adjacent dormitories, built for rent to Hong Kong business corporations, haphazardly lined stretches of the road. Encouraged by the easy money that had been made through such structures, every village and town along the way seemed to be jumping on the bandwagon by constructing a similar industrial zone of its own. As far as the eye could see, stretching into the distance on both sides of the road, wetland rice fields were being filled in with clay and rock debris by armies of bulldozers and trucks. Films of red and yellowish dust blanketed the terrain. At least temporarily, large parts of a

*A New Market-Town Factory. Built on recently reclaimed
farmland; upstairs is the workers' dormitory.*

district that only recently had contained some of the richest farm-
lands in China resembled nothing less than the surface of the moon.

As of 1990 Chen Village sat near the outer edge of one scarred
corridor of this chaotic would-be conurbation. Even the town
which had served as the former commune headquarters (the term
"commune" had been expunged from official terminology in the
mid-1980s and replaced by the term "township"), which lay a few
miles down the road from the village, had been utterly transformed
from a sleepy market town into a bustling center of labor-intensive
light industry. Every few minutes, buses plying between Shenzhen
and outlying counties pulled into the main street of the town to
disgorge passengers; and taxis regularly pulled up to deposit or pick
up Hong Kong business managers out for the day to inspect their
factories.

To travelers accustomed to other parts of East Asia, the town's
architecture and general ambience seemed strikingly reminiscent of
the rapidly industrializing towns of two decades earlier in Taiwan:
the same cacophony of motor scooters; the same crowded family-

run shops that stayed open into the night, selling a motley range of cheap and expensive merchandise; the same large flashing neon signs advertising tiny unhygienic restaurants; the same lack of pedestrian sidewalks despite dangerously heavy through-traffic and incompetently aggressive drivers; the same unplanned sprawl. Much of the town's populace had arrived in recent years from elsewhere, drawn in from poorer rural districts by the coveted chance to work in the factories of Hong Kong entrepreneurs. Some 90 percent of the town's population were now non-native to the area.

Chen Village was only fifteen minutes away by car along a newly paved road. But as of 1990 it remained far enough back from the burgeoning town and the main traffic routes to retain an aura of rural placidity. From afar, rice fields and fish ponds, picturesquely backed up by the foothills of a mountain range, greeted visitors much as when the sent-down youths first arrived in 1964. But close up, the entrance to Chen Village had been altogether transformed. A row of large, modern, lavishly tiled three-story houses, each fronted by walled courtyards and ornate gates, ostentatiously lined the entry road; and close by, on what until recently had been ricelands, stood an impressively large primary school, similar in architecture to the schools of Hong Kong.

The Village Expands.
New homes encroach upon rice paddy.

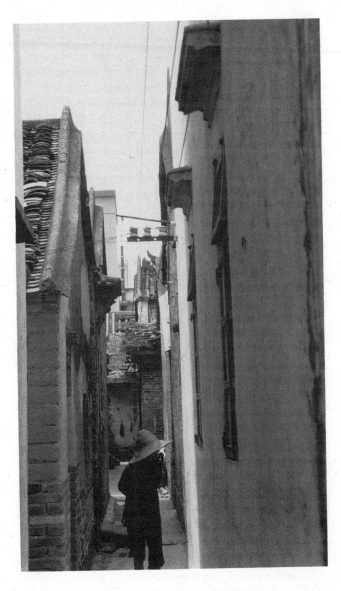

Old Lanes of the "Inner" Village

A hundred yards further on lay the old maze of village lanes, still crowded wall-to-wall with small one- and two-story houses, but manifesting a new prosperity. The lanes were uniformly well paved in concrete, with no remaining traces of the dirt and mud mixed with refuse that had greeted walkers in the early eighties.

At the center of this labyrinth of narrow lanes, the main village square now teemed with commerce for a few hours every morning. Villagers were plainly eating very well: there were four butchers' stalls, a dozen vegetable stalls, and two fresh-fish stalls, some run by villagers and some by outsiders. One vendor had even opened a daily furniture stall in the square. A decade earlier, there had been no such daily market; few villagers had had any cash on hand. Now, they were very much part of a consumer cash society, spending money freely on a regular basis. The Chens had their pick first; and the laborers from poor inland counties who worked in the village then bargained for the final leftovers: the animal heads, fat, and vegetable rejects.

In the past decade, life had been transformed for the Chens not just materially, but, just as obviously, politically. The only political slogans in sight adorned the walls of dilapidated public buildings, and the slogans were so faded as to be barely legible. The physical traces of the Maoist era had all but disappeared.

The Lost Generation

Chen Village had never had it so good, and very few in the village would ever have countenanced a return to earlier times. But whatever the material improvements in the peasants' lives, the village was, tragically, *too* close to the wealth of Hong Kong.

Living under the shadow cast by Hong Kong, the young men in particular were acutely aware that their relatives who had left for the British colony in 1979, when the borders were last open, were now making vastly more money than they themselves could ever hope to earn, even in this prospering region of China. Almost all of the two hundred Chen Village men who had fled to Hong Kong had become construction workers—such former Mainland peasants today make up the bulk of Hong Kong's building trade—and by the close of the 1980s they were earning some HK$10,000 (US$1300) a month, and almost double that amount when overtime work was available. They could earn, in short, some ten to twenty times more than their younger brothers and cousins in Chen Village could possibly make as farmers or as workers in the sweatshop assembly plants of the local industrial towns. This invidious comparison rankled; and it drained the young men of Chen Village of any desire to enter the workforce. Rather than labor all day for what their kin across the border could afford to spend on just a couple of packs of cigarettes or one dish in a restaurant, they preferred to live as dependents on their Hong Kong relations. Few of them deigned to hold a job, unless a Hong Kong–based relative was willing to buy them a truck that would elevate them to the prestigious status of an owner/driver.

The majority of the young men lounged around the village, and many of them passed the time by gambling at mahjongg for heavy stakes. Such idleness now passed as a sign of status. Those with Hong Kong relations set the standard: that it was beneath contempt for a man to enter the local factories for such seemingly paltry wages. Some of the young men who did not have any kin in Hong Kong, desperate to keep up with their friends' lifestyles, turned instead to petty crime to support their gambling habits and their liking for Marlboros. A few became engaged in petty smuggling, helping to carry contraband further inland. Others turned to theft, the incidence of which climbed precipitously during the latter half of the eighties. Traditionally, theft had been common in the Chinese countryside, but robbers normally had been careful to steal from *other* villages, not from their own community. Now, in a sign of how far the sense of local community had declined, most of the house theft in Chen Village could be traced to the village's own young men. In the 1960s and 1970s, villagers usually had left their doors unlocked when they went out to work. Now, they not only found it necessary to lock up; they had installed massive iron-grill outer gates as an extra precaution.

If the generation of youths of the 1970s had been dissatisfied, this younger generation, throughout the county, seemed to their elders to be irredeemably "lost." Hard drugs were not yet a problem in Chen Village, but growing numbers of the young men who had grown up in the nearby market towns reportedly had turned to heroin, smuggled in by Hong Kong's secret societies, the so-called triads. In the 1980s these triad criminal organizations had spread rapidly across the border, recruiting young local hoods. The local triad groups now operated protection rackets in the nearby market towns, bleeding the private stall-holders and shopkeepers. A war to control such "protection" territories nearly broke out in the late 1980s between the triad gang of Chen Village's township and the gang of a neighboring township. Fighting was averted only at the last minute when triad emissaries from Hong Kong arrived to adjudicate the dispute.

Even though the village was unable to immunize itself against petty crime, the quarter-hour motorbike ride from the market town still kept Chen Village at arm's length from the hard drugs and underworld activity. Parents could console themselves that whatever the malaise in the village, life there continued to hold some advantages over the nearby urbanizing centers. But they nevertheless were deeply perplexed and worried by their sons, and by the frustrated dreams and daily boredom that undermined the young people's spirits.

Looking backward in time for some solution, the father of a twenty-year-old, in conversations with us, lamented the evaporation of the community structures that in his own day had provided organized activities and camaraderie for village young people. In the mid-1970s, this man had been one of the earliest to leave for Hong Kong, so dissatisfied had he been at the stifling collectivism of that period. But now, a decade and a half later, he looked back at the collective life through different spectacles, nostalgically comparing it to the less cohesive community where he now spent his weekends twice each month:

> Before, the brigade at festivals would organize a basketball competition between the production teams, and it would allocate money toward lion dance groups and martial arts groups. Now, instead of such community get-togethers, people just watch TV and video cassettes in their own homes. Before, even watching TV was done all together on the village's only set, at the community hall. Now even the hall has been rented out to a Hong Kong businessman as a factory.
>
> Before, as teenagers graduated from school they joined the village militia or the Communist Youth League. They moved from one sort of community organization to another as they grew up. Now the Youth League has almost no meetings, and almost no members. And the village militia doesn't

even exist any longer. Now the young people have no sense of belonging to anything, and they have nothing to do with their time. I think that contributes to the crime rate. People don't do anything together any more, except gamble. Before, the young men would go down to the river to bathe together: now it's too polluted, and even that's gone, even bathing. The entire sense of community life is gone, and I regret it deeply.

Do I have any aspirations for my son? Just that he be a bit filial, and that he not go around stealing like so many others. That's all you can hope for these days.

Industrious Daughters

The young women of Chen Village remained more obedient to their parents and less rebelliously frustrated than the young men. Raised to have fewer ambitions than their brothers, they seem to have found it easier to accommodate themselves to the gap between local realities and the frustrated desires for Hong Kong lifestyles. Whereas the young men of Chen Village largely refused to enter the factories, daughters were considerably more amenable.

This is not to say that the teenaged girls looked forward with positive feelings to factory work. In fact, many of them tried to delay their entry into the workforce by staying on at school as long as possible. In this, too, they were quite different from their brothers, who despaired of any future and looked at education and a school diploma as "useless." Often, to the consternation of parents, they dropped out before graduation in order to join their friends on motorbikes, at pinball arcades, and at mahjongg.

Whereas in the early 1980s many of Chen Village's young women had left home to work in the factories of Shenzhen city, it no longer seemed worthwhile to do so after factories opened within pedaling distance from home. Though local salaries remained a bit lower than in Shenzhen, at home a young woman could save considerably on dormitory fees and eating expenses. Almost all of Chen Village's unmarried young women now pedaled off to work every morning either at the township headquarters town or at the headquarters town of the township next door, for wages ranging from 200 *yuan* to 500 *yuan* monthly.

This factory work expanded their social horizons. They were intermingling at work with women from other villages and even other counties, and in the towns were meeting and being wooed by young local men from the surrounding villages. Consequently, whereas most betrothals in Chen Village through the 1970s were with fellow villagers and fellow Chens, by the late 1980s the majority were being consummated with young people from other communities in the area. Yet this in no sense reflected any reversion to traditional custom. Unlike the betrothals of traditional times, these marriages were not arranged by parents on behalf of youngsters who had never met; instead they were "romance" marriages of the young people's own doing, a reflection of the young women's widening range of contacts. And a young woman was not severing frequent contact with her own parents and relations by moving into a different village. Motorbikes had greatly reduced the friction of distance between villages; a daughter who lived in another village was now mere minutes away from her parents' home, almost as close at hand as if she lived within the village itself, and was conveniently returning home several times a week.

Despite the shift back to cementing marriages outside the village, the bride price demanded for a daughter's hand remained low. Partly it was because parents recognized that much as with intra-village marriages, they would not altogether be losing their daughter to another family. But perhaps a more important part of the explanation for low bride prices lay in a shift in the villagers' sense of their own wealth. Similar to the truly wealthy of traditional China, and similar too to the European wealthy of several centuries ago, a young woman's parents were now tempted to show off how much they could afford to spend in giving away their daughter. As a Chen Villager whose child had recently gotten married explained:

> Before, people were poor, so if you gave away your daughter you felt you were losing something and wanted something in return, a good bride price. Now, because people are well off, they feel, when I marry off my daughter I want to look good. A high dowry looks good.

If the family had a source of funds from Hong Kong, a daughter thus carried into marriage a trousseau that included a wealth of jewelry, often including a couple of expensive necklaces, several silver bracelets, and several dozens of rings. And for herself and her husband the dowry would include a color television set, a large motorcycle, and other ostentatiously expensive items.

The government had raised the legal age of marriage to 22 for men and 20 for women, but a great many were now getting married in their late teens.[1] One villager strongly hinted to us that a recent rise in pre-marital pregnancies explained many a hurried marriage; but it also seems, quite simply, that many of the families saw early marriage as desirable *per se*. In traditional times, and even under the collectives, early marriages had been associated with prosperity; most weddings had had to be delayed while the groom's family labored and saved to build the requisite new home (see pp. 194–95). Now, prosperity had arrived in the form of Hong Kong remittances, and families could afford that luxury of an earlier wedding. And they no longer felt inhibited by regulations. As the women's representative made clear to us, with the break-up of the collectives the state no longer had the means at its disposal to enforce the marriage-age laws.

After they married, most of the young women continued to work in the factories. A great many of them continued to work even after they had children, so long as a mother-in-law was available to look after them. Thus, while husbands stayed at home, the young wives frequently had become the family's main local source of financial support. But even the women imposed strict limits on the type of work they were willing to do. They, like their unemployed husbands, refused to be seen in the farm-fields. During the 1980s a prejudice had rapidly developed in Chen Village against agricultural labor, even though farming one's own land could net about the same amount of pay as factory work. But farmwork had come to be seen as "backward" and physically onerous, unlike the "modern" and thus more high-status factory labor.

Only some of the villagers over the age of forty were willing to go out into the fields any longer. Most of the other villagers shied

---

1. These young couples go through a wedding ceremony at the home of the groom's parents, which in the eyes of the peasantry legitimates the marriage, more so than an official registration of it at the market town. The young couple openly take up married life together until they come of legal age and then belatedly register the marriage.

away from it entirely, to the extent that some of the families with relatives in Hong Kong even had begun buying all of their vegetables in the market rather than maintain a small vegetable patch.

Symbols of Prestige

It did not go unnoticed among Chen Village emigrés that relatives back home were disinclined to work—all the while that they themselves in Hong Kong labored ten or more hours a day. Some of the emigrants were painfully aware, moreover, that pouring financial support into Chen Village had undermined the initiative and self-respect of the young men. But given the undeniable fact that only two or three days of Hong Kong wages would support their relatives' expenses in China for a month, they had difficulty reducing their remittances. On their trips home, they would have been laid open to the terrible embarrassment of seeming unfilial and ungracious. It would go against everything that they had been taught while young about family obligations.

For some of the emigrés, it was much more than just a question of a few dollars a month. They found themselves trapped in a competition among themselves to seem generously wealthy within the village, a competition encouraged by their relatives. New neighborhoods of ostentatious villas on the outskirts of the village bore testimony to this competition. The exteriors of these villas of two, three, and even four stories were lavishly and sometimes garishly tiled to impress, and inside boasted such modern amenities as tiled bathrooms with flush toilets. (The effluents were discreetly piped into the nearby fishponds to be eaten by carp that ended up on unsuspecting Hong Kong tables.) The villas had cost their donors dearly. More often than not, the men who paid to have them built lived, incongruously, in a single cramped rented room in Hong Kong—while vying to prop up the lifestyles of close kin, and their own reputations, back home.

An additional irony was attached to this competitive effort. Not all of the beneficiaries even felt comfortable in the new villas. An emigrant who built for his parents one of the grandest in the village explained:

Modern House. An emigrant who cannot afford to build a grand villa provides his relations with a tiled two-story home.

My mother refused to move into the new house; she prefers to stay in the old one. And my father stays overnight in the new one just to keep it guarded. But we got the house built rather than invest the money in some business because all villagers *have* to show first that they can afford one of these new houses. And when families do move into the new one they won't want to sell the old one, feeling it would be a loss of face to be seen selling off an ancestral home. So the old houses just lie empty.

The emigrants who bankrolled their kin in Chen Village were paying a very high price for status.

Two Nations

Not far from the largest and flashiest of these neighborhoods of new villas lay another new neighborhood of a very different sort.

Tent Housing Immigrant Workers

It consisted entirely of flimsy tents stitched together from plastic sacks. These were the homes of some of the temporary workers from the poorer parts of Guangdong. The number of such laborers in Chen Village had grown since the early eighties, apace with the decreasing inclination of the Chens to do their own work.

Whereas Chen Village in the 1960s and 1970s had organized construction squads to go seek work outside the village during slack seasons, the Chens were no longer willing to undertake such work even in building their own homes, and had begun to rely entirely on such construction squads from poorer districts. (The special irony here is that villagers who now considered such work beneath their dignity had become the dependents of relatives in Hong Kong who were, precisely, construction workers.) A squad of ten building workers from an inland hill district, interviewed during a rest break, related that they were earning 200 *yuan* a month, but from that had to spend 30 *yuan* just to buy free-market rice; they but rarely ate any meat. In their home district there was no steady work; otherwise they would never have come. They could afford to travel home only once a year for the Chinese New Year.

More permanent immigrants, whole families that crowded into their employers' storage sheds, now undertook almost all of the farming in the village. It was usually on a sharecropping basis in which, among other things, they agreed to pay the grain levy imposed by the state and to supply their hosts with a year's supply of rice for home consumption. One couple whom we interviewed, squatting amidst four small ragged children in a tiny shack, had not yet been able to secure such a sharecropping arrangement, and so for the past five years the husband and wife had been scooping up sand from the river for a living.

The giant community hall that had been built under Longyong's aegis had now been rented out to a Hong Kong capitalist as a small plastic toy factory. When we visited, the dozen workers inside, all young men from one impoverished Guangdong county, were idle: the village was in the midst of an electricity blackout, a common occurrence in a district that was expanding at a pace quicker than the infrastructure could handle. (Chen Village was in the process of buying its own electric generator for use during such blackouts.)

The young workers slept nights in the hall's balcony. They had all bought temporary permits to live in the county. Had they not, whenever they ventured outside the village they would have run the risk of being questioned by police, and if they did not have the money to pay a heavy fine would be badly beaten. As outsiders, they needed also to pay the township a residence tax of 6 *yuan* a month. They resented the unfairness of the treatment meted out to them as non-locals, and resented too the precariousness of their lives, but realized full well there was not much they could do about it. Life, they said, was very hard back home, and here at least they had enough to eat.

The two hundred immigrants in the village had no legal rights to settle there permanently; they were there only at the sufferance of the village government and could be evicted at any time. Even if resident for a long period, they held no rights to share in the distributed agricultural land and could only remain in the precarious status of a tenant. Nor did they hold any rights to build their own homes,[2] nor the right for their children to attend school on the same basis as the local children. In their own country of birth, they were in a situation no better than the "guest workers" in Europe or the illegal Mexican immigrants in America. They did not possess even the rights of "second-class citizens."[3]

Such hired labor had been introduced only with the reforms of the eighties. One might, without exaggeration, call it exploited labor. Yet the policies of the collective era, which all but banned labor mobility and such wage labor, had not necessarily been preferable. For when the hiring of migrant labor was terminated in the mid-1950s, the peasants from the poorest districts had been forced back upon the resources of their own villages. Deprived of any means to escape from their community, they were consigned for two and a half decades to a hopelessly meager livelihood. No socialist policies were devised to bring underemployed labor to where it was temporarily needed, say at harvest time. Instead, to the economic detriment of all sides, each village was left to fend for itself. This self-reliance most hurt the destitute areas, which generally lacked the climatic and soil conditions conducive to developing food production. Over those two decades, consequently, *per capita* income differentials substantially widened between the better-off and poorer districts.[4] In short, even under Mao the Chinese countryside had consisted of

[2] In Chen Village, the arable land remained under the ownership of the former production teams and could only be parceled out as use rights to team members. But land designated for building sites could be bought and sold. However, only the local villagers were allowed to participate in such transactions.

[3] In response to the boom times in Guangdong Province, several millions of these immigrants had flooded into the Pearl River delta by the close of the eighties. During one week alone, during the Chinese New Year in 1989, approximately 100,000 a day were pouring into the province from other provinces, eager to find any available work. (*Zhongguo jinbao,* a Guangdong newspaper, March 3, 1989, p. 1) Nor was the flood confined to Guangdong. Across China, laborers from China's impoverished regions have been moving in large numbers into the prospering districts.

[4] See Peter Nolan and Gordon White, "The Distributive Implications of China's New Agricultural Policies," in Jack Gray and Gordon White, eds., *China's New Development Strategy* (London and New York: Academic Press, 1982); also Nicholas Lardy, *Agriculture in China's Economic Development* (Cambridge: Cambridge University Press, 1984), Chapter 4.

"two nations," of have and have-not localities—indeed, more so, it seems, than might have been the case had less inflexible and less "socialist" policies prevailed.

However, in previous decades, with the best-off and worst-off communities isolated from each other, this chasm between incomes had had fewer political and social ramifications. In contrast, within the richest communities across China today, sizable groups of poor immigrant laborers are living cheek to jowl with the most fortunate of the rural populace, as in Chen Village;[5] and the "two nations" of rich and poor accordingly are all too aware of the discrepancies in earnings and lifestyle. Already, several tens of millions of poor migrants reside semi-permanently in these anomalous circumstances, and they cannot be expected to continue to accept meekly their current lack of all security in residence rights and their abysmal living standards. A very special type of class conflict is likely to trouble China's countryside in the decades to come.

By the end of the 1980s, the tensions were already there—and they were mutual. Chen Villagers distrusted and feared the outsiders who did all of their dirty work for them. The Chens gossiped among themselves that most of the newcomers were untrustworthy, that one could never entirely be sure who they were and where they came from, that they were likely dangerous. The Chens reasoned that if they were in the outsiders' shoes—still impoverished and living next door to idle occupants of villas such as their own— *they* would feel resentful, and so they imputed such hostility—and vengeful acts—to the newcomers. Two recent murders in the neighboring township, villagers were sure, must have been perpetrated by out-of-county people. Within Chen Village, the rising crime rate was generally laid at the door of the immigrants within the village—even though the thieves who were caught usually turned out to be young local men. When an out-of-county intruder, a total

---

5. As just one example, in 1988 one of us visited a rural township of non-Chinese hill peoples in Yunnan Province that has become wealthy on the proceeds of village- and township-owned mines. There, much as in Chen Village, most of the farming and almost all of the heavy labor was being done by impoverished immigrants. (This wealthy township is discussed in Jonathan Unger and Jean Xiong, "Life in the Chinese Hinterlands under the Rural Economic Reforms," *Bulletin of Concerned Asian Scholars* 22, no. 2 [April 1990], esp. pp. 11–12.)

stranger, did get apprehended in the dark of night stealing from a fruit orchard, a crowd of Chens furiously beat him to death.

Uneasy though they felt about their new neighbors, most of the villagers were willing to tolerate them on a semi-permanent basis, for they needed the cheap labor force to do all of their work for them. A different strategy prevailed in a village only some five miles from Chen Village. As of November 1989, signs had been posted throughout that village warning that, as a safeguard against crime and to protect "hygienic standards," all non-locals other than a small number of tenants and factory workers would have to vacate their premises and move out of the village within the following three days, or face a 200-*yuan* penalty fine. This village apparently feared that non-locals would soon outnumber the locals—and the village was moving to preempt such a possibility.

Chen Villagers felt that immigrants from relatively nearby hill counties were more to be trusted than those who came from further afield. The families that were allowed to sharecrop the village lands derived almost entirely from such nearby counties. This same standard was being applied throughout the district: a caste system of sorts had been put in place based upon the immigrants' place of origin.

In the industrializing market towns, for instance, factory wages were pegged to one's origin. As of 1990, workers from the county in which Chen Village is located and from the immediately surrounding counties could earn up to 400–600 *yuan* a month, almost as if they were members of a special guild, while those from further afield in Guangdong found themselves earning some 150 to 350 *yuan*. Immigrants discovered, moreover, that jobs in most of the factories informally were reserved for Guangdong residents and Cantonese speakers from Guangxi Province, and that others would have to content themselves with the dirtier and more low-paying jobs outside the industrial sector. An important exception to this general rule comprised factories that, through labor recruitment agencies, had been directly recruiting large groups of female workers from other parts of the country. In a village almost next door to Chen Village, a former villager who over the course of several decades had become a Hong Kong millionaire had triumphantly returned to erect a vast textile factory that almost exclusively employed young women recruited in Hunan Province. Other young women were now arriving on their own accord from Hunan to seek work alongside their sisters and cousins on the production line. But such opportunities were reserved for new arrivals from southern provinces such as Hunan and Fujian. Immigrants from more distant provinces had to make do with jobs far lower on the status scale.

Near the bottom of this pecking order were the migrants from Sichuan, the inland Mandarin-speaking province that lies on the far side of the Yangtze gorges. They were consigned to jobs as agricultural laborers on the large vegetable farms owned by Hong Kong capitalists.

Exports of fresh vegetables had become big business in the county. From this county alone, the value of agricultural exports to Hong Kong had risen from US$3 million in 1979 to more than $70 million in 1988,[6] and the greatest part of this came from fresh vegetables. Yet most of this income was being reaped by Hong Kong entrepreneurs. A number of these investors were reportedly former vegetable farmers from Hong Kong's New Territories who had sold their own lands in Hong Kong for housing developments and now had considerable capital to spare. They held a decided advantage over the local peasants, in possessing a far greater knowledge both of modern agricultural techniques and of the Hong Kong markets. Just as important to their success, in the mid-1980s the Chinese authorities, to ensure that vegetable prices in Hong Kong remained high, had decided to establish export quotas on vegetables; and in one fell swoop the Hong Kong investors managed to secure the great bulk of the new export quota allotments. The local Chinese peasantry, cut off from exporting their own crops to Hong Kong, were now increasingly willing to get out of agriculture entirely by renting their lands cheaply to the Hong Kong businessmen. A woman from a village not far from Chen Village, who was now running a tiny roadside snack stand, related that she had signed a four-year contract handing over her family's five-sixths of an acre of fertile land for a paltry annual rent of 900 *yuan* (US$190). Comparatively little of Chen Village's croplands had been given over to Hong Kong interests in this fashion; but in the rural district immediately surrounding Chen

[6.] *Zhongguo Jinbao,* June 16, 1989.

Hong Kong–Owned Vegetable Agribusiness

Village about a third of all the irrigated land was now in the hands of absentee Hong Kong vegetable growers.

Quite strikingly distinct from the irregular patchwork of small plots that characterized the resurgence of family farming in China in the eighties, the fields in this new agribusiness were vast rectangular fields watered at exactly spaced intervals by perfectly straight irrigation channels, much as in publicity photographs of Mao's period. And again as in the collective agriculture of the 1960s and 1970s, large squads of workers labored together on these expansive fields in tight-knit groups under the supervision of a squad leader. All that was missing were the red flags of Maoist-era propaganda shots. China had reverted to family farming, it has been said, because individual peasants can intensively cultivate a Chinese garden-style agriculture more efficiently than a large-scale farming operation can. Yet here, in what arguably is the most efficient free-enterprise agriculture in China, were the resurrected fields and work squads of yesteryear.

About a mile from Chen Village, a large encampment housing 300 farm laborers from Sichuan stood in the middle of the vast vegetable acreage controlled by a single Hong Kong investor. The encampment consisted of primitive one-story adobe dormitories whose dark interiors were entirely taken up by cramped rows of crude narrow double-decker plank beds. When we visited, a group of young laborers, men and women alike, were outside cooking up a dinner of left-over vegetables in huge communal cooking pots. Wages, they said, ranged from 150 to 250 *yuan*. They could not get any jobs outside of agriculture, they complained, because of the discrimination against them. The 26-year-old work squad leader, who had been working in these fields for the past three years, told us that he was afraid to go into the market town, or even out to the main road, because groups of young locals, teenagers aged 16 or so, would beat and rob him. The gangs usually included the sons of local cadres, so there was nothing he could do about it.

Spawned by the rapid social and demographic dislocations in this district, in less than a decade an entirely new and finely graded structure of discrimination had been erected in place of the caste-like class-label structure of the Maoist era.

Because these new patterns were set in place through informal, unofficial rules, they have taken a form peculiar to this particular small region. The old patterns had been shared across the nation: under Mao, every village had had its officially persecuted four-bad types and its favored poor and lower-middle peasants. In contrast, not every village today has a mistrusted and despised outgroup of immigrant farm laborers camped nearby or, within village boundaries, groups of immigrant tenant farmers and factory laborers. In post-Mao China each village and region has been wrestling with its own new sets of circumstances.

What particular interests were the Chens trying to protect by enforcing discrimination? On the one side, obviously, they wanted to assure themselves a comfortable lifestyle by having others undertake all of the heavy manual work at relatively low pay; on the other, in the factories of the nearby towns they wanted to ensure relatively high rates of pay for their daughters and wives despite the huge influxes of poor laborers from other parts of China. The erection of discrete labor markets, reserving high-paid jobs for local people, met these twin desires. Foreign employers went along with this: it enabled the employers to retain access to cheap immigrant labor for most types of work, while assuring the active cooperation of the local population in keeping the immigrant workforce "in its place."

There was also a psychological dimension to this finely drawn structure of discrimination: the local populace's desires for status. Awkwardly dependent upon and thus in an inferior position to their relatives in Hong Kong, villagers could take pleasure in their assured superiority *vis à vis* outsiders from elsewhere in China, and especially the denigrated Sichuanese.

As has been seen, the villagers were not attempting to escape the discomfort of dependency by turning to greater personal industriousness. Rather, dispirited by the Midas touch of nearby Hong Kong, they retreated, the young men in particular, into a restless indolence. Unable and unwilling to seek a higher status in life through their own endeavors, they used relatives' money to invest heavily in costly symbols of status. They were competitive among themselves, but for most it was a competition to consume wealth rather than to create it.

□ *12* □

Entrepreneurs and Gamblers

Not all of the villagers were lacking in entrepreneurial spirit, to be sure. But only a small minority of them were in a good position to take advantage of the boom times in the county. They were largely the very same men who had learned how to take charge under socialism. The socialist era favored them, and now, ironically, the demise of agrarian socialism likewise benefited them.

Local Successes

A clear illustration is provided by the younger brigade-level cadres of the 1970s, who for the most part were able in the 1980s to convert their managerial experience into decent incomes. Of the four men who, when teenagers, had been named as "revolutionary successors" by the sent-in workteams of the 1960s and who subsequently rose to brigade posts, two managed factories for Hong Kong corporations as of 1990. Foolish ran a metal-door factory in a nearby town and a second "revolutionary successor" was in charge of the plastics factory in the converted Chen Village community hall, while Baodai, another of the four "revolutionary successors," now held command of the village's public affairs as party secretary. All three of these men could count themselves successes, but they had all stayed on the safe path of paid employment.

Only the fourth of the "successors" chose to risk his future entrepreneurially. In the mid-eighties he resigned from his job as the brigade's administrative head (Longyong's old post), and borrowed heavily from the banks to plant extensive fruit orchards on the hillsides.[1] But his orchards had not yet begun to reap adequate returns, and as of 1990 he was anxiously trying to keep his head above water. To protect his investments, he had equipped his main orchard with a watchtower where a hired hand slept nights. The man had also purchased a shotgun, and his landholdings were surrounded by signs proclaiming that the owner will take no responsibility if any intruder is wounded in the course of arrest.[2]

The former production team heads similarly had managerial experience to draw upon, and one might have expected that they would have comprised the largest pool of entrepreneurs in the village. But only a few of them had the courage to take risks or, when they did, the capability, connections, and luck to invest wisely in endeavors.

The ordinary villagers were poorly equipped to take a similar entrepreneurial plunge. Unlike former cadres, they were not used to handling large sums of money and were inexperienced in managing anything more complex than ordinary farm tasks. In the first half of the 1980s, the county, flush with money, had made it easy for the local people to secure bank loans at favorable rates for investment purposes, but few dared.[3]

---

[1] Although the village administration is no longer officially titled a "brigade," villagers normally continued to refer to it as the brigade.

[2] The local legal system appeared to be blatantly partial to the rights of property owners. When the stranger who trespassed on a different villager's orchard was beaten to death (see Chapter 11), neither the proprietor nor any of the other villagers involved were ever prosecuted.

[3] Although the villagers were generally intimidated by the amount of debt burden involved in such bank loans, in reality there turned out to be little genuine risk involved. One of the two former landlords in Chen Village had been among the few who plucked up the courage to apply for a bank loan, and in the spirit of the times was granted 100,000 *yuan,* but he was not able to turn a profit. So too, the former head of the No.1 production team, Qingfa's old ally, borrowed heavily and lost most of the money. But since they had had no collateral to back up their borrowings, and since the banks were reluctant to foreclose on their homes, they were not made to pay any real penalties for their indebtedness.

Only two men in the village had the wherewithal and the daring to become truly successful in the private sector.[4] One of them, a man in his forties named Chen Chongyin, had served ten years as a production team head. He was descended from the village's most wealthy family (see page 21), but his father very fortunately had received his share of the family lands at the time of his wedding before the revolution—and thus, unlike the two younger brothers in the family, he had been designated a middle peasant during the Communist land reform. Chongyin had inherited this middle-peasant label, and that was good enough to enable him to enter senior high school in the early 1960s, and later to become a team head. In that position, Chongyin had shrewdly stayed on Qingfa's good side during the 1970s, and he profited from the relationship after the brigade's property was rented out through auction at the start of the 1980s. As a relative of Chongyin explains:

> He did favors for Qingfa, and benefited in return. For example, at the very beginning of the eighties Chongyin rented out the village's store and a brigade fish pond, both at a very cheap price, and Qingfa thereafter could always get his cigarettes from the shop for free. And then when the dike broke and swept away a few of my relative's fish—just a few, really—Qingfa said, "Okay, because some of your fish were lost, I'll reduce the rent by quite a bit." People were angry about that.

A few of the villagers who tied themselves to Qingfa's coattails found themselves cut off when Qingfa fell, with all their contracts rescinded. Chongyin, though, had successfully gambled on a series of other ventures in the early 1980s when most of the other villagers were still unwilling to trust the government's promises. He had fairly and successfully bid for a grove of several dozen lychee trees on a fifty-year contract for only a couple of hundred *yuan* a year, and a grove of bamboo, and then other groves and orchards as they became available. He took out bank loans to fertilize them and greatly increased their productivity. He parlayed these assets into developing a new twenty-acre orchard of orange trees.[5] From there he pioneered a large chicken

---

[4.] As noted earlier, Qingfa was well on his way to becoming the third such success story before his death.

[5.] The deal in establishing new orchards on unused brigade land was that the land was free for the taking, and for the first twenty years there would be no rent due, but farm, a row of ramshackle brick halls each containing about 3,000 chicks, with an annual output capacity of some 40,000 chickens.

Despite their growing wealth, he and his wife did not rest on their laurels. They worked a seven-day week, every week, and plowed the earnings back into new investments. When we hiked up to the chicken farm in 1989, Chongyin's wife was in the midst of busily feeding a dozen purebred hogs in the new piggery they had just established as yet another commercial venture. Unlike their neighbors, they lived frugally, intent upon future gains and further expansions of their ventures. They displayed a work ethic altogether at odds with, and disdainful of, the prevailing village ethos of idle consumerism. Theirs was an ethic shared by only a few other village families, a small band of household heads who insisted upon pursuing the notion that success and self-worth are tied to frugality and hard work. Other families, awed by what they perceived as the near impossibility of ever achieving a Hong Kong–style livelihood through personal effort, held these several families in bemused respect, as if such efforts defied imitation.

Chongyin and his family started to build a new villa in the village, but then left it standing half-built in the realization that they would have no time to bask in its luxury and that their money could be put to more productive purposes. They lived instead in relative deprivation in a three-room temporary-looking mud-brick house at their chicken farm a couple of miles outside the village. The dwelling differed little from the one next door occupied by their hired hands. Chongyin had moved up here from the village because he was reluctant to delegate responsibility for guarding his property to any hired personnel, even someone from Chen Village. Chongyin's cousin, who opened a chicken farm not far away, likewise slept nights with his wife at their farm's storeroom rather than trust an employee. Even those like Chongyin who exhibited the most vision and who were able to expand their endeavors into sizeable operations continued to hold to a "small producer mentality." The growth of their business ventures was limited to what they could physically keep their eyes on.

Though rich by Chen Village standards, Chongyin did not wish his children to pursue a similar livelihood. He bought a house

---

thereafter through the fortieth year the orchard owner would get half of the yield and the brigade half, and after forty years the trees and land would revert to the brigade.

in the county capital in order to enable his children to transfer their residence permits there. (This was permitted under a moneymaking scheme by the county government, which had put these homes on the market.) Chongyin felt it was a good investment: with residence cards, his children could now obtain an education in the county town; and even more importantly, with their new urban residence permits they would not have to become farmers even if government policy should be reversed in future years. Through Chongyin's house purchase, they had already leaped the greatest divide in social status and livelihood in China—the divide between the countryside and the cities.[6]

Only one man in Chen Village achieved greater economic success in the 1980s than Chongyin—and that was Longyong. "Of course Longyong succeeded," remarks a former production team cadre:

> He knew the enterprises, he knew how to handle a business, he knew officials, he knew the banks and how they operate. Compared to everyone else in the village, he was used to dealing with things on a big scale . . . So it isn't as if Longyong's type of success was open to everyone in Chen Village. . . . There's an ironic twist in it, you know, since by the end of the 1970s even Longyong hadn't had much success with the collective enterprises. Today, all that's left of his grandiose collective endeavors is a big water pump that had been put in at great expense to get water up to the collectives' hillside orchards. But he learned about business through his mistakes—even though it was a learning experience that cost the village a lot—and that's now benefiting him in his private ventures.

Longyong was the first in the village to perceive that good prospects existed for large-scale chicken farming. Hong Kong had recently placed tight restrictions on such operations within the Crown Colony in order to reduce pollution from waste-matter runoffs, and the closing of Hong Kong's operations opened an enormous opportunity for China's border counties. Under a county plan to encourage modern chicken farming, large bank loans, interest free if repaid within three years, were being made available to any groups of households that

---

[6.] Chongyin's decision to secure his children's future in this manner turned out to be a wise move. A few years later, in the early 1990s, Chongyin fell seriously ill, and he passed away prematurely in the late 1990s before he could parlay his early entrepreneurial successes into a solid financial position for his children.

applied to run the operations cooperatively. Longyong canvassed his neighbors to find willing partners, but all of the families that he contacted did not dare to take the risk. The only volunteers were two brothers, one of them a former team head, whom he had not initially approached. Together they secured a 100,000-*yuan* loan, succeeded in paying it off in time, and began taking home 10,000 *yuan* apiece in profits each year. Longyong and his partners expanded the operation into orchards that they fertilized with the chicken manure. They quarreled, however—few partnerships last long in Chen Village. As a consequence they sold the chicken operation for 400,000 *yuan* in 1987 to a man from the county, who needed a safe haven for a fortune he reputedly had made in less-than-scrupulous ways. Longyong plowed part of his profits from the sale into a modern three-story villa. To further celebrate his success, when one of his sons in Hong Kong married he invited one representative from every family in Chen Village to an enormous wedding feast.

Longyong also quickly invested part of his proceeds into a large hog-raising operation on the flats near the river. It contained some sixty modern sties, each equipped with running water and each containing one pink Western-breed hog. To guard the property, Longyong's brother loyally lived amid the stench in a one-room shed; even Longyong could trust only close kin to protect his assets.

Within another year, Longyong sold the sties to the brigade, netting a tidy profit of some 20,000 to 30,000 *yuan*. Having witnessed a phenomenal growth in the county's economy of 30 to 40 percent during that one year, the brigade foresaw that construction materials would be commanding ever-higher prices. It seemed profitable to buy up and demolish Longyong's new sties in order to build a sizeable brickworks in its stead, to take advantage of the clay deposits that lay along that stretch of the river. As part of the deal, Longyong acquired 20 percent of the brickworks. The brigade took a large chunk of shares, and most of the rest was offered as a joint venture to a capitalist from Fujian Province. Some forty workers from Henan Province in north China were hired as a squad through an old-style labor contractor to man the kilns.

Longyong had softened with the years. In his new role of private entrepreneur, he no longer needed to assert control over his fellow villagers, and no longer saw a need to be hard on both himself and others. As one villager put it:

Nowadays, Longyong gets on quite well with other villagers, and he himself has become plump and fair-skinned, now that he no longer does physical labor. He spends his time drawing up contracts and so forth for his business, and doesn't come into conflict with other villagers. He no longer exercises power. But Baodai, the party secretary, still seeks out Longyong's opinion over important decisions. You might say Longyong serves as a consultant.

No, folks don't think badly of Longyong that first he pushed socialism so fiercely and worshipped Mao and then turned around and is now making piles of money for himself. In both cases, they feel it's the political climate of the times. The younger generation is envious that he's doing well financially, but envious in a positive sense—because his money is not made from bribes. They look up to that. The older folks know, though, that he's had tremendous advantages because of his experience as a cadre.

The poorly educated and inexperienced young men of Chen Village felt that any similar success was totally beyond their capacities. To them, Longyong seemed all too knowledgeably sophisticated in the ways of business. Yet Longyong himself obviously realized that he could only operate within the context of the village world that he knew. He restricted his entrepreneurial investments to strictly rural-style ventures: a crude village brickworks, orchards, and chicken farms. These were the types of endeavors that were too small-scale and peripheral to attract Hong Kong investors: a rural lacuna in which people of peasant stock like Longyong might hope to compete. The locals could not hope to start their own manufacturing enterprises. We were told by an agent for Hong Kong manufacturers, who frequently visited the county's factory sites, that some 90 percent of all the manufacturing plants in the county were controlled by Hong Kong companies as of 1990, and that the preponderance of the remaining plants were owned by local government administrations. Local private entrepreneurs simply did not have the manufacturing expertise, or the knowledge of the market, or the same access to capital, or sufficiently secure sources of supply to compete in the same arena as Hong Kong firms. Very little of the extraordinary upsurge of manufacturing in the district was locally spawned.

Interviews in 1989 and 1990 with people from more than a dozen other villages in Guangdong revealed an interesting pattern in this respect. In the several border counties, local entrepreneurship was restricted to relatively marginal activities, much as in Chen Village, whereas the Pearl River Delta counties on the far side of Canton, in contrast, were witnessing an extraordinary flowering of indigenous rural entrepreneurship. Such counties were too far from Hong Kong to fall within the immediate orbit of direct Hong Kong investment, yet were sufficiently within transport range of Canton and Hong Kong to profit from the surge of trade flowing across Guangdong's borders.[7]

From the extraordinary developments in those rural districts, it is obvious that, given the right market conditions, villagers in this region of China were quite capable of complex entrepreneurial activity, including manufacturing. But in Chen Village's county, smothered by the embrace of direct Hong Kong investment, such entrepreneurship never had a chance to surface.

The New Face of Village Government

In addition to Chen Village's several private entrepreneurs, an additional important economic actor was active on the local scene — Baodai. As party secretary, he had under his charge a village budget of 600,000 yuan a year. He was risking some of this capital in new investments, much as the brigade had during the era

[7.] One example will suffice. Two of us spent several days in 1986 in a village some two hours beyond Canton, in a rural district that before the 1940s had been a major center of rural silk-textile production. Starting in the early 1980s, peasant entrepreneurs revived the industry, to the extent that almost from scratch this small district of a few rural market towns quickly became one of the three major silk-manufacturing areas in China, and from there developed into a major manufacturer of synthetic cloth such as nylon. Our host in the village, a former production team head still in his thirties, had borrowed 150,000 *yuan* from a bank to open a factory with his brother-in-law and several minor partners. The factory was so successful that within a few years he was flying to business negotiations in diverse parts of the country, as far away as Beijing. He imported his raw material—artificial silk threads—from South Korea and sold his cloth throughout China, especially Manchuria. (Despite his success, he was obviously worried that government policies might change. As of 1986 he purposely had not reinvested much in the factory's premises, which were ramshackle temporary structures. And his wife, rather than stay at home or work in his firm, was bicycling off every morning to work on the production line of a county-owned textile factory. It was not for the pay, which they did not really need; it was to retain a secure job with pension benefits just in case the national regime shifted course dramatically, as had occurred so often before in socialist China's history.)

of collective agriculture. But given the competition posed by Hong Kong investors, the brigade under Baodai pursued much the same narrow range of endeavors as Longyong and Chongyin. Above all, it successfully poured money into two large chicken farms, which it eventually contracted out. But the brigade also embarked on a path that was beyond the reach of the village's private entrepreneurs: it sought to take direct advantage of the influx of foreign companies. In the late 1980s, like so many other villages in the region, it borrowed almost two million yuan from the bank to construct two factory buildings for rental to foreign firms. The buildings stand in an industrial park in the township's market town, on a site offered by the township government. Such official efforts to be actively entrepreneurial were commonplace elsewhere in China at the time.[8] In fact, in a large part of the countryside, especially in China's richer regions, the village, township, and county governments didn't just build factory premises; they started manufacturing operations under their own managements. This phenomenon was on such a wide scale that the industries owned and run by rural administrations in China expanded at a faster rate during most of the 1980s and the first half of the 1990s than any other sector of the national economy. Seen in this light, the entrepreneurial efforts of Baodai and the officialdom of Chen Village's township pale in significance. Faced by the too-stiff competition that Hong Kong firms posed in manufacturing, the local governments and private entrepreneurs alike in the border counties opted out. Except for the new village brickworks, the Chen Village government preferred to set itself up simply and purely as a landlord, collecting its rents every year.

That left Baodai with free time on his hands: he even found the time to embark on private ventures (without much financial success) in developing an orchard and chicken farm. But he continued to put most of his effort into ensuring that he still reigned supreme in all aspects of the village's public affairs. "The party secretary does just about all of it," remarked one of the villagers; "he's the one key actor left." Baodai sat on a five-member village administrative committee,[9]

---

8. On this, see Jean C. Oi, *Rural China Takes Off: Institutional Foundations of Economic Reform* (Berkeley: University of California Press, 1999).

9. The central government has renamed this committee of village cadres the "villagers committee" *(cunmin weiyuanhui)*, which has fooled some observers into the mistaken

but with the withdrawal of the village cadres from daily control over the local economy, the committee had comparatively little to do, and the other members retained very little say. In this vacuum, Baodai effectively gathered into his own hands whatever economic decision-making powers remained. According to the official rhetoric in China, under government reforms of the 1980s the local party leadership and the local government administration were supposed to be separated into two distinct spheres of activity *(dang zheng fenkai)*; but this does not appear to have held true either for Chen Village or for other villages that we know about.

As party secretary, Baodai ran the entire show, dominating the village's party committee, which had been reduced to only three people. One of the three members was the village administrative head, Longyong's old position. Baodai inserted into this post a baby-faced twenty-three-year-old whose main responsibility was to serve as Baodai's chauffeur. (As the ultimate in prestige items, the village had imported a Japanese minibus to transport Baodai and his colleagues to functions.)

The third member of the party committee was the women's representative, a vivacious woman in her forties who openly confessed to us that she held no influence. Her main responsibility was to enforce the government's birth-control policies, a thankless task that she undertook with good cheer and very limited expectations. She dutifully visited homes to provide a two-child-policy lecture to each young bride, which everyone politely accepted as a required formality. But even she shrugged her shoulders at the impossibility of enforcing the edict. As she explained:

> There's a fine of 1,200 *yuan* for having the third child, but people consider that as nothing serious. The pregnant women just run away into hiding with relatives in other villages. When they come

---

belief that these are democratic assemblies of all villagers. Instead, as of 1990 the "villagers committee" consisted of only five members in Chen Village: the party secretary, the village head *(cunzhang)*, the deputy village head, the administrative secretary *(wenshu)*, and the women's representative. Ostensibly, during the 1980s there were village-wide elections to select the committee, but there were no nominations and the slate of five committee members was determined beforehand; only those five stood. Afterward, the five formally decided among themselves how to divide up the posts, similar to the procedure of previous decades.

back with the newborn they just pay the fine and that's that. . . . The child grows up like any other children. Since it wasn't its fault the child shouldn't be discriminated against in schooling and so forth. . . . Normally, though, Chen Villagers are happy not to have a third child if they already have two boys or have one boy and one girl. Nowadays people think it's best to have one of each, since daughters are considered more filial than sons and more caring toward elderly parents. But if a couple only has two girls, they'll definitely keep trying, since a daughter is still seen as getting "married off" to other people.

Baodai, as party secretary, was held responsible by the government to set a firm example for his charges in abiding by the government's birth-control program. But he himself refused to stop short with two girls. With three young daughters, his wife gamely went into hiding in 1987 to have a fourth child—this time a son.

Whereas previously the brigade committee apportioned the various administrative responsibilities, for the most part Baodai managed single-handedly. Most importantly, infractions of village rules and quarrels between families used to be dealt with by a brigade-level public-security officer, but that post was abolished and Baodai took over its duties. "Whenever anything happens you go to him and him alone," said a villager. "In a village there are always quarrels, you know, like when two neighbors are building houses or if some tree along a property line dies. People come to look up Baodai to arbitrate day or night, even when he's eating." Villagers also had to come to him to obtain permits to build new homes. Both formally and informally, Baodai played the role of mayor, prosecutor, and judge, and through a myriad of discretionary acts he had it within his power to favor some families and obstruct others. He did not do so blatantly; he appeared to maintain a relatively even hand. But it is little wonder that to keep on his good side, just in case, almost all families plied him with small gifts. Baodai did not have to go out of his way or resort to literally corrupt activities to generously supplement his salary.

But even though Baodai's power over the village populace remained substantial, in an era of economically independent households he exercised far less power than village leaders of previous decades. As one of the Chens relates: "Before, during the period of the collectives . . . you had to ask for favors for everything. Now, you largely do things for yourself, and for most people most of the time, you don't need the cadres." Baodai was fully aware that a leader's power to exact cowed compliance from the peasantry was a thing of the past, and he generally intruded on the affairs of his neighbors only when mediation was called for.

Baodai could attempt to bolster his political sway through his control of brigade revenues. For the most part, these were utilized to support the village's public services. If Baodai generated profits he could play the role of the village's patron, much as Longyong had with his initial burst of economic successes in the 1970s. With the revenues from the village government's chicken farms and brickworks, he was able to claim responsibility for helping to get the road to the township market town paved and a new wider bridge built across the river. Perhaps most importantly, the brigade proudly helped finance the construction of the impressive new school at the entrance to the village.[10] But more recently the brigade had incurred heavy debts as a result of new investments, and it was not able to cover all of the school's ongoing expenses.[11] This depletion of brigade profits removed another card from Baodai's hand.

Loyalty Networks: Production Teams and Lineages

A full decade after the return to independent family agriculture, the production teams continued to own assets and received ongoing revenues from the rental of fish ponds and orchards and from the sale of team land for new housing.[12] But without any economic functions

[10.] For both the road paving and construction of the school, all of the remainder of the needed funds came from production-team coffers, much as had been the case in the 1960s and 1970s.

[11.] "Theoretically," Baodai admitted to us, "schooling is compulsory and free; but in reality it isn't." Each student was required to pay a tuition fee of 150 *yuan* a year, *plus* book charges, renovation fees, snack fees, and so forth to help support the eleven teachers' salaries. Almost all of the Chen Villagers could afford these various school fees, though there were grumblings. The charges put the school altogether beyond the reach of the migrants' children—but that aspect did not particularly upset the villagers.

[12.] Whereas the teams' agricultural land ostensibly remained team property, having been placed in 1982 in the farming families' hands for a period of fifteen years, building sites could be sold outright by the teams. The new owners received legal deeds to the property.

The Primary School

to perform other than those of a landlord, the teams no longer needed a full-fledged team committee, just a very part-time team head and cashier, and a part-time accountant shared with a second team. Little power or perks adhered to these positions — since the team structure remained far more democratic than at the brigade level. For decisions of any significance, meetings were convened of all the men in a team over the age of thirty. (With the breakup of collective agriculture, women receded into the background and were no longer called to such meetings, even when they headed households. So, too, the traditional weight given to seniority in age had reasserted itself in the tacit expectation that only men over the age of thirty should attend.) Discussions at the meetings usually centered on how to spend the team's income. Some of it was to pay the team officers and to provide for team services, such as modest support for any indigent elderly, or to pave the pathways within each team's neighborhood. Some of it went toward village-wide services, such as the financial support each of the teams equally provided toward the construction of the new school and lighting for the village lanes.

The limits in community cohesion were felt in 1988 when no one could agree on who should pay what fair share of the year's electric bill for lighting these pathways. The brigade declined to do so, since it was strapped for cash due to its plunge into financing the market-town factories; and each of the teams bridled at the thought that it might be paying more than its fair share to light the way home for other teams' members. The expenditure involved was quite small, since Chen Village contained only some ten street lamps, but before the quarrel could be resolved the village's streets were pitched into darkness for some months.

At each team's meetings, much of the team funds normally were allocated to the team's own collective entertainment. A team would send its teenagers free of charge on a tour of Canton; or, in the case of one team in the mid-1980s, even sponsored a free bus tour for team members to Guilin, the famous tourist city in neighboring Guangxi Province. As of late 1989, all of the teams were sponsoring team-paid outings to Shenzhen restaurants and hotels.[13] Such tours and outings served the special function of reinforcing and celebrating the members' feelings of identity with their teams. Such feelings could be observed, too, at times of weddings, when most families formally invited to the wedding feast one representative from each of their team's households. That same sense of continuing team identity also could be seen in the sites chosen for the new villas at the edges of the village. The members of each team tended to group their new houses together, preserving, as it were, their team neighborhood in a new location. The owner of one such villa remarked, "I don't know why it is, but team members don't want to scatter; they want to live among each other."

One reason, it appears, was a felt need to preserve a sense of community membership at a level closer at hand than the village-wide

---

13. This reportedly was in response to pressures from on high, since the tourist trade was suffering badly in Shenzhen in the wake of the Beijing massacre. Some six to seven years earlier, there had been a similar surge in such visits to Shenzhen, again reportedly at upper-level urgings, at a time when the Shenzhen Special Economic Zone was first developing and had not yet attracted sufficient foreign visitors. In short, it appears that even where the teams' entertainment budgets were concerned, bureaucratic interference occasionally could still be felt.

conglomeration of a thousand people. Close kinship provided a very strong bond among some households, but that could incorporate only a very narrow band of families. At the next remove, people could use their common team membership as a benchmark in determining whether to lend money to each other or otherwise help each other out. The teams provided villagers with a structural network of neighboring households, much as peasants before the revolution had identified themselves, at a sub-village level, as members of a lineage branch.

In very important respects, the teams now served as the equivalent of lineage branches. The five Chen lineage branches of times past had been organized around a common vested interest in lineage-branch property, property that had been bequeathed by their ancestors to all of the branch members as a group. So too, team members in the 1980s shared in common inherited property holdings—the team's property. And much as the teams were now doing, before the revolution the lineage branches had used the rentals from their common property to support celebrations that affirmed their group identity.[14] The central sacred rite of lineage-branch membership had involved the solemn distribution of a section of pork to each male member of the branch each year. Under socialism, the teams had displaced the lineage branches as the foci of sub-village identity, and in keeping with this, each year during the 1960s and 1970s the Chen Village teams, at the Chinese New Year festival, provided a free piece of pork to each member household. This no longer contained any sacred ritual significance, of course, but the pork distributions by the teams similarly symbolized the common bond shared by member families. In keeping with the continued sense of a common bond after the return to family farming, some families in the late 1980s even individually took it upon themselves to give pork to neighbors from their production team during the Chongyang festival. This is an occasion at which the Chinese traditionally present cooked pork at their ancestral graves and then later consume the pork to enhance their own luck. Ordinarily, only kin are allowed to eat this efficacious pork; to disburse such luck among

---

[14.] In the earlier half of the twentieth century, only the Lotus Branch, Qingfa's lineage branch, had had enough property to afford to pay great attention to such celebrations. And as noted in Chapter 1, it was the Lotus Branch that had maintained the firmest sense of identity.

neighbors and teammates signifies that the households share in a special relationship.[15]

At the same time that team membership took on some of the attributes of the old lineage branches, the lineage branches of tradition were reviving. At the Chongyang festival the families from a couple of the branches visited the graves of their founding ancestors as a group, and distributed pork afterward to all of the male descendants in the branch. Much as with the teams, families now looked to their lineage branch, too, as a means of providing a meaningful sub-community and as a means of identifying which households they could hope to turn to for mutual help and loans. But these feelings were not strong enough to spur personal donations to support branch activities. The five branches' ancestral halls in Chen Village (and the grand main ancestral hall as well) remained in a dilapidated state in 1990 and were variously being used as warehouses, shops, or as sleeping quarters for migrant workers. Rather than spend money to restore them as lineage-branch halls, branch members preferred to forgo having any halls. Even the annual branch rites and pork distributions relied largely upon financing from several of the elderly Chens who had migrated to Hong Kong before the revolution.

Which, then, was more important to villagers: their production team or their lineage branch? One of our acquaintances insisted to us in 1989 that it was the production team:

> Even in the Lotus branch, if it weren't that the annual rites were paid for by some people in Hong Kong, they probably wouldn't be held. Not all of the men bother to attend, only from some ten families that are mutually close, families that were richer before 1949. The older people who are keener on this kind of thing are dying, and the young people don't know the rituals and don't care. In ten years' time, no one will even know how to.

---

[15] In traditional times, too, such pork occasionally was provided to non-relatives: "The ritual pork is not an ordinary offering because once it has been placed before the ancestors it takes on a sacred, magical quality and is believed to be especially lucky. All Chinese like to eat pork from a good grave, and sometimes even non-lineage members are offered some as a prized gift." Jack Potter, "Wind, Water, Bones and Souls: The Religious World of the Cantonese Peasant," *Journal of Oriental Studies* 3, no. 1 (January 1970): 151.

*The Main Ancestral Hall. Used as sleeping
quarters for the sent-down youths in the 1960s,
as the village school in the 1970s, and as a dormitory
for migrant laborers in the 1980s.*

Yet such a view was contradicted by his friend, a man of forty, who adamantly insisted that his lineage-branch identity is far more important to him and to his relatives than is their production team. An important distinction among villagers was distinctly felt here: the first interviewee, who gave primacy to the team, was of poor-peasant class label. The second interviewee was from a family that held a rich-peasant label, and he explains his preference:

> The very idea of a production team was associated with the party's rule, and I was terribly discriminated against and felt under terrible pressure from other members of the team during the period of the collectives. So I don't feel entirely comfortable today with such an organization, one that's been shaped by the party.

Yet even this man's family still participated actively in the affairs of its team: his uncle, in fact, had served recently as the team head and his father as the team accountant. And the first interviewee admitted to feeling closer to certain other families because they belong to his own lineage branch. In short, two different means of defining one's place within the Chen Village community coexisted, one a heritage of the collective era and the other from a more remote past, and just about every family was employing both references. It was merely a matter of which of the two the family gave greater weight to. At a time of rapid social and economic change, it became an advantage to be able to turn to more than one sub-community structure as an anchorage for support.

A Religious Gamble

Just as lineage feelings had reemerged in a weakened form, traditional religious beliefs also made a partial comeback, now that the state and its ideological demands had receded from the village scene. Almost every home reinstalled an ancestral altar, where incense is offered to the deceased. And it became popular for housewives to visit the same two female shamans who two decades earlier had been hounded into quitting their trade. For fees that could range up to a hundred yuan, the old women became possessed and spoke in the voice of their god or in the voice of one of the client's dead relatives, who helped to resolve problems and improve the family's fortunes. (However, people no longer turned to the women shamans to cure the sick; doctors and medicines had long since won the villagers' allegiance.) Men in the village almost never consulted these female shamans. Instead, they frequented a couple of blind male fortune-tellers. There now existed a distinct gender division in Chen Village in the pursuit of supernatural advice.

Frequently, the questions that villagers asked of the shamans and blind oracles involved desperate efforts to augment luck: to know the future in order to manipulate it so as to win big money easily. Most other aspects of religious practice were given short shrift. No efforts have been made to rebuild the old village temple that was destroyed in the Cultural Revolution, nor had the village god that used to safeguard village affairs been resurrected, since no one was willing to contribute to purchase a new effigy.[16] (As of 2007, some two decades later, the

---

[16.] Except when wealthy elderly emigrants in Hong Kong have sponsored the rebuilding of a temple, few of the villages in the district have raised the money to do so. This community still has not built a temple.) Moreover, few efforts were made to remember all of the ritual involved in caring for the spirits of the dead. Although religion in Chen Village had revived, it was as truncated religion. What people one-sidedly emphasized in the late 1980s were religious beliefs that could be given a cargo-cultist twist. This was especially true for the young men. As in a cargo cult, they were fixated on obtaining a lucky break out of their predicament, the fantastical stroke of fortune that would bring them, entirely free of any dependency on relatives, the consumer goods from Hong Kong that they so achingly desired.

Their passion for gambling was also tied to these cargo-cult dreams—of a sudden effortless rise into wealth. It was a passion not confined only to the young men. The gambling fever gripped much of the village populace, male and female alike: the middle-aged, the elderly and, in imitation, even children were caught up in it. Gossip among neighbors frequently revolved around who had become addicted to gambling and who among them had been showered with good luck or faced ruin.

Dilemmas at the Turn of the Nineties

For all their uncertainties and discontents, the villagers felt that they were fortunate compared with their previous poverty. They feared that any rocking of the boat might endanger their present lifestyles, and therefore there was little sympathy in the village for the protests that swept Chinese cities in the spring of 1989. "Despite seeing all the footage of the Beijing massacre on Hong Kong television," observes one interviewee, "the older men in the village argued that the demonstrators had gone too far, and that they deserved what they got."

Nevertheless, the Chen Villagers' exposure to Hong Kong for the past decade was shaping a quiet revolution in their understanding of the world and in their own relationship to the polity. We were taken aback when one of the village cadres, at a dinner with other villagers,

---

was made clear to us in an interview with a *fengshui* (geomancy) master in Hong Kong, who made the bulk of his living by giving advice in the nearby Chinese countryside on the efficacious siting of special buildings. If only the construction of new temples and ancestral halls were popular, he told us in 1990, he would enjoy a far brisker business.

began expounding eloquently upon the virtues of constitutionalism and judicial independence as checks against the autocracy of officials.

A large number of the Chen Villagers were beginning to visit their relatives in Hong Kong, and a few went on business. Qingfa was in Hong Kong twice in the early 1980s, and Baodai now made the trip regularly. We met Baodai for breakfast at a Hong Kong restaurant in the autumn of 1989 when he and the party committee's women's representative were on an "inspection tour" of the colony. Their one-week trip had been paid for by the Hong Kong businessman who owned the plastics factory in Chen Village's former assembly hall.

Baodai's hope of wooing other Hong Kong businesspeople to set up manufacturing facilities was suffering a setback, however. The months following the Beijing massacre of June 1989 brought troubles for the county and village. Hong Kong industrialists, panicked and appalled by the political events in China, shied away from any new investments in China, and the brand-new factory buildings that had been erected everywhere in the county stood empty as prospective renters pulled back. The two factory premises that the Chen Village government had built in the market town with bank loans of two million *yuan* had just been completed, and Baodai, anxious for tenants, needed to find 30,000 *yuan* a month in mortgage repayments. (He asked us, desperately, whether we happened to know any Hong Kong capitalists whom we could persuade to relocate there.) Aggravating Baodai's anxiety was the fact that as the county's construction boom screeched to a halt the price of bricks suddenly dropped by half, and the brigade's new brickworks stopped making any profits. The brigade government was caught in a severe financial bind.

Exacerbating these difficulties, the handful of private entrepreneurs in Chen Village had shown a naive ignorance of the forces of supply and demand. In Chen Village and elsewhere, orange orchards had been planted speculatively earlier in the decade and the first harvests had brought high profits, so everywhere, in this and all the neighboring counties, entrepreneurial peasants like Chongyin had eagerly expanded their orchards. In some districts, even the rice paddy fields were converted into pocket orange orchards. As could have been predicted, this rapid expansion of acreage oversaturated the local market for oranges, and the price plummeted. Nor could these counties find markets beyond the region. The quality of the oranges was far too inferior to compete with American Sunkist on the Hong Kong market, and the national transportation system was too overloaded to transport them to markets in other parts of China. After the harvest of 1989 Chen Village found itself sitting on a 550-ton mountain of unsold oranges. When we saw Baodai late that autumn, he was scratching his head over how to ride out the region's economic recession. He found himself overburdened by concurrent responsibilities for the two empty factory buildings, looming bank-loan repayments, and his own and other people's hillocks of oranges.

He and all the Chen Villagers would soon be rescued by the rapid march of globalization. Within a few years, the village land would become far too valuable for oranges.

▫ *13* ▫

Globalization and Transformation

In 2006, as we traveled toward Chen Village after an absence of sixteen years, the road from the township's capital town was crowded with heavy trucks and packed buses. Nothing along the route resembled the former countryside. The rice fields and verdant hills had all disappeared, replaced by a vast agglomeration of grim factories and row upon row of workers' dormitories — grey rectangular concrete structures four or five stories high, with laundry hanging from windows. Lingering piles of roadside rubble signaled where buildings had recently been demolished for redevelopment. Further along lay a dense cluster of low apartment buildings, cheap hotels, and stores, followed by a row of relatively fancy restaurants where factory managers congregated in air-conditioned comfort, and beyond that a small hospital and a clinic. From the roadway, it would have been impossible to tell where one administrative district ended and another began, except for a huge roadside sign announcing "Chen Village Industrial Zone No. 3." We had arrived.

It was lunchtime, and thousands of workers in their teens and twenties, often wearing distinctively colored shirts and badges that identified their places of employment, hurried toward cheap eating places that lined the industrial zone's main street. These variously advertised different regional foods—even halal Muslim food—to meet the tastes of workers from across China, but most of the eateries specialized in the dishes of one or another of the poorer inland provinces.

During the Maoist era, Chen Village was a fairly typical farming community for this part of China, buffeted from above by common political forces but retaining its territorial integrity and many of its local traditions. By the close of the 1980s, it had become an anomaly, a village of dependents in a microregion that had been uneasily drawn into the economic pull of the semiforeign city of Hong Kong. Most of the region around it had undergone rapid industrial transformation, but the full force of this transformation had not yet reached Chen Village. Now, within the past decade and a half, it has.

Chen Village is today an integral part of an industrial region that stretches all the way from Hong Kong to Canton, and far beyond. The entire region is crisscrossed by modern highways, and, hour after hour, drivers speed past an almost unending sequence of factory zones, punctuated by brief flashes of the tiled homes of former villages. The region has become one of the world's industrial heartlands, feeding foreign department stores, electronics companies, and discount emporiums with much of their merchandise.

This is not the only part of China that has been dramatically affected by global demand for inexpensive mass-produced goods. Up and down the country's east coast, once-rural districts have filled up with factories churning out export commodities and, increasingly, producing for an expanding domestic market. Chen Village is no longer a typical village—it is no longer a village at all. But it is a typical part of a globalized industrial development that is engulfing ever more space and people in China.

The Industrialization of Chen Village

Chen Village first began to give up its agricultural land only a couple of years after the post-Tiananmen recession of 1989–90. The scare among investors over Tiananmen had receded. New industry once again was pouring into Guangdong's border districts from abroad, and industrial estates were again expanding outward from the nearby market town. In 1992 a consortium of Taiwanese developers approached Baodai to lease a stretch of rice fields on which to construct worker dormitories. The deal with the Taiwanese investors was soon dwarfed by a rapid succession of other land deals, and by 1994–95

Reshaping the Landscape

all of the village's agricultural fields and fish ponds had disappeared under concrete and asphalt. Rather than rest on its laurels, the village leadership quickly began looking toward the nearby hills as a means to expand Chen Village's land leases.

In the late 1980s we had clambered up and down a succession of rolling hills to reach orchards and chicken farms a couple of miles from the village. Now, almost all of those hills have disappeared, blasted away in the latter half of the 1990s to provide additional space for factories. The earth and rock have been carried off over the years by a relentless army of trucks, which poured out their loads elsewhere in the Pearl River region as landfill to create other industrial sites. Today, most of Industrial Zone No. 3 is comparatively flat, yet it sits where those substantial hills once stood.

Half hidden by factories, Chen Village's original residential district remains largely intact. A visitor walking in from the industrial zone first encounters a new outer residential ring, several blocks wide, filled with relatively recent (and already rapidly aging) five- and six-story apartment buildings that Chen households have erected as rental properties. Some of the Chens have moved out

Rental Apartments

here, but most of the residents are new arrivals from elsewhere in China who can afford to live outside of the industrial zones—foremen, technicians, and the most prosperous of the immigrant store owners. Further in from this outer residential circle stand the tile-covered villas built from the 1980s onward, with new cars parked

*Living Well. A Chen mansion built at the
turn of the 21st century.*

inside the gates of a number of them. Wandering toward the center
of the village, one comes upon the old warren of village lanes,
crowded with old tiny peak-roofed dwellings and the small brick
houses built in the Maoist era. Walking from the industrial zone
through the newer layers of housing and into the old heart of Chen
Village is like stepping back progressively through recent history.
Some of the buildings in the old lanes date back to well before the
Communist revolution. Up one lane, dilapidated wooden gates lead
into the narrow courtyard of a small former lineage-branch hall,
which later became the headquarters of a production team during

Playing Chinese Chess

the Maoist period, and now houses a migrant family. Under an old beam carved with traditional motifs, a large faded mural of Mao's face incongruously smiles down on the migrant family from the hall's rear wall.

Almost all of the industrial workers have arrived without families and live in packed dormitories out in the industrial zones, a distance from the Chen residences. But some migrants, akin to this family, occupy the run-down old dwellings at the village's center. Many doors are left wide open even on winter days to circulate air in the heat that now envelops the region during most of the year, and passersby can glimpse married couples with children and sometimes even grandparents in the cramped shabby interiors. Inside some of the other houses, groups of young men or women live amid crowded rows of bunk beds. Former homes in a few of the wider alleys have been converted into makeshift beauty parlors and electronic-games arcades, overflowing with migrant workers during their off-hours. Clusters of men squat outdoors in the lanes playing cards and Chinese-style

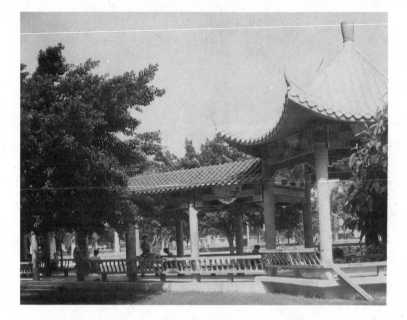

Park Portico

chess. Several ancient Chen ladies live among them in this old quarter, chatting or dozing at their door stoops, unwilling to move out of the homes where they had spent most of their lives.

Further on lies the village square and main ancestral hall, which had previously opened onto a vast rectangular fish pond (see page 4). Land has since become far too valuable to be wasted on a pond, and it has been entirely filled in. A police station and several commercial and apartment buildings stand on part of the reclaimed land, and the rest is devoted to a small park. It has a lawn, shady trees, benches for the elderly, and basketball courts for the more vigorous. Offering extra shade and benches, open porticos border two sides of the park, their ceilings adorned with brightly colored paintings of Daoist saints and figures from Chinese legends. The several times that we visited during late afternoons, old grandmas sat quietly with friends or grandchildren and school kids with backpacks played on the grass.

An Exclusive Welfare State

All told, slightly over 1,000 Chens co-exist today with some 50,000 to 60,000 "outsiders." The vast majority of the latter live in Chen Village's territory on temporary permits, which means, among other things, that they have no say in the governance of the territory and no claim on any welfare benefits allocated through the village government. Even more strikingly than in the 1980s, the Chens and migrant workers comprise "two nations" of haves and have-nots.

Many of the Chens lead middle-class lifestyles based on the proceeds of rental properties. They are also the beneficiaries of a mini-welfare state that is theirs alone to enjoy. Among the benefits, they receive heavily subsidized medical care. All adult Chens are entitled to free annual medical examinations, from blood tests and eye examinations to tests for breast cancer—the works.[1] When sick, the Chens pay only one-fifth of the bill at local medical clinics and the village government covers the rest. If hospitalized, a Chen pays only a token part of the cost and enjoys coverage of up to 100,000 *yuan*.

The Chen Village government has built an apartment building to provide very inexpensive rental housing for any Chens in need, especially single women and the elderly. Nearby, an old people's home takes care of other elderly Chens who can no longer look after themselves.

Taking over from the former production teams, the village government foots half the bill for biannual tours, open to all adult Chens, to popular destinations such as Beijing, Shanghai, and Xi'an, and, in a recent year, all the way to South Korea by plane.

Of far greater importance, all of the Chens of working age are guaranteed an easy job. The village government requires each factory that operates in its territory to hire a Chen as a factory official, at a salary of approximately 1,500 *yuan* (US$200) a month. Assigned to the factory by the government, they bear the grandiose title of "Chinese-side factory head" *(Zhongfang changzhang)*. Their main duty, though, is simply to serve as a liaison between the village

---

[1.] In keeping with the national government's policy to promote one-child families, the only Chen children who qualify for free annual medical examinations are those without siblings. As a villager explains, the policy is premised on the argument that there is a special need "to ensure that an 'only child' grows up healthy."

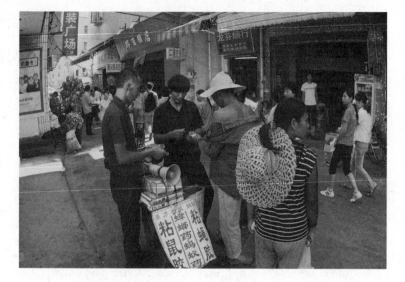

*Bustling Shopping Street. A decade and a half
earlier, Chen Village contained only a handful of
general stores and an outdoor morning market.*

authorities and the factory. They also take an elementary course in occupational health and safety, supposedly to help reduce the shockingly high rate of industrial accidents in local factories.[2] But they are not expected to take this very seriously. Several Chens confided that their job requires, at most, only a few hours each week. Their "factory head" salary really amounts to a disguised fee that the factory pays to bolster the living standard of a Chen family. For the factory, the cost comes to only about US$200 a month, a comparative pittance; but for the lucky Chen recipients, it is a meaningful contribution to their welfare–state benefits.

[2.] Hospitals in the Pearl River Delta region (where Chen Village is located) dealt with more than 40,000 fingers that had been chopped off by machinery in a single year. (*China Work Safety News* [in Chinese], February 24, 2005, p. 4.) An academic specialist in Beijing recently told one of this book's authors that some 17,000 workers in Shenzhen lose a limb in industrial accidents each year.

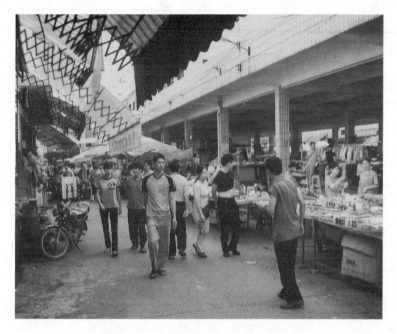

The Open-Air Market Transformed. Chen Village's first supermarket is located nearby.

There are not enough factories in the zones to provide a "factory head" income for every working-age Chen, and so the village government itself hires a considerable number of them. We encountered two young men leisurely going from home to home, unnecessarily sharing the task of reading water meters, and chatting with residents along the way. A woman whom we met disburses oral polio vaccines to migrants' children for a few hours a week. These very part-time posts pay approximately the same as the "factory head" jobs.

This is not the only income provided to them. Every Chen, child and adult alike, is entitled to a cash payment each year of about 10,000 *yuan* as a "dividend" from the village's land leases and investments. This dividend payment alone is about three times the total per capita rural income in China, and is equal to the per capita net annual income of the average *urban* Chinese.[3]

This dividend income is distributed not by the village government but by the Chen Village Shareholding Company, Inc. *(Chencun Gufen Youxian Gongsi)*. Into the early 1990s, all of the fields had been owned by the former production teams, but that system had run into problems as the village began to lease out land to industry. It soon became apparent that land-use planning was needed, with some land zoned profitably for industrial sites and other land for public infrastructure. But that would have benefited some teams more than others, and thus would have created intravillage conflict. So here and elsewhere in the industrializing districts, the regional government decreed in the 1990s that the teams' lands were to be combined village-wide. The new entity was designated a shareholding company. This terminology was imposed by the regional government and was meant to suggest that the former production teams' assets were being "corporatized" and that stock shares were to be handed out to each individual villager as a form of privatization. Each of the former teams' heads was to sit on a board of directors.

Each village was permitted to determine how to distribute shares, and the village adopted a method that reflected the communal values of the socialist era rather than the individualism of Western-style capitalism. Rather than hand out a share to each Chen as an irrevocable private possession that could be inherited, every child received half a share, which automatically converted into a full share at the youth's eighteenth birthday. Henceforth, as new children were born, each received a newly minted half share, and when a person died his or her share disappeared. When a young woman married out of the community she lost her share, but simultaneously gained a share in the community she married into. When a family moved away from the community it similarly lost its shares and dividends, but the shares could be reclaimed if and when the family moved back.

All of this is similar to how production teams used to determine who shared in the pool of team incomes in the days of Mao. Children

[3.] As of 2005, the average per capita rural income in China was 3,255 *yuan,* and the net per capita income in urban China stood at 10,493 *yuan. 2006 China Statistical Yearbook* [in Chinese] (Beijing: National Bureau of Statistics, 2006), Table 10.2.

born then to team members had gained a share in the team assets and had been entitled to a given portion of grain each year, with adults allotted a higher portion, while women who married out of the team had lost team membership and their share of team assets, as did families who moved away.

A Confucian twist has been added. In deference to the Chinese tradition of respect for the aged, an extra 250 *yuan* a month (3,000 *yuan* each year) is handed out to elderly Chens as so-called fruit money (that is, as a gift dividend ostensibly to enable them to buy delicacies). A neighboring village devised a variation on this, in which children received one share, young adults two shares, and older people were provided with an extra share and corresponding dividends.[4]

A decade passed before the higher authorities in this part of Guangdong intervened to enforce permanent ownership of shares—stipulating in 2004 that each native villager is to hold one share, period. No new shares would be issued henceforth to newborns or new daughters-in-law. Nor are shares to be taken away when a villager dies: they are now privately inheritable. But this has been implemented in a way that ensures that the Chens and their descendants will remain the sole owners: the shares cannot readily be sold. And the show of respect for old people has been maintained. Elderly Chens still receive monthly "fruit money."

Though originally decreed from on high in the 1990s, the formation of a shareholding company is very much to the benefit of the Chens. Had the land become the property of the village government,

---

[4.] In some other parts of Guangdong, respect for older people has been incorporated into a more intricate age-based distribution of shares. In an industrialized rural township on the far side of Canton that two of us have studied, a village "shareholding company" distributed one share to the native young people up through the age of 17. Between the ages of 18 and 35, a villager held two shares; between the ages of 36 and 55, three shares; and over that age, four shares. A nearby village in the same township provided one share to each child between the ages of 1 and 7, two shares between the ages of 7 and 12; 2.5 shares at ages 12 to 20, and so forth, with up to 4 shares for each village member over the age of 40. In short, different villages have worked out different formulas, but the guiding principle that each village separately has worked out appears to be quite similar regarding a link between community membership, respect for age, and dividends. Jonathan Unger and Anita Chan, "Inheritors of the Boom: Private Enterprise and the Role of Local Government in a Rural South China Township," *The China Journal,* no. 42 (July 1999), pp. 61–64.

as the successor to the brigade, the new arrivals from across China could become eligible to share in the village government's largesse if the Chinese government decided in the future to allow the migrants to become permanent residents rather than temporary permit holders. But no matter how national residence regulations may change in years to come, the shift of all the landed assets into a private shareholding company perpetuates the Chens' exclusive ownership and control over the territory's land and collective investments. The monetary handouts and the mini–welfare state that has been erected for the Chens will continue to be safely theirs alone.

All the same, in terms of daily operations it is often difficult for villagers today to distinguish between the Chen Village government and the shareholding company. The CEO of the company is the Chen Village party secretary, and the company's building is part of the village government compound. One villager assured us, "The village's governing committee runs the shareholding company committee."

Governing Chen Village

It is now customary in China for a city to administratively absorb the surrounding counties so as to form a geographically vast metropolis. As a consequence, Chen Village is now officially titled an "urban neighborhood" (shequ),[5] the lowest administrative level of a city, and its township (which used to be designated a commune) is now designated an urban district (jiedao)[6] of XX City.

But the reality is that Chen Village is not treated like an "urban neighborhood." An "urban neighborhood" has no real governing power in China. It does not raise its own revenues, control its own police force, contribute to its own urban planning, or set local regula-

[5] The Chinese term shequ literally means community, but the word has been transformed in China over the past two decades to mean the smallest geographic jurisdiction of an urban administration, which coincides with what we normally would call an urban neighborhood.

[6] Formerly a commune that was renamed a rural township in the early 1980s, it has now been officially labeled a jiedao. The word literally translates as street, but it is the urban administrative term for an urban district containing about 100,000 people.

The Chen Village Government Headquarters

tions. Chen Village does. A genuine "urban neighborhood" simply contains an office comprised of a half-dozen or dozen personnel who serve as local welfare agents of the urban government. Chen Village's government, in contrast, controls its own turf as much as it did in previous decades when it was officially a village.

Since the sizeable industrial zones must be planned, developed, and supervised, the government/company employs approximately a hundred full-time white-collar staff. Some of them have been brought in from outside to provide the necessary technical expertise and managerial skills. Not one of the Chens who are employed in the government has a college education. But the Chens reportedly occupy all of the vital decision-making positions.

Here and in neighboring communities, the salaries of the Chens who are employed as ordinary full-time personnel amount to only about 2,000 *yuan* a month. This is not much more than is handed out for those very part-time posts such as reading water meters. But as one man noted, "The full-time personnel also receive annual bonuses of 20,000 to 30,000 *yuan,* and if you're high like the party secretary you receive considerably more than that. And they have [an inside track to] property, which they can place under relatives' names. . . . So people want to hold a cadre's position."

Given the stakes, a contest arose to control the village government, and in 2000 Baodai lost his position as party secretary. The villagers with whom we spoke could only guess at the reasons. But they emphasized that he did not suffer much financially. As one person put it:

> The party looks after its own, and under the early retirement system [Baodai] was given a very good job. He now works as an official at the publicly owned waterworks company. [This is co-owned by Chen Village and a neighboring village.] The salary isn't much, only a few thousand a month, but at year's end there can be a huge bonus, up to 200,000 *yuan.*

Baodai's successor is a younger man—still only in his mid-thirties when he attained the position. A senior high school graduate, he had first obtained a job as an accountant in the village government office. Next, he was put in charge of granting permits of all sorts, and as he rose, he sought party membership. By the time Baodai withdrew from contention in 2000, the young man had maneuvered himself into position to win the intraparty election to become party secretary. As in earlier times, it is the party post—not a village government position—that determines who is the powerful political kingpin.

The Chinese government has passed a law stipulating that villages must hold competitive elections every three years for the village government leadership, and so Chen Village holds elections. Though its territory contains some 50,000 to 60,000 people, only Chens are enfranchised to participate. We were in Chen Village in January 2006 during the lead-up to an election. A group of elderly Chens all concurred that the impending election was important to them because their incomes depended upon having a capable village leadership. But in reality, the election provided little choice. There was a preselected slate of candidates. The incumbent committee of village officials had provided a list of names to the village's thirty-odd party members, who drew up the final list of nominees. As one man subsequently explained, "They know who's good. They know how to find the right people, the most capable. . . . It's democratic and free. The party decides, and then there is no objection from the people. This is democracy. The candidates have to be vetted, and it's not a process that's taken lightly." Notably, the real power in the community, the party secretary, was not even on the ballot, since who holds that vital post gets determined entirely within the ranks of the party.

The ballot listed eight names in all (with blank spaces for scattered write-ins), and six candidates were elected. So the voters' choice was essentially limited to eliminating the two least popular among the listed candidates. It was not listed on the ballot who would be elected to which post. Instead, just as in Mao's time, this would be formally determined by the elected committee after the election. But again, just as in Mao's day, "when you go to elect the committee, you already know who is supposed to take up which position." In Chen Village, there were no surprises. The incumbents on the ballot were all reelected.

Not one person with whom we spoke expressed any dissatisfaction with the procedures. They had no particular desire to throw out the incumbents, and no particular complaints about how the village was being run. Not knowing any other system, they accepted its premises as democratic.[7]

Although the Chens seem largely satisfied with the status quo, there are numerous reports of violent conflicts elsewhere in rural China over the procedures for industrial transformation. A common complaint is that village officials corruptly connive with higher-level officials to cheat ordinary villagers out of the profit from selling their land to indus-

---

[7.] This is not true for all Chinese villages. In some, there have been protests about the procedures or angry protests against the election results. In some other villages across China, various types of genuinely democratic processes have been installed to forestall discontent. In the most democratic and transparent, titled the "sea selection" method, each villager is able to nominate someone for direct election as village head, and all of the nominees subsequently get voted upon. In one version of the "sea selection" method, the top five or six vote-getters become the official nominees for village head; a second village-wide vote is then held to determine the two final candidates; and a third and final round of voting by secret ballot decides who of the two becomes village head. This was the procedure used in a village in Qinghai province visited by one of the authors. Jonathan Unger, *The Transformation of Rural China* (Armonk: M.E. Sharpe, 2002), pp. 219–220. On why and how village elections occur, see Daniel Kelliher, "The Chinese Debate over Village Self-Government," *The China Journal,* no. 37 (January 1997), pp. 63–86; Kevin O'Brien, "Implementing Political Reform in China's Villages," *The* trial developers. Typically, the village and higher-level governments give the farmers minimal compensation for their land. Then the local officials sell the land at market value to developers and keep the profits for themselves. Protests against such confiscations have been the single most frequent cause of mass disturbances in China in recent years.

In contrast, in Chen Village, as in most villages in its county, a generous share of the proceeds from redevelopment are distributed to the villagers; and much of the rest is being plowed back into new property developments for further collective enrichment. As seen in the case of Baodai and his successor, the village leadership benefits more handsomely than ordinary villagers. But there is so much wealth being generated in this region by the tens of thousands of disenfranchised migrant workers (most coming from impoverished villages in the interior) who labor in the local factories that all Chens can receive a package of income and welfare benefits that well exceeds previous expectations.

The Chen Village government is similar in this respect to the two villages that border it. Their leaders similarly strive to maintain generous mini–welfare states and to distribute sizeable dividends, and interviewees from these villages express satisfaction with their governments. Common factors obviously come into play. Among other things, all of these are lineage villages. They also all come under the same higher organs of government authority, which in this corner of Guangdong has seemed favorable to the welfare and prosperity of native residents.

Australian Journal of Chinese Affairs, no. 32 (July 1994), pp. 33–59; Lianjiang Li and Kevin O'Brien, "The Struggle over Village Elections," in Merle Goldman and Roderick MacFarquhar (eds.), The Paradox of China's Post-Mao Reforms (Cambridge: Harvard University Press, 1999), pp. 129–144; and Li Lianjiang, "The Empowering Effect of Village Elections in China," Asian Survey 43, no. 3 (August 2003), pp. 648–662. Also several chapters in Larry Diamond and Ramon H. Myers (eds.), Elections and Democracy in Greater China (Oxford: Oxford University Press, 2001), pp. 101–175; and a special issue of The China Quarterly on elections: no. 162 (June 2000), pp. 465–559. The director of the State Council's Village Economy Research Section has written an excellent report analyzing the various types of corruption and abuses of power that local cadres perpetrate in villages, and he concluded by pressing arguments on behalf of village democracy. Zhao Shukai, "Shequ chongtu he xinxing quanli guanxi" [Community Conflict and New Forms of Power Relations], Nongcun diaoyan [Village Investigations and Research], no. 146 (November 21, 1998) [a publication of the Development Research Center of the PRC State Council], 22 pp.

Village Identity

Although the neighboring villages are equivalent in economic prosperity, they also reveal certain differences that we believe reflect different degrees of community identity. As observed in Chapter 1, back in the pre-Communist period Chen Village had maintained a strong sense of collective village-wide identity and loyalty that had helped it to fend off its larger neighbors (see page 17). That heritage had strengthened brigade-level authority and activity during Longyong's tenure in the period of collectives, and it still appears to bear an influence on Chen Village today. In contrast, the two neighboring villages are larger and apparently did not traditionally need to hold to that same degree of beleaguered loyalty and identity—and again we believe this may be reflected in those villages today. As one quite visible example, in the two neighboring villages litter is scattered throughout the streets and drifts into unsightly large piles. In Chen Village, which is no more prosperous, a corps of sixty immigrant street cleaners constantly scours the streets to pick up litter with brushes and pans. Even the small lanes in the old village center now inhabited by poor outsiders are noticeably clean.

The village government pours considerable money into bolstering the Chen community's sense of identity and pride. To glorify the village and lineage, in 2004–05 it dismantled the main ancestral hall and erected an improved replica in its place—what the Chen ancestors presumably would have built had they the funds. The Chinese conception of architectural heritage does not entail preserving the actual materials that a building is composed of, and almost all of the original hall was discarded.[8] The new replica is outfitted with more solid pillars, new beams fancifully painted with motifs from Chinese legends, and a new large altar, upon which sit newly carved tablets of the ancestors.

Once a year at the autumn Chongyang festival, the village authorities sponsor lineage ceremonies at the hall and, using public funds, two pigs are roasted and the meat ceremonially divided among all of the attending male Chens. But at all other times of the year,

---

[8.] This conception of architectural heritage is the focus of Pierre Ryckman, *The Chinese Attitude toward the Past,* 47th George Ernest Morrison Lecture (Canberra: Contemporary China Center, The Australian National University, 1986), 22 pp.

The Lineage-Hall Altar. The sacred tablets are inscribed with the names of lineage founders and illustrious ancestors.

Entrance to the Ancestral Hall. The calligraphy hanging
at the entrance celebrates a recent wedding at the hall.

the hall has become the daily meeting place for a few dozen elderly
Chens. There is a distinct gender division among this generation: the
old men chat, smoke, and drink tea near the hall's main gates; the old
women set out folding tables in the main hall (traditionally exclusively
men's territory, where women were prohibited from congregating)
and spend the day there absorbed in mahjongg. The village government has moved quickly to accommodate the hall's new functions,
and during 2006 several new rooms were under construction off to
one side of the hall to provide community-center facilities for the
elders.

Reconstructing the main lineage hall was not considered a suffi-

The Second Ancestral Hall

ciently strong statement of Chen identity and pride, and so the village government immediately began erecting a second main lineage hall a block away. It stands on the site of the old Lotus lineage-branch hall,[9] but has been built anew to celebrate the glory of the entire lineage. Ancestral halls traditionally were rather austere, but this new second main hall is expensively gaudy, almost in the fashion of a Chinese religious temple. Enormous brightly painted front doors open onto a rich interior of elaborately carved woodwork, much of it covered in dazzling gold leaf. The village government has spent a million *yuan*

[9.] Neglected during the 1980s (p. 324), the lineage-branch halls have never been restored by members. All of them either have been converted to other uses, knocked down, or left to decay. A burnt-out wreck of a hall, its roof half caved in, lies at the end of one of the old lanes, and no one cares even to clear away the mess. Focusing on the glory of the lineage as a whole and the distinctiveness of the Chens has become a bulwark against the community's absorption into the surrounding sea of outsiders. In this light, to focus on one's own lineage branch would only serve to play up traditional internal divisions.

on gold alone. It appears to be competing against other villages in this show of opulence. In late 2006 the hall was on the verge of being officially opened, and in the village next door a very similar gaudy gold-laden ancestor hall was nearing completion.

Public Entrepreneurship

Like other villages in the township, the Chen Village government and its shareholding company have invested heavily in developing the industrial zones. The government's initiative has been vigorous. From the beginning, it took responsibility for clearing away the hills, laying roads and sewerage pipes, building factory buildings, and attracting foreign industry to set up production.

It found itself hard put to raise enough money for all of this. Industrial Zone No. 3 has a wide main street that is more than a mile long, but only one-third of that length had been built when the village ran out of funds. So it appealed to county authorities. The village government argued that, since Chen Village was further out, it was several years behind other villages in getting its industrial zones up and running, and a plea was made for the higher authorities to take over the road's construction. The appeal worked. Chen Village was declared a "late developer," and poverty-alleviation funds *(fupin kuan)* were allocated to complete the road. In China, poverty-alleviation funds normally are supposed to be allocated only to villages in the most impoverished parts of China that are suffering from malnutrition. But the county was flush with money and so Chen Village became an odd beneficiary.

Walking the road today, it is obvious at what point the county took over its construction. Where the village government had paid for and overseen it, cracks are already visible and the road edge is chipped. Starting at the point in the road where the county took over, it remains in excellent shape. A Chen Villager who had been a construction worker in Hong Kong and has now gone into the construction industry in the village walked the road with us. He explained that the higher-level governments know how to monitor contractors better; they also know that enough money needs to be spent to ensure that good materials are used and that proper storm-water sewers are installed. He pointed out where, even today, infrastructure projects under contract to state-owned construction companies are better built than those let out to private contractors. The Chen Village government and the new private construction companies have been on a learning curve.

Short on money and expertise in the 1990s, the village government could develop only a portion of the new industrial sites. So the township government entrepreneurially came in to erect some of the factory buildings, and continues to collect rents from these. Other undeveloped sites were leased for fifty years to foreign companies that constructed their own factory buildings. Other sites, some of them very sizeable, were let out to foreign land developers, which built gated industrial parks each containing a number of factory premises for rent. Other smaller sites were leased individually to Chens. One Chen entrepreneur estimates that, all told, more than 80 percent of the village's land has been leased out.

That still leaves a considerable amount of land. The Chen Village government/shareholding company has, over the years, constructed a fair number of factory sites on its own and has become a major property owner. In late 2006 it had just completed an enormous factory complex for a single Hong Kong electrical-goods manufacturer—a vast, walled compound containing ten large four- and five-story factory buildings alongside row upon row of multistory worker dormitories. The Chen Village authorities can expect a very substantial rent from these premises.

The 10,000 *yuan* of dividends that each of the Chens receives each year seems generous when compared with the incomes of most Chinese, but when computed in terms of foreign exchange rates it amounts to only US$1,300. In light of the vast amount of property development in Chen Village, including the buildings owned by the village shareholding company, the dividend might seem unusually low. But the Chens collectively pay close attention to the village's financial situation, since their own incomes depend on it, and they consider the amount reasonable. A dozen villagers observed to us that it had been very costly to rip out the hills, build the roads, install electricity, construct factory buildings, and hire security—and that paying back loans to cover these expenses ate up much of the local tax revenue and rental income. They also are in agreement that the ground rents need to be kept at a reasonably low rate: "There's a limit to what Chen

Village can charge, or else we can't compete with all the other places in the region that are trying to attract businesses."

Despite this, the general opinion is that the prospects are favorable for a boost to their own incomes. Villagers reason that since most of the potential land has been occupied, the village authorities' reinvestment in infrastructure and buildings will soon begin to slow down, and the dividends will accordingly begin to rise. One Chen who is knowledgeable about financial matters relates that the dividend may possibly increase to about 30,000 *yuan* per person within a few more years.

Through their private endeavors, however, some villagers already earn far more than this.

· 14 ·

Lifestyles of a Middle-Class Community

Two decades earlier, many of the parents of young men were in despair. A father whose son had just turned twenty lamented to us in 1989 (page 295): "Do I have any aspirations for my son? Just that he be a bit filial, and that he not go around stealing like so many others. That's all you can hope for these days."

Times have changed. The son, Chen Liming, is today a multimillionaire in U.S. dollar terms. One interviewee estimates that more than half of the Chen households today hold private invested assets worth a million *yuan* or more. They have all benefited from the village government's policy to give the Chens a monopoly over several types of private property development. A dozen or so households, Liming's among them, have been able to convert this advantage into considerable property empires.

Becoming Rich

Liming owed his start in business to his father, who had become a construction worker in Hong Kong. When Chen Village began to level hills in the mid-1990s, he had Liming bid to take up some of the excavation work. The father recruited other relatives to put up money, bought a bulldozer, and returned from Hong Kong for a year to assist. Renting additional bulldozers, the father and son took turns supervising the excavations day and night. A continuous stream of trucks was hired to cart off the dirt, and Liming's father stood there in the small hours of the night keeping track of each truck's load. "This type of work had to be done by relatives," he explains, "since cheating is easy." Even today, Chen Villagers do not readily expand their businesses beyond what they and close relatives can directly supervise.

Liming parlayed the profits from the excavation work into property development. Each new property has served as collateral for ever-larger borrowings to purchase new building plots from the Chen Village government, on which he has constructed factories, dormitories, apartment buildings, and commercial premises.

Even though foreign companies have been permitted to construct their own factory premises and attached dormitories, and land-development corporations can develop big factory estates, all other types of property development are reserved for the Chens alone. As one example, once it became clear that storefronts are profitable investments, it was decreed by the Chen Village government that henceforth only Chens and the village government/shareholding company could construct them. A high-rise factory building recently constructed by an outside firm faces a commercial street, and part of the ground floor suspiciously resembled storefronts, so the authorities insisted that the company seal off the premises with a high brick wall. Across the street sits one of the apartment buildings erected by Liming, containing a bustling restaurant and stores.

Most recently, though, Liming has not been allowed to purchase any new land from the village government. His father puts this down to the authorities' "red eye disease," a Chinese term for envy—but in the next breath he adds that the village authorities feel Liming is already very wealthy and that, for reasons of equity, the authorities believe the opportunity to become rich ought to be spread among a wider range of villagers. However, Liming is still able to purchase and redevelop sites that already contain old buildings. On an enormous block of land that had contained several one-story corrugated-iron factory buildings, he has begun constructing four very substantial multistory factories and a number of high-rise dormitories. It is a joint investment with two Chen Village officials, one of whom sits on the village's governing committee.

Such partnerships are open knowledge in Chen Village, and vil-

Property Development. The building to the left, on the broad main street of one of the industrial zones, was constructed by Liming. Above the stores, he rents out the three stories of dormitory rooms to migrant workers, eight to a room. Beyond are rows of new worker dormitories owned by the village government/shareholding company, which have been rented on a long-term lease to a foreign manufacturer.

lagers seem to consider it a matter of good business sense. A developer needs to cultivate connections and backing, after all. As for the propriety of the officials' participation, it is taken almost for granted that one of the purposes of holding an official position is to reap advantages. So long as the amount of money available to the villagers through dividends remains unaffected, so be it.

Liming and his wife and four children live in a four-story villa, built in the 1980s through the father's remittances from Hong Kong. A maid answers the door. The couple drives new cars, an upscale Toyota and Honda with leather seats. They are no misers. But they live well below their means. The home, for instance, is filled with ordinary well-worn furniture, and no remodeling has been undertaken since they moved in in the 1980s. Given their wealth, they live and dress simply, and both work hard. Though Liming's wife holds one of those "factory head" posts that takes little of her time, she is busy the rest of her day collecting rents and doing the accounts of the family business.

Rather than live better, they are intent upon reinvesting the great bulk of what they earn in new property ventures. They are motivated by a Chinese-style work ethic similar to Chongyin's family on their chicken farm two decades earlier. Liming and his wife and father today share the ethic that self-worth and satisfaction are tied to success in business and to a frugality that helps achieve this. Two decades earlier as a young man, Liming had been a bored, free-spending school dropout who had seen no way forward for himself. With opportunities, a different side of his character has emerged. In middle age, he is self-confident, articulate, and holds to an ethos that is congruent with his father's aspirations. The father, who is a silent partner in Liming's operations, can be considered a millionaire in terms of his family's assets, but much of the year he and his wife live in a tiny apartment at a public housing estate in Hong Kong.[1] In the 1980s he had put most of his income from Hong Kong into constructing the four-story villa back home in an effort to display his status. Today, he lives almost as frugally in Hong Kong in order to invest most of his earnings through his son, to gain the satisfaction of their achieving in Chen Village what is today most highly valued—a major family stake in property investments.

The grounds for achievement having shifted, the family holds no sentimental feelings toward their four-story villa. The house occupies a quarter of a large walled block of land that contains a garden and ornamental trees—and it is located in the most valuable section of the residential district, facing the park. Other families have begun leveling their twenty-year-old villas in order to construct apartment buildings, and Liming and his family have made a decision to do the same. A six-story building will be erected over the entire site, containing stores on the ground floor and forty apartments above. One of them, the family's new home, will be enormous.

---

[1] Having become a Hong Kong resident three decades ago, the father no longer counts as a Chen Village community member and cannot directly engage in the property transactions there. Even if he were to return to live in Chen Village permanently, he would not receive dividends or restored community rights, as his move abroad changed his status within China.

The Leisured Middle Class

Although unusually successful, Liming is not Chen Village's only type of success story. In the late 1980s, Chen Dawei and his young wife were operating one of the chicken farms we had visited up in the hills. They were among the small group of entrepreneurial families in Chen Village who were seeking to prosper through their own hard work. Still in their early twenties, they were living in a storeroom amid the chicken coops. They had begun branching out into pigs, and were trading ideas and experiences with Dawei's older cousin, the entrepreneurial Chongyin. With several hired hands from Sichuan, Dawei would soon begin planting what would ultimately become a very extensive lychee orchard of 3,000 trees spread across more than twenty acres of hillside.

While a magnet for local entrepreneurship up through the mid-1990s, endeavors such as animal husbandry and orchards became increasingly marginalized by the more lucrative opportunities available through property development. When the expansion of Chen Village's industrial zones finally reached his properties in 1999 and the village government wanted to level hillsides containing fifteen acres of his orchards, Dawei was happy to accept the compensation offered and moved down from the chicken farm.

The compensation was extremely generous. On the proceeds Dawei has been able to construct two six-story apartment buildings in the residential district, where only Chens are permitted to own property. His family occupies the entire second floor of one of these buildings, with a spacious living room that sports decent Western-style furniture and a huge flat-screen TV. A one-car garage on the ground floor houses Dawei's new Toyota Camry, next to an apartment set aside for his parents

Dawei is in the midst of expanding his holdings. In exchange for some additional hillside land that the village government recently needed, he was offered a free building site and has begun to erect a third large apartment building. In the old warren of lanes, Dawei's family also continues to own two small homes that they rent out. He and the other Chens want to entirely redevelop the run-down village center and to construct high-rise apartment buildings there, but they feel stymied by tradition:

Collectibles. Corner of a Chen living room.
(Photo by Ao, 2007)

> This is ancestral land that goes back many generations in the same family. People wouldn't at all mind redeveloping it themselves, as the land would remain in the family. But you can't build much on these tiny parcels of land, and nobody is willing to lose face by selling off their ancestral property so that some other family can put up large buildings.

They are waiting expectantly for the village government to cut this Gordian knot. The idea is for the authorities to organize the area's redevelopment as a collaborative venture among all the Chen families, so that no family will be put in the position of selling off ancestral land.

Dawei continues to supervise seven acres of lychee orchards, but this keeps him busy only part of the year. During most months, tending to his rental properties and to his post as a "factory head" occupies only part of his day. Like most Chen Villagers, he has time to spare, and he whiles away some afternoons with friends. Though still entrepreneurial, he has joined a rentier class, a leisured group of property owners that from all appearances have become numerous in the once-rural districts surrounding China's cities.

Leisure and boredom continue to feed a gambling habit among a portion of the Chens. Many villagers play mahjongg for small stakes as a social activity, but a minority of them gamble for high stakes, and not just at mahjongg. A man whose son-in-law ruinously gambles notes that the circle of gamblers is composed largely of people who have not been able to rise much beyond what they receive as village-government largesse. They have nothing to motivate or preoccupy them, he laments, and too much time to kill. Several have lost their homes through gambling.

The passion for gambling is not as widespread, however, as it was in the 1980s. Prosperity has largely dissolved villagers' frustrated envy regarding the incomes of kin in Hong Kong and has cured the community-wide fever to win personal fortunes through the miracle of good luck. It has become obvious that Liming, Dawei, and dozens of others within the village have been able to amass larger invested holdings than the relatives who departed. In fact, the opportunities in Chen Village to make good money have expanded to the extent that some of the Hong Kong émigrés have returned home.

Insiders and Outsiders

Two decades earlier, the local villages had erected a finely graded structure of discrimination against the migrant workers pouring into the region. Feeling awkwardly dependent upon, and in an inferior position to, their relatives in Hong Kong, they had taken pleasure in their own superiority vis-à-vis the migrants from elsewhere in China, especially the Sichuanese.

That finely drawn system of discrimination has broken down. Workers today arrive from countless poor corners of rural China to labor in the factories. The Chens accept the workers' presence, as their own prosperity both as rental-property owners and as dividend recipients depends upon the district's industrialization. One acquaintance, gazing at a street of newly built and still unoccupied factories, observed with satisfaction that thousands of additional workers would soon be arriving, all of whom would need to rent accommodation.

But although the Chens no longer feel overtly prejudiced against the migrants' arrival, they are distinctly aware that they themselves comprise a mere 1,000-plus people in a sea of more than 50,000 outsiders. As a community, they have become intent upon protecting their own identity and projecting their control.

Control is manifested in a police corps. It is formally titled a public-order corps and it does not count as a full-fledged police force, which only higher levels of government can establish. A detained suspect is supposed to be handed over to higher-level police to be formally charged. But the Chen Village corps, with more than a hundred uniformed men and a small squad of police cars, looks and behaves like a police force. Some of the members sit in police boxes that are strategically located every few blocks, while others go on patrol. Most of them are themselves immigrants, but the supervisors are Chens. Longyong's son, in fact, serves as deputy commander. (Longyong himself passed away in 2005.)

The corps' main daily concern is theft, which is rife in the region. Their efforts to guard against this are bolstered by hundreds of private security guards employed by factories. Organized gangs have been known to steal even large bulldozers during the night using cranes and heavy-duty trucks. To coordinate policing efforts, the Chen Village corps has formed a joint force with a neighboring village. The borders between the two villages' industrial areas are no longer readily distinguishable, and police boxes throughout the border areas now carry signs reading, "Li and Chen Villages Police Substation" *(paichusuo)*. Traditionally, before the revolution, Chen Village had semihostile relations with the Li lineage, but common economic and security concerns have cemented close cooperation between them today (for instance, they also co-own and co-manage the local waterworks company). Li Village has installed closed-circuit cameras to monitor its residential district, and Chen Village might well follow suit, as both villages very often adopt similar practices.

Conversations in Chen Village suggest that the dozens of police boxes and the uniformed patrols serve a purpose beyond public order and the deterrence of theft. They visibly make the statement that, in a broader sense, things are under control. In the midst of the district's rapid transformation and their own submersion in a flood of outsiders, the Chens can feel reassured.

The Chen Village government also actively pursues policies to accentuate and perpetuate the Chens' collective identity and separateness. One element is to physically seal most of the Chens off from the outsiders by building a luxurious gated community exclusively for their own use. A wooded hill had been preserved at the edge of the residential district, and half of it has now been removed to create a huge block of level land beneath a cliff face. Foundation pilings have already been driven, and two sixteen-story and nine eleven-story apartment buildings will rise on the site, set in landscaped gardens. The walled complex will have tennis courts and a swimming pool and will be guarded by a corps of security personnel. The village government, which is constructing the project, plans to sell the large apartments at cost. For Chen families that cannot afford to buy these luxury apartments, a low-rise housing estate is under construction nearby that will contain small apartments for sale at a heavily subsidized price.

The rules for the two housing estates will be strict. Only Chens will be allowed to purchase an apartment, and resale or even rental to an outsider will be forbidden. But there will be two exceptions. The emigrants to Hong Kong, though no longer officially members of the Chen Village community and unable to participate in the shareholding company or receive welfare benefits, will be allowed to purchase an apartment in the luxury estate and retire there. They are, after all, members of the Chen lineage. But the other exception goes against traditional notions. Chen daughters who have married outsiders will be permitted to purchase an apartment on the same terms as other Chens. Patrilineal descent no longer counts for all. A daughter's family today is also allowed access to village welfare benefits when in need—including a subsidized apartment. As a man remarked to us, "Some young women may be ugly or have some other problem, and so they settle for marrying a migrant. If they don't have a home to live in, we think it's reasonable to give them one."

Realigning Identities

By tradition, once a year lineage-branch identity gets accentuated. At the Chongyang festival many of the men go out to ancestral graves for three days running—on one day to visit the graves of their immediate kin, on another day to pay respects as a group to the lineage-branch ancestors, and on a third day to pay respects to the long-dead ancestors of the whole lineage. As they regroup day by day in these larger contingents of kin, they are acting out how, traditionally, identities and mutual loyalties were supposed to be organized.

But these rites are not taken particularly seriously. Several men emphasized to us that people attend only if they do not have other things to do on those days. Bucking tradition, women are allowed to tag along and watch the proceedings, though few do.

For the first time, the rituals are carried out at a cemetery, not at a series of grave sites scattered across the hills. With the development of industrial zones and the leveling of the hills, the graves of the Chens and of other lineage villages all needed to be relocated, and a large, beautifully landscaped cemetery for the deceased of several villages has been opened by the township government up amid the steep foothills of the mountain range. The cemetery lies inside Chen Village territory, and so the Chens were given first choice on where to site their graves. *Fengshui* masters were hired, and they chose a particularly auspicious location on a cemetery slope where good aura flows across from neighboring hills. On a series of terraces that rise up the slope, the Chen graves radiate outward by generation and ancestral bloodline. Near the center lie the gravestones of Chen Village's founding fathers, who were from the Chen lineage's eighth recorded generation, while several terraces away lies a kinship group containing a very recent burial site from the twenty-fourth generation. Due to the layout of the new cemetery it has now become possible, for the first time ever, for the Chens to visually trace the proximity of their relation to every other male Chen simply by strolling across the terraces.

Although the layout of the cemetery displays how the lineage is divided into different branches, the Chens are now much more focused on what unites them rather than what divides them. In the late 1980s an interviewee from a family that had held a rich-peasant label observed that his lineage-branch membership was meaningful to him (page 325), but his younger brother, standing with us in the cemetery, today shrugs off its importance. Close relatives count, "but we're sometimes several hundreds of years apart from other lineage-branch members; it's too distant."

While lineage-branch identity persists at a very low pitch, production-team identity has become even more attenuated. Whereas two decades earlier in the 1980s, team membership had *(continued)*

Burial Urns (above). In parts of south China, including Cantonese-speaking areas, the custom has been to bury the deceased in a coffin for about five to ten years and then to exhume and cleanse the bones and place them in urns. At a considerably later date, the bones sometimes were reburied in a grave or tomb. To save land, the Chinese government has decreed that corpses must be cremated, and while the older of these urns contain bones, the newer ones contain ashes. The man in the photo is pointing to the space reserved for his own burial urn and ashes. A solitary cross designates the urn of a relative who converted to Christianity.

The Cemetery (top, opposite).

Memorial Graves (bottom, opposite). Five similar adjoining graves com-memorate five of the village's founders. The number of these memorial graves coincides with the number of Chen sub-lineages.

provided villagers with a level of community that they could turn to for mutual support and loans, identity with the team shrank dramatically after the teams' landholdings and revenues were combined into the shareholding company in the 1990s. A group of elderly men at the ancestral hall murmured assent when one of them observed, "We no longer have any sense of a production team because there isn't any economic base for the teams." Once the teams no longer had any land-rental incomes, they no longer supported any group activities and no longer convened any meetings. Nor were most of the members any longer neighbors. They have moved into new homes that increasingly are scattered across the new residential districts.

But the team heads have remained in place. As Dawei notes, "Before, we all sat together and chose the team head, but now that we're not officially a village they're not elected. The same people just stay in the position, inherited from the previous system." They are now officially titled "residents' small-group heads" (jumin xiaozu zhang), which is the title of the lowest grassroots urban post, but Dawei and others always continue to use the old rural term team head, just as they often continue to speak of the village government as the "brigade": habits die hard. The five former team heads now hold full-time salaried positions and occupy desks in what is titled the Monitoring Office (Jianshi Bangongshi) at the village government headquarters. Each also oversees one of the five electoral districts in Chen Village. Most important of all, they all sit on the board of directors of the shareholding company. The teams are gone, and the Chens' sense of team identity has all but vanished over the past one and a half decades, but the former team heads have been incorporated into Chen Village's governing structure.

The Influence of Hong Kong

The Chens' views of the world and of their own government continue to be influenced by the community's proximity to Hong Kong. They remain close to the relatives who had emigrated to Hong Kong, many of whom regularly come back and forth across the border; and with major improvements to transportation links the Chen Village residents themselves can now visit Hong Kong for a day and be home before bedtime. During evenings, Chen Villagers usually watch Hong

Kong TV game shows, comedies, and dramas, and have become attuned to Hong Kong's social mores. Rather than attempt to block the broadcasts, the Chinese authorities have been accommodating. In fact, the regional government has come to a commercial agreement with the Hong Kong channels, and whenever the Hong Kong TV shows have advertisement breaks, commercials for regional Chinese advertisers appear on Chen Village screens.

Everywhere in China, fads in music, hairstyles, clothes, and popular literature have washed across from Hong Kong and Taiwan, but in the counties near Hong Kong the penetration of foreign ideas has been broader and deeper and reaches back further in time. Two decades earlier, a Chen Village official at a dinner gathering openly had expounded upon the virtues of constitutionalism and judicial independence (page 328). The Chinese government is not particularly concerned about music and fashion styles, but in this border region it has reacted to reduce the influence of imported political knowledge and ideas. Nowadays, every time one of the Hong Kong channels launches into a news show, the television screen suddenly switches to a TV station that has been established in the township, which substitutes a local news broadcast. The government is intent upon retaining some control over the content of local thinking.

In some other respects, the influence of Hong Kong runs strong. This can be seen clearly in local marriage ages. Whereas two decades earlier young women had normally married in their late teens (page 297), they tend today to marry considerably later, between the ages of twenty-two and twenty-five, and men today delay marriage until the ages of twenty-five to thirty. Several Chens concurred that the reason for the delayed marriages is simple: young people marry later in Hong Kong. (They note, by way of comparison, that the outsiders residing in Chen Village normally marry three to four years earlier.)

At the same time, several of the customs that had arisen in the 1980s have persisted. Among these is the dowry. With growing prosperity, the dowry has risen substantially in value as families compete to show how much they can afford to provide their daughter. In addition to a complete set of furniture, TV, and refrigerator, a wealthy family may buy their daughter a car or even an apartment. All of this is displayed with fanfare on the wedding day. If the groom's parents are wealthy, they may be equally or even more generous, albeit not as publicly. This cannot be considered a bride price, though, as it

A Modern Wedding Procession

goes directly to their own son, not to the family of the bride. The bride price itself has become insignificant: the groom's family often simply pays for the tins of Western-style cookies and the cake vouchers that the bride's family distributes to its close acquaintances. The groom's side also pays for a wedding reception. But even though the groom's family could afford to splurge on this, the reception often is catered at the ancestral hall to save the cost of renting out a restaurant. Traditionally, both the bride price and the groom's family's wedding banquet signified the departure of the bride from one family line to join another. The new practices, by being relatively modest in cost, implicitly downplay the significance of the woman's change of status.

Bringing Up the New Generation

One thing has not changed over the past two decades: the importance of having a son to carry on the family line. Back in 1989 couples were willing to pay fines of 1,200 yuan in order to give birth to an extra child in hope of a son (page 318). In line with increased prosperity, they are willing to pay far more today.

Dawei is among them, and a good deal of his financial resources have gone into the quest for a son. Under tighter family-planning regulations that were introduced in this region in the 1990s, if the first child was a son, a couple was no longer allowed to have a second child. If the first child was a daughter, the couple was allowed to try again for a boy, but they were legally limited to a second child. Dawei had two daughters, and felt he was wealthy enough to pay the fine for having a third child—who also turned out to be a girl. The monetary penalty for violations climbed for each extra child. For a fourth child in Chen Village, it stood at 150,000 *yuan* in 2000. Under pressure from higher authorities, the Chen Village government also decreed that having an extra child would mean forfeiting seven years of a family's dividends. Dawei and his wife agreed it was worth the cost, and she became pregnant, left the village, and went into hiding elsewhere for the duration to avoid being pressured into an abortion. The fourth child was a boy, and Dawei says he considers himself lucky that the son was born in 2001, since the penalty for a fourth child had, by 2006, risen to 300,000 *yuan*.

The local birth-control policy also kept tightening. When Chen Village's official status was converted from rural to urban, it was given a grace period up to July 2007 to adopt urban birth-control rules. Whereas rural parents in China are legally permitted to have up to two children, urban regulations decree one birth, period, regardless of whether the child is a son or daughter. Wealthy Chen Villagers anxious to have a son can be expected to keep trying, but they now have to pay a fine even for the second birth.

Ironically, Dawei's wife, a mother of four, is employed part-time at the village government's family-planning department, where her job is to prevent migrants from giving birth to unauthorized children. She makes the rounds of the apartment buildings that house workers, and if a migrant woman has two children she is supposed to persuade the woman to have a tubal ligation, though she shrugs off this part of her job as useless talk. She is also supposed to be on the lookout for swelling tummies. But she notes,

> The migrants can get away with having children more easily than us. If a migrant woman becomes pregnant here, how do we know whether it's her first child or if she also has a couple of kids back in the home village? She'll only get in real trouble when she goes back to the village to register the child. She'll have to sooner or later, since if the baby isn't registered it can't get an identity card or go to school.

Her own son is now of nursery school age. A brightly painted three-story nursery school has opened in Chen Village, on the very spot where the auditorium had previously stood. The Chen Village English and Chinese Languages Nursery School is part of a private chain of nursery schools whose promise is that the children will be familiar with English by the time they enter primary school. In China, many parents are seeking any advantage for their children in the ultra-competitive effort to climb the school ladder into university, and knowing English at an early age is supposed to provide a leg up. The nursery is relatively expensive, but the appeal works—especially among the many technicians and factory managers who live in Chen Village's vicinity. According to the nursery school's director, it enjoys an enrollment of two hundred, some thirty of whom are Chens. Some of the other children come from surrounding villages, but the bulk of the pupils are from the families of the "outsider" white-collar staff and store owners. The most affluent Chens do not consider even this nursery school to be good enough for their little ones. Dawei, for instance, prefers to drive his son twenty minutes every morning to an even more expensive nursery school located in the township's capital. He himself feels unconcerned about whether his son gets an early start in learning English, since he is not particularly anxious about whether or not his little son gets into university. He just wants the best for him.

As exemplified by Dawei, parents today are willing to go out of their way from nursery school onward in support of their children's education. In the 1960s and 1970s, they looked upon themselves as being poorly educated peasants, and they did not expect—and were not expected by the schools—to be involved in their children's education in any way. Today they exhibit an active interest, which the schools encourage. When we dropped in at Dawei's home one day,

The Nursery School. (To preserve the anonymity of Chen Village, the village's real name has been digitally erased from the school and the school bus in this photo.)

he and his wife were hurrying off to the high school to see their elder daughters' classes perform on sports day; and when we arrived at Liming's house the following morning, he and his wife were about to leave by car for the open-house day at the primary school.

The primary school is at a driving distance because the Chinese government decreed in the late 1990s that rural primary schools should be combined into large schools in order to provide better facilities. The new school that Chen Village now shares with two neighboring villages is located at the far end of one of the other villages. A lot of money has been poured into it. Surrounded by well-tended lawns and bestowed with a ceremonial clock tower and grand foyer, it looks more like a hotel or city hall than an elementary school. Plaques at the main gate proclaim the various awards it has won for foreign-language teaching, ecological awareness, and academic excellence.

*The Primary School. At the left side of the photo, a teacher in
jacket and tie is leading an outdoor exercise class dancing
to the beat of Cantonese pop music.*

While rural public schools elsewhere in China charged considerable tuition fees up until the central government reformed the system
in 2007, in Chen Village's area, as part of the largesse of the mini-
welfare state, schooling has been free for all of the local children since
some time in the 1990s. Affluent outsiders such as factory managers
and university-trained technical specialists are permitted to buy places
in the school system for a very steep price. But money alone is insufficient. The fashionably dressed wife of a high-level technician said
that to get her seven-year-old son admitted she had had to produce a
lot of documents to prove that her husband holds the type of job status
and credentials that the local authorities want to attract to the district.
Admission is so restricted that in her son's class only five of the thirty
pupils (a student-teacher ratio that is excellent by Chinese standards)
are non-locals. The children of the less-wealthy and less-qualified
outsiders have to make do with a private elementary school that has
leased an abandoned school building in one of the villages.

Into the 1990s, children from Chen Village had attended the village school up through junior high school. Relatively few of them went on to senior high school, and so they grew up knowing and playing only with other Chen Village children. That situation has been transformed. About 90 percent of them today go on to senior high school, and throughout the six years of junior and senior high school, they attend—and live at—a giant public high school with other local teenagers from throughout the township. They have grown up with the children of all the nearby villages and towns, and consequently many of their best friends are not Chens. The younger generation has developed far broader social networks and a correspondingly broader sense of identity than their parents. While the Chen Villagers are erecting a strong sense of their own distinctiveness as Chens vis-à-vis the sea of "outsiders" among whom they now live, the younger Chens' sense of separateness simultaneously has largely evaporated vis-à-vis their own generation of local Lis, Wens, Huangs, and Liangs from the surrounding villages.

The high school, which opened in the late 1990s in the township capital, looks much like an American college. Set in a lovely campus of shaded lawns and ponds, it centers on a sprawling modern six-story classroom building surrounded by five-story dormitories. These accommodate almost all of the school's 3,200 students, eight to a room. Though the students from Chen Village live only twenty minutes away by bus and go home to spend weekends, one of the staff explained that if the teenagers were allowed to live at home throughout the week, "they'd be out all over the place, playing video games, shopping, and so on." On weekdays they are not allowed to leave the school grounds. Instead, they attend seven and a half hours of classes till 5:00 P.M., and then return to their classroom after dinner for homework sessions.

The central government is aware of the downside of having students cram to pass competitive exams, and it has been beating the drum about the importance of "quality education" *(suzhi jiaoyu)*. In keeping with this, a school administrator launched into a discussion about how the school emphasizes a quality education. But he stopped in mid-sentence, laughed, and corrected himself: "Really it's not about quality. It's all about grades, and whether you can get into a university or not. Not that we don't care about [quality] education. But nowadays if you don't have good grades, what's the use?" The school uses its wealth to recruit teachers from across China who have success-ful records in preparing students for the university-entrance exams. English is one of the core subjects in the exam, and to assist students in this the school has hired two teachers from the United States.

The administrator boasted of the school's success rate and proudly reeled off figures about how many of the school's graduates attend prestigious universities. But in contrast to the school's claims, several villagers observed that relatively few of the Chen teenagers enter higher education. Unlike the rest of China, a university credential is not viewed in Chen Village as a necessary stepping stone to a decent salary. Financially, a youth can do just as well staying within the community, collecting dividends and going into property develop-ment. Local high-school students who are successful in their studies are caught between the ethos of academic striving and achievement that is instilled at the school, and their parents' ambivalence about the strategic value of their going on to university. Nonetheless, if a young person from a well-off household wants to continue, the parents are sometimes loyally supportive. Liming's daughter, for one, is a first-year biology major at a regional university, and her parents feel proud of her accomplishment.

There is an alternative to university available. A group of entre-preneurs from elsewhere in China founded a for-profit private voca-tional school in Chen Village in 2003, offering majors in computer skills, auto mechanics, basic accounting, and the like. Starting with a lease on Chen Village's abandoned primary school, the school campus rapidly expanded into a few additional classroom buildings and sev-eral six-story dormitories. The principal, who is from Shandong, said that the 1,700 students come from throughout China, but not a single young person from Chen Village attends the school. None of them needs to learn the vocations taught there because they already enjoy sufficient means to earn a decent income.

The principal spoke about the quality of the training and claimed that graduates are recruited by firms such as the giant Taiwanese com-pany Foxconn (which manufactures most of the world's iPods) and by Japanese companies in the region. But in reality, all was not well at the school. Two days after our interview, a large crowd of students staged a boycott of classes, unfurled banners, and yelled slogans. They complained that the school had suddenly demanded that its students pay the next year's tuition well in advance, within one week's time, and that if they could not, they would immediately need to go work at local factories as migrant laborers in order to come up with the fees. The school appeared to be in financial trouble, and had come up with a plan to contract out its poorest students to factories in the nearby industrial zones.

This effort to force them into factories highlights the precarious circumstances in which many of Chen Village's "outsiders" find themselves. Similar to these students, a great many of the migrant workers lead a hand-to-mouth existence. Most of them, workers and vocational students alike, have arrived in Chen Village in hopes of improving their lot, and many find their hopes dashed. There is a substantial flow of people into and out of the territory, as people flood in but then find they cannot sustain themselves, or become exhausted from long work hours, or decide to seek better prospects elsewhere, or simply give up and return to their home villages. Most of the people living in Chen Village are caught in these situations, and the contrast between their livelihoods and the middle-class lifestyle of the Chens is, to say the least, striking.

· *15* ·

Outsiders

The vast numbers of people moving into and out of Chen Village in the search for work cannot disguise an important trend. An increasing number of "outsiders" are settling there, despite their lack of official residence rights *(hukou)*. The newcomers are highly stratified socially and economically. Some of the factory owners who have arrived to manage their own businesses are wealthier than the richest of the Chens. Other immigrants have brought modest savings with them to start small family businesses that they try to build into permanent livelihoods. But a majority of the new settlers are impoverished migrant laborers who seek to stay on, working themselves to the bone in hopes of a better chance in life.

Business Immigrants

The upper crust of Chen Village's outsider residents are factory owners and managerial staff from Taiwan and Hong Kong. Most of them leave their families back home and travel back and forth several times a year to see their wives and children. Some live a double life. It is widely claimed in China that some of the Taiwanese and Hong Kong businessmen and factory managers have taken mistresses or "little wives" and now have second families in China. Some others frequent prostitutes, large numbers of whom display their charms in the streets and entertainment spots of the nearby township capital. Most of the prostitutes were originally poor young women from the countryside who dropped out of factory jobs, and are now exploited in a different fashion by the foreign management staff away from home.

Increasingly, though, as the infrastructure and amenities in Chen Village and the surrounding district improve, the arrivals from abroad have begun to bring their families with them to China. In the former commune town, there are now schools that cater specifically to their children. One advertises that it adheres to a Taiwanese school curriculum; another that it provides a standard Hong Kong education. The foreign families (all of them ethnically Chinese) occupy some of the best rental properties in Chen Village, but a few now want to live in their own houses. The Chen Village government has been accommodating. It has set aside a block of land where they can purchase sites to construct their own mansions.

They are not the only wealthy newcomers. A number of successful businesspeople from within the People's Republic, having built up their own manufacturing businesses elsewhere in China, have moved their factories to the coast to facilitate exports. An example is a factory owner from Gansu Province, who has registered his business in Hong Kong and claims it to be a "foreign-funded" enterprise in order to pay lower taxes for his Chen Village factory than would a Chinese business.

Somewhat less affluent are the Chinese-born managers and technicians who help run the foreign-invested factories. Many of them have earned a tertiary degree in China or occasionally even abroad, and some can speak passable English or another foreign language. Within this region their tastes are considered sophisticated and their example helps set the standard for a middle-class lifestyle. They and the Chinese-born factory owners often send their children to the excellent local government schools—and as a result their children grow up with friends among the local youngsters. This is the one group with family members who intermingle socially with the Chen community.

A substantial number of storekeepers, owners of food stalls, and proprietors of small service businesses have also taken up residence on a semipermanent basis. They arrive with a bit of capital and are thus a notch above the migrant workers, but they normally have very long workdays, and the living conditions of many of them are no better than those of the workers.

*Leisure Time. Storekeepers eager to sell snacks
provide chairs for off-duty workers.*

This is evident among the storekeepers. At a small grocery near
the entrance to one of the industrial zones, a family with two small
children is attempting to make a go of it. They are from a nonindus-
trialized part of Guangdong Province. The man explains, "At home
there's no work. . . . Everyone is coming to this part of Guangdong in
search of opportunities." The store is clean but not well stocked: a limited variety of food staples alongside some boxes of washing powder,
soap, toothpaste, and other household essentials. It is partly a result of
how much the new storekeeper can afford to stock and partly that the
migrant workers who patronize the store can themselves afford to buy
only the most basic of supplies, "just a *yuan* here and a *yuan* there." To
make ends meet, the store opens from early morning till bedtime, and
the whole family works, eats, and sleeps on the premises. A miniscule
kitchen and squat toilet are hidden in a curtained cubicle at the rear
of the store, and directly above it is an open concrete ledge four feet
below the store's high ceiling, just wide enough to accommodate a

*A Bit of Extra Cash. The proprietor of a small
store supplements his income by guarding bikes.*

mattress that the whole family sleeps on. The store's proceeds are too
low to enable them to live elsewhere.

Down the block, a small television store has the same arrangement—an open sleeping ledge above, and the storekeepers' two
little children running around underfoot. The main item on sale is
a small color TV in multicolored plastic that sells, remarkably, for
only US$30. It was past 9:00 P.M., but the hardworking couple was
busily repairing electronic goods while awaiting customers. "Most of
the store's business is at night," the man explained, "after the workers get off work. They have an hour off at 5:30 P.M. to eat and then
they go back to their factory jobs at 6:30, doing overtime work till
10:00, 11:00, or midnight. Some come in after midnight to shop, so
we stay open till 1:00 A.M. Actually, when a factory has rush orders
they may have to work up to seventeen or eighteen hours a day."
While running his store requires a seven-day workweek, a factory
job is far more grueling.

Factory Workers

Despite the fatigue of laboring from early morning to late at night, some of the factory workers say they want long overtime hours, as this is the only way to have a bit of money left over to send home to their families. They are trapped in a choice between exhaustion through long, fast-paced work or extreme poverty.

The post-Mao years had been unkind to farming families in the poorer inland parts of China. From the mid-1980s up through the early 2000s, the real prices they received for their crops had declined, while expenses had risen. Exacerbating their financial difficulties, increasingly high fees began to be charged in the countryside for public services like education and health care. In poor inland villages, a family without an outside income often was hard pressed to keep its two children in primary school. At the same time, local taxes and charges kept rising as corrupt and inefficient rural bureaucracies became bloated with officials' relatives and cronies.[1]

The family of one twenty-three-year-old factory worker from the countryside, named Li, experienced exactly this situation. During the 1990s, she and her brother had been raised by grandparents in a village in Guangxi Province while her parents worked all year long in a coastal city. They needed the outside income, since there were six family members, only a quarter acre of farm plots, and high local taxes and fees. Even with her parents' migrant labor, Li had been obliged to drop out of primary school because they could not afford to continue paying her tuition fees.

When Li was eighteen, her parents decided that they were too old to keep up with their low-paid work in the urban service sector, and they returned to the village to live. It became the children's turn to leave home, as a second generation of migrant workers. Like most workers from the countryside, Li and a friend sought jobs in a factory district where they already had contacts with migrant workers from back home. Her first job was gluing leather belts at a factory not far from Chen Village, working at times until 1:00 in the morning. The overtime rate only came to 2.8 *yuan* (US$0.33) an hour, and after the factory deducted the cost of meals she received only 400 to 500

---

[1]. Thomas Bernstein and Xiaobo Lu, *Taxation without Representation in Rural China* (New York: Cambridge University Press, 2003).

Back to Work

yuan (US$55 to $65) at the end of the month. So after four months, she returned home exhausted and then left again to work at a factory that makes plastic hangers. The smell was unbearable; each work shift often amounted to twelve hours; and her take-home pay came to only about 600 *yuan* (US$80) a month, but her options elsewhere were no better, and so she stayed there for one and a half years. But then factory orders dwindled and her pay at the end of the month dropped, "so I went back to my village for a few months before joining a friend to look for work in Shenzhen." They found jobs in a watch-strap factory, where dust from polishing the metal straps bothered her lungs. (Health hazards and industrial accidents in the export factories are common; Li's brother died in a work accident about this time at a nearby factory.) Frightened about possible damage to her lungs, Li quit her job to work in an electronics factory in one of Chen Village's industrial zones, where she takes home a bit more than 700 *yuan* a month for up to eleven hours a day of rapid work. In her spare time, she says, she

Bed Space

likes to go window shopping. Her daydream—and the dream of her friends, she says—is to escape factory work by miraculously marrying a well-off husband.

Her work experiences have been no worse than most of the other migrant workers from the countryside with whom we have spoken. In fact, women like her have had an easier time than men in finding employment, and very often earn more. Up until about 2004 the export factories normally would not hire men for production-line jobs, but only for heavier manual work such as loading and unloading or for the relatively few technically skilled tasks. As a result, men comprised only about one-tenth of the manual workers at most of the factories in the Chen Village region. Managers explain that they preferred young women because they are more obedient *(tinghua),* easier to manage, have nimbler hands, and are more meticulous.

Many of the job recruitment posters outside factory gates in this region simply used to read, "Women workers needed: ages 18–23." Crowds of job seekers would gather at factory gates, and the factory managers could pick and choose: as one manager told us, "We took only about one in five." They were not interested in women older than twenty-three because it was said that by the age of twenty-four, rural women returned to their hometown to get married, and the factories did not want to deal with problems related to pregnancy. The factory managers also calculated that by the time a woman reached her late twenties, she was physically too old to keep up hour after hour with the rapid pace of work.

Up into the early years of the twenty-first century, so many young people were seeking work at the factory gates that the employers could impose tough work conditions. One of this book's authors conducted a survey in 1996 of workers in footwear factories operated by owners from Taiwan and Hong Kong, and found that 81 percent of the respondents reported restrictions on workers going to the bathroom.[2] In some factories in this region, workers were regimented as though they were in the military and were marched to and from their production lines and dormitories and mess halls.

Monetary penalties against workers were also commonplace in the export industries in Chen Village's region, and cut into the workers' take-home pay. Fines were sometimes levied for being even a few minutes late, for not turning up for work even if ill, and for making mistakes on the production line. Fines were also sometimes imposed for talking at work, for littering, and even for an untidy dormitory space. Factory managers and foremen sometimes even felt they could get away with physical abuse. In the survey of footwear factories, one-third of the surveyed workers reported that their factory resorted to physical punishments.[3]

Workers who resented a factory's treatment felt inhibited from leaving because the factories made this prohibitively expensive. One of the most common means was to demand a "deposit" from newly hired workers that was the equivalent of two to four weeks' wages, which workers would forfeit if they quit before the next Chinese New Year. Many factories deliberately were also weeks or even months in arrears in paying workers, and then refused to disburse any of the

---

[2] Anita Chan, *China's Workers under Assault: The Exploitation of Labor in a Globalizing Economy* (Armonk, N.Y.: M.E. Sharpe, 2001), p. 10. Other results from this survey are reported in Anita Chan and Zhu Xiaoyang, "Disciplinary Labor Regimes in Chinese Factories," *Critical Asian Studies* 35, no. 4 (December 2002), pp. 559–584.

[3] Chan, *China's Workers*, p. 10.

Hard Labor

owed wages if a worker quit.[4] Notwithstanding the financial loss they would incur by leaving, many young workers became burned out physically and mentally, and the job turnover rate tended to be high in the export industries.[5] It was common for workers to suddenly quit, recuperate in their home village, and go out again in search of a job.

Because of the discriminatory hiring practices, many of the male migrants either sought construction jobs or, along with women beyond their mid-twenties, settled for very low-paying jobs in sweatshops and

[4.] *Ibid.*

[5.] In a formerly rural industrial zone elsewhere in south China, two of us conducted extensive research in 2002 at a massive Taiwanese-owned factory that produces running shoes for one of the world's most prestigious brand names. To work there was considered highly desirable compared with what was on offer elsewhere in the area, and the factory had its pick of young workers. We attended one of its hiring sessions, during which 400 eager applicants were prodded to test their muscle tone and underwent a medical examination to ensure they would be able to withstand long hours of fast-paced labor. But the rapid work tempo and numbingly long hours proved too much for most recruits. The factory's management reported that in the previous year 43 percent of its 13,400 workers had dropped out, unable to last until the Chinese New Year.

cottage-industry workshops.[6] A male worker in Chen Village named Wang, for instance, relates that since 1998 he had moved across China from one very poorly paid job to another. But returning to farming is not an alternative. In his village in Henan Province in northern China, his parents, with three grown sons, possess only a bit more than an acre of land.

In 1998, at the age of eighteen, Wang followed a fellow villager to one of Henan's cities to work in a small woodworking factory. He earned a mere 200 to 300 *yuan* a month plus food, and after the third month the factory collapsed and did not pay what it owed him for the previous month's work. Wang moved onward to Beijing, where he found work at a local workshop that made carts pulled by tricycles. As an apprentice solderer working seven days a week, he earned only 230 *yuan* a month without food, just a bed space. By the second year, his salary had risen to 900 *yuan,* but the business was on the verge of bankruptcy. So when he returned home at Chinese New Year, he stayed in his village for a year, helping with the farming and making furniture for fellow villagers. "But the problem was that when they got married and I made furniture for them, they didn't have the money to pay me." So he went to work at a small county-town factory, where after half a year he was injured. The factory had no insurance cover, and the owner simply gave him 1,000 *yuan* and sent him home. When he recovered, he found a job at a small factory in Canton, but the pay was so low that after a month he realized he was actually losing money. In all, he held a dizzying succession of nine different jobs over a period of six years—paint-spraying Christmas toys, making cheap furniture for export, sawing the parts for wooden loudspeakers. Finally, he decided to use his life savings of 1,500 *yuan* (US$200) to attend a technical school for two months to learn how to operate a forklift. He received a certificate, but then could not find a forklift job. He had to go back to working at a small factory at very low wages, where "even when they cheated and paid me only two and a half *yuan* (US$0.33) an hour for overtime, there was nothing I could do." By 2006, at long last, he had found a job niche where he could support himself, as an independent

6. Most of China's construction workers are migrant workers from the countryside. Both in Chen Village and elsewhere in China, it is common for them to live at the construction site. Once a ceiling is in place, workers often set up makeshift sleeping quarters inside the building they are constructing.

Young Migrants at a Chen Village Barbershop

solderer who takes on temporary contracts at factories for repair jobs, from which he can earn some 2,000 *yuan* (US$270) a month.

Wages have been so low and the work conditions so grueling that eventually fewer would-be workers began showing up at factory gates. Starting in 2004, the international press began reporting that China's export industries had begun facing shortages of workers, especially in south China, and that as a result, workers' wages there were rising sharply. However, contrary to the news reports, as of 2006–07 big wage rises were not evident in Chen Village or in the surrounding region. In many cases, the take-home pay of factory workers in Chen Village's industrial zones did not rise even when higher minimum legal wages were announced. [7] A Taiwanese-owned factory where we conducted

---

[7]. To avoid charges of illegal conduct, most of the employers in export industries set their production workers' monthly pay at almost precisely the same level as the local legal minimum wage. (Beijing does not set a national minimum wage but rather lays down the criteria for determining local minimum wages based on a formula that includes local inflation rates and the median wage of local residents.) In the Chen Village region, the legal minimum wage, when adjusted for inflation, had not increased during the decade

interviewing in early 2007 is a case in point—with the manager and workers telling very different tales. The manager complained that he was caught in a squeeze between higher wages and the demands of his customers for ever-lower prices.[8] He claimed that his workers' monthly wage now came to about 1,600 *yuan*, and that the basic wage [for the first forty hours per week] alone amounted to 700 *yuan* a month. But the workers, here and at other factories, told an entirely different story. At the gate of this factory, a security guard said that the job turnover rate "is very high because the wages are too low. My own monthly pay is 900 *yuan* for twelve hours a day, with only one day off a month." Several young women workers who were leaving their shift gave similar accounts, and noted that their take-home pay had not gone up even when the local legal minimum wage had been increased by 120 *yuan* in July 2006. The factory had immediately increased its deductions for food, utilities, and accommodation by 120 *yuan*, exactly offsetting the wage increase. "Now, even if we don't eat at the canteen they still deduct 200 *yuan* for food." At the end of the month, they were left with 400 *yuan* (US$55) in take-home pay. Are there better factories? No, they answered, "they're all about the same."

---

from 1993 through 2003, and in fact had decreased slightly in real terms during most of that period. In 2004 the local metropolitan government finally raised the minimum wage by more than one hundred *yuan*, though this was partly offset by local inflation. The minimum wage rose again in real terms in 2005 and in 2006. Some factory employers began complaining that this imposed a new cost on them. So in 2007 the region's authorities, in keeping with a reputation for siding with manufacturers, declared there would not be any annual increase in the minimum wage for the year to come, despite an accelerating inflation. (Food prices in China at the time were rising at an annual rate of about 15 percent).

8. This complaint seems valid. Factory managers from Hong Kong and Taiwan note that when their companies had initially set up production in China in the 1990s their profit margins had been high since it was cheaper to produce in China than in the factories back home. They therefore could undercut their competitors' prices and still make a handsome profit. But as very large numbers of corporations from Hong Kong, Taiwan, and elsewhere have transferred production to the mainland, this advantage has been erased. The manager of a Hong Kong-owned factory that sells to Wal-Mart confided to us, "Before, our profit margin was high, at 30 percent. Now, even if we get 10 percent, it's already good. Now a buyer like Wal-Mart can easily use email to ask for quotes from a lot of suppliers, and we have to compete. Doing business is getting more and more difficult." He and other managers have often tended to respond to the price squeeze by attempting to squeeze workers in their wages and conditions.

Instead of increasing their workers' real wages in a meaningful way, factories have become less selective in their hiring policies. The manager of a Hong Kong–owned lighting factory explains,

> Although we previously only wanted women as they're easier to manage, we no longer have any restrictions. Either sex is fine. Now, we have three men to every two women. Before, we only took workers up to the age of twenty-two or twenty-three, but now we accept workers from eighteen up to thirty-five-year-olds. We actually now prefer thirty-year-olds because they're more stable. They don't leave since it's not easy for them to find other jobs. . . . We now give a reward to our workers who introduce a friend to work here. If they bring in a man we pay sixty *yuan*, if a woman, then eighty *yuan*.[9]

Still, the small placards that are mounted outside factory gates do not advertise openings for ordinary production-line workers. They specify only skilled posts—lathe operators, technicians, and the like. People without such skills are still expected to gather at the gates in small knots to await an opportunity to find out if any jobs are available. But they no longer are in a situation of having to jockey desperately for factory jobs, and one result is that the factories in the Chen Village area are no longer in a position to demand deposits of money from newly hired workers.

The young people from the countryside feel under less pressure to take a job under any conditions because their families' circumstances in the villages are no longer as desperate. After dropping for more than a decade and a half, crop prices began rising again in 2003–04. By then, the Chinese government, worried about the prospects of rural unrest, was already passing laws and regulations to assist farmers. Starting in 2001, it took measures to force rural county governments to reduce the farmers' tax and fee burdens, and in 2006 the

---

9. The manager of a Taiwanese-owned factory told us that he still declines to hire men or any women over the age of twenty-five: "Once a woman's married she has lots of family matters, and so today she'll ask to be let off work and tomorrow she'll again ask to be let off work, and she'll tell lots of lies, such as her papa's ill or has died." Question: Why won't you hire married men? "Boys *(nan haizi)* are difficult to control. Some of them join gangs. So in order to protect the women workers I don't hire men." We nevertheless noticed a number of male workers, one of whom commented, "What a terrible *(hen hei)* factory."

agricultural land taxes were entirely eliminated and a small per-acre subsidy was granted to grain farmers. Giving further relief to village families, at the beginning of 2007 rural school tuition fees (though not textbook fees) were abolished nationwide up through grade nine. Nevertheless, many villagers, including Wang's parents, continued to feel hard pressed. Rising costs for fertilizers and other inputs ate into profits, and the Wangs still earned less than 1,000 *yuan* of cash income in 2006 from their tiny landholdings. Their new annual land subsidy amounted to a paltry seventy *yuan*. Consequently, people like Li and Wang need to continue to seek factory employment, and large numbers of younger people continue to pour out of the countryside into industry. It is just that they no longer exceed the needs of industry to such an extent that they have to crowd outside factory gates.

Even though the pay remains quite low and the hours are exhausting, some of the workers are beginning to settle down in the Chen Village area. The great majority of the young women who had come out from their villages to work in the 1980s and the early 1990s had permanently left factory work when they returned home to marry. But by the latter part of the 1990s increasing numbers began returning to factory or service-industry work after marriage and even after giving birth, often accompanied by their husbands.[10] It was too difficult to make ends meet otherwise. It has become increasingly common now in poorer parts of China's agricultural heartlands for villages to be occupied largely by grandparents and children, with the younger adults returning once a year at Chinese New Year. Like Li's parents, they normally return to their village permanently when too old to keep up with the rigors of factory and construction work, but even that pattern appears to be changing. As just one example, Wang has married a young woman he met at a factory. Wang's father had just joined them in the late autumn of 2006 to work as Wang's assistant, and it remains uncertain whether any of them will ever return permanently to the countryside. Wang's wife was pregnant, and Wang mused that it might be better for the child to be brought up back home by his mother, "But my wife wants to raise the kid here and to bring

---

[10.] On this phenomenon see Kenneth Roberts, Rachel Connelly, Zhenming Xie, and Zhenzhen Zheng, "Patterns of Temporary Labor Migration of Rural Women from Anhui and Sichuan," *The China Journal*, no. 52 (July 2004), pp. 49–70.

*Family Labor. Grandparents in a migrant household assemble
cheap plastic dolls. To help make ends meet, older migrants
sometimes take up very low-paying "putting out" work.*

over my mother to help out." As whole families settle in, the composition of Chen Village's permanent population is becoming increasingly mixed—with still-unknown social and political ramifications.

The permanent relocation of such families into the district has been made possible by the erosion of the temporary-residence permit system. Without a temporary-residence card they faced arrest up into 2003. Wang recalls, "A fellow from my village was working in the township next door [to Chen Village], and he was detained by the police for not carrying a temporary permit. They'd put you in detention, with awful food, and would make you labor. Someone I knew was arrested right outside my factory for not having a permit, and he had to pay one hundred *yuan*. The boss had to come to bail him out." Migrants who looked unemployable were forcibly shipped back to the countryside after detention.

Times have now changed, due in part to a well-publicized incident. In 2003 a university graduate employed at an industrialized "village" near Canton was apprehended for not carrying a permit card and was beaten to death at a detention center. Although such events were not unknown among migrant workers, the brutal death of a university graduate struck a raw nerve in Internet chat rooms, and the case quickly mushroomed on the Web into a national *cause célèbre*. In June 2003 the State Council in Beijing reacted to public pressure by abolishing the detention centers and the forced repatriation of migrants. In China, national decrees regarding the treatment of migrant workers are often ignored by local authorities, but this particular decree coincided with manufacturers' complaints of "labor shortages." As a result, in Chen Village and elsewhere in the region the police have become more circumspect and relaxed in their treatment of migrant workers. The temporary-residence permit has become easy and inexpensive for a migrant to obtain, and workers are no longer at the mercy of impromptu police checks. Wang claims he doesn't even need a permit anymore. Whole families like his from poor regions of China are now able to move into Chen Village essentially unimpeded. Even though they remain second-class "guest workers" ineligible to obtain public health care, schooling, or any other benefits, and even though this lack of access exacerbates the precariousness of their daily lives, a sizeable and relatively rapid relocation of such families—here and elsewhere in China—is under way. Over time, the wave of new settlers looks likely to alter dramatically the overall composition of Chen Village's permanent population.

Past, Present, and Future

It was observed in the previous chapter that the Chens have been vigorously attempting to set in stone their own self-willed image of Chen Village as a single-lineage community, but it is in fact a community in flux, as an accelerating number of new residents like the Wangs move permanently into its territory. As beneficiaries of the foreign companies' exploitation of factory workers, the Chens at once welcome the inpouring of labor and yet endeavor to keep the new residents at arm's length and in all respects disadvantaged. This may not be a sustainable situation, since the Chens comprise only about

2 percent of the populace that now resides in the territory, and since the number of new permanent residents will soon begin to greatly outnumber the Chens.

Outside forces are at play that are greatly altering access to Chen Village within the region, portending further major changes in the community's circumstances. A new rapid-transit commuter rail line has been laid, and a train station was scheduled to open in 2009 on Chen Village's doorstep, not more than ten minutes' drive away. Chen Village is being integrated into a vast, sprawling conurbation, and within a few years' time it will be no more than a heavily industrialized commuting suburb of XX City. In such circumstances, power cannot forever be monopolized in the hands of the Chens as though this were still a village. As was observed in Chapter 13, on paper Chen Village has already legally been designated an urban neighborhood (shequ), though in practice it continues to maintain its own rural-style government structure. But throughout China, higher levels of government have been moving to absorb urbanized neighborhoods directly into metropolitan administrations, and where this has occurred the village administrations have entirely disappeared, along with their local regulations and controls. This will most likely be Chen Village's fate, and probably sooner rather than later. The Chens will remain prosperous property owners and shareholders, but they will become urban residents with the same rights as other urban residents. Eventually, the families that have newly settled in Chen Village presumably will also hold urban residence rights. For the sake of the struggling families of newcomers, let us hope so.

But whatever the future scenario may prove to be, the fate of the community and its people will continue to lie in the grip of large regional, national and, indeed, global forces. External forces have, of course, weighed heavily in the tale of Chen Village for the past half century and more. Village life was strongly penetrated by the Maoist polity, with its intricate structures of power and control, its party-dominated organizations, its cadre workteams, Mao Thought counselors, and incessant campaigns. Chen Villagers had to learn how to cope with radically new, sometimes beneficial, but often unpredictable and arbitrary political programs and fiats emanating from Beijing. Then, in the space of only a few years, decisions from above swept the village headlong into Deng Xiaoping's version of coastal economic reform, with its "special economic zones," easy money, and new status symbols. Once again, forces external to the village—entailing new debilitating economic dependencies and values centering on Hong Kong—penetrated Chen Village during the 1980s. The two decades since then have witnessed new shifts in the community's circumstances that have been just as profound—the extraordinary local industrialization generated by economic globalization.

Throughout it all, village life provided a thread of continuity—a shared history of the personal struggles among village leaders, of material improvements, of marriages, funerals, and the slow succession of generations—that partially buffered, and placed on a human scale, the vast social, political, and economic forces that surrounded and were wrenchingly reshaping village life.

It has not always been a particularly pleasant chronicle. But we are grateful to our friends from the village for sharing this history with us, so that we too have had a human scale, a scale the size of one community's territory, by which to measure the changes that have swept and are sweeping China.

Epilogue

An Unbroken Thread

THE SENT-DOWN YOUTHS AND CHEN VILLAGE

In the summer of 2007, each of the sent-down youths who had lived in Chen Village during the 1960s and 1970s received a handsomely printed invitation to a reunion. In flowery language, the invitation read:

> The sweat from your labor has watered the soil of Chen Village. Your friendship with us is as wide as the earth and high as the heavens. Since the Reform and Opening, Chen Village has undergone earthshaking changes, and the villagers will never forget the sent-down youths who gave up their youth to contribute to building our village. The Chen Village governing committee warmly invites you to the 2007 reunion of villagers and sent-down youth. The governing committee will provide food and lodging and travel expenses from Canton and Shenzhen. We sincerely hope that you can accept our invitation.

Included with the invitation was a commemorative booklet, containing old black-and-white photos of the teenagers taken when they had lived in the village and, in color, a group photo of the well-dressed middle-aged men and women who had attended the first reunion ten years earlier in 1997, which the former sent-down youths themselves had organized. The booklet also included a small collection of poems and essays that some of them have more recently written about Chen Village. Devoid of bitterness, the tone is one of nostalgia for the past and happiness at the village's current success. Ao penned the longest essay, in which she observed:

> Every time we return to Chen Village we walk to and fro as if intoxicated—we can't get enough of the sights. It is a tremendous delight to wander everywhere, stepping on familiar ground . . . remembering those days of common struggle.
>
> Throughout all our years of toil with the cadres and masses, we were only able to bring about gradual change. Now, fortunately, under China's policy of reform and opening, within twenty years the village has undergone an earthshaking transformation. It has not only become a new socialist village but part of a city, and its people are urban residents. We sent-down youth are fortunate to see with our own eyes Chen Village's rise to eminence. . . .
>
> I have been to many cities in America and throughout the world and I have countless acquaintances. None of my new friendships are closer than those I have with the people of Chen Village.

The reunion was celebrated with fanfare in October of 2007. Chen Village literally rolled out a red carpet—flanked by lion dancers and musicians—for the visitors. During the two days of reunion activities, the former sent-down youths had opportunities to exchange news about their lives. About 40 percent of them were now living in Canton, and another 40 percent in other parts of China, especially in Shenzhen. From what they reported, fortune has been kind to most of them, and in late middle age many of them maintain a solid middle-class lifestyle. Those who swam out to Hong Kong in the 1970s have also generally done well in life. Some went on to earn higher degrees and became prosperous engineers, teachers, and journalists, and some succeeded in going abroad. Ao, for one, has settled in the United States, where she obtained a university degree while working full-time, raised a family, and proudly saw her two daughters graduate with honors from Yale law school and Oberlin.

To close out the reunion, the fifty-one who had returned for the occasion contributed US$7,000 to host a gala music-and-dance performance for the whole Chen community.

Whatever the circumstances in the 1970s that caused them to leave Chen Village, many of them had possessed a genuine idealism and they had identified deeply with its residents—and the villagers have reciprocated. Time and again, the Chens told them at the reunion that

Homecoming, 2007, in front of the fancy new ancestor hall.

"we will never forget you," and as proof of this the village government made an offer: they could purchase burial plots in the new cemetery. A dozen of them, including Ao, have accepted the offer. Their ashes will someday be interred along with all the members of the Chen lineage. Chen Village has become their adopted ancestral home.

Other Writings
on Chen Village

Chan, Anita. *Children of Mao: Personality Development and Political Activism in the Red Guard Generation.* London: The Macmillan Press; Seattle: University of Washington Press, 1985. Ao provides one of the four case studies in this book.

Chan, Anita and Jonathan Unger. "Grey and Black: The Hidden Economy of Rural China." *Pacific Affairs* 55 (Fall 1982): 452–471. Chen Village is one of four villages discussed in terms of the second economy in the countryside.

Madsen, Richard. *Morality and Power in a Chinese Village.* Berkeley: University of California Press, 1984.

———. "Harnessing the Political Potential of Peasant Youth." In *State and Society in Contemporary China,* edited by Victor Nee and David Mozingo, 244–263. Ithaca, NY: Cornell University Press, 1983.

———. "The Maoist Ethic and the Moral Basis of Political Activism in China." In *Moral Behavior in Chinese Society,* edited by Richard W. Wilson, Sidney L. Greenblatt, and Amy Auerbacher Wilson. New York: Praeger, 1981.

Unger, Jonathan. "The Class System in Rural China: A Case Study." In *Class and Social Stratification in Post-Revolution China,* edited by James L. Watson, 121–141. Cambridge University Press, 1984.

———. "Remuneration, Ideology, and Personal Interests in a Chinese Village, 1960–1980." In *Chinese Rural Development: The Great Transformation,* edited by William L. Parish, 117–140. Armonk, NY: M.E. Sharpe, 1985.

Index